REVISE

A2 PSYCHOLOGY

KEY TOPICS

We have tried to ensure that the information presented in this book maps exactly on to the latest version of the AQA-A A2 Level Psychology Specification. However, in case of changes, please visit the AQA website directly.

REVISE

A2 PSYCHOLOGY

KEY TOPICS

DIANA DWYER
(The Joseph Whitaker School, Rainworth, UK)

CLARE CHARLES
(North Leamington School, Leamington Spa, UK)

Ψ Psychology Press
Taylor & Francis Group

HOVE AND NEW YORK

First published in 2003 by Psychology Press Ltd
27 Church Road, Hove, East Sussex, BN3 2FA

This updated and amended edition published 2006

http://www.psypress.co.uk
http://www.a-levelpsychology.co.uk

Simultaneously published in the USA and Canada
by Taylor & Francis Inc
270 Madison Avenue, New York, NY10016

Psychology Press is part of the Taylor & Francis Group, an informa business

AQA examination questions are reproduced by permission of the
Assessment and Qualifications Alliance.

British Library Cataloguing in Publication Data
A catalogue record for this book is available from the British Library

ISBN13: 978-1-84169-649-2
ISBN10: 1-84169-649-8

Cartoons drawn by Sean Longcroft, Beehive, Brighton, East Sussex
Cover design by Richard Massing
Typeset in the UK by Facing Pages, Southwick, West Sussex
Printed and bound in Italy by Legoprint.

Contents

Chapter 11
Perspectives: Debates   285

Chapter 12
Perspectives:
Approaches in Psychology   307

Diana Dwyer

To a wonderful fiend (sorry, Freudian slip—friend) Lesley McDonough whose wit and wisdom have been an inspiration to me.

With much love and gratitude Les, Di.

Clare Charles

Love to Mum, Dad, Lesley, Martin, and especially Stephen for encouraging and enabling me to complete this.

Preparing for the Exam

You've coped with the demands of AS—well done! Hopefully the AS exam is well behind you, but the knowledge you gained from revising and the exam itself should still be with you, and this will help you to succeed at A2.

If you've forgotten some of the revision and exam techniques suggested in Brody and Dwyer's *Revise Psychology for AS Level* then a quick review of this is a good idea. Now think about how you can apply these to A2.

A2 PSYCHOLOGY OVERVIEW

3 MODULES
Unit 4 30% of A2 mark
Unit 5 40% of A2 mark
Unit 6 30% of A2 mark

Halve the percentages to get the total A level marks at A2, as your total A level grade comprises 50% AS and 50% A2. We will focus on Units 4 and 5 in this revision guide, as Unit 6 is coursework.

The A2 course consists of options, particularly in Unit 4, the *options paper*, and to a lesser extent in Unit 5, the *synoptic paper*. What follows is a list of the options available in this revision guide, which have been selected based on the findings of a survey on popular A2 choices and match our textbook *A2 Psychology: Key Topics, Second Edition* by Michael W. Eysenck.

Options available in this revision guide

UNIT 4: PYA4
Social psychology: Relationships, Q2
Social psychology: Pro- and anti-social behaviour, Q3
Physiological psychology: Biological rhythms, sleep, and dreaming, Q5
Developmental psychology: Cognitive development, Q10
Developmental psychology: Social and personality development, Q11
Comparative psychology: Evolutionary explanations of human behaviour, Q15

UNIT 5: PYA5
Individual differences: Psychopathology, Q2
Individual differences: Treating mental disorders, Q3
Perspectives: Issues, Q4 and Q5
Perspectives: Debates, Q6 and Q7
Perspectives: Approaches in psychology, Q8

On the table above, highlight the options you have studied for Units 4 and 5. The question numbers refer to the exam papers. It a good idea to make a mental note of these so that you can immediately turn to the questions you will be answering in the exam.

One question is guaranteed per option. You need to have covered a minimum of three options for the Unit 4 exam paper, but may choose to do more than this to give you a choice of questions. For the Unit 5 exam paper you may choose to do Psychopathology or Treating mental disorders or both for Section A, Issues or Debates for Section B, and the Approaches are compulsory for Section C.

THE EXAM FORMAT

Unit 4 Exam Paper	Unit 5 Exam Paper
1½ hours	2 hours
3 x 24 mark essay questions	2 x 30 mark essay questions and 1 structured question on the Approaches
30 minutes per question	40 minutes per question

Using this Revision Guide

Each chapter is organised on broadly the same format, minor variations may occur as appropriate to the content.

- **What's it about?**—Introduces each chapter.
- **What's in this unit?**—Maps directly onto the Specification.
- **Ask yourself**—Introduces each of the sub-sections within each option.
- **What you need to know**—Identifies key content in each sub-section.
- **Content summary**—Includes theories and explanations.
- **Research evidence**—Where appropriate, this is divided into "for" and "against".
- **Evaluation**—Where possible, positive and negative points have been made.
- **Over to you**—Possible exam questions.
- **Questions and essay plans**—These provide guidance on the range of potential exam questions and suggestions on how to tackle them.

This revision guide has sufficiently detailed content, when combined with study, to enable you to achieve the maximum grade, but it doesn't inundate you with too much content that you never end up using! This is because content has been restricted to manageable amounts. Where there are more than two theories, two of them have been covered in depth, including content summary, research evidence, and evaluation; additional theories are covered superficially, i.e. content summary only. Thus, you have additional content to provide breadth in your answers and these can also be used as counter-perspectives as part of the evaluation. This approach is preferable to covering all theories equally as this often means that none of the content really achieves depth and you would have a lot more material than you need.

This approach matches what is expected of you in the exam, which is that *you should know two theories in depth and use others as support*. Thus, you can be confident that what is included in this revision guide provides you with sufficient material to achieve breadth and depth and so meet the assessment requirements (see the information on "AO1 and AO2 assessment").

QUICK CHECK

- Do you know the options you will focus on in revision?
- Do you know how these will be approached in this revision guide? Have a look at one of the chapters to get a better idea.

NOTE: Throughout the text we have referred to *A2 Psychology: Key Topics, Second Edition* (A2PKT) by Michael W. Eysenck. You can cross-reference this book with the page numbers we have supplied.

How Does A2 Differ from AS?

The type of exam question. A2 requires essays rather than structured answers, except for the Approaches question.

The ratio of AO1 to AO2 is now 50:50. It is not 60:40 as at AS and so you need more analysis and evaluation at A2.

The emphasis on synopticity. The difference in the number of essay marks between Units 4 and 5 is due to synoptic assessment. Synopticity is not that different from AO2 skills, e.g. methodological criticisms and the use of counter-perspectives. So there is no need to see this as something new; you probably already have synoptic skills.

Options rather than compulsory content. So choice, self-responsibility, and independence, rather than prescription! You can choose which topics to cover with your teacher's approval, and you have a choice over which content you revise as this depends on what you want to put into your essay. This means that, more than ever, your success is down to you and how well prepared you are to answer the range of exam questions. This is finite and so with thorough preparation you can prepare for all eventualities—even your least favourite questions, as it's best not to leave these out!

REVISION TIPS

Think back to the AS topic on memory and no doubt you will remember that organisation, repetition, and making information meaningful all improve memory. So bear this in mind during your revision programme. Also consider what has worked for you up to now and what hasn't, if appropriate. See how your strategies compare with the following "do"s and "don't"s.

DO	DON'T
Start now—the exams are not ages away.	Procrastinate, i.e. put off until another day.
Organise the information, e.g. mind-maps, flow charts, tables—anything that summarises and condenses the information.	Write pages and pages of disorganised notes.
Make revision personally meaningful and ACTIVE, i.e. do something with the information—use colour, images, make your own revision aids.	Just read your notes—most people don't learn enough from reading as it is passive and lacks meaning.
Practise exam questions.	Leave a question out because it is difficult.
Leave time for repetition, i.e. revise a topic more than once.	Think you can learn it all at once.
Revise where there are no distractions.	Tell yourself the TV or music is helping.
Have regular breaks, of 5–10 minutes, not an hour!	Cram with hardly any breaks or sleep!

More Revision Tips

Think about how you learn and revise most effectively, note down any further strategies that work for you and USE THEM!

- **Know what you need to cover.** Make a checklist of what you need to cover and don't *keep* revising what you know; move on to what you don't.

- **Time management.** Create your own revision programme, which includes all of your subjects and time off. If you lapse, don't bin it! Keep to the revision timetable and try to make up the missed revision in your time off.

- **Be active.** Do something with the material. For example, an IT revision aid, a mind-map, sticky notes, revision cards, a revision audiotape or CD; present it to a friend, parent, pet, whoever you can get as a captive audience…just don't be passive!

- **Make reading meaningful.** Use a highlighter pen for key points in this revision guide. Think about the meaning before continuing on to the next section. At the end of a chapter assess how much you know. Be honest! Then re-read to increase your understanding and recall.

- **Use the Essay Plans provided in this revision guide to create your own model answers.** Revise the Essay Plans, then cover them up and see if you can remember the key points. Compare your plan with the original plan and then try writing it in timed conditions. This gives you the opportunity to interpret the question for yourself. It will show if you are forgetting key content and the more you do something the faster and better you get! The model answers you produce will be much more useful as revision aids than the Essay Plans supplied.

- **Use your own words.** When making notes and revision aids, or writing essay plans or answers always use your own words, as this will increase your recall and understanding. Plan so content is enough but not too much—a plan is essential. So simply note down the number of paragraphs you are going to use (we suggest 6 for Unit 4 and 8 for Unit 5) and summarise in a word or two what each paragraph will be about. Ideally you should have a plan for every possible exam question!

- **Practise.** To achieve grade A essays you need to practise. Knowledge alone is not enough, you need to be able to present this effectively in essay form. Practice in revision should guard against the "gibberish effect" in the exam!

- **Use your knowledge of stress management.** So do not displace, you are in control!

- **Use your knowledge of memory.** Mnemonics, e.g. acrostics, acronyms, method of loci. According to context-dependent memory we remember best if the cues at retrieval are the same as at encoding, so try to match your revision to the exam conditions—both with the environment, i.e. quiet and distraction free, and your internal state, which will hopefully be energised but not too stressed, both in revision and the exam!

- **Create your own exam.** Put possible questions into two envelopes, one for the Unit 4 exam paper and one for the Unit 5 exam paper, so that you don't know which question will come up, just like in the exam. This is the only way to get used to the "No, not that question" phenomenon.

- **Use a variety of revision methods.** There's no denying it, revision can be tedious, stressful, and a living hell so try to make it more bearable with a variety of techniques.

- **Prioritise.** There is no such thing as a photographic memory, which I think is a good thing because I certainly don't have one! This means the only way to cope with the vast amount of information you need to know for the exam (!!) is to prioritise key points and learn a manageable amount of these.

- **Reinforcement.** If you have worked hard be nice to yourself.

- **Don't give up.** It is not all or nothing.

AO1 AND AO2 SKILLS

As you are no doubt well aware from AS, Assessment Objective 1 (AO1) requires *knowledge and understanding* and Assessment Objective 2 (AO2) requires *analysis and evaluation*.

The AO1 part of the question usually begins with the injunction *"describe"* or *"outline"* and the AO2 part of the question usually begins with one of the following injunctions: *"evaluate"*, *"assess"*, *"criticise"*, *"critically analyse"*, or *"critically assess"*.

Alternatively, the exam question could begin with one of these: *"discuss"*, *"critically consider"*, *"compare and contrast"*, or *"distinguish between"*, which are both AO1 and AO2 terms.

The remainder of the question will then specify what you need to apply the injunctions to: psychological theories, terminology, concepts, studies, methods, perspectives, and applications.

If the question asks for *research*, theories or studies could be used.

If the question includes a *quote*, you must reference it, so comment on it in the introduction and conclusion.

The A2 Specification contains all the possible exam questions, so you can now work out the range of potential exam questions for the options you are studying by combining the following question stems with the content identified in the Specification.

> **Outline and evaluate…**
>
> **Describe and assess…**
>
> **Discuss…**
>
> **Critically consider…**

I won't go on as I'm sure you can now add to this list yourself.

What you need to be aware of is that the question may be split into two parts, where (a) usually requires AO1 content and (b) mainly AO2. The marks may be spread equally so 12:12 or 15:15, or unevenly, e.g. (a) = 6 and (b) = 18 on Unit 4, and (a) = 10 and (b) = 20 or (a) = 5 and (b) = 25 on Unit 5. Or the question may be just that, one question, where the AO1 to AO2 ratio is always a 50:50 split.

AO1 AND AO2 ASSESSMENT

To achieve highly it is important to develop *précis*. This is the ability to write concisely and so summarise information succinctly. This will improve your AO1 and AO2 performance, as it's important to condense description and evaluation in order to cover sufficient content in the tight time limits of 30/40 minutes. The best way to practise this is to focus on always using your own words when noting content from this revision guide and to write only as much as *you* can realistically include in an essay in timed conditions. The Approaches question is quite distinct from the essay questions and will be considered in detail in the Approaches chapter. However, the suggestions on how to gain marks on AO1 and AO2 are relevant, as is *précis*, so although the structure of the question is different, the skills you need to bring to it are the same.

Look closely at the mark schemes for Units 4 and 5 (see A2PKT p.15), to get further insights into how to gain, and not lose, marks. Do you agree with the following suggestions?

AO1

How to gain marks	How to lose marks
Know your stuff so your answer is accurate and detailed.	Bluff and write only in generalities.
Show a clear focus on the question by using link sentences (see Exam Technique).	Waffle, lack focus, write a meandering answer.
Be selective; only the most relevant content to the question should be included.	Write everything you know about the topic that may or may not answer the question.
Plan, so you know what's going in each paragraph and the conclusion.	Write for the entire exam with no thought to planning. This will make your answers lack structure, the content order illogical, and your writing incoherent.
Write about some content in detail (depth) and some content superficially so your answer also achieves breadth.	Write about only one theory/study but in little detail so it looks like you've only learnt one thing, not very well.
Balance breadth and depth, write about two things in depth and identify alternatives but don't go into detail.	Take a narrow approach so achieve depth only, or an expansive approach, which achieves breadth but no depth and so your answer is imbalanced.
Show synopticity by identifying methodological approaches and criticisms, and use counter-perspectives.	Show no knowledge of methodology and ignore alternative perspectives.

AO2

How to gain marks	How to lose marks
Use material effectively by selecting evidence that relates well to the question and give balanced analysis (different strands, e.g. for and against) and evaluation (strengths and weaknesses).	Lack selectivity and give a one-sided answer, e.g. only evidence for or only weaknesses—these are very common mistakes!
Use evidence effectively to support evaluation.	Ignore evidence to support evaluation and instead make personal criticisms about the psychologist. For example, "he took cocaine and was sex-mad" is not appropriate!
Coherently elaborate the criticism, i.e. explain it and assess the consequences of the strength or weakness.	State, but don't elaborate, the criticism.
Comment on the meaning of a theory or research study, give different interpretations and conclusions *throughout* your answer.	Give limited, or no, commentary and conclusions.
Show synopticity with methodological criticisms and evaluation of the theoretical perspective, using counter-perspectives as evaluation.	Fail to comment on the methodology and make no reference to counter-perspectives.

How to Get Synopticity in Your Answers

Look at how this is assessed on the mark schemes for Unit 5, AO1 and AO2.

Synopticity means having an overarching knowledge and critical understanding of fundamental psychological content, in particular *methodologies* and the different *approaches/perspectives.*

What follows is a summary of each different approach, the methodologies favoured by each approach, and an evaluation. You need to know at least two of these approaches well to achieve highly on the Approaches question on Unit 5. You should also review Research Methods covered in Unit 3 at AS, as this is a key source of synopticity.

BIOLOGICAL APPROACH

Genetics.

Methods: Twin, adoption, and family concordance studies.
Evaluation: Not 100% concordance; small samples and so limited population validity; cannot separate out nature and nurture. The method is natural experiment as genetic relatedness is a naturally occurring IV, which means cause and effect cannot be inferred, as the IV is not manipulated.

Neurological.

Methods: Brain scanning techniques (e.g. CATs, PETs, and MRIs) and brain-wave recordings.
Evaluation: The reliability, i.e. consistency of the measures, is an issue. Also, the interpretations of such data may be subject to bias and error, which reduces confidence in the validity of the methods.

Biochemical.

Methods: Levels of neurotransmitters and hormones are measured.
Evaluation: Physiological measures have objectivity, but it is not clear if the levels are a cause, effect, or correlate of the phenomena they are linked to.

Overall.

The method tends to be experimental, which means research has objectivity and so scientific validity. However, experimental trials may be artificial and so effects lack validity, as demonstrated by the placebo effect. The physiological measures are objective and precise, which increases confidence in the validity of the data. But the biological approach is reductionist as it reduces complex behaviour to oversimplified factors and ignores psychological factors, and so may overestimate the role of nature and underestimate the role of nurture. Thus, psychological approaches must also be considered. The approach is also weakened by determinism, as it tends to ignore the free will of the individuals to control their own behaviour, as it suggests that behaviour is determined by biology.

BEHAVIOURAL APPROACH (LEARNING THEORIES)

Classical conditioning.

Methods: Laboratory experiments, where Pavlov showed that a stimulus–response bond could be formed by pairing a neutral stimulus with a stimulus that produces an automatic response.
Evaluation: Limited generalisability as it can only explain behaviours that are in some way linked to an automatic response, and so works best for explaining emotional responses.

Operant conditioning.

Methods: Laboratory experiments where Skinner demonstrated that behaviours followed by positive consequences (positive and negative reinforcement) are more likely to be repeated and those followed by an unpleasant consequence (punishment) are likely to be stamped out.

Evaluation: Explains a wider variety of stimulus–response bonds, as spontaneous operants are shaped into more fixed behaviours through reinforcement. It is not always possible to distinguish between classical and operant conditioning.

Overall.

The theories are based on observable and measurable research and so are supported by objective, scientific data. They are criticised as being mechanistic as they reduce men to machines due to the assumption that behaviour is programmed by the environment. Not only is this reductionist and environmentally deterministic, it ignores psychological factors such as cognition as much of the research is conducted on animals and so extrapolation is an issue. Neo-behaviourists have expanded on traditional learning theories, e.g. Bandura's Social Learning Theory, and this does take into account cognition and social factors.

COGNITIVE APPROACH

Mental processes (thinking, attention, memory) are believed to be the determinants of emotion and behaviour. The information-processing model and the computer analogy are key features of this approach. A breakdown in information processing results in faulty thinking, i.e. cognitive distortion.

Methods: Laboratory experiments where attempts are made to operationalise cognition, e.g. number of words remembered, measures of cognitive dysfunction. Also, the computer model, where a computer represents the brain, has led to research into artificial intelligence, which is related back to human cognition.

Evaluation: The cognitive approach is supported by experimental data and so has scientific objectivity but may be biased by artificiality and researcher and participant effects. Such findings would lack experimental validity, both internal and external, which reduces the value of the research. Researcher bias is a particular problem with cognitive dysfunction as this involves value judgements to determine whether cognition is faulty or not. Another weakness is that research on thought depends on self-disclosure and so may lack validity, as people do not always say what they really think. The computer analogy has considerably advanced understanding but is limited, as even the most sophisticated computer does not compare to the human brain. It is mechanistic and reductionist as, of course, we are not machines and the focus on cognition means emotional, motivational, and social factors are ignored.

PSYCHODYNAMIC APPROACH

Freud founded this perspective with psychoanalysis, and the term psychodynamic means "active mind", i.e. the psyche, as this is the focus of Freud's and neo-Freudian theories (Jung, Adler, Erikson).

Methods: Freud used the clinical interview to compile case studies. He claimed that adult behaviour is determined by unresolved conflicts from childhood, based on the opposing needs of the id, ego, and superego. Id impulses are our evolved animalistic tendencies, the sexual (libido) and aggressive drives, which motivate behaviour, and conflict with the ego and the superego. Such conflicts are repressed into the unconscious, which can lead to fixation or regression to earlier psychosexual stages, and the anxiety caused by such conflicts may trigger defence mechanisms and poor ego development.

Evaluation: Freud conducted the clinical interviews, which means they are vulnerable to researcher bias and participant reactivity, and validity must be questioned. Freud's research cannot be tested empirically as concepts such as the unconscious cannot be operationalised and so the research lacks scientific validity and can be neither verified nor falsified. A restricted sample of neurotic Viennese women was used so population validity is low. Freud's theory may be era-dependent and context-bound as repression is likely to have occurred a lot in Victorian society, but given the permissiveness of today's society it is difficult to see the need for repression. Freud was the founding father of the psychological approaches and was the inspiration for much further research. Thus, his contribution to psychology should not be underestimated, and many of his ideas underpin psychotherapy today. There are also ethical implications as, to a certain extent, parenting is called into question due to its contribution to childhood conflicts.

EVOLUTIONARY APPROACH

Darwin founded the evolutionary perspective with his theory of natural selection, which proposes that evolution is a gradual process where changes in genetic make-up are selected if they are adaptive, i.e. help the individual better fit its ecological niche. Adaptive characteristics or behaviours increase survival and reproductive potential, as species with these traits are more likely to survive and reproduce and so transfer these adaptive characteristics into the next generation. Hence, they have been passively (i.e. naturally) selected and so goes the process of evolution. Sociobiologists have expanded on Darwin's original theory, as his concept of individual fitness and survival did not account for social behaviours, whereas inclusive fitness and kin selection do. Environmental change and competition drive the process of evolution as they exert selective pressure. Key assumptions of this approach are that behaviours are genetically predisposed and that these behaviours must be adaptive or neutral to have been selected and to have remained in the gene pool and that these would be universal.

Methods: The fossil record, natural experiments, and naturalistic observation have provided some evidence to support evolutionary explanations. Naturalistic observation has provided a great deal of evidence on variation between and within species that supports evolutionary principles. Selective breeding provides further support.

Evaluation: Research into genetics provides some support but there are many criticisms of this. Also, the evolutionary concept of the gene is questionable, as complex behaviours are not coded in the way suggested by evolutionists. Evolutionary theories are post hoc (after the event) and this means they are speculative rather than based on hard evidence, as this is difficult to acquire. The research methods are subject to researcher bias and other confounding variables, and cause and effect cannot be inferred from such research. This has led to the explanations being described as "evolutionary stories" and certainly they lack empirical support and so scientific validity. Extrapolation is also an issue as most of the evidence is derived from animal research. The evolutionary perspective is reductionist as it focuses on only one factor, the gene, and it is biologically deterministic as predisposition is inconsistent with free will. In particular, social and cultural factors are ignored as the perspective only accounts for nature, not nurture. Postmodernism, social constructionism, and feminism challenge evolutionary explanations. The missing links in the evolutionary time line are also a weakness, but do not disprove the perspective, as there is insufficient evidence to either verify or falsify it. Consequently, evolutionary explanations are often contradictory, as just about any pattern of findings can be explained by the evolutionary approach seeing as how they cannot be falsified!

All these perspectives can be evaluated positively based on the insights they provide and the useful applications they have generated.

Hopefully the above gives you an idea of the range of content you have to draw upon to increase synopticity in your answers. This provides only an overview of the approaches—they are covered in more detail in Chapter 12.

Synoptic Rules

1. Know the range of methodological criticisms and how to integrate them into your answer.

2. Identify perspectives and evaluate them using the alternative perspectives, and conclude that a multi-perspective (e.g. diathesis–stress) is optimal.

EXAM TECHNIQUE

ANSWER THE QUESTION—It sounds obvious, yet it's not always done.

1. Check the injunctions to see whether AO1, AO2, or both is required.
2. If there is a quote, use it.
3. If the question says *"including"* you must write about whatever is specified. If it says *"e.g."* you can choose alternative content if you prefer.
4. Leave spaces between paragraphs so that you can expand on your link sentences if you have time or feel you need to change them as you go along.
5. If the question says *"explanations"*, *"theories"*, or *"two or more"*, you must cover two or more explanations of theories.

The way to make it clear to the examiner that you are answering the question is to use *link sentences*, i.e. re-phrase the words of the question and make a mini-conclusion, one per paragraph, so it's clear that whatever you've written about in that paragraph is relevant to the question. This is a good check for you as well, because if you can't make a link sentence then the chances are the material isn't relevant!

BE SELECTIVE—You can only write a limited amount in 30 (Unit 4) or 40 (Unit 5) minutes.

1. The content you select must be the most relevant possible!
2. Don't go into lengthy descriptions that are an unnecessary amount of detail and which reduce the time you have for more relevant material. For example, when describing a piece of research, give the findings and conclusions only—the aims and procedures are too much detail.
3. Having selected the most relevant material, describe and evaluate two areas in detail to achieve depth, and write about alternative content superficially so that your answer shows a wider understanding and achieves breadth.

BE INFORMED—Make sure your use of material does you justice, i.e. you do show how much you have learned in psychology. To do this, AO1 must be accurate and detailed and AO2 must make effective use of research evidence

ESSAY PLANS—These, of course, should be second nature as a result of planning in revision!

1. In the exam use the first minute allocated to do an essay plan. Write the numbers 1 to 6 (Unit 4) or 1 to 8 (Unit 5) along one line and underneath briefly note what will go into each paragraph, this may be as little as one word, as you do need to move quickly onto your answer.
2. Leave space so that you can add in anything else that occurs to you as you do the essay. The stress of exams can affect memory so if you think of something really good for paragraph 5 or the conclusion add it onto the plan in case you forget it by the time you get to that paragraph.
3. Don't cross the plan out—this can only be credited if it's not crossed out so tick content, if you like, to check off what you've done.

BE BALANCED—AO1 and AO2 achieve equal marks.

1. Make sure that AO1 and AO2 are balanced at the planning stage.
2. Provide evidence for and against to achieve balance.
3. Give positive and negative evaluation.

TIME MANAGEMENT—Manage your time in the exam very carefully: on the Unit 4 exam paper you have 30 minutes per question; on the Unit 5 exam paper you have 40 minutes per question. Resist the urge to spend a disproportionate amount of time on your first essay, just because you could make it really good with 10 more minutes. One brilliant answer is no good—it is better to have three very good answers, than one brilliant and two average ones!

DON'T JUST STATE, ELABORATE—To achieve a grade C or above your answer must not be superficial. This often occurs when criticisms are merely stated as it's easy to say a study lacks ecological validity, or is reductionist, deterministic, etc. You could simply learn a list of AO2 phrases and hardly know what they mean! So, unsurprisingly, stating criticisms achieves few marks. To go beyond mere statement you need to provide commentary:

1. Explain what the criticism means.
2. Make a conclusion by assessing the consequences of the criticism, e.g. if the research lacks validity then this reduces its value and so it does not provide strong support for ...... theory, which may reduce its explanatory power.
3. Relate this conclusion back to the question. Write a link sentence, e.g. if the question had asked you to assess the contribution of ...... explanations, and you have reached the above conclusion, then you can say, "The theory lacks empirical support as the validity of the research evidence can be questioned and so there is a need for further research to substantiate the explanation. This means whilst it may appear to make sense we cannot fully accept the insights the explanation provides and so it lacks explanatory power. Furthermore, this explanation takes only one perspective, whereas a multi-perspective best accounts for ......". Note in this example the use of "and so" and "This means". There are many useful phrases (see A2PKT p.19) that you can use to ensure your answer does contain commentary and does link back to the question.

MASTER AO2—What is commentary? It is interpretation, analysis, evaluation, and conclusions. Does your answer have MERIT? Use this mnemonic to check your answer is evaluative:

Methodological criticisms. Criticisms of the research methods, design of the research, and the sample, all of which have implications for reliability and validity.

Ethics. Do the ends justify the means? Much research has ethical implications so consider whether it should have passed the cost–benefit analysis.

Real-life validity, explanatory power, and applications. How well does the theory/explanation/research relate to and explain real-life phenomena? In other words, is it psychologically real? Does it have face validity, i.e. seem plausible? If so, can the information be used in a positive way (i.e. applications)? If not, the theory/explanation/research may lack value and explanatory power. See the conclusions in the Essay Plans, as this is often a useful way to complete an essay.

Individual, social, and cultural variation. Has such variation been accounted for? Are explanations culturally relative or universal? If cultural relativism has not been acknowledged the research may be ethnocentric. Remember, to some extent, all research is a product of the time and context in which it was carried out. So contextualise the research and assess whether it is era-dependent and context-bound, and consider the consequences in terms of ecological validity (can it generalise to the present context?), population validity (can it generalise to other populations?), and temporal validity (can it generalise to more recent time periods?).

Theoretical. Reductionism and determinism can be used to evaluate most theories. Nature/nurture can also be used to assess theoretical perspectives. Don't forget to show that you *understand* why they might be relevant to the question you are answering. Use counter-perspectives as evaluation and conclude that a multi-perspective is optimal.

Different sources of AO2 marks, e.g. ethics, validity, etc. can be used in various essays. So it's a good idea to create your own AO2 revision sheet of criticisms with elaboration and commentary.

HOW TO WRITE A GRADE 'A' ESSAY

You know one when you read one! Perhaps you have been supplied with model answers in class and so can tell when an essay is really good. But how do you make yours equally so?

Begin by knowing what you are going to write about in each paragraph, what conclusion you are heading towards, and make sure that what you have planned is what you can feasibly write in timed conditions. You should have a plan for the range of potential exam questions committed to memory, so that you spend only a minute noting it down in the exam, as there isn't time for any longer.

DO	DON'T
Know which question numbers you have prepared for.	Spend the first 5 minutes of the exam finding the questions.
Answer the question set by noting the injunction and the specified content.	Interpret the question to suit yourself and the essay you prepared earlier.
Get straight to the point.	Say what you intend to cover—just do it!
Use commentary, where criticisms are elaborated and conclusions linked to the question.	List criticisms with little elaboration.
Make sure content is relevant by using link sentences.	Avoid finding out content is irrelevant by refusing to link to question.
Use *précis*.	Write in an over-wordy or long-winded style.
Write an informed answer by using research evidence to support and challenge, and explain why. Base conclusions on this evidence.	Write the "man on the street" answer with only your own opinion and anecdotes about yourself as evidence.

Well that's the end of my advice. Do understand that I am a teacher and so bound to go on a bit, but that at the same time I just might know what I'm going on about. So please do follow the advice in this chapter!

Good luck!

Work hard and you should be celebrating in August!

Social Psychology

What's it about?

Theories of interpersonal relationships are concerned with the factors that determine who we like and dislike, the features that influence our friendships and sexual relationships. In this unit, we start by looking at the determinants of initial friendships and attraction. We then consider theories that explain why some relationships endure, perhaps going from strength to strength, while others break down. We continue by looking at the differences in relationships between cultures and sub-cultures, for example, the difference between arranged marriages and those based initially on romantic love. Finally, we will consider relationships that have attracted research attention only recently, such as homosexual relationships and those formed over the Internet.

What's in this unit?

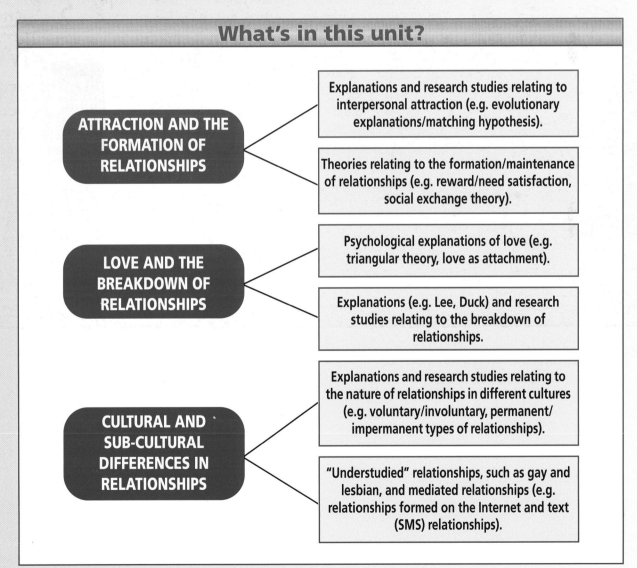

ATTRACTION AND THE FORMATION OF RELATIONSHIPS

- Explanations and research studies relating to interpersonal attraction (e.g. evolutionary explanations/matching hypothesis).
- Theories relating to the formation/maintenance of relationships (e.g. reward/need satisfaction, social exchange theory).

LOVE AND THE BREAKDOWN OF RELATIONSHIPS

- Psychological explanations of love (e.g. triangular theory, love as attachment).
- Explanations (e.g. Lee, Duck) and research studies relating to the breakdown of relationships.

CULTURAL AND SUB-CULTURAL DIFFERENCES IN RELATIONSHIPS

- Explanations and research studies relating to the nature of relationships in different cultures (e.g. voluntary/involuntary, permanent/impermanent types of relationships).
- "Understudied" relationships, such as gay and lesbian, and mediated relationships (e.g. relationships formed on the Internet and text (SMS) relationships).

ATTRACTION AND THE FORMATION OF RELATIONSHIPS

ASK YOURSELF

Think of three close friends you had at primary and secondary school. What attracted you to those particular people? List as many factors as you can.

Were the same friendships maintained from primary to secondary school? If not, think about the reasons why they did not continue.

Consider any friendships you have outside school or college. How did you meet these friends? Are these friendships the same or different from the ones at school or college?

With respect to romantic relationships, what features attract you to a particular person? Do you think your friends find the same features attractive or are they looking for different ones?

WHAT YOU NEED TO KNOW

FACTORS THAT ATTRACT PEOPLE TO ONE ANOTHER

- Physical attractiveness (including the matching hypothesis)
- Proximity
- Attitude similarity
- Demographic similarity
- Similarity in personality

THEORIES OF THE FORMATION OF RELATIONSHIPS

- Social exchange theory
- Reward/need satisfaction theory

To read up on attraction and the formation of relationships, refer to pages 25–48 of A2PKT.

THE FIVE MAIN FACTORS DETERMINING INTERPERSONAL ATTRACTION

Many factors are involved in the formation of interpersonal relationships. The five main factors are:

- Physical attractiveness.
- Proximity.
- Attitude similarity.
- Demographic similarity.
- Similarity in personality.

Physical Attractiveness

Research indicates that being physically attractive makes people more popular and that this applies in friendships as well as personal relationships. Features that make women attractive include large eyes, small nose, small chin. In men, attraction is related to a square jaw, small eyes, and thin lips (Cunningham, 1986, see A2PKT pp.25–26).

RESEARCH EVIDENCE

- Brigham (1971, see A2PKT p.26), in a review of stereotypes, showed that people prefer those who are physically attractive, believing them to be interesting, poised, exciting, and sexually warm.
- Walster et al.'s (1966, see A2PKT p.27) "blind date" study. Students were randomly paired at a huge blind date dance and, during the interval, were separated and asked to give a rating of their date. It was found that the only significant predictor of how highly people were rated was their physical attractiveness. Characteristics such as personality, interests, and intelligence made little difference to the ratings.

EVALUATION OF THE IMPORTANCE OF PHYSICAL ATTRACTION

- **Supporting evidence.** Walster et al.'s (1966) "blind date" study demonstrates strong support for the importance of physical attractiveness in interpersonal relationships.
- **Individual differences.** Towhey (1979, see A2PKT p.28) demonstrated that some people are more influenced by physical attractiveness than others.
- **Importance in long-term sexual relationships.** Murstein and Christy (1976, see A2PKT p.28) found that the importance of physical attractiveness continues throughout a marriage and is therefore not just of importance in the initial courtship period.

The Matching Hypothesis

Although we may prefer to be with people who are very beautiful, in real life this is obviously not possible. The *matching hypothesis* states that we tend to pair with individuals who have a similar level of attraction to ourselves, both in friendships and romantic relationships.

RESEARCH EVIDENCE

- Walster and Walster (1969, see A2PKT p.27) repeated the "blind date" study but students met beforehand. This time, they expressed the most liking for those with the same level of physical attractiveness as themselves.
- Murstein (1972, see A2PKT p.28) found that engaged and married couples were judged to be of a similar level of attractiveness.
- Silverman (1971) conducted a field study in bars and similar places and found that couples were rated as similar in levels of physical attractiveness.

EVALUATION OF THE MATCHING HYPOTHESIS

- **First meetings.** It is not supported by Walster et al.'s (1966) initial "blind date" study, perhaps because of the artificial nature of the study.
- **Subsequent meetings.** Many other studies, including field studies, and Walster and Walster's (1969) follow up "blind date" study, support the hypothesis.

Proximity

The single most important factor in predicting our likely choice of friends is the "nearness" or proximity between us and them. Because of where we live, work, or go to school we have close contact with particular people and it is this contact, caused by the physical arrangement, that influences who we choose as friends and lovers.

RESEARCH EVIDENCE

- Bossard (1932, see A2PKT p.29) examined the pre-marital addresses of 5000 couples and found that half of them lived within short walking distance of each other.
- Deutsch and Collins (1951) found that people assigned to rented housing made friends regardless of race. This has obvious implications for racial harmony.

EVALUATION

- **Proximity is an obvious determinant of relationships.** We cannot get to know people unless we meet them. It may be the amount of contact rather than proximity that is the crucial determinant.
- **Temporal validity.** Bossard's (1932) study is rather dated and may not necessarily apply nowadays when people are far more mobile and travel greater distances. Also, Internet relationships have allowed proximity to be less important in certain types of relationships.
- **Proximity does not always lead to liking.** Intense dislike as well as strong attraction can result from proximity. Ebbesen, Kjos, and Konecni (1976, see A2PKT p.29) found that if people have enemies, they are also likely to live close by. It may be that a lot of contact results in intense emotions, whether positive or negative.

Attitude Similarity

The more similar the attitudes are between two people, the greater the likelihood of friendship and romance. This particularly applies to important attitudes.

RESEARCH EVIDENCE

- In a series of studies known as "bogus stranger studies", Byrne et al. (1968, see A2PKT p.30) found that people shown a questionnaire about another person's personal characteristics tended to express liking for them in direct proportion to the number of attitudes they shared with them. The questionnaires were fake, hence "bogus stranger" studies.
- Werner and Parmalee (1979, see A2PKT p.30) demonstrated that friendships depend on shared interests, such as leisure pursuits, more than on other attitude similarities.

EVALUATION

- ☹ **It only applies to important attitudes.** Shared interests are more important than other attitudes in friendships (Werner & Parmalee, 1979). However, in marriage, other important attitudes (not shared interests) such as political convictions tend to dominate. This is probably because men and women do not expect to share interests—you do not have to go to every football match with him in order for him to fall in love with you (but it probably helps!).
- ☺ **It is generally, but not always, supported by research.** Buss (1985) found a great degree of similarity in attitudes in married couples but Gold et al. (1984), in an artificial laboratory study, demonstrated that sometimes "love is blind". Overall, however, the rule still applies. Cattell and Nesselrode (1967) found that the most stable marriages are those between couples who are similar in attitudes.

Demographic Similarity

Demographic factors such as age, religion, social class, sex, and ethnic background are important determinants of relationships; people generally prefer those who are demographically similar to themselves.

RESEARCH EVIDENCE

- Kandel (1978, see A2PKT p.30) examined the characteristics of best friends in secondary school students and found great similarity in these factors.
- Newcomb (1961, see A2PKT p.30) demonstrated that when people were allocated a room with a person who held different attitudes and beliefs, 25% were friends after a year, demonstrating that when obliged to mix, some very different people can grow to like each other. Nevertheless, a much greater percentage (58%) of those allocated a room with someone with similar attitudes and beliefs to themselves became friends.

EVALUATION

 Supporting evidence. Kandel's study and similar research supports the idea that demographic similarity is influential.

 Correlational limitations. Remember, however, that the association between age, religion, sex, social class, and ethnic background is *correlational* so there's not necessarily a direct cause–effect relationship between these factors and attraction. It's possible that we feel more comfortable with those from a similar background so we don't try to mix with people who are different. This may account for Newcomb's findings.

 Implications. Breaking away from demographic ties can result in a person being isolated or rejected from their community; hence this could explain some instances of why demographic similarity dominates.

Similarity in Personality

The idea that "opposites attract" and "birds of a feather flock together" have both been explored. Generally, evidence indicates that similar people are attracted to each other, and that opposites do not attract. However, Winch (1958, see A2PKT p.31) argued that people are compatible if they have complementary *needs* (e.g. a dominant person with a submissive one).

RESEARCH EVIDENCE

- Burgess and Wallin (1953, see A2PKT p.31) looked at the personality characteristics of engaged couples and found significant within-couple similarity.
- Winch (1958, see A2PKT p.31), however, explored complementarity rather than similarity in the needs of married couples and found that couples with opposing personalities were happier than those with similar ones.

EVALUATION

 Individual differences. Some couples are happier in a relationship with an individual whose personality is the opposite to their own, as long as their needs are complementary, whereas some are happier with a partner similar to themself.

The Importance of All Five Factors

Similarity appears to be an over-riding factor in relationship formation. Why is it important? Rubin (1973, see A2PKT p.31) suggests that it is for a number of reasons:

- Similar people are likely to like us.
- We like those who we think like us.
- It is easy to communicate and feel relaxed with similar people.
- People who hold similar attitudes validate our own attitudes and thereby increase our self-esteem—it is a strong positive reinforcer.
- People who are similar to us enjoy the same activities.

GENERAL EVALUATION OF RESEARCH

☹ **Much research lacks ecological validity.** Many of the studies involve very artificial situations. For example, some involve questionnaires in which a description of a person (e.g. their age, interests, likes/dislikes, attitudes) and perhaps a photo is provided and the participant estimates how much they would like them (the "bogus stranger" studies). In real life, we actually meet people and there may be a host of other factors that determine whether or not a relationship will form.

☺ **Validity.** However, in real life people do occasionally use written profiles as a basis for choosing a partner (such as using newspaper "dating" ads), and they choose on the basis of similarity, so the method is not entirely without validity.

☺ **Individual differences.** It is possible that there are large individual differences in the degree to which these factors influence friendships—some people may be more tolerant of different age groups, different interests, or different ethnic groups; indeed, some people may seek variety. At present these individual differences have not been widely researched.

☹ **Lack of qualitative data.** The post-modernist approach would point to the lack of qualitative data, which is perhaps more appropriate for study in this area.

Real-life relationships are based on more than just physical attractiveness.

THEORIES AND RESEARCH RELATING TO THE FORMATION OF RELATIONSHIPS

Evolutionary Explanations

Evolutionary or sociobiological theories (see A2PKT pp.32–33) are based on the premise that evolution has shaped the behaviour of all organisms so as to maximise the propagation (passing on) of their genes. This involves behaviour that increases survival of the individual (since the longer you survive, the greater the opportunity for reproduction) as well as reproductive behaviour. In humans, this means that *all* relationships (even friendships) have evolved to increase survival of the individual and opportunities for successful reproduction. With regard to sexual relationships, Buss (1989, see A2PKT p.32) argues that women seek older, successful men who can support them and their children. Men prefer younger women because they are likely to be more fertile than older ones. Both prefer attractive partners because this indicates healthiness. With regard to families, it is inherent in us to form close family relationships since these help to propagate any shared genes. We have therefore evolved to protect our children, grandchildren, nieces, etc. The closer the genetic relationship, the more we are prepared to sacrifice in order to protect our relatives (see Fellner & Marshall, 1981, A2PKT p.33). This is known as *kin selection,* the notion that survival of an individual's genes is ensured by helping the survival of close relatives.

RESEARCH EVIDENCE

- Singh (1993) reported that men are attracted to women with a low waist-to-hip ratio and this is related to child-bearing potential.

- Buss (1989, see A2PKT p.301) conducted an extensive cross-cultural study that demonstrated that men and women seek different things in long-term sexual partners in ways that correspond to evolutionary theory; for example, men valued physical attraction while women were concerned with the ability to support a family.

- Davis (1990, see A2PKT p.270) considered the content of personal ads in newspapers and found that women emphasised their beauty, whereas men emphasised their wealth and other resources; women stated they were looking for status and good earning potential in a man, whereas the men were looking for a physically attractive, younger woman.

EVALUATION

- **Validity.** These theories help explain several aspects of relationships, such as why men and women seek different things in partners and why enormous emotional energy is devoted to children.

- **The theory is non-scientific.** In general, sociobiological theories are unable to make predictions, the essence of a good theory. They take existing aspects of relationships (such as why men and women seek different things), often only considering Western relationships, and then create a hypothesis that fits into the overall theory. For example, they suggest that physical attraction is a desirable feature because it indicates health and therefore child-bearing ability, which is not necessarily true.

- **It cannot explain all important relationships.** The approach does not adequately explain some important and quite common relationships, such as homosexual relationships and close friendships (attempts have been made but the arguments are weak). If genes are the most influential factors, why do women love their best friends as much as their lover and like them more (Sternberg & Grajek, 1984, see A2PKT p.34)?

Reward/Need Satisfaction Theory

This theory (see A2PKT p.34) is based on *learning theory* and states that we form relationships that provide rewards (reinforcement) and satisfy our needs. Rewards include companionship, being loved, sex, status, money, help, and agreement with our opinions, as shown by Foa and Foa (1975, see A2PKT p.35). Both operant and classical conditioning are influential. Byrne (1971, see A2PKT p.35) pointed out that by *classical conditioning* we come to like people with whom we associate enjoyment and satisfaction even if they are not directly responsible for the positive experiences. When we experience enjoyable shared activities with people they create in us a positive emotional feeling, known as a positive *affect*. By operant conditioning, we like those who provide us with rewards and dislike those whose presence is unpleasant because they are, for example, tedious, boring, or argumentative.

RESEARCH EVIDENCE

- Veitch and Griffitt (1976, see A2PKT p.35) demonstrated that people who interact with a stranger against a background broadcast of good news rate them more positively than when they meet a stranger while listening to a broadcast full of depressing news items.

- Rabbie and Horowitz (1960, see A2PKT p.35) found that strangers preferred those who they met while winning a game rather than when losing it.

EVALUATION

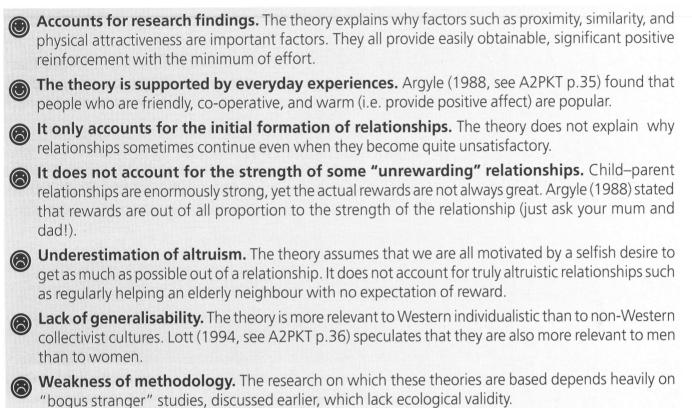

- 😊 **Accounts for research findings.** The theory explains why factors such as proximity, similarity, and physical attractiveness are important factors. They all provide easily obtainable, significant positive reinforcement with the minimum of effort.
- 😊 **The theory is supported by everyday experiences.** Argyle (1988, see A2PKT p.35) found that people who are friendly, co-operative, and warm (i.e. provide positive affect) are popular.
- ☹️ **It only accounts for the initial formation of relationships.** The theory does not explain why relationships sometimes continue even when they become quite unsatisfactory.
- ☹️ **It does not account for the strength of some "unrewarding" relationships.** Child–parent relationships are enormously strong, yet the actual rewards are not always great. Argyle (1988) stated that rewards are out of all proportion to the strength of the relationship (just ask your mum and dad!).
- ☹️ **Underestimation of altruism.** The theory assumes that we are all motivated by a selfish desire to get as much as possible out of a relationship. It does not account for truly altruistic relationships such as regularly helping an elderly neighbour with no expectation of reward.
- ☹️ **Lack of generalisability.** The theory is more relevant to Western individualistic than to non-Western collectivist cultures. Lott (1994, see A2PKT p.36) speculates that they are also more relevant to men than to women.
- ☹️ **Weakness of methodology.** The research on which these theories are based depends heavily on "bogus stranger" studies, discussed earlier, which lack ecological validity.

THEORIES OF MAINTENANCE AND DISSOLUTION OF RELATIONSHIPS

Economic Theories: Social Exchange Theory

The basic assumptions of social exchange theory (SET) are that relationships provide both rewards (e.g. affection, sex, emotional support) and costs (e.g. providing support, not always having your own way). Everyone tries to maximise rewards while minimising costs. People also expect to receive as many rewards as they provide, so that "give and take" is equal. Relationships tend to break down when rewards and costs are no longer balanced, or the rewards are not what the person thinks they deserve. Alternatives are also taken into consideration—a person may stay in a bad relationship because they are scared of the alternative of being alone. On the other hand, some people leave fairly ordinary marriages when they meet a new, exciting, alternative partner.

Levinger (1976, see A2PKT p.44) focuses on marriage and argues that three factors are likely to lead to a marriage breaking down:

1. Low amounts of positive satisfaction (few rewards).
2. No great barriers to leaving the marriage (barriers include the hurt you may cause, the social stigma, the financial constraints).
3. A high number of attractive alternatives, such as the possibility of a more interesting new partner.

Economic Theories: Equity Theory

Equity theory is an extension of exchange theory. The basic assumption is that people only consider a relationship to be satisfactory if what they gain from it reflects what they give to it. This means that if one person contributes more, they feel they should get more out of it. Equity is especially important at the beginning of a relationship rather than when it is firmly established.

RESEARCH EVIDENCE

- Hatfield, Utne, and Traupmann (1979, see A2PKT p.37) looked at people who felt under-benefited (got less than they should) or over-benefited (got more than they should) in a relationship. They found that the under-benefited people felt angry, resentful, and deprived. Those who were over-benefited felt guilty and uncomfortable.

- Argyle (1988, see A2PKT p.37) explored gender differences and found that over-benefited women are less satisfied that those in equitable marriages, whereas with men, over-benefit brings little dissatisfaction. Under-benefited men feel more aggrieved than women in the same situation.

- Buunk and Van Yperen (1991, see A2PKT p.37) found that those in marriages perceived to be equitable were found to be the happiest, whereas those who perceived themselves as under-benefited were the unhappiest. But this applied only in relationships high in exchange orientation, i.e. where rewards given by one partner are expected to be reciprocated by the other partner.

EVALUATION OF SOCIAL EXCHANGE THEORY

 Explanation of individual differences. Levinger's theory takes account of at least some of the complex reasons why people remain in marriages or leave them. By doing this, it explains why there is not a strong relationship between levels of satisfaction and likelihood of leaving the marriage. People in very unsatisfactory marriages often do not dissolve them, yet those in mediocre marriages sometimes do. If the barriers to leaving are high and the alternatives not very attractive, then people tend to stay.

Does not account for change over time. SET does not explain why an initially successful marriage becomes unhappy.

Underestimation of altruism. SET assumes that people are self-centred whereas many relationships are not based on this principle (see evaluation of reinforcement and need satisfaction theories, in the previous section).

Cross-cultural criticism. These principles apply more to individualistic than to collectivist cultures.

EVALUATION OF EQUITY THEORY

 Explains influences on relationships. The theory takes account of rewards and costs and thereby explains the matching hypothesis. It explains why people are usually equally physically attractive as well as equal in other ways, but also why, for example, a rich, unattractive man can attract a younger, far more attractive woman.

Supported by research studies. There is considerable research evidence in support of equity theory, see above.

Does not account for change over time. Because equity is more important at the beginning of a relationship and people are quite tolerant of some inequity once the relationship is well established, it has limited value in explaining the maintenance and dissolution of relationships.

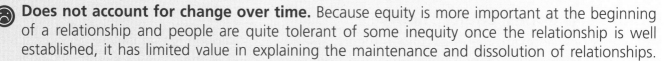

Some research contradicts the theory. Not all research evidence supports equity theory. Some research (e.g. Buunck, 1996, see A2PKT p.38) indicates that there is no association between the degree of equity and the future quality of the relationship.

Individual differences. There are strong individual differences in the degree to which people expect equity (e.g. Buunk & VanYperen, Clark & Mills), so the theory does not apply to everyone.

Underestimation of altruism. Like SET, it assumes people are self-centred (see evaluation of reinforcement and need satisfaction theories, in previous section).

Cross-cultural criticism. These principles apply more to individualistic rather than collectivist cultures.

Not all marriages are based on equity. Clark and Mills (1979, see A2PKT p.38) contend that most marriages are not based on exchange principles. They believe that in many marriages people gain satisfaction by responding to each other's needs.

SO WHAT DOES THIS MEAN?

Researchers and theorists of interpersonal relationships face many problems. There is an enormous number and type of relationships and many theories are not specific about the type of relationship to which they apply. Relationships form and evolve over a very long period of time, making the processes involved difficult to research and not very amenable to the typical methods used. Duck (1992, see A2PKT p.35) has been particularly critical of the use of artificial arrangements, especially the "bogus stranger" studies, in which people have little other than a questionnaire on which to base their opinions. When we interact with people in real life there are a host of other influences that affect our judgement. Nevertheless, the research has revealed useful pointers to the most important influences on the formation of relationships and has formed the basis on which more realistic research can be founded.

OVER TO YOU

1(a). Describe research studies relating to interpersonal attraction. **(12 marks)**

(b). Evaluate these studies with reference to theories of interpersonal attraction. **(12 marks)**

LOVE AND THE BREAKDOWN OF RELATIONSHIPS

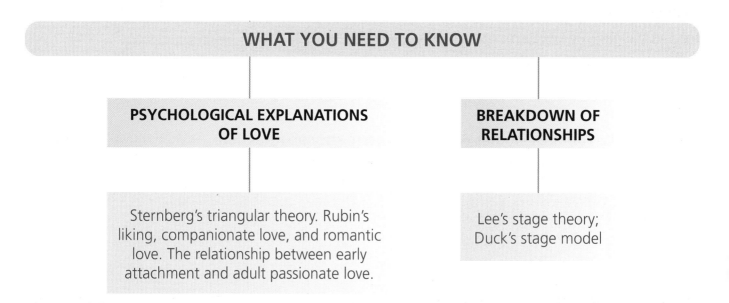

Think about one or two friendships you used to have but that no longer exist. What factors contributed to the end of those friendships? Was their dissolution sudden or gradual? Did you "fall out" or just "drift apart"?

Consider some friendships that have lasted a number of years. Why do these carry on while others break up?

Do the same with respect to some romantic relationships—both your own and those of other people. Think about the reasons why they endure or end. Are these factors the same as or different from those that influence friendships?

What factors do you think contribute to increasing divorce rates?

ASK YOURSELF

WHAT YOU NEED TO KNOW

PSYCHOLOGICAL EXPLANATIONS OF LOVE

Sternberg's triangular theory. Rubin's liking, companionate love, and romantic love. The relationship between early attachment and adult passionate love.

BREAKDOWN OF RELATIONSHIPS

Lee's stage theory; Duck's stage model

EXAM ADVICE: Social exchange theory (SET) and equity theory relate to the formation as well as the maintenance and dissolution of relationships, so could also be discussed in the context of the previous section.

PSYCHOLOGICAL EXPLANATIONS OF LOVE

Sternberg's Triangular Theory

Sternberg (1986, see A2PKT pp.49–50) defines love as:

- *Intimacy* (sharing mutual understanding and emotional support).
- *Passion* (involves physical attraction and sexual desire).
- *Decision/commitment* (involves the short-term decision that you love someone and a longer-term commitment to maintain that love).

These three components of love can be combined in different ways to produce seven varieties of love (see table below). Thus, liking involves only intimacy, infatuation involves only passion, romantic loves involves both intimacy and passion, and so on.

Type of love	Intimacy	Passion	Decision/commitment
Liking	✓		
Infatuation		✓	
Empty love			✓
Romantic love	✓	✓	
Compassionate love	✓		✓
Fatuous love		✓	✓
Consummate love	✓	✓	✓

EVALUATION

🙂 **Applications.** The theory has practical applications—it is possible to measure the components in the two parties and then analyse the differences in the types of love shown by each partner. It helps pinpoint areas where change and compromise may be necessary.

🙁 **Vagueness.** The components are rather vague, especially commitment, and it is therefore difficult to judge the basis on which one person decides to love another.

Liking and Loving

Psychologists distinguish between liking and loving and between different types of love, mainly companionate and romantic (passionate) love.

- *Liking* is the affection we feel for casual acquaintances.
- *Companionate love* is the affection we feel for those with whom our lives are deeply entwined.
- *Passionate love* is a powerful emotional state that involves overwhelming feelings of tenderness, elation, anxiety, and sexual desire.

RESEARCH EVIDENCE

- Rubin (1970, see A2PKT p.50) devised a Love Scale and a Liking Scale. The Love Scale measures the desire to help the other person, the degree of dependence on the other person, and feelings of absorption and exclusiveness. The Liking Scale measures respect for the other person's abilities and the degree of similarity in attitudes and other characteristics.

EVALUATION OF RUBIN'S SCALES

- 😊 **Provide useful information.** For example, the scales show that men tend to love only within a sexual relationship but women experience deep companionate love within a wide range of relationships.
- 😊 **Predictive ability for love.** The Love Scale can be used to see how successful a relationship is likely to be over a six-month period (Rubin, 1973).
- 😊 **Can be applied to same-sex friendships.** The scales look at all types of relationships, including ones that are sometimes rather neglected, like same sex friendships.
- ☹️ **Do not clearly differentiate between loving and liking.** Sternberg and Grajek (1984, see A2PKT p.50) found a high positive correlation between Rubin's two scales.

The Relationship Between Early Attachment and Adult Passionate Love

Hazan and Shaver (1987, see A2PKT p.50) compiled the "love quiz" and found that patterns of adult loving reflected the type of attachment styles that people showed in infancy (Ainsworth and Bell's Strange Situation, covered in the AS course). Securely attached people were trusting, confident, and had stable relationships; those who were anxiously attached were uncertain and insecure in their relationships; those who were avoidantly attached were detached and unresponsive in adult relationships.

Romantic and Companionate Love

Berscheid and Walster (1978, see A2PKT p.51) distinguished between liking, and two types of love, with the following characteristics:

Companionate love	Romantic/passionate love
On a continuum with liking	Entirely different from liking
A totally positive emotion	Involves a mixture of positive and negative intense emotions: joy, elation, anxiety, deep despair
Tends to deepen and intensify with time	Tends to become diluted over time
Based on mutual actual rewards and familiarity	Based on imagined gratification and fantasy
Founded on certainty and predictability	Thrives on novelty and uncertainty

BREAKDOWN OF RELATIONSHIPS

Models of Relationship Break-up: Lee's Stage Model

Stage models (see A2PKT pp.51–56) list the stages through which people are likely to pass in the breakdown of a relationship. One such model is that of Lee (1984, see A2PKT pp.51–52) who looked at premarital romantic break-ups. Lee's model focuses on the process involved while there is still some hope for the relationship.

Dissatisfaction—one or both recognise there are real problems

Exposure—dissatisfaction brought into the open

Negotiation—discussion of issues raised

Resolution—both parties try to find ways to solve the problem

Termination—if resolution attempts are unsuccessful, the relationship ends

EVALUATION OF LEE'S STAGE MODEL

☺ **Supported by research evidence.** Lee's model is based on studies of over 100 premarital break-ups.

☺ **It has practical implications for the repair of relationships.** The research and theory has been useful in counselling.

☺ **Corresponds to common-sense expectations.** As predicted by everyday experiences, the strongest relationships take the longest time to pass through the stages.

☹ **Rigidity of stages.** All stage theories are rather inflexible in that they assume every broken relationship goes through the same stages. This may not always be the case: not enough account is taken of individual differences.

☹ **Theory is descriptive rather than explanatory.** It describes the stages but does not explain why people go through each one.

Models of Relationship Break-up: Duck's Phase Model

Another stage or phase model is that of Duck (1982, see A2PKT p.52). Unlike Lee, Duck's model focuses on the processes involved after it is clear that a relationship is at an end. At each stage, the dissatisfied

Intrapsychic phase—thinking about problems in the relationship but not speaking out

Dyadic phase—confronting partner and trying to sort things out

Social phase—decision to leave is made and discussed publicly in order to gain assistance from others and each gives their own version of events

Grave-dressing phase—self-justification: marketing one's own version of the break-up and its causes; especially important if they intend to go into new relationships

partner in the relationship reaches a point that tips him or her over into the next stage. These breaking points are called thresholds. The thresholds that lead into each phase are: "I can't stand this any longer" (intrapsychic); "I'd be justified in withdrawing" (dyadic); "I mean it" (social); "It's now inevitable" (grave-dressing).

EVALUATION OF DUCK'S PHASE MODEL

- **Addresses cognitive not just behavioural aspects of relationships.** It considers the effects of people's feelings and attitudes, not just the effect of their actions.
- **Important applications.** The theory has practical implications for the repair of relationships and has formed the basis of a new model that looks at strategies to repair a relationship (Duck, 1994, see A2PKT p.52).
- **It is descriptive not explanatory.** It does not provide reasons for breakdown; it simply describes the stages.
- **Individual differences.** Like other stage theories, it is rigid in that it assumes every breakdown goes through the same stages and this may not necessarily be the case.

SO WHAT DOES THIS MEAN?

All models describing the course of a relationship can inevitably be criticised on the grounds of being rather rigid and not taking sufficient account of the distinctiveness of relationships. Nevertheless, there is often a general pattern that can be seen in the course a relationship takes when it is breaking down and this has important implications and applications. For example, Duck's model of relationship breakdown has been used to develop a new model that looks at strategies whereby a relationship can be repaired. He suggests that in some phases certain behaviours will be more effective than others to put things right.

OVER TO YOU

1. Describe and evaluate explanations of the breakdown of relationships. **(24 marks)**
2. Critically consider two psychological explanations of love. **(24 marks)**

CULTURAL AND SUB-CULTURAL DIFFERENCES IN RELATIONSHIPS

ASK YOURSELF

What are the essential differences between arranged marriages and those based on choice? What problems are there in assessing whether one is more "successful" than the other?

Even in cultures in which gay and lesbian relationships are reasonably acceptable, those in such relationships experience considerable problems. What are these problems? Why is it usually much easier to be heterosexual?

Have you read about people forming romantic liaisons after "meeting" on the Internet? List as many differences as you can between these relationships and those formed by meeting people face to face. What do you think are the pros and cons? Can you imagine your life without your mobile phone? Do you think there are differences in the way males and females and different age groups use their phones?

WHAT YOU NEED TO KNOW

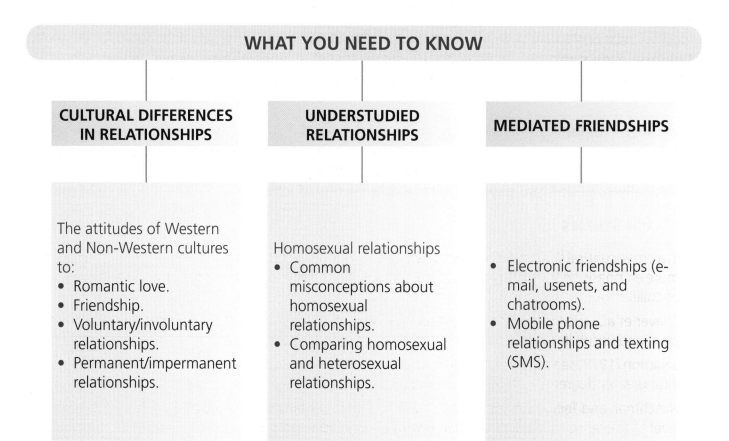

CULTURAL DIFFERENCES IN RELATIONSHIPS

The attitudes of Western and Non-Western cultures to:
- Romantic love.
- Friendship.
- Voluntary/involuntary relationships.
- Permanent/impermanent relationships.

UNDERSTUDIED RELATIONSHIPS

Homosexual relationships
- Common misconceptions about homosexual relationships.
- Comparing homosexual and heterosexual relationships.

MEDIATED FRIENDSHIPS

- Electronic friendships (e-mail, usenets, and chatrooms).
- Mobile phone relationships and texting (SMS).

To read up on cultural and sub-cultural differences in relationships, refer to pages 58–70 of A2PKT.

DIFFERENCES IN RELATIONSHIPS BETWEEN CULTURES

Most research on interpersonal relationships has been carried out in Western cultures, and has traditionally focused on heterosexual relationships that involve choice. More recently, researchers have begun to look at homosexual relationships, and at relationships based more on obligation than on choice. We will now consider research in these areas.

Much of the cross-cultural research in social psychology is based on a difference outlined by Hofstede (1984) between individualistic and collectivist cultures. Western cultures are considered individualistic; most Eastern nations are considered to be collectivist (Goodwin, 1995, see A2PKT p.58). Individualistic nations emphasise self-interest and the interest of one's immediate family, personal autonomy (making your own decisions), and individual initiative, achievement, and independence. Collectivist cultures emphasise loyalty to the group, interdependence, and the belief that group decisions are more important than individual ones.

In terms of relationships, the table below summarises some of the important differences between Western and non-Western cultures:

Romantic love	There is a strong tendency for members of individualistic societies to regard romantic love as the main basis for marriage, while collectivist cultures put little emphasis on its importance.
Friendship	People in individualistic cultures have more friends than do those in collectivist cultures, but these friendships tend to be more superficial.
Voluntary/involuntary relationships	In non-Western cultures, arranged marriages are common and are based on social status. In individualistic cultures, the individual chooses their own partner, usually on the basis of romantic love.
Permanent/impermanent relationships	Divorce is tolerated far more in some cultures than in others, but it is a fallacy that it is increasing in all societies; in some the rates are dropping substantially.

RESEARCH STUDIES

- In a cross-cultural study, Levine et al. (1995, see A2PKT p.59) found that individualistic cultures put far more emphasis on the importance of romantic love as the basis for a happy marriage than did members of collectivist cultures.
- Shaver et al. (1991) found that the attitude of the Chinese to romantic love is that it causes sorrow, pain, and unfulfilled affection rather than excitement and satisfaction.
- Salamon (1977, see A2PKT p.59) found that friendships were far closer in Japan than in Germany, with a far greater degree of self disclosure and mutual trust.
- Hirschman and Teerawichitainan (2003) found that in certain Muslim groups there is a relatively high level of tolerance for divorce compared with other Muslim groups.

- Yelsma and Athappily (1988, see A2PKT p.59) compared Indian arranged marriages with Indian and North American "love" marriages and found little difference in satisfaction.

- Gupta and Singh (1982), however, drew different conclusions. They investigated the amount of loving and liking in Indian marriages, half of which had been arranged and half based on love, comparing these feelings in short- and long-term marriages. They found that love increased in arranged marriages and steadily declined in "love" ones until in the 10-year marriages, the arranged marriage couples showed far greater love than those in the "love" ones. The same applied to liking but the differences were not so extreme.

- Dion and Dion (1993) argue that the self-centredness of individualistic societies makes it difficult to sustain a stable, happy marriage.

- Goodwin (1999, see A2PKT p.60) reports on different attitudes to the breakdown of marriage. In China divorce is viewed as shameful and there is a 4% rate, whereas in the US, it is far more acceptable and has a rate of 40–50%.

EVALUATION OF THE DIFFERENCES BETWEEN WESTERN AND NON-WESTERN RELATIONSHIPS

☹ **Comparisons are rather simplistic.** The divide between collectivist and individualistic cultures is rather crude and the differences are not entirely clear-cut. For example, even in cultures in which marriages are arranged there is some degree of individual choice (they are not forced marriages), and in individualistic societies parents and social groups do have a strong (if more subtle) influence on people's choice of marriage partner.

☹ **Cross-cultural research is riddled with problems.** It is very difficult for psychologists from one culture to appreciate the complexities of another culture.

SO WHAT DOES THIS MEAN?

The types of relationships studied by Western psychologists are very biased. The emphasis is on initial attraction, friendships, and long-term sexual relationships, all of which are important in the mobile, urban, Western world. However, kinship (family relationships), which is extremely important in all societies but especially collectivist ones, has received relatively little attention. A more thorough cross-cultural perspective on interpersonal relationships would contribute greatly to a sensitive understanding of the nature and importance of such relationships both within and between cultures.

UNDERSTUDIED RELATIONSHIPS

The term "understudied" refers to the fact that certain relationships have been studied less than others, due to their newness and/or relatively recent acceptability. Most research into understudied relationships has focused on gay and lesbian relationships and, more recently, electronic relationships started over the Internet.

Homosexual Relationships

There are some common misconceptions about homosexual relationships that can be summarised as follows:

- Homosexual relationships tend to be short-lived. However, Peplau (1991, see A2PKT p.62) showed that 50% of gay men and 65% of lesbians are in a stable relationship at any one time.
- There is less love and commitment in homosexual relationships. Yet Kurdek and Schmitt (1986, see A2PKT p.62) found that love and liking was just as high for homosexual as heterosexual couples. In fact, the lowest level of liking was amongst cohabiting heterosexual couples.

HOMOSEXUAL AND HETEROSEXUAL RELATIONSHIPS COMPARED

Homosexual and heterosexual relationships are similar in that, whether homosexual or heterosexual, people have an urge to form a monogamous, central, committed relationship. Couples also tend to get on better if they share similar attitudes and interests.

There are several differences between homosexual and heterosexual relationships:

1. Homosexuals, especially male ones, are more likely to have an additional sexual partner outside the relationship (10 years after the start of a committed relationship 94% of gay men, 43% of lesbians, 30% of heterosexual men, and 22% of heterosexual women report having sex outside the relationship—Blumstein & Schwartz, 1983, see A2PKT p.62). When considering these statistics we do, however, need to bear in mind that it is extremely difficult to undertake research into affairs since the participants may not be totally honest, either keeping their affairs secret from everyone or pretending to have more affairs than they do in reality.

2. Homosexuals experience more prejudice and related stress than do heterosexuals.

3. More importance is attached to power and status in heterosexual than in homosexual relationships (Blumstein & Schwartz, 1983).

4. Married couples tend to stay together longer than cohabiting couples, whether homosexual or heterosexual. This is probably due to the greater social, cultural, economic, and religious support for marriage.

EVALUATION

- **A broadening of information.** The study of both heterosexual and homosexual relationships provides greater mutual understanding. At present the vast majority of research on relationships concerns heterosexual ones. This excludes a great many individuals and undervalues their experiences.

- **Medical applications.** In light of the AIDS crisis, it is essential to understand the risks, activities, and attitudes in all sexual relationships.

- **Research difficulties.** There are considerable problems with researching homosexual relationships. Due to prejudice and discrimination, it is almost impossible to obtain a representative sample of homosexual individuals.

SO WHAT DOES THIS MEAN?

We need to be aware that homosexuals are attempting to build relationships in a completely different social context from that of heterosexuals. While heterosexual relationships are valued and celebrated in all walks of life, homosexuality is ignored, condemned, or penalised. A deeper understanding of homosexual relationships and the ways in which they are affected by power and social structures can provide an insight into ways in which society influences all our private relationships.

MEDIATED FRIENDSHIPS

Mediated relationships are relatively new. There are two main areas:

- *Electronic relationships* are all relationships operated through the medium of the Internet.

- *Mobile phone friendships* are those based on calls, texts, or both.

EMOTICONS
Happy :-)
Devil with grin >:-)
Angel with halo O:-)
Surprised :-0
Sad :-(
Wink (sarcasm) ;-)

Electronic Relationships

Electronic relationships are those formed through the medium of the Internet. These can take several forms:

- *Emails* are "letters" or messages sent electronically from one user to another.

- *Usenets* are a newsgroup (forums) related to a particular topic.

- *Chat rooms* are a means by which people can communicate with one another in real time.

(See A2PKT pp.63–67 for more details.)

Electronic communication (e-mail, usenets, and chat rooms) is fundamentally different from most other forms of communication since it conceals all nonverbal cues (facial expression, tone of voice, etc.). These cues are important in any relationship since they express true feelings. A new form of communication to express emotions, termed "emoticons" in its later visual version, has developed in chat rooms (and in emails and mobile phone text messaging) in order to express emotions. For example, the typing of ":)" depicts happiness, automatically producing "☺" as an emoticon. However, these are obviously contrived and convey exactly what the sender wishes to and no more, and so can provide the means of deliberate deception.

RESEARCH ON ELECTRONIC RELATIONSHIPS

- Parks and Floyd (1996, see A2PKT p.65) investigated newsgroup users and found that 61% had formed a personal relationship, of which 98% communicated directly by e-mail, 33% by telephone, 28% via the postal service, and 33% met in person. Women were significantly more likely than men to form relationships online. As in real life, these relationships ranged from superficial and short-lived to deep, intense, and committed; many conversations were not related to newsgroup topics, demonstrating the breadth of the relationships. Further research is necessary to see how the rewards and costs that operate in traditional relationships affect online ones.

- McKenna and Yael (1999, see A2PKT p.66) conducted a series of studies involving Internet users via participant observation, in-depth interviews, a survey of nearly 600 newsgroup users, and two laboratory experiments. In terms of personality, the anxious and lonely were more likely to use the net to form relationships. Those who felt they could express their "real self" on the Internet were more likely to interact offline (either by phone or face to face). Laboratory experiments showed that people have a greater liking for those with whom they initially "chat" online and, not surprisingly, that they tend to present more idealised pictures of themselves when interacting online than when first meeting face to face. Both the survey and experiments demonstrated that online relationships develop more quickly and easily than do face-to-face ones. Eventually many relationships that have started online develop into real-life, offline ones.

COMPARISON WITH TRADITIONAL RELATIONSHIPS

Factors such as similarity, especially similarity in values and interests, are still important (Hultin, 1993, see A2PKT p.66). Online, attitudes can only be judged by open expression of them, while offline we often make assumptions based on age, dress, and other aspects of physical appearance. Proximity is irrelevant in Internet relationships but familiarity (measured by the number of times people interact) is still very important. One significant difference is that the frequency of interaction can be controlled entirely online but not offline. Physical attributes obviously play virtually no part in online relationships while they are crucial in traditional ones. Cooper and Sportolari (1997, see A2PKT p.66) state that romantic and/or erotic relationships are based on emotional intimacy rather than physical attraction.

Cyberaffairs

Some people use the Internet as a type of "dating agency" with the intention of using the net as a means of finding a suitable partner for a real-life romantic relationship. Others use it as a means of having sexual exchanges online (cybersex) with no intention of any real-life encounters. Griffiths (2000, see A2PKT p.67) lists reasons why such relationships are seductive and addictive:

- The Internet is easy and affordable to access.

- Cyberaffairs are easy to conduct.

- Fantasies can be indulged anonymously.

- They provide emotional and mental escape from real life, especially for the shy and lonely, or those who feel trapped in unhappy real-life relationships.

- They are popular with those working long or unsociable hours.

Cooper (1998, see A2PKT p.67) calls this the Triple A Engine: access, affordability, anonymity.

Problems with Electronic Affairs

People can masquerade as someone else, which leads to mistrust. Even though pretending to be someone else could possibly increase understanding (by putting yourself in the role of a different gender or culture), it is ethically unsound and deceitful. Vulnerable individuals can become emotionally involved in unsuitable relationships, which may replace real-life ones. See A2PKT p.68 for an interesting case study entitled "Love at First Byte".

The Use of Mobile Phones

Research on mobile phone conversations:

- Gossip is the main use of mobile phones. 33% of men and 26% of women gossip on mobile phones every day (Fox, 2005, see A2PKT pp.68–69).

- 65% of mobile phone time involves social relationships, especially personal ones.

- Although men and women spend the same amount of time on social relationships, men spend 66% of the time talking about their own relationships compared with only 33% of the time for women, who appear to talk more about other people's relationships than their own! (Fox, 2005, see A2PKT p.69.)

Research on texting:

- 16–24 year olds do far more texting than calling (Fox, 2005, see A2PKT p.69).

- Women text more than men. However, men are more inclined than women to use texting in order to avoid talking, perhaps due to shyness or laziness (Fox, 2005, see A2PKT p.69).

SO WHAT DOES THIS MEAN?

The formation of relationships over the Internet provides exciting opportunities for people from very different walks of life to interact and begin to appreciate contrasting lifestyles. The "rules" that operate in the formation and maintenance of such relationships are very different from those in traditional relationships. Nevertheless, some of these relationships do eventually develop into more traditional "face-to-face" ones. From the point of view of psychologists, this area of research is in its infancy and we have yet to appreciate the full implications of the advent of this new technology on the field of interpersonal relationships.

The advent of mobile phones has led to another revolution in communication and therefore relationships, especially for the young. Mobile phones provide a very easy way of maintaining social relationships. Calls can be made at almost any time or place, whilst the ability to text provides a cheap and convenient way of keeping in touch, and is especially useful on occasions when the individual does not want to have a conversation. There is much research still to be done in this area, and one interesting angle may be to investigate whether differences in the use of mobile phones between the older and younger generations could be summed up by the greeting "Where are you?" as opposed to "How are you?".

OVER TO YOU

1. **Discuss sub-cultural and cultural variations in the nature of relationships.** **(24 marks)**

2. **Discuss research into relationships that can be considered "understudied" such as homosexual and "electronic" relationships.** **(24 marks)**

Question 2 adapted from AQA A2 [Summer 2002] Psychology Examination Papers.

QUESTIONS AND ESSAY PLANS

1 Outline and evaluate the contributions of psychological research (theories and/or studies) to our understanding of the formation of relationships. **(24 marks)**

There is a huge amount of information that could be included here, so you need to be selective and ensure that enough AO2 is included. Do NOT try to cover all theories and research. In the conclusion, you could mention that there are other theories that could have been included.

Paragraph 1 Introduction

Make sure this involves giving a definition of relationships and of interpersonal attraction. Outline the problems of conducting research in this area, of the artificial nature and lack of external validity of much of it. This is covered on page 21.

Paragraph 2

Outline the five main factors that determine interpersonal relationships: physical attractiveness, proximity, attitude similarity, demographic similarity, similarity in personality. Bear in mind the *contribution of psychological research* and give a piece of research for each factor.

Paragraph 3

Evaluate the five factors. Again, mention research that has modified and extended our knowledge of the role of these factors.

Paragraph 4 Economic theories and learning theories

Outline the theories briefly; be careful not to include too much detail—this is all AO1 and you cannot afford to spend too much time on it. Include some AO2 by mentioning problems with the research. This will follow up the comments made in paragraph 1 with reference to specific pieces of research. For example, Veitch and Griffitt (1976) do demonstrate an important point but the research set-up is far more simplistic than would be found in real life.

Paragraph 5

Evaluate economic and learning theories. Research using "bogus stranger" studies can be criticised; research only covers initial stages of a relationship; the theories assume basic selfishness, and so on. It is always a good idea to mention cultural factors, so include the fact that the research has mainly been done on Western societies and the theories apply more to individualistic rather than collectivist cultures.

You may well have written enough by now and should go straight to a conclusion, but if you have time, you could include the next two paragraphs.

Paragraph 6 Sociobiological/Evolutionary theory and supporting evidence

Outline the theory including research evidence (positive evaluation) such as Buss (1989) and Davis (1990).

Paragraph 7

Criticism of sociobiological/evolutionary theory. The emphasis on the gene is biologically deterministic because it suggests our genes control us, which ignores free will. Also, it is reductionist because it only accounts for one influence and so does not account for psychological explanations, e.g. social factors/nurture. For example, relationship formation is probably better explained by the social context and social constructions, e.g. increasing permissiveness of society—does this lead to more open relationships or serial monogamy? Also ethics—it provides scientific support for the double standard, which is criticised as sexist by feminists.

Paragraph 6/8 Conclusion

Consider the cultural bias of all these explanations. They are based on the Western concept of romantic love and the increasing research on relationship formation in collectivist cultures shows that explanations and processes are very different. The explanations have explanatory power for Western relationships but little for collectivist relationships. Also, different perspectives need to be considered together to account for formation of relationships, as this behaviour exists at different levels: biological, behavioural, cognitive, and social. Thus, a multi-perspective reveals the most insight.

2 Describe and evaluate explanations of maintenance and/or breakdown of relationships. (24 marks)

You first need to decide whether you will cover just maintenance, just breakdown, or both. In this plan, we will cover both, but you may prefer to concentrate on one or the other; there is plenty of material to do this.

Paragraph 1 Introduction

Define relationship and explain how some of the explanations account for *both* maintenance and breakdown, as it is a lack of the factors that maintain a relationship that cause breakdown.

Paragraph 2 Economic theories: Social exchange theories (SET) and equity

Outline the actual theories and explain how they can account for maintenance *and* breakdown. Basically, if costs outweigh rewards, the relationship may break down. If the reverse is true, so there is a "profit", then the relationship is likely to be maintained. Remember, both parties must show a profit. In terms of equity, this must be equal to what was invested by each party.

Paragraph 3 Evaluation of economic theories

There are two separate strands to evaluation—the methodology and the actual theories. Mention the problems of methodology, and there is more specific evaluation as applied to SET that can be included (page 24). The theory assumes selfishness; does not allow for strength of parent–child relationship; and applies to Western cultures rather than collectivist ones. In general, Clark and Mills' (1979) research shows that not everyone uses exchange principles.

Paragraph 4 Stage theories of breakdown

Refer to Lee's (1984) model of breakdown and Duck's (1982) stage model. Outline the stages; it may be better to cover only one theory if you are limited on time.

Paragraph 5 Evaluation

Describe how these models are mainly descriptive, not explanatory. They also assume that every relationship follows the same course in rigid stages. It is difficult to gain scientific evidence for social phenomena, as it is difficult to control social behaviour. Thus, rather than a quantitative approach, a qualitative approach is taken, which rejects scientific validity as the only desirable goal of research; instead the focus is on meanings. The models do have real-life explanatory power but scientific validity is lacking and so they do not necessarily offer genuine insights into maintenance and breakdown. On the positive side, they have practical applications, since they are useful in charting a possible breakdown and implying ways in which it could be helped at different stages.

Paragraph 6 Conclusion

A key criticism of the explanations is that they try to explain maintenance and breakdown in terms of factors within the relationship, which ignores the impact of society. We need to consider historical factors in relationships. For example, changing attitudes to divorce might best account for the decrease in maintenance and increase in breakdown in the West. Neither do these models adequately explain the real reason why many collectivist cultures have so little breakdown as this is very much due to cultural norms. The research is based on white Western culture so has limited generalisability to alternative relationships. Also, whilst the explanations account for many factors within the relationship, they need perhaps to focus on characteristics and emotions of the individual (such as self-esteem and whether people feel they deserve more).

3 Describe and evaluate **two** explanations of love.   (24 marks)

Paragraph 1 Introduction

Outline all the different ways in which love is defined, explaining that the word has a multitude of meanings. Many of the explanations of love are ethnocentric as they focus on Western idealised romantic love.

Paragraph 2 Liking and loving

Explain the difference between the two (Rubin, 1970): love is based on intimacy, dependence, and support, whereas liking is based on respect and similarity. Evaluate these in terms of methodology. Rubin's love and liking scales are measured using questionnaires—outline the problems of such questionnaires. Liking and loving correlate positively, which means the test does not discriminate well between them. The scales do, however, provide useful information and have predictive power in terms of how long a relationship may last.

Paragraph 3 Sternberg's (1986) triangular theory

Comment on the components of commitment, passion, and intimacy, which yield different types of love (give an example). A combination of all three is optimal consummate love. Evaluate how reductionism of any classification means explanatory power may be limited as people may not fall neatly into one category or they may exhibit multiple types of love. Also the decision/commitment component is vague. But it can be applied well to relationship counselling.

Paragraph 4 Hazan and Shaver's (1987) research

Assess the relationship between adult love and early attachment styles. In terms of evaluation, this model is explanatory, not just descriptive, and is supported by developmental research (the work of Bowlby, 1946, and Ainsworth et al., 1978).

Paragraph 5 Cultural and sub-cultural differences in concepts of love

Outline the difference between Western and non-Western societies and the importance of different types of love in such societies. Mention the difference in the types of love that are used as the basis for marriage.

41

There is a good deal of evaluation, including the simplicity of the divide between collectivist/individualistic societies, the Western bias of research, and the difficulty of conducting cross-cultural research.

Paragraph 6 Conclusion

Some models concentrate on differentiating between different types of love and this is useful in itself but will inevitably be rather simplistic given the very complex nature of relationships and the enormous variety of them. Other models, notably Hazan and Shaver (1987), offer explanations that relate types of loving styles to life experiences and have predictive power as well as having practical implications for counselling. Inevitably, there are the usual problems of conducting cross-cultural research but this should not detract from its importance. It indicates that there are substantial differences in the relative importance placed on different types of love across cultures.

Social Psychology

PRO- AND ANTI-SOCIAL BEHAVIOUR

Specification 13.1

What's it about?

It is obviously of considerable importance to society to understand the circumstances under which people act in anti-social or pro-social ways. In this section we focus on aggression as a specific type of anti-social behaviour, and altruism and helping as forms of pro-social behaviour. We start by looking at how aggression is defined and the forms it can take, before considering social psychological theories that seek to explain its causes. Certain stressors in the environment may be responsible for various forms of aggression, from mild irritability to rioting and even murder. We consider what research tells us about these. We then focus on the reasons why people behave in a pro-social manner and whether or not this behaviour is ever truly altruistic, that is, whether people ever act in a way that benefits others but offers no advantage to themselves. Finally, we look at what conclusions can be drawn from research on the effects of the media on both pro- and anti-social behaviour and consider reasons why the media may be influential.

What's in this unit?

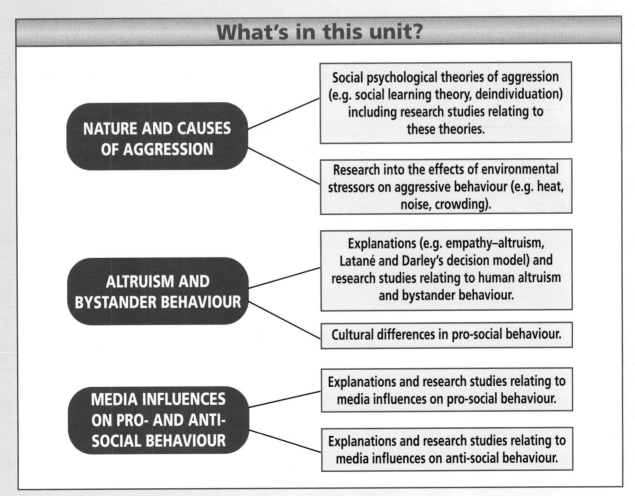

NATURE AND CAUSES OF AGGRESSION

- Social psychological theories of aggression (e.g. social learning theory, deindividuation) including research studies relating to these theories.
- Research into the effects of environmental stressors on aggressive behaviour (e.g. heat, noise, crowding).

ALTRUISM AND BYSTANDER BEHAVIOUR

- Explanations (e.g. empathy–altruism, Latané and Darley's decision model) and research studies relating to human altruism and bystander behaviour.
- Cultural differences in pro-social behaviour.

MEDIA INFLUENCES ON PRO- AND ANTI-SOCIAL BEHAVIOUR

- Explanations and research studies relating to media influences on pro-social behaviour.
- Explanations and research studies relating to media influences on anti-social behaviour.

NATURE AND CAUSES OF AGGRESSION

ASK YOURSELF

In your experience, do aggressive people have aggressive children? If so, do you think this is due to genetics, or simply due to the example set by the parents?

Do you think being part of a big, excitable crowd might make peole get carried away and behave more aggressively than they would usually, without pausing to consider their actions?

What types of situation are most likely to make people aggressive? Is there anything society can do to control this?

WHAT YOU NEED TO KNOW

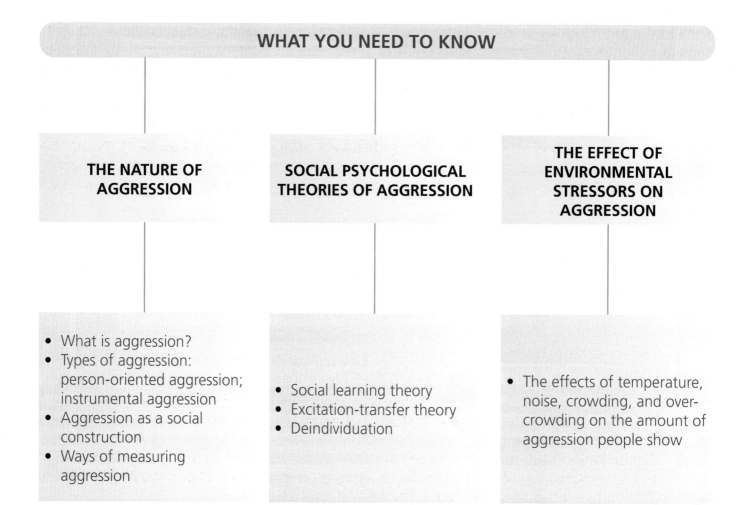

THE NATURE OF AGGRESSION

- What is aggression?
- Types of aggression: person-oriented aggression; instrumental aggression
- Aggression as a social construction
- Ways of measuring aggression

SOCIAL PSYCHOLOGICAL THEORIES OF AGGRESSION

- Social learning theory
- Excitation-transfer theory
- Deindividuation

THE EFFECT OF ENVIRONMENTAL STRESSORS ON AGGRESSION

- The effects of temperature, noise, crowding, and over-crowding on the amount of aggression people show

To read up on the nature and causes of aggression, refer to pages 75–91 of A2PKT.

THE NATURE OF AGGRESSION

What is Aggression?

Aggression involves deliberately hurting or attempting to hurt someone. The intention to harm is crucial to the definition—harming someone by accident is not aggression. A definition from Baron and Richardson (1993, see A2PKT p.75) is: "any form of behaviour directed towards the goal of harming or injuring another living being who is motivated to avoid such treatment". Aggression is not necessarily physical but can be verbal, such as swearing at someone.

Types of Aggression

- *Person-oriented aggression* is aggression whose main purpose is to hurt for the sake of hurting—e.g. punching someone who has annoyed you.
- *Instrumental aggression* is aggression aimed at getting something you desire, such as pushing someone against a wall so you can get past them or punching them so you can grab their bag while they are off-guard. This includes self-defence, such as grabbing and twisting the arm of someone who is about to attack you.

Aggression as a Social Construction

One of the reasons why aggression is difficult to define and to measure is that what you are dealing with is not an action in itself but the *intention* behind the action. A single action, such as pushing someone, may be an accident, an attempt to save the person from injury, or an aggressive act. Only by knowing what the intention was can we judge the behaviour as aggressive or otherwise. The problems of measurement were shown by Blumenthal et al. (1972, see A2PKT p.85) who asked participants from different social groups and with different attitudes to judge the behaviour of police in a student demonstration. Those who sympathised with the demonstrators judged the behaviour as much more aggressive than those who were unsympathetic towards them. In essence, when we label a behaviour as aggressive we are not simply describing an action but making a value judgement based on our own belief system.

Ways of Measuring Aggression

For reasons mentioned above, the measurement of aggression in psychological studies is a considerable problem. It has been done by several means including aggressive play, punching a doll, and willingness to give electric shocks or blasts of white noise to someone.

SOCIAL PSYCHOLOGICAL THEORIES OF CAUSES OF AGGRESSION

Social Learning Theory

The main principle of social learning theory is learning by *observation*. As well as learning by direct reinforcement and punishment (as in classical learning theory), people learn by indirect or *vicarious reinforcement,* that is, seeing someone else reinforced or punished for certain behaviour. The behaviour that is observed may not be copied immediately but may be seen some time later. This means that the behaviour is represented internally, so that *cognitive processes* are involved.

Bandura (1973, see A2PKT p.76) believes that the models that are imitated determine three aspects of aggressive behaviour:

- The exact type of aggressive behaviour shown (e.g. kicking, swearing, punching).
- The frequency of the aggression shown.
- The targets for the aggression—who or what the aggression was directed towards, such as women, members of minority groups, toys.

THE BOBO DOLL STUDIES

Bandura conducted a number of studies (e.g. Bandura, Ross, & Ross, 1961, see A2PKT p.76) in which children observed an adult being aggressive towards a Bobo doll and showed that they learnt new, unusual, distinctive forms of aggressive behaviour (types of aggression the children had never seen or shown before).

The studies showed that people are likely to copy another's behaviour if:

- The model is similar to them (e.g. in sex and age).
- The model is admired (e.g. a pop star or footballer) and has desirable characteristics (e.g. is attractive).
- The model is rewarded.
- They are directly rewarded for the behaviour. This is more effective than seeing the model rewarded.

EVALUATION

 Support from laboratory studies. Studies such as those of Bandura's Bobo dolls and many others support the view that people learn by imitating others. They also demonstrate the conditions under which participants are most likely to imitate and which types of models are most influential. As with all carefully controlled laboratory studies, cause and effect can be established.

Lack of ecological validity. However, such studies are set in artificial environments. In particular, with reference to the Bobo doll studies, the doll was designed to be hit so it was not really surprising that it was, and does not mean that children would necessarily hit a real person. In ordinary life aggressive behaviour is observed in a certain context (such as watching a film with parents who comment on the violence).

Real-life research. Patterson et al. (1989, see A2PKT pp.78–79) demonstrated that role models are important in the development of anti-social behaviour and that parents are the most important ones. Surveys/questionnaires found that very aggressive ("problem") children are raised in homes of high aggression, little affection, and little positive feedback (a "coercive" pattern). Eddy et al. (2001) found this applied to girls as well as boys. However, not all children raised this way show anti-social behaviour patterns.

Cross-cultural studies. As predicted by social learning theory, there are cultural differences in aggression. The Arapesh is an example of a non-aggressive culture in which aggression is not admired (reinforced) or modelled by adults. The Mundugumor show the opposite pattern, in which violence is the norm and status is determined by the amount of aggression shown (Mead,1935, see A2PKT pp.79–80).

 Studies of media influences. As predicted by the theory, there is a great deal of research evidence that watching violence in films and playing violent video games can increase aggressive behaviour. This is covered in detail later.

 Practical implications. Patterson's research (referred to earlier) gave an indication of what patterns of parental behaviour lead to problematic behaviour at home and at school, which offers ways of teaching parents better techniques. Research on media influences is of value in identifying which aspects of the media, which particular individuals, and the specific context in which such influences can be negative or, indeed, positive.

SO WHAT DOES THIS MEAN?

On the positive side, social learning theory can account for individual and cultural variation in aggression but it is unlikely that learning accounts for *all* aggressive behaviour. In nearly every society, men are more aggressive than women. Twin studies (e.g. McGue, Brown, & Lykken, 1992, see A2PKT p.80) indicate genetic differences in aggression. This indicates that social learning theory may have underestimated the role of *biological factors* in determining aggressive behaviour. Also, the psychodynamic approach offers an alternative account, seeing aggression as an instinctive force present from birth.

Excitation-Transfer Theory

There are circumstances under which we experience increased bodily arousal—our heart beats faster, we sweat more, and so on. When we feel aroused, we also experience an emotional feeling, such as excitement, joy, or fear. Usually, we know why we are aroused and respond accordingly. Sometimes, however, we transfer the arousal caused by one stimulus and add it to the arousal caused by a second stimulus. Zillmann's *excitation-transfer theory* (e.g. 1979, see A2PKT p.82) proposes that if an individual is already aroused (for example, because it is hot) and then encounters provocation, they may assume the arousal is a form of anger and lash out in aggressive behaviour. If you are, for example, aroused at a rugby match and your team is losing, then someone bumping into you may provoke an unusually aggressive response.

Pre-existing aggression **+** Anger generated by provocation **→** Increased likelihood of aggression

EVALUATION

 Validity. This can account for why people sometimes respond aggressively to mild provocation. It could, for example, explain why people can be aggressive and irritable during hot weather or when in a crowd.

 Supporting research evidence. For example, Zillmann, Johnson, and Day (1974, see A2PKT p.83) demonstrated that, when provoked, people who have been aroused by exercise are more aggressive after a rest, when the arousal cannot be attributed to the exercise, than immediately after the exercise, when they believe their arousal is due to the exercise.

☹ **Individual differences.** It does not account for individual and cultural variations in aggression.

☹ **It only accounts for a small amount of aggression.** In everyday life, we usually know why we are aroused and the theory does not apply in such cases.

Deindividuation

Deindividuation is the loss of our sense of identity and social responsibility and may occur when we become *anonymous* by, for example, wearing a uniform or being part of a crowd. This can lead to aggression due to the lessening of regard for social constraints.

Two possible reasons for deindividuation leading to violent behaviour are:

- People feel less accountable because it reduces the likelihood of being identified.
- Lower self-awareness makes people more likely to follow others.

RESEARCH EVIDENCE

- Zimbardo's "prison" study (1973, see A2PKT p.83). Those dressed in guards' uniforms acted aggressively towards the "prisoners".
- Zimbardo (1970) found that participants who wore overalls gave greater shocks than those who wore normal clothes and name tags.
- Rehm et al. (1987). In this study schoolchildren in handball teams were randomly assigned to two conditions, one wearing identical outfits and the other wearing their own clothing. The "anonymous" group was far more aggressive in play.

EVALUATION

☹ **Does not account for all aggression.** It can account for some aggression but by no means all. It only accounts for aggression that occurs when people become anonymous. It does not attempt to account for other forms of aggression.

☹ **Lacks consistency.** Being in a crowd does not always lead to anti-social behaviour. It may lead to other types of impulsive and friendly behaviour such as singing in a crowd or doing a Mexican wave.

☹ **Being anonymously dressed can lead to non-aggressive behaviour.** A uniform does not always result in people acting aggressively towards others. If dressed in a nurse's uniform people are less likely to give electric shocks (Johnson & Downing, 1979).

SO WHAT DOES THIS MEAN?

It would seem that deindividuation leads to a *loss of personal control*, which in turn leads to greater conformity. Whether this leads to an increase in aggressive behaviour depends on the circumstances. Only if the surroundings and situation foster hostility, is there likely to be an increase in aggression.

THE EFFECT OF ENVIRONMENTAL STRESSORS ON AGGRESSION

Temperature

RESEARCH EVIDENCE

- Baron and Bell (1976, see A2PKT pp.85–86) conducted a laboratory study that measured levels of aggression by the intensity of electric shocks participants believed they were giving to others. They found a *curvilinear relationship* in that aggression increased up to about 34°C and then decreased.
- Baron and Ransberger (1978, see A2PKT p.86). In a naturalistic correlational study, they found that violence was highest at around 29°C, but it then declined as the weather got hotter.
- Anderson (1989, see A2PKT p.86), however, found that acts of extreme aggression continued to increase as the temperature rose.
- Rotter (1993) also found that violent sex crimes occur more frequently with higher temperatures.

Noise

RESEARCH EVIDENCE

- Glass et al. (1969, see A2PKT pp.86–87). In a laboratory study, they compared task performance and galvanic skin response (GSR) of participants when working with random noise, predictable noise, and no noise. The random noise condition produced the most errors and the highest GSR, with the no-noise condition producing the fewest. Unpredictable noise can act as a stressor and any stressor can increase the likelihood of aggression.
- Geen and McNeil (1969) conducted research that indicated that people are liable to be aggressive in noisy conditions if they are in an environment that suggests violence, such as being provoked or watching a brutal film.
- Donnerstein and Wilson (1976), in another laboratory study, measured aggression by the administration of electric shocks. They found that noise had the greatest effect when participants had already been provoked. Noise did not cause anger in the first place but did increase the likelihood of it being displayed if the atmosphere was already aggressive.

Crowding and Overcrowding

RESEARCH EVIDENCE

- Loo (1979, see A2PKT p.87). In a naturalistic study, Loo found young children were more aggressive in their nursery school the greater the density. Loo suggested a curvilinear relationship similar to that for temperature. Moderate density leads to increased aggression but, as crowding gets more intense, aggression declines and people withdraw into themselves.

- Rohe and Patterson (1974). This study suggests that the aggression may be due to frustration caused by lack of toys rather than density *per se*.
- McCain et al. (1980, see A2PKT p.87) found more rioting and assaults in high density than in low density prisons.
- Calhoun (1962, see A2PKT p.87). This, and other animal studies, demonstrated high levels of aggression in rats that were in an over-crowded cage. Young rats were killed or had their tails bitten off and some males showed unusually aggressive sexual behaviour. Nevertheless, not all of the animals responded aggressively; many rats simply withdrew and tried to hide.

The "negative affect escape" model advanced by Baron (1977, see A2PKT p.88) suggests that, up to a point, negative feelings caused by environmental stressors increase aggression but after that aggression is reduced because the most appropriate reaction is to attempt escape rather than to become aggressive.

EVALUATION

🙂 **Some support.** Baron's theory is supported by laboratory studies but not by real-life correlational ones. This is not easy to explain. Laboratory studies lack ecological validity and do not measure real-life aggression. On the other hand, the real-life studies cannot measure temperature or levels of aggression very accurately. It is also possible that in real-life situations the stimuli that provoke people are more intense and therefore more likely to stimulate aggression.

🙁 **Other theories also explain our behaviour.** For example, the excitation-transfer model also accounts for why we tend to be more aggressive when stressed.

SO WHAT DOES THIS MEAN?

It is difficult to draw definite conclusions about the effects of environmental stressors on aggression. Laboratory studies are very limited in the conditions they can practically and ethically arrange, while real-life studies involve a whole host of uncontrolled variables that might contribute to aggression. There does seem to be convincing evidence that increase in stressors is associated with increased aggression up to a point, but whether aggression continues to rise with increasing stress or whether it then levels off or decreases remains debatable.

OVER TO YOU

1. **Describe and evaluate research into *two or more* environmental stressors on aggressive behaviour.** **(24 marks)**
2. **Describe and evaluate *one* social psychological theory of aggression.** **(24 marks)**

ALTRUISM AND BYSTANDER BEHAVIOUR

ASK YOURSELF

Do you think that there is such a thing as truly altruistic behaviour—actions that help others with no "pay back" at all for the helper? Or do you think that there's always some benefit, even if it's simply feeling good about yourself?

We've all heard of heroic acts of self-sacrifice, such as someone rushing into a burning building to rescue a person trapped inside. On the other hand, we unfortunately also hear of incidents in which people scream for help but are ignored. What causes this contrast? Is it simply that some people are much more caring and brave than others, or is it more to do with the actual situation?

Different cultures have different norms of caring. Does this mean there are cultural differences in pro-social behaviour? If so, how do they show themselves?

WHAT YOU NEED TO KNOW

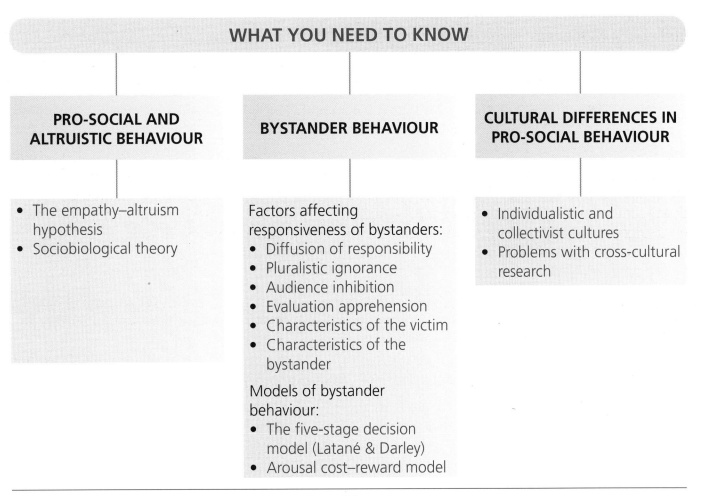

PRO-SOCIAL AND ALTRUISTIC BEHAVIOUR

- The empathy–altruism hypothesis
- Sociobiological theory

BYSTANDER BEHAVIOUR

Factors affecting responsiveness of bystanders:
- Diffusion of responsibility
- Pluralistic ignorance
- Audience inhibition
- Evaluation apprehension
- Characteristics of the victim
- Characteristics of the bystander

Models of bystander behaviour:
- The five-stage decision model (Latané & Darley)
- Arousal cost–reward model

CULTURAL DIFFERENCES IN PRO-SOCIAL BEHAVIOUR

- Individualistic and collectivist cultures
- Problems with cross-cultural research

To read up on altruism and bystander behaviour, refer to pages 93–109 of A2PKT.

PRO-SOCIAL AND ALTRUISTIC BEHAVIOUR

- *Pro-social behaviour* is behaviour that benefits others and includes a wide variety of actions such as complimenting someone on their outfit, giving someone a lift to the shop, donating to charity, and helping in an emergency.
- *Altruistic behaviour* is a form of pro-social behaviour that is costly to the individual who is behaving in this way. Hence, driving out of your way to give someone a lift when you expect nothing in return is altruistic, whereas doing the same thing because you want a lift next week is pro-social but not altruistic.

The Empathy–Altruism Hypothesis

Batson (e.g. 1987, see A2PKT p.93) argues that humans act altruistically because we have the capacity to show *empathy*. Empathy is the ability to share the emotions of another person and to understand that person's point of view. Batson's empathy–altruism hypothesis holds that when we see someone in trouble, we feel *personal distress* (shown by emotions such as fear and anxiety) and *empathetic concern* (such as sympathy and tenderness). The feelings of empathetic concern and the desire to reduce the person's distress may lead to altruistic helping, which is help designed to relieve the victim's suffering.

An important aspect of this hypothesis is that it suggests that humans are truly altruistic, whereas other explanations contend that there is no such thing as truly altruistic behaviour, only egoistic self-interest.

RESEARCH EVIDENCE

- Batson et al. (1981, see A2PKT p.94) arranged for participants to believe that they were watching a distressed individual being given shocks in an "important" study that could not be discontinued. They were given the opportunity to change places and receive the shocks themselves. The degree to which they could escape was high or low (they were made to watch or allowed to leave) and the degree of empathy was also high or low (the victim had the same or a very different score from them). When escape was difficult, the participants offered help (regardless of the degree of empathy), presumably to relieve their own distress. More significantly, those in the high empathy–easy escape condition also offered to change places. This supports the empathy–altruism hypothesis since their only motivation for offering help was empathy. Batson concluded that people are capable of true altruism.

EVALUATION

- **Research support.** It is supported by the above study and other similar studies (e.g. Batson et al., 1988, see A2PKT p.94).
- **Other factors.** Factors other than altruism may have affected their behaviour. In the Batson et al. (1981) study participants may have offered to change places not because of altruism but due to factors such as fear of disapproval or the demand characteristics of the experimental situation.
- **Artificial research.** The research does tend to be rather artificial in the measures of empathy. They involve only short-term instances of altruistic acts that have little impact on the participants' everyday lives, whereas real-life altruism may be much more demanding.

Support from other theories. The hypothesis is supported by the theories of moral development. These are covered in the Cognitive Development chapter of this book. They demonstrate that, in accordance with the predictions of the hypothesis, as egocentrism decreases and the ability to empathise increases, the likelihood of altruistic behaviour increases.

Everyday experiences. In ordinary life there are a great many instances of truly altruistic behaviour in which people risk their lives for others (sometimes over a long period of time, as in the case of people sheltering Jews from the Nazis).

Does altruistic behaviour exist? Some argue that there is no such thing as truly altruistic behaviour. For example, a theory known as the negative-state relief model suggests that pure altruism is a myth and that people only help if they stand to gain by it, even if it's simply because they avoid feeling guilty, or it makes them feel good about themselves.

Sociobiological Theory

Sociobiological theory provides an alternative to social psychological approaches, as it is an evolutionary (biological) theory. Sociobiological theory states that any behaviour that promotes an individual's genes, or copies of their genes, is likely to be passed on to subsequent generations and therefore eventually become embedded in the genes. This leads to two main behavioural characteristics:

- *Kin selection*—we tend to act pro-socially towards our own family members, especially our children, because they carry copies of our genes. The closer the kin and the higher their breeding potential, the more likely we are to help them.
- *Reciprocal altruism*—we also behave altruistically towards familiar people because they could be of help to us in return at a later date.

This behaviour is innate rather than voluntary and also occurs in nonhuman species. It provides a biological rather than a psychological explanation for altruistic behaviour. Such behaviour is referred to as "apparent altruism" because it is not truly altruistic, as it benefits the individual in terms of improving the likelihood of them passing on their genes.

Biological Versus Psychological Altruism

- Some altruistic behaviour can probably be accounted for in terms of biological altruism, as suggested by sociobiological theory.
- However, it is unlikely that this can account for all altruism in humans—we are thinking reasoning beings who make voluntary decisions and are guided by social norms and by our own moral values.

SO WHAT DOES THIS MEAN?

Some theories see humans as basically selfish creatures who act in their own interests either because selfishness is innate at the gene level and behaviour is only superficially altruistic, as predicted by sociobiology, or because people wish to protect themselves from sadness and guilt, as proposed by the negative-state relief hypothesis. Alternatively, the empathy–altruism hypothesis views humans as having the capacity to be altruistic (even though their altruistic urges are often over-ridden by egoistic ones). At present, there is no consensus amongst social psychologists on whether true altruism actually exists or is just a myth.

BYSTANDER BEHAVIOUR

The tragic case of Kitty Genovese (see A2PKT pp.97–98), who was raped and stabbed to death in and around an apartment block while onlookers in nearby flats did nothing to help, instigated the study by social psychologists of bystander behaviour. Why was no help forthcoming for Kitty, yet in January 1982 a man sacrificed his life to save others when a jet plane crashed into the Potomac River (see A2PKT p.97)?

Factors Affecting Responsiveness of Bystanders

DIFFUSION OF RESPONSIBILITY

Ironically, if there are many people who witness an event, it is less likely that help is offered than if only one person sees it. People may fail to help because they believe someone else will. Because there are other witnesses, they do not feel personally responsible. *Diffusion of responsibility is the belief that the responsibility to act is shared amongst onlookers and no single individual feels responsible.*

PLURALISTIC IGNORANCE

When people are uncertain as to whether an event is an emergency, they may look to others for guidance. However, since everyone is doing the same, and not intervening, they take their cues from them and do nothing. *Pluralistic ignorance is the mistaken belief of a group of bystanders that other onlookers think an emergency situation is harmless.*

AUDIENCE INHIBITION

Sometimes people don't help because they are afraid of acting inappropriately and making a fool of themselves. This is especially likely to happen when a situation is ambiguous. *Audience inhibition is a person's reluctance to help for fear of making a bad impression on others.*

EVALUATION APPREHENSION

People may be reluctant to help in an ambiguous situation when they are not sure if it is an emergency and if the person in trouble actually wants to be helped. This can happen, for example, if two people are having a violent argument and you are not sure whether they would rather be "left to it" or whether the weaker one may require assistance. *Evaluation apprehension involves the concern an individual has when they feel they are being judged.*

CHARACTERISTICS OF THE VICTIM

Unsurprisingly, people who are perceived as deserving of help are more likely to receive it than people who appear undeserving. Piliavin, Rodin, and Piliavin (1969, see A2PKT p.100) found that people were more likely to help an individual who collapsed on a train if he appeared to be disabled than if he appeared to be drunk. We are also more likely to help people we perceive as similar to ourselves in a moderately ambiguous situation; in a clear-cut emergency, this becomes irrelevant and people help regardless.

CHARACTERISTICS OF THE BYSTANDER

One factor involves expertise and skills; people are more likely to help if they have the required skills. This includes those trained in life-saving, medicine, first-aid, and self-defence. Also, gender seems to play a part. In a review of studies, Eagly and Crowley (1986, see A2PKT p.101) reported that men are more likely than women to offer help in situations involving danger. These studies have been criticised for concentrating on situations in which men are likely to have greater skills or expertise and not on ones where women may feel competent (such as helping someone whose baby buggy has collapsed). Men are more likely to help women than men, especially if the woman is attractive; women offer assistance to men and women equally.

Models of Bystander Behaviour

THE FIVE-STAGE DECISION MODEL

According to this model, put forward by Latané and Darley (1970, see A2PKT p.102), whether or not people intervene in an emergency depends on a series of decisions. Only if the answer is "yes" at each stage will help be given. The decision-making sequence is as shown overleaf.

EVALUATION

- **Practical application.** The model has been extremely useful in pinpointing reasons why people do not intervene and this can be used in education programmes that encourage pro-social behaviour. It also helps on an individual level since people can be offered advice on the best way to encourage others to help them in an emergency situation.

- **Supporting evidence.** There is a great deal of supporting evidence for the model. We have briefly covered some research studies that support the model and there are many others, some of which had previously unexpected results (such as the more people who witness an emergency, the less likely that help will be forthcoming).

- **Cannot account for all research findings.** This model is limited in that it does not explain certain aspects of helping behaviour, such as why some individuals are more likely than others to receive assistance.

- **Does not account for all factors.** It does not consider motivational and emotional factors in helping. This model considers the practical aspects of helping but not the underlying emotions involved. It does not, like the altruism–empathy model, consider the role of empathy and sympathy in pro-social behaviour. Neither does it consider the role of such emotions as fear and anxiety in the decision about whether or not to help. The decision-making process is unlikely to be followed carefully by onlookers who are terrified or otherwise extremely aroused. They are more likely to act impulsively, in whatever way.

THE AROUSAL COST–REWARD MODEL

This model put forward by Piliavin et al. (1981, see A2PKT p.103), and sometimes referred to as the bystander calculus model, also suggests that there are five stages that people go through when faced

The Five-Stage Decision Model

1. Notice the event

There are several reasons why you may not notice, such as paying attention to something else or being in a rush.

Research evidence: Darley and Batson (1973) arranged for people to be told to go from one lecture to another and pass a groaning person *en route*. Only 10% of those told to hurry noticed the person and helped, as opposed to 45% who believed they had just enough time and 63% who were told they had plenty of time.

2. Decide it is an emergency

Some events can be ambiguous and people are not sure whether help is needed.

Research evidence: Clark and Word (1972) found that every participant helped a man in the next room who feigned falling from a ladder when he shouted for help, but only 30% went to see if help was needed when there was a crash but no sound from the victim. Pluralistic ignorance may be operating here.

3. Assume responsibility to do something

As mentioned earlier, when a lot of people are around, diffusion of responsibility is liable to occur and no single individual may feel it is their responsibility to help.

Research evidence: Latané and Darley (1970) arranged a situation in which a fellow student of the participants could be heard having an epileptic fit over an intercom. 100% of participants who believed they were the only person who heard summoned help, but this was reduced to only 31% when people thought they were one of six.

4. Decide how to help

Even if people are fully aware of an emergency and believe they are the only ones who can help, they will not do so if they feel they are not capable of offering useful assistance.

Research evidence: Huston et al. (1981, see A2PKT p.100) report that this contention is supported by real-life studies. Compared to non-responders, significantly more of the people who intervene in emergencies are trained in life-saving, first-aid, self defence, or crime prevention. Cramer (1988) also found that when non-nurses and nurses are present, nurses are far more likely to respond (although if non-nurses are on their own, they will offer help).

5. Actually provide help

Sometimes, even if all other decisions have been affirmative, people may not help for fear of appearing foolish. Audience inhibition may lead people not to help. Other practical considerations may also prevent help being forthcoming, such as someone else getting there first or the victim refusing the help that is offered.

The Arousal Cost–Reward Model

1. Becoming aware of the need for help
As in the previous model, people do not help unless they have paid enough attention to the situation to be aware that help is required.

2. Experiencing arousal
Once the situation is recognised as one that might require action, the bystander experiences physiological arousal—the heart beats faster, sweating occurs, and so on—as the body prepares itself for action. If the situation is very urgent, there is a feeling of tension and stimulation.

3. Interpreting the cause of the arousal
We are automatically programmed to seek the cause of the arousal. There are two different emotions that we may consider are causing the arousal:

i. If we believe we are experiencing anger or nervousness, this decreases the likelihood of helping.
ii. If we believe we are experiencing concern or distress, this increases the likelihood of helping.

Whether or not we actually help also depends on the next stage.

4. Carrying out a cost–benefit analysis
We now weigh up the potential rewards and costs of helping. The bystander calculus model suggests four sets of costs/benefits:

i.   The costs of helping include possible physical harm, embarrassment if the help is not wanted, loss of time, and general inconvenience.
ii. The costs of not helping include feelings of cowardice and shame and the possible disapproval of others.
iii. The benefits (rewards) of helping include admiration and gratitude from others, feeling good about ourselves, even material gain.
iv. The benefits of not helping include being able to carry on as usual without disruption or loss of time.

5. Making a decision whether or not to help and acting on it
The final decision of whether or not to help depends on the balance of costs, in the following way:
- If the cost of helping is low and the cost of not helping is high (e.g. rescuing a child who may otherwise die), then helping is likely to be direct and swift.
- If the cost of helping is high and the cost of not helping is low (trying to intervene in a nasty fight) then it's unlikely that direct help will be given; the bystander will probably leave the scene or deny there's an emergency.
- If both types of costs are low then behaviour depends largely on the norms of the situation, mainly whether or not the particular bystander believes they should help.
- If both costs are high, the situation is difficult for the bystander. Some will try to summon help from elsewhere (dial 999); some will justify doing nothing (e.g. by believing that the victim shouldn't have got themselves in that mess), while others may risk their life.

Impulsive helping
A later version of this model allows for circumstances in which the situation is so dangerous and urgent that there is no time to consider costs and rewards. In cases in which there is a very high risk of loss of life unless action is taken swiftly, the bystander becomes so highly aroused that he or she focuses all their attention on the situation and acts on impulse without regard to costs.

with an emergency, but they do not all involve a decision. Rather, this model takes account, in the early stages, of our emotional response to an emergency. See the model on the previous page.

EVALUATION

- **Experimental support.** Many studies, both in the laboratory and in the field, support the idea that people weigh up benefits and costs before taking action. For example, in the study by Piliavin et al. (1969, see A2PKT p.100) on the New York underground, people were more likely to help a disabled person than a drunk person. The costs of not helping a disabled person are high whereas they are low in the case of the drunk; similarly costs of helping a disabled person are low, whereas a drunk might become aggressive or be sick on you, so the costs may be high.

- **Some non-obvious predictions are supported.** The findings from the Piliavin et al. study are as expected but other findings that support the model are not. In a variation of this study, two girls got up to help a collapsed victim until they saw blood coming out of his mouth. They then sat down again. Many people would expect help to be forthcoming to such a victim but this model predicts that the cost may be too high.

- **Methodological limitations with the supporting studies.** Some of the studies that support this model are laboratory based and therefore lack ecological validity and cannot necessarily be generalised to everyday life. Others are based in the field, which increases the ecological validity but also means there is a variety of uncontrolled variables (such as the particular group of people present) that may affect the outcome; therefore we can be less confident about cause and effect.

- **Allows for physiological influences.** The model allows for both psychological and biological reasons for helping. Unlike the empathy–altruism model, this model allows for the physiological influences in helping. The modified version in particular allows for the effects of emotional arousal as well as for the decision-making process involved in cost–benefit analysis.

SO WHAT DOES THIS MEAN?

The decision model of bystander behaviour focuses mainly on the cognitive factors involved in deciding whether or not to help. The arousal cost–reward model, in contrast, takes more account of the effects of physiological and emotional factors, and is therefore a more well-rounded model. The modified version of this model also allows for occasions, sometimes reported in real-life incidents, when people impulsively risk their lives to try to help others without consideration for the costs or benefits. It is quite possible that no single model can account for all helping behaviour. It is quite likely that the processes operating in a sudden emergency are not the same as those that take place when there is more time to reflect on the situation.

CULTURAL DIFFERENCES IN PRO-SOCIAL BEHAVIOUR

Most research on pro-social behaviour has been conducted in the USA but these findings cannot necessarily be generalised to other cultures that have a different set of values. We will first look at these different values, then at cross-cultural research on pro-social behaviour.

Individualistic and Collectivist Cultures

In the sections of this book on cultural bias (in Chapter 10: Issues, and in Chapter 2: Relationships, see A2PKT pp.443–451), we distinguish between individualistic cultures, typified by most Western countries, and collectivist cultures, such as Israeli Kibbutzim, and many African and South American countries. In terms of altruism and pro-social behaviour, the important differences between these cultures are that:

- *Individualistic* nations emphasise self-interest, the interest of one's immediate family, personal autonomy (making your own decisions), achievement, and independence.
- *Collectivist* cultures emphasise loyalty to the group, interdependence, and the belief that group decisions are more important than individual ones.

The values of the collectivist cultures lend themselves much better to pro-social and altruistic behaviour than do the individualistic ones.

RESEARCH EVIDENCE

- Mead's "New Guinea tribes" study (1935, see A2PKT pp.79–80). Margaret Mead found considerable differences in pro-social behaviour in her classic studies of native tribes. At one extreme were the cooperative, altruistic, and empathetic Arapesh, at the other there was the ruthless, uncaring Mundugumor. However, the reliability of this research has been called into question.
- Whiting and Whiting's cross-cultural study (1975, see A2PKT p.105). They compared everyday behaviour of young children (aged 3–10) in six cultures and found altruism ranged from 100% in Kenya to only 8% in the USA.
- Eisenberg and Mussen's review of cross-cultural altruism studies (1989, see A2PKT p.106). This analysis found that children raised in rural Mexico, Hopi reservations, and Kibbutzim in Israel were more considerate, kind, and cooperative than children in the USA. Children in the kibbutzim continued to cooperate on a task even when offered rewards for individual achievement. In contrast, children from Europe and America continued to compete even when cooperation would have given them a better overall achievement.
- With respect to helping behaviour in adults, the results are not clear-cut. Generally, people in all cultures tend to be more willing to offer help to those who are similar to themselves, but there are some intriguing exceptions. For example, in Athens, foreigners who asked a favour received more help than native Greeks. In some collectivist cultures non-natives are treated better than natives.

Problems with Cross-cultural Research

- There are very few cross-cultural studies in pro-social behaviour and several of these few are now very dated. Others only involve asking a single favour so do not tell us much about everyday, long-term pro-social behaviour.
- There are serious problems with trying to carry out cross-cultural research. It is extremely difficult for psychologists from one culture to objectively measure behaviour in another. As well as the obvious problems of language, there are numerous problems of understanding and interpretation of nonverbal communication that make objectivity very difficult indeed.
- When observations are carried out, participants are almost always going to change their behaviour as a result of being observed, especially when the researchers are from another culture.

SO WHAT DOES THIS MEAN?

There are several aspects of a culture that either foster or discourage pro-social and altruistic behaviour. Whiting and Whiting (1975, see A2PKT p.105) suggest that children are least altruistic when they have to compete in schools and are given little responsibility for other members of the family, as in individualistic cultures. Pro-social behaviour is fostered when children have to care for younger siblings, as in collectivist cultures. Fijneman, Willemsen, and Poortinga (1996, see A2PKT p.106) point out that since this behaviour is expected it may be pro-social but not necessarily altruistic.

Despite limitations in the research, it is apparent that there are wide variations in the degree of pro-social behaviour shown in different cultures. These findings lend support to social learning theory, that our behaviour is learned through socialisation.

OVER TO YOU

1.(a) Outline research evidence into bystander behaviour. **(12 marks)**
  (b) Discuss the extent of cultural differences in pro-social behaviour. **(12 marks)**
2.(a) Outline *two* explanations of human altruism. **(12 marks)**
  (b) Evaluate these explanations with reference to research studies. **(12 marks)**

Question 2 adapted from AQA A2 [Winter 2002] Psychology Examination Papers.

MEDIA INFLUENCES ON PRO- AND ANTI-SOCIAL BEHAVIOUR

ASK YOURSELF

Do you think that watching violent television programmes or films can cause people to become aggressive? Do you think children are more easily influenced than adults?

Should we censor certain violent films in order to prevent "copycat" crimes? Or is this an unfair infringement of the liberty of the vast majority of mature adults who would never behave in such a way?

Now that the media is such an important part of children's lives, should society be using television to encourage kind and cooperative behaviour? If so, are there any programmes from your childhood that you believe could do this?

WHAT YOU NEED TO KNOW

EXPLANATIONS OF MEDIA INFLUENCES

MEDIA INFLUENCES ON PRO-SOCIAL BEHAVIOUR

MEDIA INFLUENCES ON ANTI-SOCIAL BEHAVIOUR

The various ways in which the media can influence behaviour including:
- Social learning theory
- Disinhibition
- Desensitisation
- Cognitive priming
- Displacement effect
- Stereotypes and counter-stereotypes

Research evidence and the limitations of such research

Research evidence and the limitations of such research

To read up on media influences on pro- and anti-social behaviour, refer to pages 109–121 of A2PKT.

EXPLANATIONS OF MEDIA INFLUENCES

There is no doubt that the media has an effect on people's behaviour. There are several suggested mechanisms by which this may occur, including the following.

Social Learning Theory

Social learning theory emphasises that children learn through observation. Bandura demonstrated that children imitate role models, including media heroes and heroines, and via this they learn new, distinctive ways of being aggressive, especially if the violence is reinforced. Although Bandura's research concentrated on the effects of violence, social learning theory also predicts that children will imitate pro-social role models.

Disinhibition

There are powerful social norms in society inhibiting us from being overly aggressive. However, a steady diet of violence can disinhibit us and make aggression more acceptable. This particularly applies to "justified violence" in which the "good guys" use violence to beat the "bad guys". In the case of pro-social behaviour the media can have a positive effect by removing inhibitions we may have towards helping others.

Desensitisation

When watching very emotionally charged television or films (such as violent programmes), we become physiologically aroused and may feel empathy and sympathy for victims of violence or other tragedies. However, this arousal is reduced by prolonged exposure and this may lead to desensitisation to everyday violence and anti-social behaviour.

Cognitive Priming

When watching violent programmes, people report feelings of anger, aggressive thoughts, and physiological arousal. The principle of cognitive priming is that aggressive cues or prompts presented in such programmes lead to aggressive thoughts and feelings. This, in turn, makes them liable to respond aggressively to similar cues, thereby increasing the likelihood of aggression occurring after watching a violent programme.

Displacement Effect

Gerbner and Gross (1976, see A2PKT p.112) suggest that exposure to mass media can give a false impression of the world based on this view. If we watch a lot of violence on television, especially that in news broadcasts and documentaries, we are likely to see the world as a threatening place and believe that the only way we can cope is by being prepared to be aggressive ourselves. This is known as the *deviance amplification effect*—the impression that there is more violent crime than there actually is. Unfortunately, news broadcasts do not focus greatly on pro-social behaviour so the displacement effect does not operate in a way that makes us kinder, although it probably has the potential to.

Stereotypes and Counter-stereotypes

Stereotyping involves placing people into certain categories and assuming they share common characteristics. Stereotypes are not in themselves bad, indeed they are an essential part of dealing with complex information. However, they can be dangerous if they portray a negative impression of groups of people, such as all skinheads being violent and all Japanese being cruel. Nevertheless, stereotypes can also be positive or neutral.

The media needs to use stereotypes to communicate a great deal of information quickly and uses them to great effect in comedy. They can, however, be dangerously misleading if they depict certain cultural and sub-cultural groups as the "enemy". On the other hand, they can also provide positive images, such as women being caring.

The use of *counter-stereotypes*, such as vibrant old people on children's television, and professionally successful disabled people, can be useful in promoting positive, pro-social attitudes rather than violent ones.

MEDIA INFLUENCES ON PRO-SOCIAL BEHAVIOUR

Although not a great deal of attention has been paid to the pro-social effects of the media (in comparison with the anti-social effects), social learning theory does predict that role models showing such behaviour should have a pro-social influence. Some media programmes, such as *Sesame Street* and *Mister Rogers' Neighborhood* in the USA, and *Barney* and *Teletubbies* in the UK, have been especially designed for this purpose.

RESEARCH EVIDENCE

- Friedrich and Stein (1973, see A2PKT p.113) found that children who regularly watched *Mister Rogers* were more helpful than those who did not watch the programme. They also looked at the joint effect of watching *Mister Rogers* and role-playing of pro-social behaviour. They found that although simply watching the programme did lead to more pro-social behaviour (compared to control groups) the effects were not long lasting. Encouraging children to act out the situations depicted in the programmes increased the effects considerably.

- Sprafkin, Liebert, and Poulos (1975, see A2PKT p.113) observed that children given the opportunity to comfort distressed puppies but who lost the chance of winning a prize in a game were more likely to do so if they had previously watched an episode of *Lassie* in which some puppies were heroically saved, than if they had watched neutral programmes.

- Baran, Chase, and Courtright (1979, see A2PKT p.113) found that children who watched an episode of the *Waltons* were more cooperative in game playing afterwards than were control groups.

- Moriaty and McCabe (1977), in a rather different type of study, found that children exposed to pro-social, anti-social, and neutral videos of athletes playing the same sport that the children regularly played found that children were influenced by the pro-social models but not by the anti-social ones.

EVALUATION

 Pro-social programmes can be effective. Hearold (1986, see A2PKT pp.113–114) analysed over 100 studies and found that pro-social programmes do foster pro-social behaviour in children. This is particularly true if there is no accompanying violence in the programme.

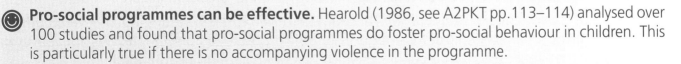 **Effects may be short-lived.** Many studies look at behaviour immediately after the programme is shown. Research indicates that the effects of a single programme may be short term, especially in younger children.

Regular watching may have longer lasting effects. Despite this, the Friedrich and Stein study (1973, see previous page) indicates that regular watching may have longer lasting effects.

 Particular effects can be durable. O'Connor (1980, see A2PKT p.114) showed a film of children playing happily together to a group of children who tended to be "loners". Afterwards, all of them played with others and the effect appeared to be long lasting.

 Effects may only apply in certain situations. Lovelace and Huston (1983, see A2PKT p.114) argue that some programmes foster only limited types of pro-social behaviour (such as heroic acts of bravery) that do not really apply in real life. For the best effect, stories need to depict ordinary everyday kindness and helping and, after the programme, adults in the child's life need to discuss the programme content with them and role-model pro-social behaviour in the course of play.

SO WHAT DOES THIS MEAN?

There is a substantial body of evidence to indicate that the media has considerable potential to encourage pro-social behaviour in children and that these effects are greatly enhanced when adults reinforce them by emphasising ways in which conflict can be peacefully resolved. There seems little doubt that the presence of pro-social role models on television has the capacity to make children more cooperative and friendly, less prejudiced, and more capable of resolving disputes without recourse to violence.

MEDIA INFLUENCES ON ANTI-SOCIAL BEHAVIOUR

There are considerable problems associated with ascertaining the effects of media violence on aggressive behaviour because of the large number of interacting influences upon children. Many studies are short term and laboratory based. Others are correlational, so conclusions about cause and effect cannot be made with any confidence.

RESEARCH EVIDENCE

- Leyens et al. (1975, see A2PKT p.115). In a comparison of the effects of a week's violent films on juvenile delinquent boys in a residential school who were high or low in aggression, half of each of the two groups of boys either watched violent or nonviolent movies, matched for excitement. The level of aggression in the groups who watched violent films rose in the following week, whereas it did not in the groups who watched nonviolent movies.

- Eron (1982) and Huesmann, Lagerspetz, and Eron (1984, see A2PKT p.116) reported results of a longitudinal correlational study over 22 years, showing a positive relationship between aggression and the exposure to television violence but only in males. They suggest that the amount of violence watched is a better predictor of later anti-social behaviour than many other factors, such as the child's IQ and the religious convictions or occupational status of the family.

- Rowell et al.'s cross-cultural study (1986). This study produced complex results, but in several cultures there was a positive relationship between aggression and exposure to violence. This was not, however, the case in the Israeli Kibbutzim, a culture in which violence is strongly discouraged.

- Wood, Wong, and Chachere (1991, see A2PKT p.117) reviewed 28 laboratory and field studies, and found that exposure to media violence invariably led to higher levels of aggression both towards strangers and friends.

- Charlton's "St. Helena" study (1998, see A2PKT p.117). In a natural experiment, Charlton and colleagues looked at the effects when television was first introduced to the island of St. Helena and found no effect at all. These children were particularly hardworking and cooperative both before and after the introduction of television.

EVALUATION

 Cause and effect. Correlational studies do not necessarily demonstrate cause and effect. It is quite possible that children who are naturally aggressive seek out violent films. Alternately, it is equally possible that another factor is causing the relationship—for example, parents who use a lot of corporal punishment to control their children may also choose to watch violent TV. The parental attitudes and aggression may cause both the high levels of aggression in the children and their high exposure to violent TV. Nevertheless, after very extensive research over many years, researchers such as Eron and colleagues believe there is evidence of cause and effect.

Limitations. Laboratory and field studies are limited in scope. Both laboratory studies and the field studies (in residential homes) only measure short-term effects either after one programme or at most a week. In addition, laboratory studies lack ecological validity so we cannot be sure that the findings generalise to real-world situations.

Consistency. Despite the limitations of research, there does seem to be a consistent finding that exposure to media violence does lead to higher levels of anti-social behaviour, at least in certain people.

SO WHAT DOES THIS MEAN?

Drawing any conclusions from research on the effects of media violence is very difficult and fraught with problems. There does seem to be convincing evidence that it can influence some individuals to become more anti-social. The effects are differential and not everyone is equally affected; those already predisposed to violence seem particularly impressionable.

However, although we cannot afford to be complacent, it is possible that the media is sometimes used as a scapegoat in a society that would rather blame the media for serious anti-social behaviour than look closely at the more deep-seated problems within it. The media is only ever likely to have an anti-social effect in a society whose norms encourage violence. As social learning theory predicts, the media can encourage pro-social or anti-social behaviour. In a society that allows its youngsters to watch, on average, 13,000 violent murders by the time they are 16, as happens in the Western world, it seems that at present its potential for encouraging anti-social behaviour is more evident.

OVER TO YOU

1. **Critically consider research relating to media influences on pro-social behaviour.** **(24 marks)**
2. **Critically consider *two* research studies relating to media influences on anti-social behaviour.** **(24 marks)**
3. **Critically consider explanations relating to media influences on anti-social behaviour.** **(24 marks)**

QUESTIONS AND ESSAY PLANS

1 Describe and evaluate *one* social psychological theory of aggression.

(24 marks)

You obviously have to concentrate on one theory but you can use others in order to evaluate the first theory. When deciding which theory to focus on, make sure you have a reasonable amount to write in terms of description and research evidence, and that any other theory you use for evaluation can be compared and contrasted with it. It is not sufficient simply to describe another theory as an evaluation—you need to draw parallels. With this is mind, we will use social learning theory as the main theory.

Paragraph 1 Introduction

Define aggression. Mention that there are many explanations for the causes of aggression and that this answer will focus on social learning theory as a *social psychological* explanation, in other words an explanation that accounts for aggression in terms of social and cultural factors rather than biological ones.

Paragraph 2

Briefly outline the main tenets of social learning theory—learning by observation and imitation. Mention that it acknowledges the importance of classical conditioning and operant conditioning as in traditional learning theory, but do not spend time describing these mechanisms. Outline the general beliefs of social learning theory in terms of methodology—a belief in carefully controlled laboratory studies.

Paragraph 3

Describe Bandura's Bobo doll studies (e.g. Bandura, Ross, & Ross, 1961) with emphasis on findings, i.e. the characteristics of the model that make one model more likely than another to be imitated. Also mention the cognitive factors that operate, i.e. that an individual won't imitate if they don't believe they are capable of performing the action. Briefly discuss the implications of this theory (this is AO2) in terms of the norms of cultures and sub-cultures and the influence of the media. With regard to the latter, this is important in our society, so mention a couple of research studies on the influence of the media. If we raise children in an atmosphere of violence, they are liable to become violent and admire that characteristic in themselves and others.

Paragraph 4

Evaluate social learning theory in terms of methodology—the positives (cause and effect clearly indicated) as well as the negatives (lack of ecological validity). You can briefly mention the ethics of Bandura's studies. Provide evaluation in terms of evidence, i.e. the theory is well supported by many studies including those into media violence (but there is no need to give details of studies). It is also supported by the extent of individual and cultural variations in aggression.

Paragraph 5

Provide evaluation in terms of limitations and alternative explanations such as social deprivation theory, deindividuation, or Freud. Learning and imitation can only account for some aggression. Twin studies and consistent gender differences in aggression indicate that biological factors must also make some contribution.

Paragraph 6 Conclusion

Conclude that social learning theory does account very well for some forms of aggression and for individual and cultural variations. However, it is unlikely to account for all aggression and there is a strong body of opinion that believes some aggression is innate.

2 Outline and evaluate *two* explanations of human altruism. (24 marks)

Paragraphs 1 and 2 Introduction

Use one paragraph to describe each of the explanations. The two explanations in the specification are the obvious choice, that of empathy–altruism and the sociobiological explanation.

Paragraph 3

We now need to go on to the evaluation (AO2). We'll begin with empathy–altruism. On the positive side, this has been supported by many research studies. Discuss the research into the hypothesis of Batson et al. (1981) and the modified version proposed in 1988.

Paragraph 4

However, there are problems with studying altruistic behaviour in the laboratory. There are limitations on the type of behaviour that can be measured, and difficulty generalising the findings to everyday life. The seemingly altruistic behaviour shown may be the result of social pressure to behave appropriately and of demand characteristics. This means that these studies do not necessarily support the hypothesis.

Paragraph 5

Briefly mention the argument covered on page 53 of this book (in the last evaluation point of this model) concerning whether true altruism really exists. The negative-state relief model argues that people never act in a purely altruistic way, they simply help others because it relieves them of the guilt they would experience if they did not. Sociobiological theory also argues that there is no such thing as altruism and therefore provides an alternative explanation.

Paragraph 6

Evaluate sociobiological theory. On the positive side, some altruistic behaviour can probably be accounted for in terms of a biological, innate drive. On the negative side, it is a very reductionist approach that explains human behaviour almost solely in terms of biological forces, and does not take account of the fact that we are thinking, reasoning beings who have been socialised within a culture. We do have some personal choice and our behaviour is therefore heavily influenced by social norms and by our own internalised moral values, none of which is considered in this theory. Note that some of the arguments that are relevant here are covered in Chapter 12 of this book, on pages 320 to 322.

Paragraph 7 Conclusion

The fundamental difference between this and the sociobiological approach is whether there is genuinely such a thing as entirely selfless behaviour, or whether we are at the mercy of biological forces that are essentially selfish at the gene level. This is not an issue that can be easily resolved as it is always difficult to ascertain and measure the underlying motivation for any behaviour.

3   "There is much public interest in the debate about the effects of violence in the media on the behaviour of young children; but why don't people focus more on the potentially pro-social influences?"
     Discuss the above quotation in relation to the pro- and anti-social effects of the media.
                                                                                    (24 marks)

There are two important points to consider with this question. First, you must address the issues in the quotation and refer to it throughout the essay, not simply make brief reference at the beginning and end. Second, since you are asked to discuss both pro- and anti-social behaviour you must be selective about the material you use or you will not get sufficient AO2 marks.

Paragraph 1 Introduction

The media certainly has an important influence on all types of behaviour but because crime and violence in general (especially in children) are of great concern and tend to be highlighted by the media, the focus is on anti-social rather than pro-social behaviour.

Paragraph 2

Briefly outline research (and I do mean briefly) that shows a relationship between media violence and aggression—hence the reason for concern. Outline the limitations of the research but also Eron and colleagues' (Eron, 1982, and Huesmann et al., 1984) conclusions about cause and effect.

Paragraph 3

Now consider research that shows that watching violent TV does not necessarily change behaviour in children who are already well balanced and cooperative. There are many other influences on children apart from the media, for example, parental style of upbringing, peer group, and culture. Present the argument that the media may be a scapegoat and we need to consider other factors such as social norms that lead us to admire aggression, especially in males.

Paragraph 4

It is true that psychologists' attention has been directed far more towards the effects of the media on anti-social rather than pro-social behaviour. This is reflected in the paucity of research on the pro-social effects. It is also demonstrated by the fact that although social learning theory predicts that pro-social as well as anti-social behaviour can be learned from models, its research has concentrated on aggressive behaviour.

Paragraph 5

Outline the research into media effects on pro-social behaviour. Again, be very brief. Despite the limitations of this research (outline these briefly), it definitely indicates that the media can have a pro-social effect, and mention the best conditions to bring this about.

Paragraph 6 Conclusion

There is a paradox in Western society. In many ways we admire aggression and enjoy watching it, hence the enormous amount of media violence that children are exposed to from a very early age. It is hardly surprising that some of it affects their behaviour. On the other hand, although research has demonstrated the potential of the media to encourage pro-social behaviour, we do not make the most of this potential. Our concentration is focused on anti-social rather than pro-social behaviour because of the media's concentration on it and our consequent fear of it. Pro-social behaviour, unfortunately, rarely hits the headlines. Maybe it's up to psychologists to take every opportunity to emphasise the potential positive effects of the media.

Question 2 adapted from AQA A2 [Winter 2002] Psychology Examination Papers.
The authors are responsible for the solutions and (a) they have neither been provided nor approved by AQA and (b) they may not necessarily constitute the only possible solutions.

Physiological Psychology

BIOLOGICAL RHYTHMS, SLEEP, AND DREAMING
Specification 13.2

4

What's it about?

Physiological psychology focuses on bodily processes and biological causes as explanations of behaviour. However, it is reductionist and deterministic to consider that behaviour is determined by physiology alone as we are not "biological puppets". Although we consider the nervous system (in particular the brain), and the effect of biochemicals such as neurotransmitters and hormones, most behaviour cannot be explained by physiology alone. It is necessary to address both physiological and psychological processes, and how they interact, in order to get a good picture of what is going on.

Thus, in this unit we will consider biological rhythms, which maintain a consistent pattern within a specific time period, and what happens when these biological rhythms are disrupted. We will then consider the physiological and psychological functions of sleep, including the effects of total and partial sleep deprivation. Finally, we will look at dreaming, which provokes the interesting question, "Do our dreams have meaning, or are they just a by-product of physiological activity?"

What's in this unit?

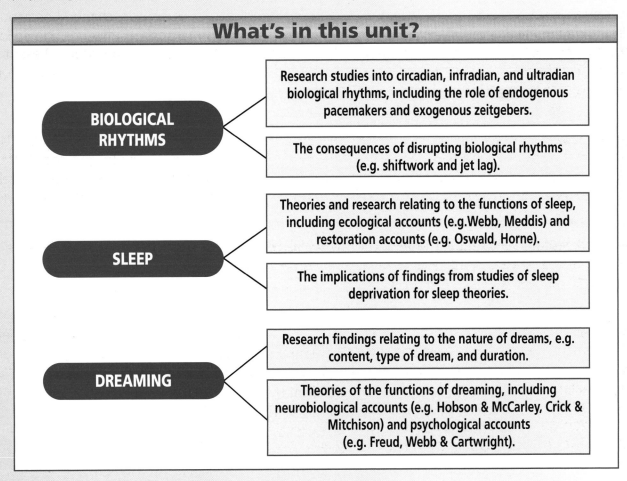

BIOLOGICAL RHYTHMS

Research studies into circadian, infradian, and ultradian biological rhythms, including the role of endogenous pacemakers and exogenous zeitgebers.

The consequences of disrupting biological rhythms (e.g. shiftwork and jet lag).

SLEEP

Theories and research relating to the functions of sleep, including ecological accounts (e.g. Webb, Meddis) and restoration accounts (e.g. Oswald, Horne).

The implications of findings from studies of sleep deprivation for sleep theories.

DREAMING

Research findings relating to the nature of dreams, e.g. content, type of dream, and duration.

Theories of the functions of dreaming, including neurobiological accounts (e.g. Hobson & McCarley, Crick & Mitchison) and psychological accounts (e.g. Freud, Webb & Cartwright).

BIOLOGICAL RHYTHMS

Are you a "morning" or an "evening" person? This links to individual differences in biological rhythms.

Do you find it easier to get up early or stay awake late? Research shows that when it comes to disrupting biological rhythms it is easier to phase delay (stay up late) than phase advance (get up early).

Have you ever nodded off and then been jolted awake by the sensation of falling? This links to the first stage of sleep.

Can biological cycles become synchronised amongst groups of people? Sometimes women's menstrual cycles synchronise if they live together.

ASK YOURSELF

WHAT YOU NEED TO KNOW

CIRCADIAN RHYTHM

24 hours, e.g. the sleep–waking cycle

INFRADIAN RHYTHM

Greater than 24 hours, e.g. the menstrual cycle

ULTRADIAN RHYTHM

Less than 24 hours, e.g. the stages and cycles of sleep

- Research studies on each of the rhythms.
- Endogenous (internal) factors, i.e. the biological clock as controlled by the suprachiasmatic nucleus (SCN, a small group of cells in the hypothalamus) and the pineal gland.
- Exogenous (external) factors, i.e. zeitgebers (time givers) such as light.
- Disruption of biological rhythms as happens with shiftwork and jet lag.

CIRCADIAN RHYTHMS

To read up on biological rhythms, refer to pages 125–138 of A2PKT.

A Circadian Rhythm: The Sleep–Waking Cycle

A circadian rhythm repeats in a cycle of once every 24 hours. Mammals possess about 100 circadian rhythms. The 24-hour sleep–waking cycle is a good example of a circadian rhythm because it clearly illustrates that circadian rhythms depend on an interaction of physiological and psychological processes. Our fairly consistent sleep pattern suggests an internal or endogenous mechanism—the biological clock. But this can be overridden by psychological factors such as anxiety.

Endogenous Factors: The Biological Clock

The suprachiasmatic nucleus (SCN) is the pacemaker of the biological clock. The SCN generates its own biological rhythm due to protein synthesis and is connected to the optic chiasm and so receives input about the amount of light, which also influences the rhythm. The pineal gland is linked to the SCN by a neural pathway and electrical stimulation of this causes it to release melatonin; when light levels are low high amounts of melatonin are released. Melatonin is a hormone that induces sleep because it enhances production of the neurotransmitter serotonin and this causes the nervous system to slow down, brain activity consequently falls, and sleep begins.

The physiological processes of the biological clock can be summarised as:

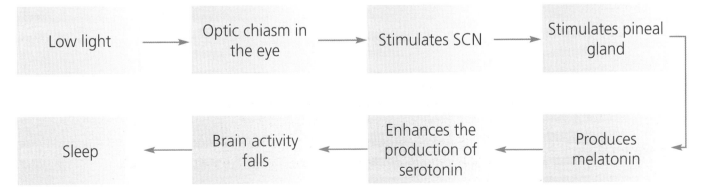

The sleep–waking cycle is 24 hours long due mainly to the above endogenous factors (in-built biological mechanisms).

RESEARCH EVIDENCE FOR ENDOGENOUS FACTORS

- Siffre's "cave study" (1975, see A2PKT p.126). Siffre spent two months in a dark cave. In the absence of light he developed a sleep–waking cycle of 25 hours, which being close to the standard 24 hours suggests the influence of endogenous factors.

- Morgan's "hamster studies" (1995, see A2PKT p.128). When the SCN was removed from hamsters their circadian rhythms disappeared. Transplanting with SCN cells re-established the rhythms, including mutant rhythms from mutant hamsters, which shows that the SCN is the main pacemaker.

- Schochat et al.'s "sleep-gate" study (1997, see A2PKT p.128). Schochat et al. found a close relationship between sleep propensity and melatonin. Six participants spent 29 hours in a sleep laboratory where for 7 minutes in every 20 they had to try to sleep. The highest sleep propensity, the "sleep-gate", was found to occur in late evening and the highest levels of melatonin preceded this by 100–120 minutes. This supports the role of melatonin in sleep propensity.

RESEARCH EVIDENCE FOR EXOGENOUS FACTORS OR ZEITGEBERS

- Siffre's "cave study" (1975, see A2PKT p.126) attempted to establish free-running, biological rhythms, so the participants were isolated from variables that would affect these, such as daylight, clocks etc. However, there was one key confounding variable–artificial, dim light. It was thought at the time that this would not affect the circadian rhythm, but this is not the case.

- Miles et al.'s study of a blind man (1977, see A2PKT p.129). The man, blind from birth, had a circadian rhythm of 24.9 hours. He had to use stimulants and sedatives to adjust his sleep–waking cycle to the standard 24 hours. This shows that light is the main exogenous factor, as it reduces the natural 25-hour rhythm to 24 hours.

- Luce and Segal 's "Arctic Circle" study (1966, see A2PKT p.129). People who live within the Arctic Circle sleep for 7 hours per night despite the fact that during the summer the sun never sets. This shows that light is not the only zeitgeber, nor is the biological clock only influenced by light. Other exogenous factors such as social customs, and psychological factors such as motivation, are important.

EVALUATION

- **Controlled conditions increase confidence in validity.** Schochat et al.'s research in the sleep laboratory took place in a well-controlled environment. The greater control of confounding variables gives confidence in the finding that melatonin and sleep propensity are associated.

- **Correlation criticisms.** Schochat et al.'s relationship is correlational not causal and so we cannot conclude that melatonin causes sleep propensity. However, the research is supported by the fact that insomniacs treated with melatonin do find it easier to get to sleep.

- **Generalisability.** Much of the research is case studies or small samples which means generalisability and therefore population validity is a weakness.

- **Validity of animal research is questionable.** Extrapolation from animals to humans is an issue in Morgan's hamster study.

INFRADIAN RHYTHMS

An Infradian Rhythm: The Menstrual Cycle

An infradian rhythm repeats in a cycle of greater than 24 hours. For example, the human menstrual cycle occurs every 28 days, although it can be 20–60 days. It is controlled by the female hormones oestrogen and progesterone, which are released by the endocrine glands. The hormones cause the release of the egg and engorging of the lining of the womb. If the egg is not fertilised the lining is shed and so menstruation is the outcome of a cycle of activity that prepares the body for conception. Menstruation is an endogenous mechanism as it is controlled mainly by internal biological factors (the hormones) but exogenous factors (external cues) can also affect the rhythm.

RESEARCH EVIDENCE

- Reinberg's "cave study" (1967, see A2PKT p.131). Reinberg investigated the effect on a woman's menstrual cycle of spending 3 months in a cave with dim lighting. Her menstrual cycle became shorter (26 days) and took a year to return to normal. It was concluded that light influences the menstrual cycle—the production of melatonin will increase due to the low light, affecting the SCN and, consequently, the lengthened circadian rhythm disrupts the infradian rhythm.

- McClintock's "synchronised menstrual cycles" study (1971, see A2PKT p.131). Women who live or spend considerable time together, such as girls in a boarding school, can have synchronised menstrual cycles. Twins can menarche at exactly the same time, including the time of their first menstruation. This may be due to pheromones, biochemical substances that act like hormones but are released in the air rather than the bloodstream. These are "chemical messengers" and so may co-ordinate the synchronisation.

- Russell et al.'s "female pheromones" study (1980, see A2PKT p.132) provides support for the effect of pheromones. Participants had donor pheromones rubbed onto their upper lips, daily, for 5 months. A control group went through the same procedure as the experimental group but was not exposed to pheromones. At the end of the 5 months four of the five women in the experimental group had menstrual cycles that synchronised with the donor.

- The "male pheromones" study (see A2PKT p.132). Women who work with men have much shorter menstrual cycles and so McClintock (1971) concluded that male pheromones might reset a woman's biological clock, increasing ovulation.

EVALUATION

- **Synchronisation is adaptive.** There is an evolutionary advantage to synchronised menstruation, as synchronised conceptions would mean that childcare could be shared (Bentley, 2000). Thus, synchronisation is an adaptive behaviour. This supports the research findings and thus validity.

- **Objective evidence.** The physiological evidence is incontrovertible and so the findings that menstrual cycles synchronise and shorten are objective and valid.

- **Problems with measurement.** Whether this is explained by pheromones is less clear. These are not consciously detectable making it difficult to measure their effect. Russell et al.'s experimental evidence overcomes this and so provides some empirical support for the role of pheromones.

- **Generalisability.** Much of the research is case studies, which means generalisability and so population validity is a weakness, particularly as menstruation is subject to great individual differences.

ULTRADIAN RHYTHMS

An Ultradian Rhythm: The Stages and Cycles of Sleep

An ultradian rhythm repeats in a cycle of less than 24 hours. In sleep the cycles occur approximately every 90 minutes and the following stages occur within these cycles. Sleep is not a total loss of consciousness but there is a descent into reduced consciousness.

The Stages of Sleep: The Sleep Staircase

Stage 1: Lasts approximately 15 minutes. The body relaxes and the individual feels drowsy. The EEG activity is characterised by alpha waves that have a frequency of 8–12 cycles per second (cps or Hz). The EOG indicates slow rolling eye movements and the EMG shows reductions in muscle tension. Heart rate and temperature also fall. A *hypnogogic* state may occur during the transition from wakefulness to sleep in which hallucinations may be experienced, e.g. the feeling of falling. As this is the lightest stage of sleep we are easily awakened and may feel as if we have been jolted awake.

Stage 2: Lasts approximately 20 minutes. The EEG activity is characterised by larger and slower theta waves (4–8 Hz) and short bursts of high frequency sleep spindles (12–14 Hz). K-complexes also occur, which are our responses to external stimuli (e.g. noise) and internal stimuli. The EOG shows little eye movement and the EMG shows the muscles are relaxed. It is still easy to be awakened.

Stage 3: Lasts approximately 15 minutes. The EEG activity is characterised by long, slow delta waves (1–5 Hz) with some sleep spindles. The EOG and EMG are the same as stage 2.

Stage 4: Lasts approximately 30 minutes. Stage 4 is also known as slow-wave sleep (SWS) because of the long, slow delta waves of the EEG. The EOG and EMG show very little activity. This is deep sleep and so it is hard to wake somebody from. Other physiological activity includes body temperature, heart rate, and blood pressure dropping to their lowest point and growth hormones are secreted. It is also the stage when sleepwalking, sleep-talking, and "night terrors" (a nightmare where the individual appears wide awake but is asleep) can occur.

Stage 5: Lasts approximately 10 minutes in the 1st cycle and builds up to an hour by the 4th and 5th cycles. The EEG activity is characterised by beta waves (13–30 Hz), which also occur during a relaxed waking state and this high level of brain activity is linked to dreaming. This stage is known as REM sleep because of the rapid eye movements and has also been called paradoxical sleep because the EEG readings show that the brain is very active, whilst the EMG readings show that the body is paralysed. Consequently it is the hardest stage to wake somebody from. This paralysis is for a good reason because REM sleep is when most (but not all) dreaming occurs and so the paralysis prevents us from acting out our dreams.

The Cycles of Sleep: Up and Down the Sleep Staircase

- **First cycle:** Go down the sleep staircase from stage 1 to 4; then ascend through stage 3 and then stage 2. Stage 5, or REM sleep, follows this and lasts for approximately 10 minutes.

- **Second cycle:** Begin at stage 2, which lasts for about 20 minutes, then descend through stage 3 to the deep sleep of stage 4, which lasts approximately 30 minutes. Then ascend through stages 3 and 2. REM sleep (stage 5) completes the cycle and again lasts for about 10 minutes.

- **Third cycle:** Enter at stage 2 and spend about an hour in this stage. Next we miss the descent of the sleep staircase by going straight into REM sleep (stage 5) for approximately 40 minutes.

- **Fourth cycle:** Enter at stage 2 for 70 minutes and then enter REM sleep (stage 5) for approximately an hour.

- **Fifth cycle:** Enter at stage 2 followed by REM sleep (stage 5). This is known as the emergent cycle because we may wake from either stage. We are more likely to remember our dream if we wake in stage 5 and can experience a hypnogogic state again and so recall vivid visual images as we wake.

Most people have five cycles that last approximately 90 minutes. Deep sleep, or slow-wave sleep (SWS), occurs in only the first two cycles; REM sleep occurs in all of the cycles, and increases during the course of the night's sleep.

> **NOTE:** As we descend the sleep staircase into deep sleep, the brain (EEG) waves become *larger* and *slower*.

RESEARCH EVIDENCE

- Electroencephalographs (EEGs) measure electrical activity or brain waves, electro-oculograms (EOGs) measure eye movement, and electromyograms (EMGs) measure muscle movement and have been used to distinguish the stages and cycles of sleep. EEG readings are normally used as the frequency (number of oscillations per second) and amplitude (half the distance between the high and low points of an oscillation) differ depending on the stage. (See the EEG diagram on A2PKT p.139.)

- Traditionally, self-report was used before the development of the recording technology.

EVALUATION

 Objective evidence. The EEG, EOG, and EMG provide objective measures of the physiology of sleep, which have greatly advanced our understanding, and the fact that they are objective means that they are less subject to bias (see A2PKT p.138).

Artificiality of the sleep laboratory. A significant weakness is that such physiological measures are gathered in a sleep laboratory, where the artificial conditions and the fact that research participants are wired up to machines may affect sleep patterns. The sleep laboratory is reductionist as it does not reflect the range of factors that can influence sleep in real life. The research lacks mundane realism and as a consequence the findings may lack generalisability to real-life sleep patterns and so ecological validity may be lacking. Consequently, the meaningfulness of the findings may be limited.

Weaknesses of the self-report method. The self-report method, used traditionally, yields subjective data compared to the objective measurements of the EEG, EOG, and EMG. Self-report is vulnerable to bias and distortion as a consequence of researcher effects and participant reactivity and so may lack validity. Furthermore, it offers no insight into the physiology of sleep.

Individual differences. Most people have five sleep cycles, which last approximately 90 minutes each. However, there is great variation in sleep patterns, as evidenced by individual differences in the total amount of sleep. For example, some people have a 9-hour sleep pattern, 7–8 hours is the average, yet many sleep for considerably less than 4 hours. Longer sleepers spend longer in REM sleep than shorter sleepers. There is also diversity in the pattern of NREM (non-REM) to REM sleep between people, and within the individual, as the pattern may vary in the same person over time.

Universality. There are some universal characteristics of sleep as stages 3 and 4 occur only in the first two cycles and REM sleep always increases in duration with each successive cycle.

OVER TO YOU

1. **Describe and assess the role of endogenous and exogenous factors in circadian biological rhythms.**

(24 marks)

DISRUPTION OF BIOLOGICAL RHYTHMS

Disrupting biological rhythms has negative consequences for the individual because this goes against a mainly endogenous, built-in pattern, and so there are physiological and psychological costs of disruption as the body attempts to readjust.

Jet Lag

Jet lag occurs when the individual crosses time zones because this disrupts the natural rhythm of the biological clock. Thus, jet lag is not caused by the rigours of travelling as is often misperceived. Instead, it only occurs when there is sufficient discrepancy between internal time (your biological clock, which is set to British time) and external time (local time of destination), which only occurs when travelling east to west or west to east, not north to south. The consequences of such disruption are a wide range of symptoms including fatigue, headache, sleep disturbances, irritability, and gastrointestinal disturbances.

RESEARCH EVIDENCE

- Klein, Wegman, and Hunt's "westbound flights" study (1972, see A2PKT p.134). Adjustment of the sleep–waking cycle was faster when flying westbound (i.e. going from the UK to the USA) than eastbound, as westbound passengers took 1 day per time zone crossed whereas eastbound passengers took 6 days for complete readjustment, irrespective of whether they were travelling home or away from home.

- Schwartz et al.'s "baseball" study (1995, see A2PKT p.135). They analysed the results of American baseball games in relation to whether the teams had to travel east to west or west to east. They found that the west coast teams travelling east lost more games than the east coast teams travelling west. This supports Klein et al.'s findings that westbound flights are easier to adjust to. However, of course, the ability of the teams studied was also a factor, which wasn't accounted for!

- Research application (see A2PKT p.134). Research findings on the circadian rhythm of the sleep–waking cycle have been applied to try to combat the negative effects of disruption. Research revealed the link between melatonin and sleepiness and so melatonin tablets have been tested as a cure for jet lag.

EVALUATION

 Phase advance vs. phase delay. The research finding that westbound flights require less adjustment than eastbound is supported and explained by the fact that when travelling west the day is lengthened and when travelling east it is shortened. It is easier to stay up late (phase delay) than get up early (phase advance). This is because the natural rhythm of the biological clock is 25 hours and so it is easier to adapt to beyond 24 hours than adapt to less than 24 hours.

 Face validity. It does make sense that it is easier to stay up late than get up early and so the research has face validity.

Shiftwork

Shiftwork causes major disruption to the biological rhythms because the individual is working when the body wants to be asleep and trying to sleep when the body wants to be awake. The consequences of this are the same as the symptoms described for jet lag. If given enough time to adjust, our bodies can reprogramme our biological rhythms and thus cope with the shiftwork by reducing disruption. The industrial accidents at Chernobyl, Bhopal, and Three-Mile Island (see A2PKT p.135) all occurred between 1am and 4am, and most lorry accidents occur between 4am and 7am, illustrating the dangers of shiftwork.

RESEARCH EVIDENCE

- Monk and Folkard's "types of shiftwork" study (1983, see A2PKT p.135). They identified two major types of shiftwork: (1) rapid rotation where the worker changes shifts approximately every third shift, and (2) slow rotation where the worker changes shifts every week or month. Both types have strengths and weaknesses, as the evaluation will show.

- Czeisler et al.'s "shift rotation" study (1982, see A2PKT pp.135–136). Given that phase delay needs less adjustment than phase advance it is better to rotate with the clock than against it, i.e. progress from early shift to day shift to night shift, rather than the other way round. Czeisler et al. tested this in a chemical plant where workers reported feeling better and less tired and managers reported increased productivity and fewer errors. Furthermore, Czeisler found that it was better to have slower shift changes. A pattern of 21 days was therefore better than 7 days, as this provided more time for the workers to adjust.

- Research application (Dawson & Campbell, 1991, see A2PKT p.135). Research findings that light acts as a zeitgeber in maintaining the rhythm of the SCN has been applied and bright light has been used as a substitute for sunlight to reset the SCN. Workers exposed to a 4-hour pulse of bright light showed improvements in work performance.

EVALUATION OF SHIFTWORK

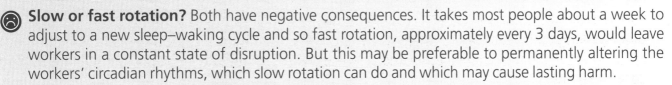 **Negative effects are well-supported.** The negative effects of shiftwork are indisputable; the accident record and workers' self-reports provide conclusive evidence of the negative consequences of disrupting biological rhythms.

Slow or fast rotation? Both have negative consequences. It takes most people about a week to adjust to a new sleep–waking cycle and so fast rotation, approximately every 3 days, would leave workers in a constant state of disruption. But this may be preferable to permanently altering the workers' circadian rhythms, which slow rotation can do and which may cause lasting harm.

Applications of the research. The successful use of light is a positive application of research into circadian rhythms.

 Individual differences. The research on circadian rhythms and on the disruption of biological rhythms may lack generalisability because the sleep–wake cycle is subject to individual differences in cycle length and cycle onset. The latter is perhaps particularly significant as the effects of disruption may vary greatly depending on if you are a "lark" (prefer to rise early and go to bed early) or an "owl" (prefer to wake late and go to bed late).

SO WHAT DOES THIS MEAN?

The biological rhythms are determined primarily by endogenous factors but these interact with exogenous factors, and physiology (the endogenous factors) can be overridden, e.g. shiftwork. Disrupting biological rhythms can have short- and long-term effects, e.g. jet travel is a temporary disruption and so although readjustment can be extremely uncomfortable it has no long-term effects. Shiftwork is a more permanent disruption experienced by many and the consequences of this can be long lasting. The negative effects can be reduced and so it is important to consider the speed and direction of the rotation.

OVER TO YOU

1.(a) Describe two biological rhythms. (12 marks)

(b) Assess the consequences of disrupting biological rhythms. (12 marks)

SLEEP

Do you ever find yourself sleeping through the day? Micro-sleep, when you temporarily lose awareness (e.g. stare blankly into space), can occur when you are sleep deprived.

How many hours' sleep do you get per night? You may have a regular pattern, or one that varies widely.

Do we sleep to be safe or do we sleep to restore the brain and body? There are several theories of the purpose of sleep.

What is the least amount of sleep you've had in one night and how did you feel the next day? Symptoms of sleep deprivation are bad enough after one night, but total sleep deprivation can be fatal.

How can the findings on sleep deprivation and illness be used to support a restorative and an evolutionary function? They show that sleep has restorative and adaptive value since it is necessary for health and ultimately survival.

WHAT YOU NEED TO KNOW

SLEEP DEPRIVATION

- Total sleep deprivation, which involves constant wakefulness, and so has been studied for short periods of time.
- Partial sleep deprivation, which involves sleep reductions, and this is something we all may be experiencing in today's 24-hour society.

Relate sleep deprivation to the theories, e.g. research on sleep deprivation supports the restoration theory and, given that it can be fatal, suggests that it is necessary for survival and so supports a restoration and an evolutionary function.

THEORIES OF THE FUNCTIONS OF SLEEP

- Restoration, i.e. repair of the brain and body, e.g. Oswald (1980, see A2PKT pp.141–142), and Horne (1988, see A2PKT pp.141–142) who distinguished between core (stage 4 and REM) and optional sleep (stages 1–3).
- Ecological or evolutionary, suggest that sleep has an adaptive function as it increases survival potential. For example, Meddis (1975, see A2PKT p.144) considered a safety function and Webb (1982, see A2PKT p.145) suggested energy conservation with a hibernation theory.

It may be that the function of sleep is that it allows us to dream. But be careful how you make such a point, as your answer must be focused on sleep not dreaming.

To read up on sleep, refer to pages 138–152 of A2PKT.

SLEEP DEPRIVATION

Sleep deprivation research has been carried out to try to clarify the functions of sleep. The reasoning being that the ill effects of not sleeping will reveal the functions of sleep.

Total Sleep Deprivation

Total sleep deprivation is when the individual experiences constant wakefulness, usually over a temporary period of time. This tends to occur very rarely in real life, as people are unlikely to subject themselves to the discomfort of total sleep deprivation. It has been investigated for research purposes but it is difficult to organise large-scale studies of total sleep deprivation due to a lack of volunteers—unsurprisingly! Consequently, the case study is the most common research method.

RESEARCH EVIDENCE

- Case studies. Peter Tripp, a New York DJ took part in a "wakeathon" for charity, where he stayed awake for 8 days (see A2PKT p.146). The effects of this included delusions and hallucinations, e.g. he thought his desk drawer was on fire. Randy Gardner, a 17-year-old student, stayed awake for 11 days and effects included disorganised speech, blurred vision, and a small degree of paranoia, which was related to the effects of the sleep deprivation as he felt people thought he was stupid due to his impaired functioning (Horne, 1988, see A2PKT pp.146–147).

- Meta-analysis by Hüber-Weidman (1976, see A2PKT p.149). Hüber-Weidman reviewed a large number of sleep deprivation studies and summarised the findings into common effects experienced over six nights of sleep deprivation. The effects included feeling distress as a consequence of the lack of sleep, a strong desire to sleep, periods of micro-sleep (a temporary loss of awareness experienced by sleep-deprived people when awake), delusions, and, by the sixth night, "sleep deprivation psychosis", which involves a sense of depersonalisation, loss of identity, and difficulty in coping with environmental demands and other people.

- The "rotating rats" study (Rechtschaffen et al., 1983, see A2PKT p.147). Two rats were placed on a disc above a container of water, one was able to sleep but the other wasn't as when the EEG indicated sleep the disc began to rotate and so the rat fell into the water. All of the sleep-deprived rats died within 33 days; the rats that were not sleep deprived appeared to suffer no ill effects as a result of the study.

- The brain-damaged patient. Lugaressi et al. (1986, see A2PKT p.147) report the case of a man who, as a consequence of brain damage, could hardly sleep at all. He was unable to function normally and eventually died.

- Fatal familial insomnia. This is a rare condition where the individual sleeps normally until middle age and then suddenly stops sleeping, which leads to death within two years.

Partial Sleep Deprivation

Partial sleep deprivation is when the individual experiences a reduction in the amount of sleep compared to normal. Partial sleep deprivation also occurs when participants are deprived of one particular stage of sleep.

RESEARCH EVIDENCE

- The "flower-pot" technique. Jouvet (1967, see A2PKT p.148) used this to test the effect of REM sleep deprivation in cats. Cats were placed on a flowerpot in a tank of water. They were able to sleep without falling off during NREM but fell off as soon as they entered REM due to the loss of muscle tone during the paralysis of REM sleep. Continued REM deprivation proved fatal.

- NREM and REM sleep deprivation. Dement (1960, see A2PKT pp.147–148) systematically deprived participants of either NREM or REM sleep to test the difference in the effects between the two. Effects of REM deprivation were more severe and included increased aggression and poor concentration. Participants deprived of REM sleep seemed to have a greater need to catch up on this than NREM deprived participants. Attempts to enter REM sleep doubled from an average of 12 to 26 times by the seventh night. When allowed to sleep normally the participants spent much longer than normal in REM sleep, as did Randy Gardner. This was named the REM rebound effect and supports Horne's concept of core sleep, which is covered in the next section.

- Reducing the total night's sleep. Webb and Bonnet (1978, see A2PKT p.149) found that participants could reduce their total night's sleep by 2 hours and reported feeling fine. In a follow-up study participants gradually reduced their total amount of sleep over a period of 2 months, where at the end of this period they slept for only 4 hours per night and reported no adverse effects.

EVALUATION OF SLEEP DEPRIVATION RESEARCH

 Case studies. The studies of sleep deprivation in humans are mainly case studies or small samples and so lack generalisability, as the effects may be due to characteristics that are unique to the individual participant. The effects experienced by Peter Tripp and Randy Gardner may not be representative of others and so population validity may be limited.

 Extrapolation. Extrapolation from animals to humans in Rechtschaffen et al.'s and Jouvet's studies is an issue; generalisability may be limited given that humans and animals differ qualitatively not just quantitatively. This is due to the greater influence of psychological factors, such as cognition, on human behaviour.

Self-reports. Results from the participants who reported feeling fine on only 4 hours' sleep contradict how the majority of us feel when we get this little sleep, which raises the issues of participant reactivity and researcher expectancy. Participant cooperation may have occurred where the participants answered as they thought the experimenter expected of them. Or social desirability bias may have occurred where the participants reported feeling fine in order to appear physically and mentally tough. Participant and researcher bias reduces the internal validity of the findings as the reported effects may be due to this rather than sleep deprivation. The truth and value of Webb and Bonnett's (1978) research is questionable and so it may not be representative of real-life partial sleep deprivation.

Correlational. The case studies involving Randy Gardner and Peter Tripp, and the man with brain damage provide correlational evidence as sleep deprivation has not been manipulated as an IV because ethically and practically this is much more difficult to do with humans. Consequently, the research evidence lacks conclusiveness, as cause and effect cannot be inferred.

 The validity of sleep laboratory research. Dement's research was an apparently well-controlled and systematic laboratory experiment that increases confidence in the internal validity. However, the sleep laboratory may well have disturbed the participants' sleep patterns, so the effects may be due to the artificiality and reductionism of the sleep laboratory, rather than just the sleep deprivation. If this is the case internal validity will be low.

Ecological validity. Total sleep deprivation is very rare in real-life sleep patterns. It is worth noting that even some insomniacs sleep for about 6 hours per night even though they may feel that they sleep much less. Consequently, research on total sleep deprivation lacks mundane realism and ecological validity. Research on partial sleep deprivation is more relevant to real-life sleep deprivation. However, as much of this research is conducted in the artificial conditions of the sleep laboratory mundane realism and ecological validity are still a weakness.

 Cause and effect. We cannot infer cause and effect in the correlational evidence; nor can we be sure of this in the experimental evidence as extraneous variables may be involved. For example, the sleeplessness will cause stress, and in real life when sleep deprivation occurs there are likely to be reasons behind the sleep deprivation, all of which may influence the effects. These confounding factors are a further threat to the internal validity of the research and so constrain conclusions on causation. However, given the amount of evidence we can be reasonably certain that sleep deprivation can be life-threatening. It is certainly one of the multiple causes of the rare medical condition fatal familial insomnia.

SUMMARY OF THE EFFECTS OF SLEEP DEPRIVATION

Individual variation

Randy Gardner showed less severe effects than Peter Tripp despite experiencing 3 days' more sleep deprivation. This shows that effects are subject to individual variation.

Effects are mainly psychological

The Hüber-Weidman review confirmed the findings of the Tripp and Gardner case studies, this being that the effects of sleep deprivation are mainly psychological, which has implications for the restoration theory of sleep.

Cognitive abilities are not necessarily impaired

The Hüber-Weidman review also showed that cognitive abilities are not necessarily impaired by sleep deprivation, as after 5 nights of total sleep deprivation abilities were fairly unimpaired. This is supported by Wilkinson (1969, see A2PKT p. 148), who investigated whether sleep deprivation reduces task performance or whether this is due to a lack of motivation. As poor performance when sleep is deprived can be improved by increasing motivation, it may well be that poor performance on cognitive tasks is due to low motivation rather than reduced capacity.

The REM rebound effect

REM sleep deprivation results in many more attempts than normal to enter REM sleep and that more time is spent in REM sleep than normal when sleep is undisturbed, as Dement's research showed. The Randy Gardner case study revealed that about 50% of REM sleep is recovered after a period of deprivation compared to less than 25% recovery of total sleep. Stage 4 recovery is even higher at 70%. This has significance for the functions of sleep as it suggests that stages 4 and 5 (REM) may be particularly important and that they may have a restorative function.

Sleep deprivation can be fatal

There is multiple research evidence that this is the case in animals and humans. The evidence thus far is that total sleep deprivation has this effect. However, current academic opinion suggests that Britain today is experiencing an epidemic of sleeplessness (partial sleep deprivation), and that this can lead to colds, 'flu, depression, diabetes, obesity, strokes, coronary heart disease (CHD), and cancer.

There are a number of explicit links between the implications of sleep deprivation research and the theories of sleep. Can you work out what these might be?

OVER TO YOU

1. **Discuss the implications of findings from studies of sleep deprivation for the theories of sleep.**

(24 marks)

THEORIES OF THE FUNCTIONS OF SLEEP

All animals sleep and this suggests that sleep serves some vital and universal function.

Restoration Theories

According to restoration theories, the purpose of sleep is to repair and recharge the brain and body through restoring energy resources, repair and growth of tissue cells and muscles, and replenishing neurochemicals. Oswald (1980, see A2PKT pp.141–142) claimed that NREM sleep restored the body and REM sleep restored the brain, through protein synthesis. Horne (1988, see A2PKT pp.143–144) expanded on this as he distinguished between core (stage 4 and REM) and optional (stages 1 to 3) sleep and claimed that only core sleep was critical for restoration of the brain as restoration of the body can occur during resting wakefulness. Restoration theories are supported by the fact that we often sleep more during times of stress and illness.

RESEARCH EVIDENCE FOR RESTORATION THEORIES

- Growth hormone. This is necessary for protein synthesis and is released during stage 4, which supports Oswald's claim that NREM sleep restores the body as the protein synthesis underpins tissue growth and repair.
- High brain activity of REM sleep. This provides evidence of brain recovery; brain processes are renewed and neurochemicals replenished.
- Babies' sleep patterns are consistent with REM as a source of restoration, as they spend approximately two thirds of the day asleep (compared to one third or less in adults) and 8 hours per day in REM sleep.
- Sleep deprivation studies. The negative effects support restoration as the function, and Horne's theory that stage 4 and REM constitute core sleep. For example, the case study of Randy Gardner (1988, see A2PKT pp.146–147) is evidence, as following an 11-day period of total sleep deprivation, Randy Gardner slept for 15 hours. He recovered only about 25% of overall lost sleep, but 70% of stage 4 was recovered and 50% of REM. This is known as the (REM) rebound effect and suggests that stage 4 and REM are more necessary than the other stages. Also, the effects of sleep deprivation shown by Randy Gardner link more to brain than body processing and this supports Horne's theory that stage 4 and REM restore the brain, not the body.
- The effect of extra activity (Shapiro et al., 1981, see A2PKT p.142). People who completed an "ultra marathon" of 57 miles slept about an hour and a half longer for two nights following the marathon, which supports restoration theory.
- Neurochemical restoration (Stern & Morgane, 1974, see A2PKT p.142). Restoration of the brain during REM sleep may rebalance the neurotransmitters, such as serotonin, noradrenaline, and acetylcholine. Evidence is that people on anti-depressants show decreased REM. This may be due to the fact that the drugs increase neurotransmitter levels hence there is less need for REM sleep.

RESEARCH EVIDENCE AGAINST RESTORATION THEORIES

- Duration of protein synthesis. Amino acids are only available for about 4 hours after eating and so protein synthesis could only occur for a very limited time within the night's sleep and so this is strong evidence against restoration theory.

- Not all lost sleep is recovered. If restoration is the main function of sleep we would expect that more of the lost sleep would need to be recovered, whereas the Randy Gardner case study suggests that only about 25% needs to be recovered.

- Increased activity (Horne & Minard, 1985, see A2PKT p.142). If restoration theory is the full explanation we would expect increased activity to necessitate more sleep. However, Horne and Minard found that participants exhausted by high activity fell asleep faster but not for longer, which contradicts Shapiro et al.'s (1981) findings.

- Neurochemicals rise and fall during sleep so are not being replenished solely during REM sleep. This explanation is too reductionist, not accounting for the complexity of neurochemical processing.

- The high activity of REM increases energy expenditure and so contradicts the energy restoration aspect of the theory.

EVALUATION

 Researcher effects and participant reactivity. All research is vulnerable to bias as a consequence of the relationship between the researcher and participant. Thus, contradictory findings on the effect of increased activity may be explained by experimenter expectancy, participant cooperation and demand characteristics. Consequently, the value and meaningfulness of the research may be limited.

Reliability and validity. The empirical support for restoration as the main function of sleep is weak as research findings on increased activity and sleep deprivation are inconsistent and so lack reliability, which means that the validity of the research must be questioned, and so it provides only weak support for restoration theory.

Face validity. Restoration as a function makes sense; it is highly plausible.

Objective measurement. The physiological measures of sleep, e.g. REM activity and levels of neurochemicals, are objective, which means that they are less subject to bias and so this research evidence has the strength of scientific validity.

 Multi-perspective. The sleep deprivation research suggests that effects are more psychological than physiological (Hüber-Weidman, 1976, and the Peter Tripp case study) and so the main function of sleep may be to recover psychological functioning. However, psychological functioning can be linked to restoration of the neurochemicals and so we need to take a multi-perspective, which takes into account the interaction between the physiological and psychological processes.

Further research. There is a need for further research into the neurochemicals, and the effect of sleep deprivation on health as the linking of this to physical illness is further evidence of a physiological restorative function. Also it may be that restoration only occurs in stage 4 and REM in which case the purposes of the earlier stages need clarification.

Ecological/Evolutionary Theories

The many variations in animals' sleep patterns suggest that sleep may serve an adaptive rather than a restorative function. This means sleep has been naturally selected because it promotes survival.

This is a gradual process where species that sleep have survived to reproduce and so carry forth sleep into the next generation as an adaptive behaviour. If it was non-adaptive, i.e. does not have an evolutionary purpose, then it should have disappeared. Thus, sleep is likely to be adaptive in some way as this is surely the reason why all animals sleep. Meddis (1975, see A2PKT p.144) suggested that sleep is adaptive because the immobility of sleep keeps animals safe from predators and that it occurs when normal activities (e.g. feeding) are impossible. Webb (1982, see A2PKT p.145) proposed the *hibernation theory* that suggested the adaptive function of sleep is energy conservation.

RESEARCH EVIDENCE FOR ECOLOGICAL/EVOLUTIONARY THEORIES

- The fatal effects shown in some of the sleep deprivation research confirm that sleep is necessary for survival.
- Variations in sleep patterns across species. The wide variations in animals' sleep patterns, and the fact that some animals are nocturnal and some diurnal, support an adaptive function of sleep and Meddis' theory. For example, humans are diurnal as nocturnal activity would be too dangerous given the handicap of poor night vision.
- The Indus dolphins. Pilleri (1979, see A2PKT p.144) reported that dolphins living in the River Indus sleep for only seconds at a time due to the threat of floating debris and the fact that they have to come to the surface to breathe, providing evidence that sleep patterns are specific to the ecological niche and so supporting Meddis.
- Predator/prey sleep patterns. The difference in predator/prey sleep patterns provides evidence that evolutionary forces are at work as predators (lions, tigers, etc.) sleep for much longer periods than prey (cattle, etc.).
- Metabolic rate and energy conservation. Smaller animals such as squirrels and shrews sleep for much longer periods of the day than larger animals. This is due to their high metabolic rate, which means they burn up energy fast and so sleep is a way of conserving energy, supporting Webb's theory. Further evidence is that cows sleep only 3 hours per day because they have a low energy diet, and so have little energy to conserve during sleep, and need to stay awake to eat.

RESEARCH EVIDENCE AGAINST ECOLOGICAL/EVOLUTIONARY THEORIES

- Ratio of predator/prey sleep duration. The ratio of predator/prey sleep duration seems to contradict Meddis' theory (Allison & Cicchetti, 1976, see A2PKT p.144), as given the claim that sleep provides protection from predators, prey should sleep longer than predators when in fact the opposite usually occurs.
- Lack of energy conservation. Sleep provides little more energy conservation than behavioural inactivity—the energy gain of sleep is equivalent to the energy provided by a slice of bread!

EVALUATION

☻ **Vulnerability.** Sleep leaves animals more vulnerable in some ways to predators as they are in a state of near unconsciousness and paralysis for some of the time. Moreover, they wouldn't be inconspicuous if they were noisy sleepers! Behavioural inactivity would provide the same protection as sleep in terms of being inconspicuous. Thus, protection is unlikely to be the main function of sleep.

Genome lag. Protection and energy conservation as evolutionary functions of sleep may have been more relevant in our evolutionary past. However, such explanations may not be true of human sleep today as predators no longer pose such a threat. If evolutionary forces do shape sleep patterns then we would expect humans today to need less sleep as survival could be enhanced by more hours in the working day! Sleep patterns have decreased due to the introduction of electricity (we don't have to go to sleep when it gets dark) but the change is fairly small. It may well be that sleep patterns will change in time as evolution is a gradual process and so the patterns we have at the moment may be due to genome lag, which occurs because the environment changes much more quickly than the genes.

 Low adaptive value. In some species if sleep were simply adaptive then it should have been selected out. For example, the Indus dolphins go to extraordinary lengths to sleep, where they've had to overcome the demands of their ecological niche.

Lacks scientific validity. Evolutionary theories are post hoc, i.e. they have been proposed in retrospect and consequently lack empirical support, and so they lack scientific validity. This means they are difficult to substantiate but also difficult to dismiss and so they are neither verifiable nor falsifiable.

Deterministic and reductionist. Evolutionary theories are deterministic as they ignore free will and are reductionist. Sleep is far too complex a process to have evolved solely as protection as this does not explain why we have the different stages and cycles of sleep or why we need to catch up on some of our missed sleep. Evolutionary theories ignore the physiological and psychological functions of sleep and so are unlikely to provide a full explanation for sleep.

SO WHAT DOES THIS MEAN?

The implications of sleep deprivation research for the theories of sleep are as follows. Sleep deprivation research supports an ecological perspective as it shows that sleep is necessary for survival. However, the evidence is neither directly consistent with Meddis' claim that sleep provides safety, nor with Webb's that it is a source of energy conservation. Neither of these explanations account for the negative effects of sleep deprivation. Restoration does, and it is this theory that the findings on sleep deprivation most strongly support. To conclude, restoration may be the adaptive function and so an interaction of restoration and ecological theories may best account for sleep function. A multi-perspective is needed to understand the multiple functions of sleep, as restoration and adaptation are unlikely to be the only functions; a cognitive function (memory consolidation) has also been identified, and further research may well reveal more.

NOTE: Evaluation of sleep deprivation research is relevant to theories based on sleep deprivation studies.

OVER TO YOU

1. **Outline and evaluate one or more theories relating to the functions of sleep.** **(24 marks)**

DREAMING

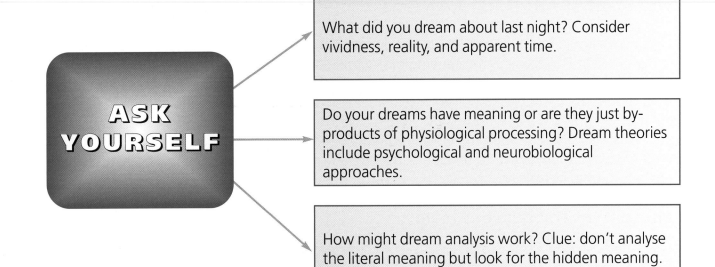

ASK YOURSELF

What did you dream about last night? Consider vividness, reality, and apparent time.

Do your dreams have meaning or are they just by-products of physiological processing? Dream theories include psychological and neurobiological approaches.

How might dream analysis work? Clue: don't analyse the literal meaning but look for the hidden meaning.

WHAT YOU NEED TO KNOW

RESEARCH FINDINGS ON THE NATURE OF DREAMS

e.g. the content, type of dream, and duration

THEORIES OF THE FUNCTIONS OF DREAMING

Neurobiological, e.g. activation synthesis (Hobson & McCarley, 1977) and reverse learning (Crick & Mitchison, 1983), and psychological theories, e.g. wish-fulfilment (Freud, 1900), problem solving (Webb & Cartwright 1978), and survival strategy (Winson, 1997). Activation-synthesis and wish-fulfilment are covered in depth, and the other theories are described so that you have enough information to achieve breadth and can use them as counter-perspectives.

As the theories of dreaming focus on REM sleep you may find it relevant to use the theories of sleep but do make sure you relate this content clearly to *dreaming* as it cannot be credited if it isn't focused on the functions of dreaming.

To read up on dreaming, refer to pages 152–163 of A2PKT.

RESEARCH RELATING TO THE NATURE OF DREAMS

Dement and Kleitman (1957, see A2PKT p.153) investigated the relationship between REM activity and dreaming, in order to increase understanding of the functions of dreaming. Participants were woken up either randomly or during alternations of REM and NREM activity, which the EEG and EOG discerned. On being woken the participant reported into a tape recorder whether they had been dreaming and the content if so. They found that most dreams were recalled during REM but that some dreaming also took place in NREM. Participants were more likely to remember their dream when awoken from REM than NREM. There was also a positive correlation between participants' estimates of the length of their dream and the length of REM activity.

Dream Content and Type of Dream

Dream content can be nonsensical as dreams can involve imaginary events (a date with a supermodel) or abilities (being able to fly), hallucinations, and delusions that are complete fantasy. However, dreams can also be rather mundane and involve real-life events; so much so that people can even get confused between things that they have dreamt and things that are real. Dreams during REM sleep tend to be vivid, detailed, and experienced as a coherent "story", whereas those in NREM sleep tend to be less detailed and coherent and more mundane (McIlveen & Gross, 2000, see A2PKT p.140). Dreams are more likely to involve negative emotions than positive; as much as 60+% may involve negative emotions, which could manifest as anxious, hostile, or unhappy dreams. Thus,

dreams can evoke powerful emotions but they can also be quite neutral. Contrary to Freud's theory, quite a small proportion of dreams have sexual content but unsurprisingly there is a gender difference as men are three times more likely to dream about sex than women! Freud's ideas about manifest and latent content could also be related to a nature of dreams exam question.

Duration of Dreams and Memory

Newborn babies spend about 9 hours per day in REM compared to 2 hours in adults, although we may dream for longer than this, as dreaming is not exclusive to REM. Dreams tend to happen in real time. This does not always appear to be the case because we may dream about events over days or weeks in one night, but the actual events we dream are in real time and the time in between is edited out, which can lead to the distortion that dreams are faster than real life. We forget more than 95% of our dreams, which shows that duration in memory is limited and that the dreams we do remember are not representative of dreams in general.

Dreaming and Consciousness

Dreaming differs from waking consciousness in that when we are awake we usually have a sense of conscious control, which we don't have in dreams. However, people can have control over their dreams, where they are able to manipulate the dream content, and these are called lucid dreams. One woman used this greatly to her advantage, as LaBerge et al. (1983, see A2PKT p.154) report that she controlled her own orgasms.

The "Singlemindedness" of Dreams

Empson (1989, see A2PKT p.155) used the term singlemindedness to refer to the fact that we are completely caught up, i.e. absorbed, in our dreams. Hence, the great relief when we realise it was only a dream! Whereas, in real life we are usually not as absorbed in our waking thoughts.

EVALUATION

☹ Subjectivity of what we recall in self-report. Self-report method is the only method available to investigate the individual's experience of their dream and so has been used by Dement and Kleitman, Empson, LaBerge, etc. However, self-reports may be biased by subjectivity and may be inaccurate due to reconstructive memory, and may be further biased by the relationship between the researcher and the participant. Researcher effects or participant reactivity may have occurred and, consequently, the validity (truth/accuracy) of the research may be limited.

☹ Artificiality of research. Dement and Kleitman's research took place in the sleep laboratory and so the findings may not be representative of real-life dream patterns. Particularly as the participants were being woken during the night and such disturbances may have resulted in REM deprivation. Consequently, more frequent periods of REM may have been detected than occur in real-life patterns of dreaming. For example, dreams in the laboratory set-up lack the emotional intensity of dreams reported in a natural environment. Thus, the research may lack generalisability and so ecological validity may be low.

OVER TO YOU

1.(a) **Describe research findings relating to the nature of dreams.** **(12 marks)**

(b) **Evaluate the research findings you have described in the question above.** **(12 marks)**

Adapted from AQA A2 [Winter 2002] Psychology Examination Papers.

THEORIES OF THE FUNCTIONS OF DREAMING

We spend about 700 hours per year dreaming, which suggests it has particular functions. Theories of dream function range from the idea that it is just a by-product of physiological processing (activation-synthesis) to Freud's theory that dreams reveal our unconscious hidden desires and so interpreting the meaning of dreams is a route to the unconscious.

Neurobiological Theories: Activation-synthesis Theory

According to Hobson and McCarley (1977, see A2PKT p.155), dreaming is a result of high levels of activation in the brain in areas responsible for perception, action, and emotional responses during REM sleep. This activation is random as signals are spontaneously generated in the hindbrain and midbrain.

Dreamers interpret these signals as if they were caused by external stimuli and this is the experience of dreaming. According to Hobson (1988, see A2PKT pp.155–156) it is the brain's "quest for meaning" that transfers the random activation into more coherent dreams.

RESEARCH EVIDENCE FOR ACTIVATION-SYNTHESIS THEORY

- Random firing of brain cells. Research on cats supports activation-synthesis as it shows that there is random firing of cells in the brain during REM sleep (Hobson, 1988, see A2PKT p.156).

- External stimuli. The theory explains why smells and tastes rarely appear in dreams as the research evidence shows that the processing of external stimuli is limited as only the parts of the brain associated with vision and hearing are activated during REM sleep and so only such stimuli is likely to be synthesised into a dream. You may have experienced the effect of external stimuli if you have dreamt of some kind of buzzer as your alarm clock went off.

- Explains how internal signals are misinterpreted as external. Hobson has also identified how internally generated signals are misinterpreted as external signals. The neurotransmitters noradrenaline and serotonin are lower during REM sleep than NREM sleep and this may lead to errors in the attentional processes that result in the misinterpretation of internal signals as external.

RESEARCH EVIDENCE AGAINST ACTIVATION-SYNTHESIS THEORY

- Dreaming is not exclusive to REM. Dement and Kleitman's research shows that dreaming also occurs in NREM sleep, whereas the evidence for activation-synthesis is limited to REM. It is possible that NREM dreaming is due to other brain activation but clearly further research is needed to confirm or challenge this. Thus, the explanatory power of the theory is limited because it only accounts for REM dreaming.

- Accounts for incoherent dreams but not coherent. Dream imagery challenges the theory, as whilst random activation accounts for the fact that many dreams are incoherent it cannot explain why many dreams are coherent and seem to have meaning. A "quest for meaning" seems rather vague and doesn't explain why people's dreams seem to relate to their current problems and coping mechanisms. Similarly, the random activation is inconsistent with the fact that many people report having recurring dreams.

- Lucid dreams. The fact that lucid dreams are under the dreamer's control contradicts the theory that dreaming is due to random activation.

EVALUATION

 Scientific evidence. There is strong scientific support for the theory as detailed research on the physiological activity of the brain during REM reinforces Hobson's proposals.

Re-activation synthesis. The theory has been expanded to account for the fact that we often dream about real-life events, as Hobson and McCarley now recognise that dreams are meaningful and that this is not just the brain imposing meaning. You may well have experienced this if your dream concerned the last thing you experienced before going to bed. According to reactivation, this occurs because during REM neurons fired during the day are reactivated and so the events of the day unfold in our dreams.

Extrapolation. This is an issue as the evidence is based on animal research and so caution is needed, as the findings may not be true of humans.

Determinism and reductionism. The theory is physiologically deterministic as it ignores the free will of the individual to control their dreams and lucid dreaming suggests we can control them. Also it is reductionist as only physiological processing is accounted for and so psychological factors are ignored.

Further research. This is needed to further investigate the neurotransmitter levels during REM sleep. The restoration theory of sleep function claims that the neurotransmitters are being replenished, which is inconsistent with Hobson's assertion that levels are low. Given these contradictions there is a need for further research into the physiology of REM sleep and, thus, dreaming. It may be that dreaming is a product of neurochemical processing, and not random activation.

Counter-perspectives. Include reverse-learning and the psychological theories (see next).

Neurobiological Theories: Reverse-learning Theory

Crick and Mitchison (1983, see A2PKT p.157) claim that the key function of dreaming during REM is unlearning, i.e. dreaming is a way of removing unimportant or "parasitic" information that is no longer needed. This frees up space in the cortex and so ensures that there is room for important information and allows the neuronal networks to function more efficiently. Dreaming is an accidental by-product of the brain-clearing function. To sum up, we dream in order to forget.

Psychological Theories: Freud's Wish-fulfilment Theory

According to Freud (1900, see A2PKT pp.158–159), the function of dreams is to provide wish-fulfilment of repressed desires. The desires are repressed into the unconscious because they are unacceptable to the individual and consequently the dream consists of the manifest content, which is the dreamer's experience of the dream, and the latent content, which is the true meaning of the dream. Symbols within the manifest content provide insights into the latent content and this can be interpreted using dream analysis, a psychoanalytical technique that provides access to the unconscious. Freud identified symbols of repressed sexual desires (e.g. poles, guns, swords, and snakes represent the penis; tunnels, caves, doors, and bottles represent the vagina; and horse riding, dancing, climbing a staircase, and crossing a bridge represent sexual relations). "Dream-work" transforms the desires into such symbols to protect the individual from the anxiety and emotional threat of their sexual and aggressive desires. However, Freud emphasised that the symbols are mainly personal, but some are universal.

RESEARCH EVIDENCE FOR WISH-FULFILMENT THEORY

- His own dreams and those of his patients. Freud (1900, see A2PKT p.158) used his own dream of one of his patients, Irma, as evidence for wish-fulfilment. Treatment had not been going well and in his dream he attributed this to another doctor and hence he was no longer to blame for his patient's slow recovery, which supports wish-fulfilment. Freud also used his patients' dreams to illustrate his theory.

- Research on giving up smoking (Hajek & Belcher, 1991, see A2PKT p.159). Participants in a programme to give up smoking reported dreams of smoking for up to a year and a half after giving up. Anxiety and panic were experienced in the dream as a result of the smoking. Participants who had the most dreams about smoking followed by guilt were less likely to start smoking again and so the dream provided wish-fulfilment on two counts.

- Physiological evidence. Research on penile erections, vaginal secretions, and clitoral enlargement support Freud's emphasis on the sexual nature of dreams.

RESEARCH EVIDENCE AGAINST WISH-FULFILMENT THEORY

- Alternative approaches to dream analysis. Jung, Adler, and Erikson have redefined dream analysis and offered alternatives to Freud. They claim that Freud underestimated the role of social factors and overestimated the role of sexual factors. However, they do support Freud on one fundamental principle, as they all believe that dreams can provide important insights into the psyche.

- Research evidence that 60+% of dreams involve negative emotions. This directly contradicts wish fulfilment, as it is unlikely that such emotionally disturbing dreams are a source of wish-fulfilment.

- Food and eating. These feature rarely in dreams and so wish-fulfilment is questionable. Clearly we would expect these to feature frequently if the main purpose of dreams was wish-fulfilment (Hayes, 1994, see A2PKT p.160).

- Only a small percentage of dreams are about sex. Research on the content of dreams reveals that sex is not always the main content of dreams.

EVALUATION

- **The first systematic account of dream function.** Freud was the first to suggest a systematic account of dream function and so deserves recognition for this and the physiological evidence on sexual activity during sleep provides objective and incontrovertible support for his theory.

- **Face validity.** Freud constructed his theory on the case studies of neurotic Viennese patients during the repressive Victorian era. Consequently, the theory has face validity as we can imagine that there was a great deal of repression of desires during this era, and the nonsensical nature of dreams is consistent with unrealistic id "thinking".

- **Era-dependent and context-bound.** Repression is less likely in today's society. Given the liberalism and permissiveness of today's society it is unlikely that repression occurs to the same extent and so the temporal validity of the research must be questioned, i.e. is it generalisable to the current context?

- **The subjectivity of dream analysis.** This means that interpretations of latent content may lack validity as they are methodologically flawed, so their usefulness and value may be limited.

- **Difficult to test.** Freudian concepts are difficult to test because they are not easily operationalised as it is difficult to measure wish-fulfilment. Consequently, the theory lacks scientific validity; it cannot be verified or falsified.

- **Only 5% of dreams are remembered.** Surely more would be remembered if dreams were a source of wish-fulfilment? A theory based on such a low percentage is not representative of the other 95% of dreams. However, an explanation for the low percentage may be that only dreams that are particularly meaningful or not as emotionally threatening are remembered.

Psychological Theories: Problem-solving Theory

Webb and Cartwright (1978, see A2PKT p.160) believe that the function of dreaming is to provide us with the opportunity to solve work, health, and relationship problems. Many people faced with a difficult problem decide to "sleep on it", which is in fact a very good solution according to the problem-solving theory as this suggests that dreams provide us with an opportunity to address current problems and cope with them. This theory also recognises that dreams may be represented in a symbolic way and so the problems may require some interpretation.

Psychological Theories: Survival Strategy Theory

Winson (1997, see A2PKT pp.161–162) provides support for the problem-solving theory, as the focus is the same but contextualised within an evolutionary perspective. Winson proposes the function of dreaming is that REM sleep is a period of cognitive processing when new information is assimilated into a survival strategy.

SO WHAT DOES THIS MEAN?

The neurobiological theories are contradicted by the psychological theories, as they do not take into account the meaningfulness and coherence of dreams. A multi-perspective is needed to best infer dream function. Dreaming may be a product of neurobiological processing, but this processing may be neurochemical restoration rather than random activation. Thus, dream imagery is not just a by-product of this but also a cognitive translation of the neurochemical processing. Thus, to understand dreaming we must consider that it exists at multiple levels and so a better understanding of dream function lies in an interaction of neurobiological, wish-fulfilment, problem-solving, and evolutionary explanations.

OVER TO YOU

1. Describe and evaluate one neurobiological and one psychological theory of the functions of dreaming.

(24 marks)

QUESTIONS AND ESSAY PLANS

Definition of biological rhythms: Physiological and psychological processes that maintain a consistent pattern within a specific period of time.

Definition of sleep: A state of altered consciousness and inactivity, which consists of five stages, NREM (stages 1–4) and REM (stage 5), which occur in cycles that average five per night. Sleep has a circadian rhythm (the sleep–waking cycle) and an ultradian rhythm (the stages and cycles of sleep).

Definition of dreaming: A state where the individual experiences thoughts and images that can interweave into a vivid and dramatic story but can also be mundane and ordinary.

1(a) Describe two biological rhythms. (12 marks)

Paragraph 1

Define biological rhythms: physiological and psychological processes, which maintain a consistent pattern within a specific period of time.

Paragraph 2

Describe circadian rhythms (i.e. they last 24 hours), such as the sleep–waking cycle. Identify the endogenous factors that constitute the biological clock, e.g. the SCN and pineal gland, and use research evidence as support, e.g. Siffre's (1975) cave study and Morgan's (1995) SCN removal and transplant studies in hamsters. Also use research evidence to support the action of exogenous factors, i.e. zeitgebers such as light, e.g. Miles et al. (1977) who studied a blind man who had a circadian rhythm of 24.9 hours and Luce and Segal's (1966) research on people living near the Arctic Circle. Biological rhythms are an interaction of nature and nurture and endogenous (internal) and exogenous (external) factors, where the endogenous factors have the strongest influence but these can be overridden.

Paragraph 3

Describe infradian rhythms (i.e. they last longer than 24 hours), such as menstruation. Explain what this involves (a cycle of 28 days) and the role of endogenous factors, i.e. the hormones oestrogen and progesterone. Use research evidence to support exogenous factors, e.g. Reinberg's (1967) cave study. Then use research to illustrate the effect of exogenous factors, e.g. McClintock (1971) and Russell et al.'s (1980) research, both of which show the effect of women's pheromones.

1(b) Assess the consequences of disrupting biological rhythms. (12 marks)

Paragraph 1

Analyse the different effects. Weigh up which flight patterns are best. Assess the different directions of flight travel using phase delay/phase advance. Use research evidence as support, e.g. Schwartz et al.'s (1995) baseball study, and Klein et al. (1972).

Paragraph 2

Consider the issue of rapid or slow rotation of shiftwork and assess the positive and negative effects of both. Use research evidence as support, e.g. Monk and Folkard (1983). Also consider the effect of phase advance/delay, i.e. it is better to rotate with the clock than against it, as supported by Czeisler et al. (1982).

Paragraph 3

Use MET (methodological, ethical, and theoretical) criticisms. Validity issues mean the truth can be questioned and this reduces confidence in the findings. This means the meaningfulness and value of the research are questionable and so conclusions must be made cautiously. But do make conclusions, e.g. suggest how consequences can be minimised.

2(a) Describe two research studies into biological rhythms. (12 marks)

Use Schochat et al. (1997) for circadian and Russell et al. (1980) for infradian.

2(b) Evaluate the studies you have described in part (a). (12 marks)

Consider which factors are not accounted for by the studies, i.e. Schochat et al. (1997) account for one endogenous factor (the influence of melatonin) but other endogenous factors (the SCN and pineal gland) are not accounted for, nor are the exogenous factors, i.e. zeitgebers such as light. Russell et al.'s (1980) research accounts for external factors, i.e. the pheromones involved in the menstrual cycle, but not other exogenous factors also identified as important, e.g. light affects the circadian rhythm, which affects the infradian rhythm. The study does not account for endogenous factors such as the female hormones oestrogen and progesterone. MET criticisms include the mundane realism and so the ecological validity of Schochat's research, particularly as researcher and participant effects and the artificiality of the sleep laboratory, may bias the findings. Consider the generalisability of both studies, given that samples were small and so population validity is questionable, and the ethical dilemma of whether the ends justify the means.

3 Discuss the role of endogenous factors in bodily rhythms. (24 marks)

Paragraph 1

Define biological rhythms and identify circadian, infradian, and ultradian. Explain what endogenous factors are, i.e. biological mechanisms, (e.g...). But there are exogenous factors that can override these.

Paragraph 2 Evidence for

Siffre's (1975), Morgan's (1995), Schochat et al.'s (1997), and Luce and Segal's (1966) research support the role of endogenous factors in circadian rhythms. Assess the consequences of disrupting the biological clock, as further evidence for endogenous factors.

Paragraph 3 Evidence against

The role of zeitgebers as demonstrated by Siffre (1975), Miles et al. (1977), and Luce and Segal (1966) support the role of exogenous factors and show that endogenous are not the only factors. Also shiftwork provides further evidence against endogenous factors, as we can go against the biological clock, but this does have consequences.

Paragraph 4 Evidence for

The female hormones support the role of endogenous factors in menstruation.

Paragraph 5 Evidence against

McClintock's (1971) and Russell et al.'s (1980) research show the importance of exogenous factors (pheromones) in menstruation.

Paragraph 6

Conclude an interaction of internal and external control. Thus, endogenous factors alone do not account for bodily rhythms.

4 Outline and evaluate theories and research studies relating to the functions of sleep. (24 marks)

Paragraph 1

Define sleep: a state of altered consciousness and inactivity, which consists of five stages, NREM (stages 1–4) and REM (stage 5), which occur in cycles. In an average night's sleep of 7 hours the individual experiences five cycles of sleep. Explain that this is unlikely to exist unless it has a function, i.e. it is adaptive (evolutionary theory), or the function may be the restoration of physiological and psychological functions.

Paragraph 2

Outline evolutionary/ecological theory (Meddis, 1975). Identify research evidence, e.g. research on differences in sleep patterns and duration. Also include hibernation theory (Webb, 1982). Research findings on the fatal effects of sleep deprivation e.g. Rechstaffen et al.'s (1983) study and Lugaressi et al.'s (1986) case study suggest that sleep is necessary for survival and so support an adaptive function.

Paragraph 3

Criticisms of Meddis (1975) are that predators often sleep longer than prey. This anomaly could be accounted for by hibernation theory as smaller animals may sleep longer to conserve energy. But does sleep conserve much energy? Also consider the vulnerability of sleep. Variation is evidence of adaptation to different ecological niches and thus evolutionary forces at work. But surely it should have been selected out when not adaptive, e.g. the extraordinary lengths the Indus dolphins go to may well be due to an evolutionary function. All the evolutionary criticisms you know for this topic—see evolutionary essay plans.

Paragraph 4

Outline restoration theory including Oswald (1980), who identified NREM-body and REM-brain processes, and Horne (1988), who distinguished between core and optional sleep. Consider the research evidence for including neurochemical restoration, and sleep deprivation research, e.g. Randy Gardner (Horne, 1988), and Dement's (1960) research, which show the REM rebound effect and so support the emphasis Horne placed on stage 4 and REM sleep.

Paragraph 5

A criticism of restoration theory is that protein synthesis has a limited time frame. Sleep deprivation research shows that activity level and sleep are not greatly related. Not all missed sleep needs to be recovered and the effects are more psychological than physiological. Neurochemical restoration may be a better explanation. But physical illness supports the importance of restoration through sleep. Although this is correlational, so causation cannot be inferred and other factors are involved.

Paragraph 6

Assess the point that both explanations may be valid and a multi-perspective is needed as this best accounts for the variations within and between species, and the fact that sleep has more than one function. But there are methodological criticisms of the research (e.g…), which means the truth/meaningfulness of the theories and research must be questioned. Neurochemical restoration may be the adaptive function but further research is needed to verify the reliability and validity of this.

5 Describe and evaluate ecological and restoration accounts of the functions of sleep. (24 marks)

Same as above.

6(a) Describe research findings relating to the nature of dreams. (12 marks)

Paragraph 1

Consider Dement and Kleitman's (1957) research on REM sleep in relation to dreaming and the content of dreams.

Paragraph 2

Assess the amount of dreams remembered (5%), duration of dreaming, and timing.

Paragraph 3

Discuss control and consciousness of dreams and Empson's (1989) findings on the singlemindedness of dreams. Also, you could use Freud's (1900) ideas of manifest and latent content.

6(b) Assess the studies you have described in part (a). (12 marks)

Paragraph 1

State the strengths and weaknesses of Dement's (1960) sleep laboratory research. It is possible to establish cause and effect because there is more control. Introduce scientific evidence. But they are artificial, reductionist, and lacking mundane realism and so ecological validity.

Paragraph 2

Weigh up the strengths and weaknesses of self-report, which is used to gather data on dream content.

Paragraph 3

Assess the validity/truth and so the meaningfulness of the findings. Reductionism means the research may not have accounted for all of the factors of the nature of dreams and so is not representative of real-life dreaming.

7 Describe and evaluate one neurobiological and one psychological theory of the functions of dreaming. (24 marks)

Paragraph 1

Distinguish between neurobiological functions and psychological functions.

Paragraph 2

Describe activation-synthesis and give research evidence for, e.g. Hobson's (1988) evidence on the random firing of brain cells and the misinterpretation of internal signals.

Paragraph 3

Give research evidence against, e.g. the coherence of dreams and the fact that dreaming is not exclusive to REM. Also consider that neurochemical processing as supported by the restoration theory of sleep may be the physiological basis of dreaming. Then evaluate, and consider that neurobiological theories ignore psychological factors and so can only be partial explanations. Consider the reductionism and determinism of the explanations.

Paragraph 4

Describe Freud's wish-fulfilment (1900) and give research evidence for, including Freud's case study evidence, Hajek and Belcher (1991), and the physiological evidence.

Paragraph 5

Discuss the research evidence against, such as the alternative approaches to dream analysis, and the lack of dreams about food and sex. Evaluate, using the methodological weaknesses of Freud's (1900) research, but also consider the strengths it considers i.e. that dreams are a way of coping with problems, which is widely accepted as a function. Use the other psychological theories as support.

Paragraph 6

Conclude that a multi-perspective is needed, as the different explanations may be valid to some extent as dreaming takes place at different levels.

Question 6 adapted from AQA A2 [Winter 2002] Psychology Examination Papers.
The authors are responsible for the solutions and (a) they have neither been provided nor approved by AQA and (b) they may not necessarily constitute the only possible solutions.

Developmental Psychology

COGNITIVE DEVELOPMENT

Specification 13.4

What's it about?

The topic area of cognitive development is concerned with the ways in which children's thinking changes (how their *cognition* develops) as they grow into adulthood. Children do not think in the same way as adults. Imagine you are playing hide and seek with a toddler. They may "hide" by putting their hands in front of their eyes and assume you can't see them: if they can't see you, you can't see them! There are many ways in which young children's thinking differs from that of adults. The above example illustrates one difference—they cannot see things from another's point of view. They also tend to view the world in very "concrete" terms rather than in the abstract.

The theories we are going to consider tend to look at the way *all* children develop—we will also look at the way children *differ* in terms of their intelligence. We will consider what is meant by intelligence and what factors affect intelligence test performance.

Finally, we will look at the way in which children develop their ideas of what is right and wrong. Several theorists, including Piaget and Kohlberg, have looked at the stages children pass through in the development of moral thinking, while Eisenberg has advanced a model to explain the development of pro-social behaviour. Are there any cultural and gender differences in the development of moral thinking? This will be our final matter for consideration.

What's in this unit?

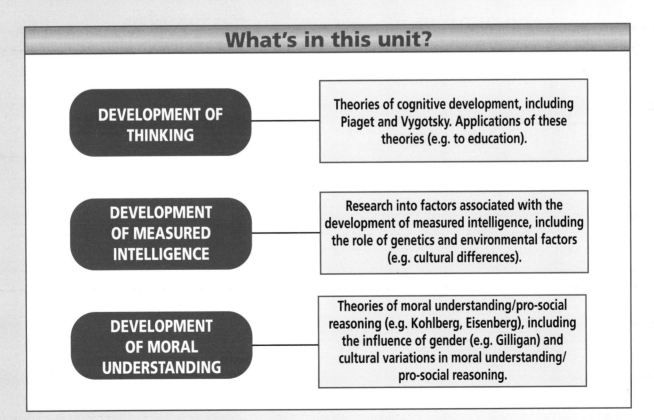

DEVELOPMENT OF THINKING — Theories of cognitive development, including Piaget and Vygotsky. Applications of these theories (e.g. to education).

DEVELOPMENT OF MEASURED INTELLIGENCE — Research into factors associated with the development of measured intelligence, including the role of genetics and environmental factors (e.g. cultural differences).

DEVELOPMENT OF MORAL UNDERSTANDING — Theories of moral understanding/pro-social reasoning (e.g. Kohlberg, Eisenberg), including the influence of gender (e.g. Gilligan) and cultural variations in moral understanding/pro-social reasoning.

DEVELOPMENT OF THINKING

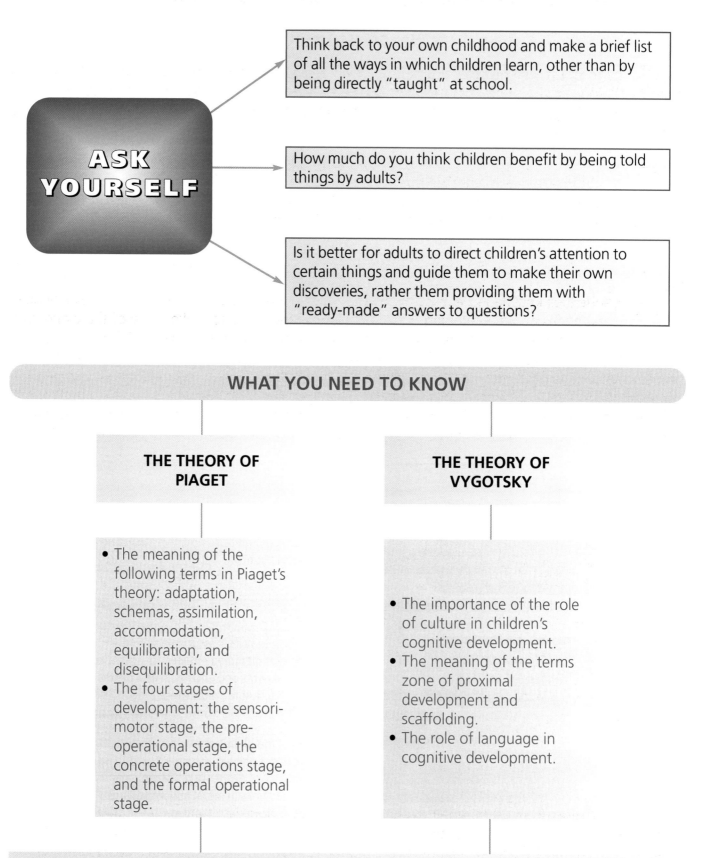

ASK YOURSELF

Think back to your own childhood and make a brief list of all the ways in which children learn, other than by being directly "taught" at school.

How much do you think children benefit by being told things by adults?

Is it better for adults to direct children's attention to certain things and guide them to make their own discoveries, rather them providing them with "ready-made" answers to questions?

WHAT YOU NEED TO KNOW

THE THEORY OF PIAGET

- The meaning of the following terms in Piaget's theory: adaptation, schemas, assimilation, accommodation, equilibration, and disequilibration.
- The four stages of development: the sensori-motor stage, the pre-operational stage, the concrete operations stage, and the formal operational stage.

THE THEORY OF VYGOTSKY

- The importance of the role of culture in children's cognitive development.
- The meaning of the terms zone of proximal development and scaffolding.
- The role of language in cognitive development.

How each of the above approaches can be used to advance the education of children.

To read up on the development of thinking, refer to pages 167–199 of A2PKT.

PIAGET'S THEORY: BASIC CONCEPTS

Piaget is the most prominent psychologist in the field of cognitive development and his innovative and thorough theory set the scene for later theories. He believed that children's thinking passes through a series of stages and that at each stage certain basic features are operating that alter the way a child thinks. These basic concepts are as follows:

ADAPTATION

Piaget believed that we are innately programmed to adapt to our environment. In cognitive development, this adaptation involves the development of an increasingly more accurate view of the world.

SCHEMAS

People organise their knowledge in terms of schemas. A schema contains all the information, experience, ideas, and memories about something. Schemas allow an individual to make sense of the world and adapt in order to have an appropriate set of responses for dealing with the world. Schemas that very young children use are simple and often inappropriate or inaccurate. For example, a child who has learnt to grasp a big rattle may use the same grip to hold everything. The "grip" schema is not yet very complex. With respect to an older child, if they have a dog called "Woof", they may call all dogs "Woof" because their schema does not allow for the fact that "Woof" is a specific, chosen name. When schemas are unsuitable, inappropriate, or inaccurate, a child's experience leads them to recognise this and change them.

SCHEMAS ARE ADAPTED BY TWO PROCESSES:

Assimilation
The process by which knowledge is incorporated into existing schemas without changing them. The incoming information is adjusted or changed to fit the existing schema. Every new object is grasped by using, for example, the thumb and all four fingers. All dogs are called "Woof".

Accommodation
The process by which schemas are changed, or new ones formed, to fit the incoming information. The child may not be able to pick up a small object by grasping with the whole hand and may learn to use the thumb and forefinger. The "grasp" schema has become more complex. They may hear the neighbour's dog being called "Snoopy" and may then refer to all dogs as "Woof" or "Snoopy". More accommodation will be necessary before the schema for dog is totally accurate.

Equilibration and Disequilibration
If new information does not fit existing schemas, then this produces a state of *disequilibrium*. This motivates children to change their existing schema or make a new one until a state of *equilibrium* is reached (which may be temporary, until some more information comes their way). *Equilibration is the process by which assimilation and accommodation are used to reach a state of equilibrium.*

PIAGET'S STAGE THEORY

Piaget believed that children pass through a series of stages and that:

- The stages are always in the same order—they are *invariant*.
- A child moves through the stages in a set order and never skips a stage.
- There are *qualitative* changes in the child's thinking from one stage to another. They do not simply acquire more knowledge (a *quantitative* change), but there is a difference in the type of logic they use.

The stages of cognitive development are:

1. The sensori-motor stage (0–2 years).
2. The pre-operational stage (2–7 years).
3. The concrete operations stage (7–11/12 years).
4. The formal operations stage (11/12 years onwards).

The Sensori-motor Stage

KEY FEATURES

- Children learn about the world through their *senses and actions*, hence the name of the stage.
- Schemas are largely based on *inborn reflexes*, e.g. sucking and grasping, and develop through refining these actions (the sucking reflex is adjusted to accommodate hard and soft objects, and so on) and by combining these actions, such as reaching for a rattle, grasping it, and putting it in the mouth.
- Children are extremely *egocentric*, not able to differentiate themselves from others.
- From 8 months they begin to develop *object permanence* but this is not fully developed until the end of the stage.
- At the end of the stage, infants show *deferred imitation*, which is imitation of behaviour seen earlier.

OBJECT PERMANENCE

The key achievement of the stage is the development of *object permanence*, the ability to appreciate that an object still exists even if out of sight. According to Piaget, children under 8 months have no object permanence (out of sight = it doesn't exist).

From 8 months, they will search for a toy if they have watched while it was hidden. From a year, they display *perseverative search* which means they will search for a hidden object but only where they saw it hidden first of all. Full object permanence occurs at the end of the sensori-motor stage when the child will look for it in the correct place.

NO OBJECT PERMANENCE

Infant under 8 months retrieves a visible object

But ...

Infant is unable to search for a fully hidden object

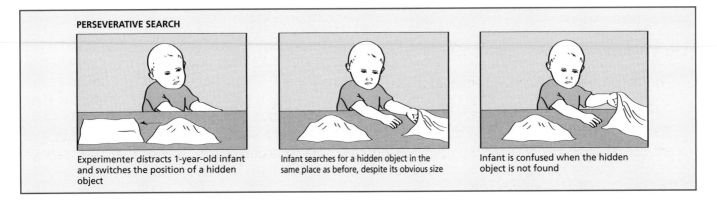

PERSEVERATIVE SEARCH

Experimenter distracts 1-year-old infant and switches the position of a hidden object

Infant searches for a hidden object in the same place as before, despite its obvious size

Infant is confused when the hidden object is not found

RESEARCH EVIDENCE

- Bower's "disappearing toy" study (1982, see A2PKT p.171). Bower believed that Piaget might have underestimated infants' abilities. His study showed that infants of 3–4 months expressed surprise when a toy hidden behind a screen was not there when the screen was lifted.
- Baillargeon and Graber's "moved toy" study (1988, see A2PKT pp.171–172). They similarly found that infants showed surprise if a toy which they had seen hidden behind one of two screens emerged from behind the "wrong" one.

The Pre-operational Stage

KEY FEATURES

- Progress from the sensori-motor to the pre-operational stage is marked by the development of symbolic thought. This is the ability to represent things internally. This is shown in several ways, including language (understanding that the sound "mummy" represents that person) and pretend play, in which one thing can represent another (e.g. a cardboard box may be used as a car).
- Children cannot perform logical operations (hence the name of the stage). They cannot reverse operations.
- Seriation—children can arrange objects in order but only on the basis of one feature, e.g. height.
- Children are still egocentric. They are beginning to recognise themselves as a separate person but still cannot fully appreciate things from another's point of view. This also includes the inability to appreciate that people think differently from yourself.
- Children are unable to conserve. Children cannot appreciate that something remains the same even if its appearance changes.

RESEARCH EVIDENCE

Studies both support Piaget's views on conservation and egocentrism and contradict them. We will consider Piaget's experiments, and then for and against both concepts.

Lack of conservation:

- Piaget's "conservation" studies (see A2PKT p.173). In these studies (see figure below), children were shown two equal amounts, such as two identical rows of counters, and asked if the number of counters in each row was the same. If they said they were, the researcher changed the layout of the counters in front of the children, by stretching out one row. They then asked the children if they were still the same. The results showed that children in this stage tended to say the second pair was different in terms of number of counters, showing an inability to conserve. This demonstrates that pre-operational children lack the cognitive operation of *reversibility*. This means that they cannot mentally reverse the operation by thinking of what happens if the counters are pushed back together. They judge by appearances and cannot take account of more than one feature (they judged just by the length of the row rather than taking account of spacing).

- McGarrigle and Donaldson's "Naughty Teddy" study (1974, see A2PKT p.181). This study showed different results. They tested 80 children in two conditions. In the first, the conditions were identical to Piaget's method but in the second, a glove puppet called Naughty Teddy appeared and made the rearrangement by, for example, spreading out the counters. Using the Piagetian method, 16% of 6-year-olds showed number conservation but with Naughty Teddy 62% thought the rows were still the same. This may be because children have the basic understanding of conservation but in the original study thought the adult must want a different answer or why ask the same question twice?

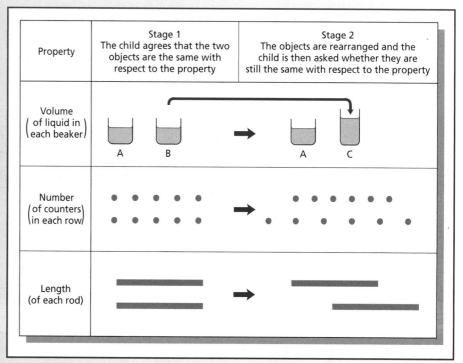

Property	Stage 1 The child agrees that the two objects are the same with respect to the property	Stage 2 The objects are rearranged and the child is then asked whether they are still the same with respect to the property
Volume (of liquid in each beaker)	A B	A C
Number (of counters in each row)		
Length (of each rod)		

- Moore and Frye's "Naughty Teddy" follow-up study (1986, see A2PKT p.182). This contradicted the findings of McGarrigle and Donaldson. They made Naughty Teddy actually take away or add counters and the younger children still tended to say the rows were the same, so perhaps they were not showing genuine conservation at all.

Egocentrism:

- Piaget's "Three Mountains" study (1956, see A2PKT p.174). This study demonstrates egocentrism. Children were placed in front of a model of three different mountains with a doll placed in another position and asked what the doll could see from locations A, B, C, and D. Four-year-old children almost always chose the picture corresponding to their own view. Six-year-olds showed a little more understanding but were

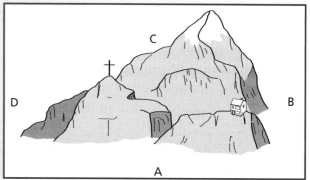

often wrong. Only children of 7–8 could succeed. This shows an inability to *decentre*, to step outside your own perspective and see things from another's point of view.

- Hughes' "Policeman Doll" study (1975, see A2PKT p.176). In this study children had to hide a boy from a policeman. This study showed less egocentrism since most preschoolers could do it. Hughes found that 90% of children correctly put the boy in section C—the only one the policemen cannot see. It may have been more realistic to them since the task related better to ordinary experiences such as playing hide-and-seek.

The Concrete Operations Stage

Children can now think logically but only if the concepts involved are tangible and familiar ("concrete") rather than abstract. Given the information that Sharina is taller than Jane but shorter than Harsa, they can work out who is the tallest and shortest. But given the information that $x>y$ but $x<z$, they would be unlikely to be able to work out the order.

KEY FEATURES

- Children can now perform logical operations and can therefore reverse concepts. This is the most important change as they no longer judge only by appearances. They can properly understand the effects of a change such as spreading out a row of counters by imagining the effects of reversing that change to get the counters back to how they were.
- Children can classify objects on more than one dimension.
- Children cannot deal with abstract concepts or hypothetical tasks.

The Formal Operations Stage

KEY FEATURES

- The individual can now deal with hypothetical situations, going beyond the realms of immediate reality.
- He or she can think in the abstract, especially in scientific thinking.

RESEARCH EVIDENCE

- Inhelder and Piaget's "pendulum problem" study (1958, see A2PKT pp.178–179). The difference between the concrete and formal operations stage is demonstrated by the pendulum problem. Children are provided with the means of making a pendulum, including some weights and a piece of string. They are asked to work out what determines how high the pendulum swings— whether it's the weight, the length of the string, the force of the push, etc. Concrete operational children try out various combinations, for example, a heavy weight with a short string, then a lighter weight with a longer string, and so on. They cannot work out a system for testing one factor at a time. But the formal operational child varies one factor while keeping others constant to see which has an effect.

EVALUATION OF PIAGET

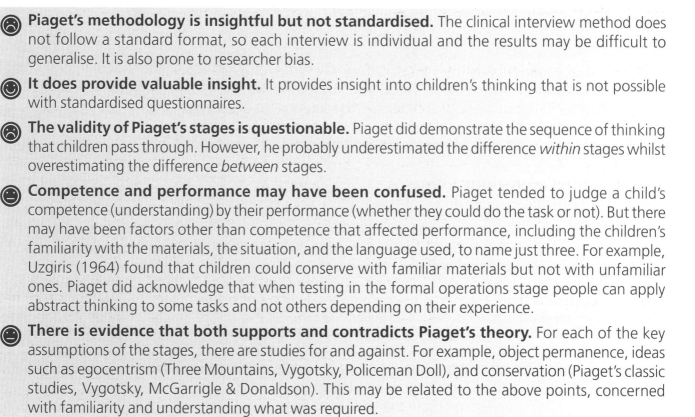

- **Piaget's methodology is insightful but not standardised.** The clinical interview method does not follow a standard format, so each interview is individual and the results may be difficult to generalise. It is also prone to researcher bias.

- **It does provide valuable insight.** It provides insight into children's thinking that is not possible with standardised questionnaires.

- **The validity of Piaget's stages is questionable.** Piaget did demonstrate the sequence of thinking that children pass through. However, he probably underestimated the difference *within* stages whilst overestimating the difference *between* stages.

- **Competence and performance may have been confused.** Piaget tended to judge a child's competence (understanding) by their performance (whether they could do the task or not). But there may have been factors other than competence that affected performance, including the children's familiarity with the materials, the situation, and the language used, to name just three. For example, Uzgiris (1964) found that children could conserve with familiar materials but not with unfamiliar ones. Piaget did acknowledge that when testing in the formal operations stage people can apply abstract thinking to some tasks and not others depending on their experience.

- **There is evidence that both supports and contradicts Piaget's theory.** For each of the key assumptions of the stages, there are studies for and against. For example, object permanence, ideas such as egocentrism (Three Mountains, Vygotsky, Policeman Doll), and conservation (Piaget's classic studies, Vygotsky, McGarrigle & Donaldson). This may be related to the above points, concerned with familiarity and understanding what was required.

SO WHAT DOES THIS MEAN?

Piaget provided a detailed and revolutionary account of how a child's thinking changes. His theory is the single most comprehensive account of cognitive development to date and has provided the foundation for further research and theory building. His theory has also been successfully applied to education, as considered later.

VYGOTSKY'S THEORY OF COGNITIVE DEVELOPMENT

Vygotsky's theory largely focuses on the role of *culture* on cognitive development. He believed that children learn in a social way through interaction with more "expert" people such as parents, teachers, and older peers. This is in contrast to Piaget who believed that children are innately motivated to discover things for themselves. Nevertheless, Vygotsky, like Piaget, believed that children are active in their own learning, not simply passive receivers of information.

The Role of Culture

Vygotsky believed that the innate mental functions possessed by children, such as attention and sensation, are transformed by learning into higher mental functions, such as problem solving. Each culture provides its children with *tools of intellectual adaptation* that enable them to use these higher mental functions, and these tools vary between cultures. For example, in the West we put great emphasis on reading, writing, and note taking in order to remember things (hence what you are doing now) but other cultures put greater emphasis on practical ways of learning and remembering. Vygotsky therefore believed that cultures teach people *how* to think as well as *what* to think.

KEY FEATURES

- **The zone of proximal development.** Vygotsky believed that children cannot be accelerated beyond their understanding but can move ahead a reasonable distance if given assistance. He used the expression zone of proximal development (ZPD) to refer to *the area between the level of performance a child can achieve alone and that which can be achieved by working with someone who has greater skills.* Suppose a child were offered some building bricks. A very young child could not build a house no matter what assistance they were given, but an older child could make a crude attempt. With adult help and advice, such as "you need to put a window in now and build bricks around it", or simply by showing the child and then leaving them alone for a while, the child can achieve more.

- **Scaffolding.** According to Vygotsky, children learn little if left alone to struggle but neither are they helped by a more experienced person taking over. What they require, and what most adults provide quite spontaneously, is scaffolding, which can be defined as *the appropriate support framework for children's learning.* Moss (1992, see A2PKT p.185) observed how mothers provide scaffolding in preschool children by (1) teaching new skills, (2) pointing out the usefulness of strategies they had spontaneously used earlier, and (3) persuading them not to use inappropriate methods. An important aspect of scaffolding is the gradual withdrawal of help as the child becomes more capable and confident and the adjustments made by parents according to the difficulty of the task. McNaughton and Leyland (1990) observed mothers helping children with jigsaws of varying difficulty. The amount of fairly direct help ("try that piece there") was higher for the more difficult puzzles and other types of guidance and encouragement ("look at that piece", "oh, well done") were again provided in proportion to the requirements of the task.

- **Language.** Vygotsky attached great importance to language. In the early years, children talk to themselves while playing. He referred to this as *private speech,* because it does not serve the function of communicating with others but of trying to plan strategies and regulate behaviour. A child might put a doll to bed and say, "you stay there, you are not well" and then introduce a doctor doll while saying, "she will give you some medicine and make you better". The language serves to sort out what is happening in the child's world. This talking out loud gradually gets less and less and is eventually transformed into thinking. Berk (1994, see A2PKT pp.186–187) demonstrated the importance of private speech by showing that children use it more when trying to do a difficult task than an easy one. Vygotsky believed that language is fundamental to the development of cognitive abilities because it serves two important functions. First, internalised language is thought; second, it is the means by which ideas are communicated and received, thus increasing understanding.

EVALUATION

- **Culture and the social context does have an important influence on development.** This has been demonstrated, and was probably underestimated by Piaget and other developmental psychologists.

- **Guidance in the form of scaffolding improves cognitive development.** Supported by Conner, Knight, and Cross (1997, see A2PKT pp.185–186) who demonstrated that in follow-up sessions, children who had received good scaffolding performed better than children who had received poor scaffolding.

The importance of private speech. Supported by Berk (1994, see A2PKT pp.186–187) who showed that young children greatly benefit from private speech when performing a task, especially new ones that they do not understand. As their skills improve, the use of private speech diminishes, in line with Vygotsky's predictions.

Vygotsky probably overestimated the role of culture. There is little evidence that children in different cultures go through different stages. Rather, Piaget's prediction that stages of development are universal has received considerable support.

Vygotsky also overemphasised the role of social factors. A child's motivation and interest are also of great importance to their cognitive development. Indeed, there are times when attempts to help or to present an opposing view can frustrate a child and make them either abandon a task or dig their heels in and become more extreme in their views.

THE INFORMATION-PROCESSING APPROACH

As the name implies, this approach (which is a collection of theories) states that the mind is an information-processing system. The theories are concerned with the ways in which the system becomes more sophisticated as children develop. The information-processing system consists of:

- A small number of *processes,* such as attention and perception.
- A number of *structures,* such as short- and long-term memory.

The way it operates can be represented thus:

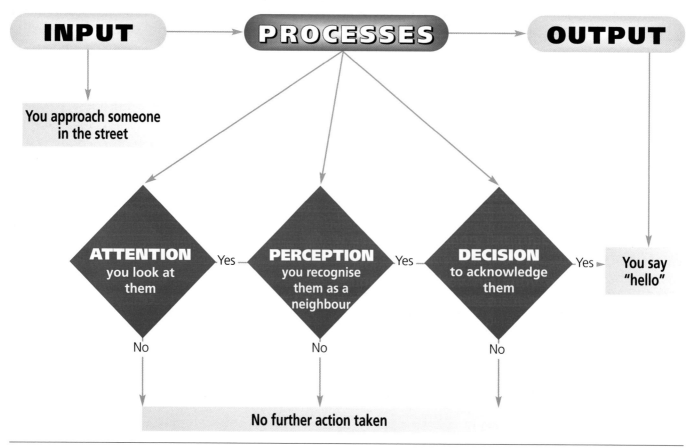

As children develop, the processes such as paying attention, perceiving, retaining information in STM, and transferring it to LTM all get more sophisticated. Alongside this, the structures also get more complex, for example STM can hold more items (a young child can only retain about four bits, an adult can hold around seven), and working memory (the capacity to manipulate information) also becomes greater. This means that problem-solving skills improve with age.

Case's Information-Processing Theory

The information-processing approach of Case is a neo-Piagetian one. It is similar to Piaget's in that it has the equivalent of the four stages of cognitive development but different in that, whereas Piaget sees each new stage as involving changes in *types* of thinking, Case sees them as more complex applications of the same processes.

KEY FEATURES

As children develop, there are two main changes. Both of these changes occur because of changes in the structure of the brain and in its operating efficiency.

- **Increase in M-space.** M-space is the capacity of *working* memory. Case (1985) showed children cards each with an addition exercise on (e.g. 3 + 5), then another one, and so on. The children had to work out the sum, then do the next card and add it to the last, and so on. Children of about 5 years could only do about two of these, but this increased to about four with 12-year-olds. Children move from one stage to another when there is enough M-space.
- **Increase in automaticity.** Many skills that older children and adults do without effort (such as reading, or calculating 17 − 6) take a lot of attention and effort in young children. As the brain matures, information is transmitted more quickly and efficiently making many skilled actions automatic. These automatic activities use very little M-space, thus increasing the amount for other use.

EVALUATION

☺ **Failure in tasks is due to processing limitations rather than lack of logic.** Evidence shows that when conservation tasks are made easier by using a container of beads rather than water, younger children can do them, whereas Piaget would predict that they still could not, because they lack the necessary logical structures.

☺ **As children develop there is an increase in M-space.** Considerable evidence supports the idea that as children develop, there is an increase in M-space and that this increase leads to more sophisticated tasks being accomplished.

☹ **There is virtually no attention paid to social and cultural influences.** This model concentrates almost exclusively on the ways in which changes in the individual nervous system (mainly the brain) affect development, not the influence that other people have.

☹ **There is little attention to the role of language.** Some developmental psychologists believe that language is fundamental to cognitive development, yet it is barely mentioned in this approach.

☹ **Descriptive rather than explanatory.** Whereas Piaget did explain how schemas change (by assimilation and accommodation), the information-processing approach simply says that inability to do a task is due to lack of M-space. This explains very little; it simply describes findings from studies in a different way.

APPLYING COGNITIVE-DEVELOPMENTAL THEORIES TO EDUCATION

Piaget's Theory

Although Piaget was not a great enthusiast for formal education, his principles have been widely applied. They have been interpreted as suggesting the importance of the following:

- **Being cognitively ready.** Children cannot be accelerated from one stage to another if they do not understand the underlying concepts.
- **Discovering for themselves and being active learners.** In order to understand concepts, children need to be active in discovering them. Simply being given information by adults does not teach anything; in fact it may inhibit learning. The teachers' role is to ask questions and use any incorrect answers to gain insight into the child's understanding. They then provide materials that put children in a state of disequilibration that enables them to modify their existing schemas. The processes of assimilation and accommodation are then used naturally by the children, thereby improving their understanding.
- **Child-centred learning.** Piaget's theory implies that, since children mature at different rates and enjoy using different materials, it is not beneficial to teach them all in the same way. They benefit greatly from peer interaction, so the ideal is to use small group activities specially designed to adequately challenge them.
- **Sociocognitive conflict.** Some neo-Piagetians, e.g. Doise and Mugny (1984, see A2PKT pp.191–192), argue that understanding is increased if children work with peers who have a different view from their own. They believe that two or more minds can sometimes generate insights that neither had thought of independently. Their emphasis, therefore, is on the importance of *social factors* in learning, that is, working alongside others. This is very much in line with Piaget's belief in the benefits of peer interaction as a means of understanding things from another's point of view.

EVALUATION

- **Some studies support Piaget's idea that cognitive development cannot be accelerated.** Gelman (1969) attempted to teach children conservation; not only was it an extremely long process but there were doubts that it was permanent.

- **Other studies contradict it.** Brainerd (1983, see A2PKT p.191) showed that preschoolers can be taught some concepts from the concrete operations stage.

- **Underestimation of the value of providing children with information.** Brainerd's (1983) study (above) implies that Piaget underestimated the value of tutorial training. Meadows (1994, see A2PKT p.191) maintains that Piaget underestimated the role of teaching and cultural influences in a child's cognitive development.

- **Active discovery learning does significantly reduce boredom in children and provides a different attitude to learning.** Children learn *how* to learn rather than simply being provided with a certain amount of information.

- **Some studies support Piaget's idea that children must work things out for themselves.** Ames and Murray (1982, see A2PKT p.192) demonstrated that children who do not understand conservation benefited more by being with children who give different *wrong* answers than by being with children who could successfully conserve, or by being told why they were wrong. This study supports the Piagetian argument that children learn by being challenged and thereby put into a state of disequilibrium, rather than Vygotsky's view that children benefit by receiving help from someone who is more "expert" than they are.

SO WHAT DOES THIS MEAN?

Piaget's ideas have had a considerable influence on British education. The Plowden report was an influential document published in 1967 and emphasised many Piagetian principles such as developmental stages, readiness, and developmental age. It recommended, for example, that children need individual and different attention and that it is a waste of time to try to make a child take a step forward before they are ready. Most importantly, children grow intellectually, emotionally, and physically at different rates and we need to take account of this "developmental age" in all three aspects. Many recommendations from the Plowden report have been implemented.

Despite criticisms and modifications, Piaget's ideas have changed the face of education. Because we now take so much of this for granted, we may lose sight of the full effect of his influence. No longer would we dream of sitting children in rows behind desks and expecting them to spend most of the school day listening to a teacher and all doing exactly the same work at the same time, regardless of ability and understanding.

Vygotsky's Theory

Like Piaget, Vygotsky believed that children are active learners who cannot be forced ahead too quickly. Since Vygotsky's theory is concerned directly with how children are taught, we can use his main principles as the basis of the key points about applying it to education.

- **Peer tutoring.** Children learn little if left entirely to their own devices but neither do they benefit from teachers who are so advanced that they do not appreciate the child's thinking processes. *Peer tutoring* is especially useful, using children a year or two ahead of those being taught. Evidence supports this in several cultures and also demonstrates that it works most effectively with two peer tutors rather than one (Ellis & Gauvain, 1992, see A2PKT p.193). As the task advances, the amount of guidance from the teacher should ideally be less and less.
- **The zone of proximal development.** This acts as a guide as to the range of abilities children can achieve with appropriate help. Teachers need to be aware of the ZPD of individual children.
- **Learning through play.** Vygotsky believed that during play, especially pretend play such as "playing shops", children operated beyond their usual level of thinking. This is related to the importance Vygotsky placed on culture. During such play children tend to use toys specific to their own culture and this enhances their learning.

EVALUATION

- ☺ **Effective learning.** There is good evidence that scaffolding provided by peers and adults can promote effective learning both at school and at home.

- ☺ **Vygotsky's methods work better with some tasks than others.** Sometimes it is more useful to discuss a task with someone of a different view (the neo-Piagetian approach), whereas at other times it is useful to be guided by an expert who can help where necessary (the Vygotsky view). On some tasks, e.g. understanding simple scientific principles such as floating and sinking, it made no difference if there was someone who knew the right answer, and the best conditions were those in which the peers started by disagreeing with each other (Howe, Tolmie, & Rodgers, 1992, see A2PKT p.194).

- ☹ **External vs. internal factors.** Vygotsky's approach tends to focus on the importance of external factors (the teacher's ability to help) and underestimate the role of the child's thought processes (internal factors).

SO WHAT DOES THIS MEAN?

Vygotsky's approach has doubtless added a new dimension to the teaching of children. He pointed out that there are important cultural differences in what children learn. Although he appreciated a child's need to discover underlying principles for themselves, he put greater emphasis than Piaget did on the value of offering direct assistance to children. Nevertheless, tutoring is not always successful. If there is a considerable status gap between the child and tutor, then the child can lose motivation and learn very little. The most effective tutors are those who can let the child get on alone when they see they are capable of so doing, and intervene only when they can provide valuable assistance. As Vygotsky demonstrated, many parents are superbly adept at this and do so automatically. However, some teaching schemes have not taken this on board and do not fully appreciate the dangers of "cramming".

The Information-processing Approach

There are various teaching strategies that are implied by the information-processing approach:

- **Tasks should be analysed in terms of what mental operations are required and what information needs to be encoded.** This enables the material to be presented in a way that children understand. It also means that teachers can analyse children's errors to see which rules or processes are being used wrongly. For example, if a child states that $74 - 26 = 58$ and $74 + 19 = 83$, then the teacher may realise that the child is operating a rule in which the tens and units have no effect on each other, rather than the child simply not paying attention. Sometimes more than one process is involved. For example, in learning to read, it may help to combine the phonetic method (a-bb-ey for abbey) with the whole-word approach (recognising a word such as "through" without trying to spell it out).
- **Present tasks in a way that does not overload the limited capacity of attention and STM.** If a problem involves several steps, it should be broken down into smaller units, none of which overloads the capacity of working memory. It is also important to practise skills in order to increase automaticity. If, for example, children learn the "times tables", then more complex arithmetic tasks can be accomplished because the M-space is not being used while doing simple multiplication.
- **Organise lessons so that children acquire metacognitive knowledge.** Metacognitive knowledge involves understanding why certain strategies are effective and applying them to other learning. Teachers need to be explicit about *what* strategies are required and *when* they are appropriate to use. For example, a child may be advised to categorise items to be remembered (e.g. putting animals into mammals, birds, fish, etc.) and then the teacher could suggest other instances when grouping is an effective strategy. Another example is emphasising to students that a theory cannot be effectively learnt by remembering individual points by rote, but only if the whole meaning is understood.

EVALUATION

- Ⓒ **Information-processing has emphasised the importance of breaking down tasks into processes and strategies.** By so doing, tasks can be presented in a way the child understands.
- Ⓒ **It is sometimes very difficult to identify the processes being used.** This is the negative side of breaking tasks down in this way.
- Ⓒ **It is difficult to estimate exactly the capacity of the M-space in any individual child.** This makes it difficult to structure a task appropriately.
- Ⓒ **How do children learn to acquire processes?** There is not a great deal of advice offered on how children can learn to acquire the processes required.

SO WHAT DOES THIS MEAN?

Although the information-processing approach does offer helpful advice, it is mainly advice that any perceptive adult could work out for him- or herself without any specific prior knowledge.

NOTE: Don't forget that one approach can be evaluated with respect to other approaches and that both differences and similarities can be used in evaluation.

OVER TO YOU

1. (a) Outline Vygotsky's theory of cognitive development. **(6 marks)**

   (b) Outline *one or more* applications of Vygotsky's theory of cognitive development. **(6 marks)**

   (c) Evaluate this application/these applications of Vygotsky's theory of cognitive development. **(12 marks)**

2. (a) Describe Piaget's theory of cognitive development. **(12 marks)**

   (b) Evaluate his theory with reference to research evidence and/or other theories of cognitive development. **(12 marks)**

Question 1 adapted from AQA A2 [Winter 2002] Psychology Examination Papers.

DEVELOPMENT OF MEASURED INTELLIGENCE

ASK YOURSELF

We often talk in terms of one person being more intelligent than another. But what exactly do we mean by intelligence? Is it just the ability to pass academic exams?

Is a car mechanic less intelligent than a teacher of philosophy? If so, why?

If some people are more intelligent than others, why is this so? Have they inherited their abilities, or had lots of encouragement, or been to a "good" school? Or is it a combination of all these?

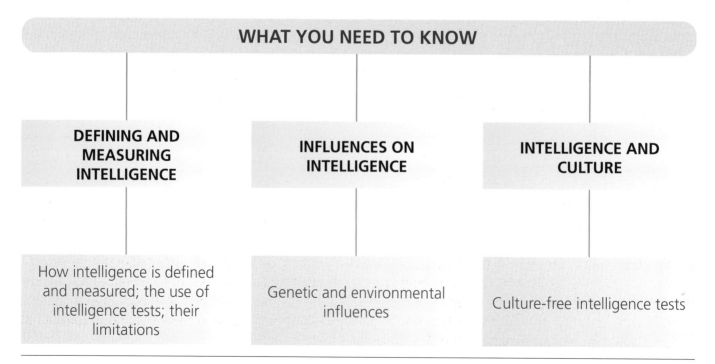

WHAT YOU NEED TO KNOW

DEFINING AND MEASURING INTELLIGENCE

How intelligence is defined and measured; the use of intelligence tests; their limitations

INFLUENCES ON INTELLIGENCE

Genetic and environmental influences

INTELLIGENCE AND CULTURE

Culture-free intelligence tests

To read up on the development of measured intelligence, refer to pages 200–216 of A2PKT.

DEFINING INTELLIGENCE

Weschler (1975) defined intelligence as "the capacity to understand the world and the resourcefulness to cope with its resources". Sternberg (1985, see A2PKT p.200) offers an alternative definition: "mental activity directed towards purposive adaptation to, and selection and shaping of, real-world environments relevant to one's life".

MEASURING INTELLIGENCE

Intelligence tests measure basic cognitive abilities but do not take account of how "streetwise" a person is—how well they cope with everyday life. Smith and Tsimpli (1991, see A2PKT p.201) give an example of a boy named Christopher who, despite having a very much below average score on an intelligence test, could speak 17 languages fluently.

Most intelligence tests have several subscales in order to measure different types of ability, for example:

- *Information*: What is the capital of the UK?
- *Comprehension*: Why do we have postcodes?
- *Spatial ability*: If you go west and then turn left and left again, which way are you going?
- *Vocabulary*: What is a rodent?

Tests should be *standardised* by being given to a large representative sample, to establish *norms* so that one person's score can be compared to an "average" score.

The best-known measure of intelligence is the *intelligence quotient* (IQ, see A2PKT pp.200–201). The test to measure IQ has a mean of 100 and a standard deviation (SD) of 16, which means that 68% of people have an IQ between 84 and 116 (1 SD either side of the mean) and 95% between 68 and 132 (2 SDs either side of the mean).

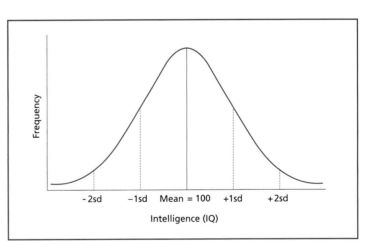

The Use of Intelligence Tests

Intelligence tests should be *reliable* and *valid*.

- *Reliability* refers to *consistency*. A test is reliable if it produces a similar score on two or more occasions with the same people. It is often difficult to test the reliability of intelligence tests due to the effects of practice.
- *Validity* refers to whether the test measures what it is supposed to measure. An intelligence test would not be valid if it measured only a very limited range of abilities, such as memory and verbal ability only. The concept of validity is especially important when we test people from social classes and cultures different from those in which the test was originally designed. It is quite possible than one culture has a different view of intelligence than does another.

LIMITATIONS OF INTELLIGENCE TESTS

- **They measure only a very limited range of ability.** Most intelligence tests lay considerable emphasis on verbal ability and abstract reasoning but little on practical problem-solving and interpersonal skills. They only really measure skills required in schools.
- **They show social class bias.** They tend to underestimate the intelligence of children from poor backgrounds for several reasons:
  - These children are not particularly motivated to do the tests.
  - They have not had experiences (such as certain play materials and certain life experiences) that enable them to understand the items.

  Studies show that when poorer children receive appropriate experience by having play sessions, their IQ scores improve far more than those of middle-class children (Zigler et al., 1973, see A2PKT p.201).
- **They are culturally biased.** They underestimate the abilities of children from different cultural backgrounds. They are devised by people from white, middle-class backgrounds and cannot easily be understood by those who have had different experiences. Williams (1972, see A2PKT p.202) devised an intelligence test based on Black American culture and found that the white children did worse on this than on standard tests. It is therefore not surprising that black children fare worse than white ones on tests designed for white culture.
- **They do not allow for cultural variation in valued skills.** Intelligence tests tend to measure only those abilities admired in a middle-class Western culture. Serpell (1979, see A2PKT p.202) found that English children do better than Zambian ones on drawing but not as well in wire-shaping.

INTELLIGENCE: HEREDITY OR ENVIRONMENT?

Why are some children more intelligent than others (as measured by intelligence tests)? Is it genetics (nature) or environment (nurture) or a complex combination of both? Some people argue that measuring the relative importance of nature and nurture is a nonsense since both are essential—it's like arguing whether the seed or soil is more important when a plant grows. Without both, nothing grows. In a similar vein, Hebb (1958, see A2PKT p.202) says that it is like arguing about whether breadth or length is more important in deciding area.

Genetic Influences on Intelligence

Genetic influences can be assessed by looking at correlations of IQ of related individuals and/or those raised together.

RESEARCH EVIDENCE

- Bouchard and McGue's "identical (MZ) twins and fraternal (DZ) twins" study (1981, see A2PKT pp.203–204) reviewed 111 studies and found an average correlation of +.86 for MZ twins and +.60 for DZ twins, implying that genetics is important. However, research shows that MZ twins are treated more alike than DZ twins, and this could account for most, if not all, of the difference (Loehlin & Nichols, 1976, see A2PKT p.204). Also, the correlation of +.60 for DZ twins is higher than that of +.47 for siblings, even though they share the same amount of genes, indicating an important environmental role.
- Bouchard and McGue's "MZ twins reared apart" study (1981, see A2PKT pp.203–204) found a correlation of +.72 in MZ twins reared apart. However, some spent several years together before

being separated and several were reared in very similar environments, sometimes within the same extended family. Nevertheless, a later study of MZ twins reared apart from birth still showed a correlation of +.75 (Bouchard et al., 1990, see A2PKT p.205). These sets of studies imply an influential role for genetics.

- Horn's "adoption" study (1983, see A2PKT p.206) reviewed findings from 500 adopted families and found a correlation of +.15 for adopted children and their adoptive mothers and +.28 for the children and their biological mothers. Both correlations are low, but they do indicate that genetics is more influential than upbringing.

- Capron and Duyne's "adoption" study (1989, see A2PKT p.207).

EVALUATION OF THE INFLUENCE OF GENETICS

 Most of the data can be used to support either side of the environment/genetic argument. Bouchard and McGue (1991, see A2PKT p.204) comment that the data from these studies are very complex and difficult to interpret and that most of the studies of family resemblance can be interpreted as either supporting the genetic or the environmentalist theory.

Children raised in the same environment do not necessarily have the same *experiences*. Variations in intelligence between children reared together may therefore be caused by these differences, as well as by genetics.

Twin studies have only been conducted in very few cultures. This means that the results, which tend to indicate 50% genetics, 50% environment, cannot be generalised beyond those cultures.

The data from adoption studies is confounded by the fact that children are often selectively placed in homes similar to those of the biological parents. This means that similarity between adoptive children and their biological parents may be due to selective placement rather than genetics.

In most studies, intelligence is measured by IQ tests. As discussed earlier, intelligence tests have serious limitations.

Environmental Influences on Intelligence

Several studies have indicated the strong influence of the home environment on children's measured intelligence.

RESEARCH EVIDENCE

- The HOME inventory. This was devised by Caldwell and Bradley (1984, see A2PKT pp.208–209) to measure the extent to which a family environment was stimulating. The six important factors were:

  - The emotional and verbal responsiveness of the parent.
  - The avoidance of restrictions and use of punishment.
  - Organisation of physical and temporal environment.
  - The provision of appropriate play material.
  - Parental involvement with the child.
  - Opportunities for variety in daily stimulation.

- Longitudinal studies indicate that the most important elements are parental involvement, variety of activities, and age-appropriate play materials (Gottfried, 1984, see A2PKT p.209). Research indicates a positive correlation between scores on the HOME inventory and IQ, implying that the home environment is important.

- Operation Headstart. This US enrichment programme for disadvantaged children indicated that environment did have an important influence on intelligence. Half a million preschoolers were placed in special programmes designed to provide the stimulation they were considered to be lacking at home. It was found that:

  - There were immediate gains in IQ but these initially appeared short-lived.

  - Long-term results were more encouraging—Headstart children were less likely to be in special schools, more likely to be employed, less likely to be underage parents, and less likely to be on welfare.

- In adolescence, the IQ of the Headstart group was higher than that of controls (Seitz, 1990, see A2PKT p.211).

EVALUATION OF THE INFLUENCE OF ENVIRONMENT

- **No conclusions can be drawn about cause and effect from correlational data.** The relationship between IQ and scores on the HOME scale is *correlational*, and so does not prove cause and effect. It may be that higher intelligence parents provide a more stimulating environment, so it may be a genetic effect that is being shown. Nevertheless, it has been found in adoption studies that when children are placed in a more stimulating environment, their IQs do increase considerably (Turkheimer, 1991).

- **There are methodological limitations with the Operation Headstart programme.** In this programme, the control group was not necessarily comparable with the research group, since children were not selected at random. Nevertheless, other research in which there was random allocation still suggests a positive effect for this programme (e.g. Ramey et al., 1999, see A2PKT p.211).

- **Gains in compensatory education programmes are influenced by environment.** Research indicates that the more extreme the deprivation, the greater the gains made from compensatory education programmes.

- **Many studies indicate a significant environmental effect.** Sameroff et al. (1987, 1993, see A2PKT p.210), in the Rochester study, showed that there is a negative correlation between IQ and family risk factors, such as mother not going to High School, having severe anxiety, and expressing rigid attitudes. This indicates that it is these factors that could influence intelligence test performance, not necessarily genetic ones.

SO WHAT DOES THIS MEAN?

It is apparent that both genetics and the environment have an effect on intelligence. A stimulating environment can greatly enhance children's abilities whilst a deprived environment can stifle opportunities for development. The problem for researchers is that it is almost impossible to separate out environmental and genetic effects. Most of the studies are correlational, showing simply a relationship between low IQ in parents and their children. Although this may indicate a genetic effect, environmental effects are almost certainly operating as well. Deprivation factors such as a mother not going to high school and lack of variety in activities are associated with low IQ. Conversely, factors such as the provision of appropriate play materials are associated with high IQ. In all these cases, genetic factors could be influencing both the home environment (because of the parents' IQ) and the IQ of the children.

INTELLIGENCE AND CULTURE

A source of great political controversy for many years, involving both psychologists and non-psychologists, has been the fact that white Americans score on average 15 IQ points higher than Black Americans.

Is This a Genetic Difference?

It has been argued by a few that this difference is due to the genetic inferiority of blacks compared with whites (e.g. Jensen 1969, see A2PKT p.212; H.J. Eysenck, 1981, see A2PKT p.212). Herrnstein and Murray (1994, see A2PKT pp.212–213) advanced the extreme view that since these differences are genetic, it is pointless to offer black children the same educational opportunities as whites as they are unable to benefit fully from them.

Or Due to Environmental Factors?

The majority (e.g. Gould, 1981) argue that this difference is due to a combination of the bias of tests and environmental disadvantage. (We have considered both of these aspects, so it is useful to recap the relevant discussions from the previous sections.)

COMMENTARY ON THIS ARGUMENT

- What is race? There are no clear-cut genetic differences between races. There is more variation *within* racial groups than *between* such groups. A "race" is not a biologically discrete group in the way, for example, that males and females are.
- Eyforth (1961) compared the intelligence of children born of white German single women but fathered by either white or black US GIs and found no differences in IQ. If the black fathers were genetically predisposed to have lower IQs, then this should have been revealed in their children.
- Mackintosh (1986, see A2PKT p.213) conducted a study in England, comparing West Indian and white children. Some groups were matched on levels of deprivation, some unmatched (in which case the West Indian groups invariably suffered greater deprivation). In the unmatched groups there was an average IQ difference of 9 points, but only 2.6 points in the matched groups (note that neither showed the 15-point difference found in American studies).
- It is impossible to measure the amount of deprivation in any family or cultural group, so these comparisons have little scientific value.
- The intelligence tests used were culturally biased, favouring white, middle-class, formally educated children. Some studies have used "culture-free" tests with mixed results (see overleaf). There are many subtle cultural effects, such as the attitude to doing an abstract task not related to ordinary life. This makes control extraordinarily difficult.
- The debate has had some extremely negative political effects, such as providing ammunition for extreme right-wing groups. For reasons already stated, the argument that blacks are genetically inferior to whites in intelligence is so weak that many argue that it should not be publicly discussed.

Culture-Free Intelligence Tests

In an attempt to reduce bias, tests have been devised that require no verbal ability or specific information. This has not been entirely successful since culture can influence the whole attitude to the testing situation. For example, some children are used to working in cooperation, not independently. An example from a culture-free test is shown below:

An item from Raven's Progressive Matrices Test: Each problem is presented in the form of a sequence of symbolic figures. The subject is required to understand the nature of the relationship within each sequence and select one figure that completes each sequence. By so doing, the subject demonstrates the degree to which a systematic method of reasoning has been developed.

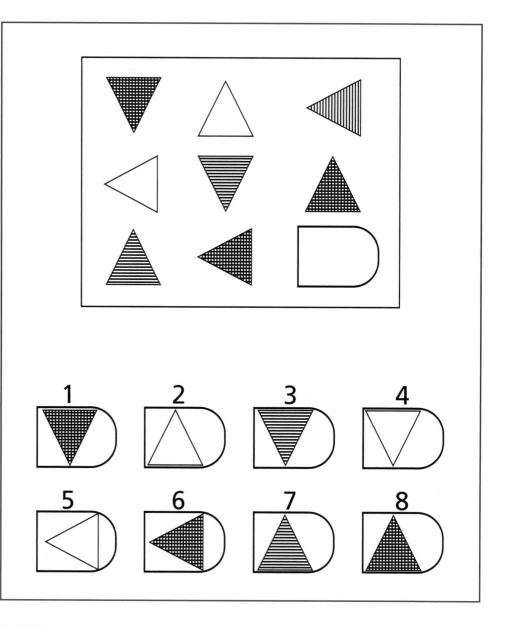

OVER TO YOU

1. **Critically consider the role of genetic factors in the development of measured intelligence.** **(24 marks)**

2. **"Today, a majority of psychologists believe that differences in intelligence result from a combination of heredity and environmental factors."**

Discuss this statement in relation to research into the development of intelligence test performance. **(24 marks)**

DEVELOPMENT OF MORAL UNDERSTANDING

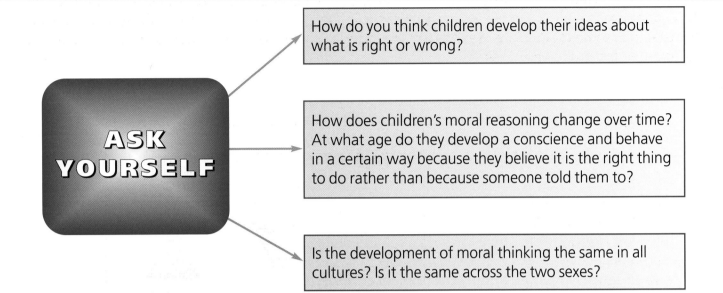

ASK YOURSELF

How do you think children develop their ideas about what is right or wrong?

How does children's moral reasoning change over time? At what age do they develop a conscience and behave in a certain way because they believe it is the right thing to do rather than because someone told them to?

Is the development of moral thinking the same in all cultures? Is it the same across the two sexes?

WHAT YOU NEED TO KNOW

KOHLBERG'S THEORY

- Pre-conventional level
- Conventional level
- Post-conventional level

EISENBERG'S THEORY

- Pro-social behaviour:

  Level 1: Self-centred

  Level 2: Needs-oriented

  Level 3: Approval-oriented

  Level 4: Empathetic

  Level 5: Internalised

THE WORK OF GILLIGAN ON GENDER DIFFERENCES IN MORAL DEVELOPMENT
Justice vs. care

CULTURAL DIFFERENCES IN MORAL DEVELOPMENT

What is moral understanding? The development of moral understanding concerns the way in which children develop a sense of right or wrong and come to adopt and internalise the rules of society.

To read up on the development of moral understanding, refer to pages 217–235 of A2PKT.

THE COGNITIVE-DEVELOPMENTAL APPROACH: PIAGET'S THEORY OF MORAL DEVELOPMENT

KEY FEATURES

- Children under the age of 5 do not have the capacity to think morally; they are *premoral*.
- From age 5 children begin to develop a sense of morality that occurs in two stages: heteronomous morality (5–10 years approximately), followed by autonomous morality (10 years onwards).
- Some children move from the heteronomous to the autonomous stage more quickly than others, and many people are never entirely autonomous.

Heteronomous Stage

- **Rules are rigid.** Children think rules come from "on high" (God or parents or teachers) and should not be changed even with everyone's consent.
- **Consequences are more important than intentions.** If a child breaks six cups she is naughtier than a child who breaks one, even if the child who broke six cups was trying to help or did it accidentally and the child who broke one was being disobedient.
- **The world is ruled according to *immanent justice*.** The world is just and fair and all naughtiness will be punished either by parents, teachers, or God. If a naughty child running away crosses a bridge that breaks, making them fall in the water, the bridge broke *because* they were naughty.
- **Obedience to adults is more important than loyalty to friends.** It's right to "tell on" your mates to a grown-up because they should not have been naughty and deserve to be punished.

Autonomous Stage

- **Rules are flexible.** Rules are designed to make things fair and it's all right to change them as long as everyone agrees.
- **Intentions are more important than consequences.**
- **Belief in immanent justice declines.** However, it often does not disappear altogether (hence the saying "what goes around, comes around"). Punishment should be used to make people behave better, not to get revenge.
- **Loyalty to friends is more important than obedience to authority.**

Reasons for the Change from One Stage to the Next

- **Changes in cognitive thinking.** As children understand more and become less egocentric, they can understand people's motives better.
- **Changes in social experiences.** As children enter into more egalitarian (equal) relationships, mixing with friends rather than authority figures, they learn to understand other people's points of view and to resolve conflicts without help from adults. They begin to understand the purpose of rules and this makes them flexible in their approach to them.

EVALUATION

- 🙂 **The methodology provides insight into children's thinking.** The use of clinical interviews in the course of playing games with children provides a detailed and naturalistic account of their thinking.

☺ **There are many studies that support the theory.** These demonstrate that young children believe consequences to be more important than intentions while older children think that intentions are more important (e.g. Piaget, 1932, see A2PKT p.222; Shaffer, 1993, see A2PKT p.224).

☺ **There is a parallel between cognitive development and the development of moral thinking.** This indicates, as the theory predicts, that advances in moral reasoning depend on the deeper understanding brought about by cognitive development.

☹ **It may underestimate the abilities of young children to appreciate intentions if the consequences are positive.** Piaget concentrated on negative consequences in his dilemma stories, but when positive consequences are involved, children seem to have a better understanding of intentions.

☹ **"Dilemma stories" are rather contrived.** They may not adequately assess a child's thinking. Discussions of real situations may be better (Karniol, 1978).

☹ **Children do not believe all rules should be rigidly kept.** Shaffer (1993, see A2PKT p.224) argues that when a rule involves something very personally relevant, such as when a parent tells you who you should have as friend, children are less likely to believe that they are fair.

☹ **Piaget's theory tends to neglect the behavioural component of morality (how people actually behave) and the emotional component (how people feel).** His theory mainly concentrates on beliefs.

KOHLBERG'S THEORY

Kohlberg based his theory on Piaget's but extended the stages considerably.

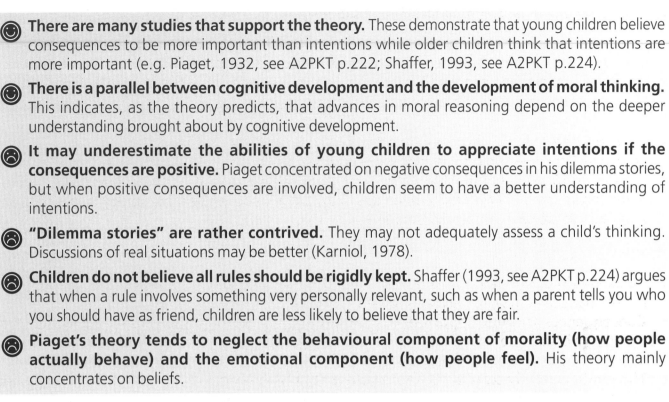

KOHLBERG'S STAGES OF MORAL DEVELOPMENT

PRE-CONVENTIONAL: LEVEL 1
ORIENTATION
Stage 1: Punishment and obedience—Children do as they are told to avoid punishment.
Stage 2: Reward—Children do as they are told to gain rewards (such as praise).

CONVENTIONAL: LEVEL 2
Stage 3: Good boy/nice girl—Children judge what is "good" or "bad" on the basis of what others (particularly authority figures) say and by social norms. Being good is important for its own sake, not just to gain rewards.
Stage 4: Law and order—People judge what is good and bad in terms of the law. If a behaviour is against the law, it is wrong.

POST-CONVENTIONAL: LEVEL 3
Stage 5: Social contract—Moral behaviour is judged by what is for the greater good. Laws should generally be kept but there should be provision to change them.
Stage 6: Universal ethical principles—People now have a set of ethical principles by which to judge what is moral. These apply universally, not just to a particular culture. It is reasonable to break a law that is considered unjust. Conscience dominates over the law.

FEATURES OF THE THEORY

- Like Piaget's theory, Kohlberg's theory (1976, see A2PKT pp.225–228) is based on the idea that movement through the stages depends on cognitive development.
- The stages are *invariant* (people move through them in the same order starting with the first one).
- Many people do not reach the last two stages (post-conventional).

RESEARCH EVIDENCE

- Invariance was shown by Snarey (1985, see A2PKT p.227). Snarey reviewed 44 studies in 26 different cultures and found that nearly all cultures went through Kohlberg's stages of moral development in the same order.
- Shaver and Strong (1976, see A2PKT p.228) found that most individuals do not move beyond law and order.

EVALUATION

☺ **There is research evidence to show that children move through the stages in the predicted direction.** Colby et al. (1983, see A2PKT pp.226–227) conducted a 20-year longitudinal study of 58 American males and found that all of the participants passed through stages 1 to 4 in the predicted sequence, suggesting that Kohlberg's stages are universal. (Nevertheless, see the negative evaluation points for differences in the post-conventional morality.)

☺ **There is also evidence that more advanced thinkers are more likely to reach the later stages.** This confirms the view that development of moral thinking depends on cognitive development (Stewart & Pascual-Leone, 1992).

☺ **The theory is detailed and covers many years of a person's life.** It is a more comprehensive theory than Piaget's and acknowledges that there are important changes in moral thinking during adulthood rather than simply the early years.

☹ **Post-conventional morality may not be the same in every culture.** Although the early stages appear similar for everyone, research indicates that the later post-conventional stages may vary from culture to culture. Kohlberg researched mainly Judaeo-Christian cultures. Miller, Bershoff, and Harwood (1990, see A2PKT p.228) found that in India the emphasis is on different values, that of duty to others rather than individual rights and freedoms as found in individualistic cultures such as the USA. See also Ma (1988, see A2PKT p.228) for research in China.

☹ **The methodology was unreliable and not objective.** Kohlberg used dilemma stories and asked very detailed questions, giving a vast amount of information, but there are problems with *inter-rater reliability* and *subjectivity*—not every researcher agreed when deciding into which stage a particular answer should be placed.

☹ **Answers to dilemma stories may not reflect how people behave in real life.**

☹ **The research has been accused of gender bias (referred to also as androcentric bias—centred only on men).** Kohlberg's research involved only males and therefore his theory should only apply to them, not to women. Yet he did apply his theory to women and judged them to be, on average, at a "lower" level of reasoning. Gilligan (1977, see A2PKT p.229) argues that men and women use different criteria for judging morality—her research is considered separately later (you will need this in order to fully criticise Kohlberg).

EISENBERG'S THEORY OF PRO-SOCIAL BEHAVIOUR

Eisenberg concentrated on the reasoning behind pro-social behaviour rather than wrong-doing. She also used dilemma stories, but rather than "naughty" behaviour as in the case of Piaget, or law-breaking as in the case of Kohlberg, Eisenberg's stories involved dilemmas of self-interest versus helping someone. For example, Mary is on her way to a party when she meets a crying child who has hurt herself and asks Mary to go and fetch her mother. Her dilemma is whether to help and miss the best part of the party or whether to carry on and not get help. Eisenberg, Lennon, and Roth (1983, see A2PKT pp.231–232) proposed that pro-social thinking advances through five stages:

Stage	Age (approx.)	Reasoning	How it is demonstrated
Level 1: Self-centred	Up to 7 years	Main concern is the self	Would not help because they may miss the party or may help if directly rewarded
Level 2: Needs-oriented	7–11 years	Expressed concern without real sympathy or feelings of guilt if they do not help	Says, "Oh dear, you are hurt aren't you?" but does not stop for long
Level 3: Approval-oriented	11–14 years	Doing things in order to gain approval	Expresses view that "It's nice to help others" but is only likely to do so if they think others will praise them
Level 4: Empathetic	Adolescence and early adulthood	Genuine empathy shown and guilt if no help is given	Shows sympathy for others' plights
Level 5: Internalised	Adulthood	Actions based on internalised set of moral values and principles	Expresses the view that if everyone helped, the world would be a better place

EVALUATION

🙂 **Eisenberg's theory considers the development of pro-social behaviour, whereas most previous research in this area did not.** It has therefore extended our knowledge in this important area. It also considers the emotions (empathy, etc.) that people feel.

🙂 **The theory has important practical applications.** It can be used as the basis for advising parents how to raise pro-social, caring children (see A2PKT p.232).

🙁 **Children may show empathy at a much younger age than this theory implies.** Zahn-Waxler et al. (1979, see A2PKT p.232) found that very young children will sometimes show distress if they see another person in obvious pain.

🙁 **The stages on pro-social reasoning do not correspond to those on moral development.** Although there are parallels between some of Kohlberg's stages and those of Eisenberg, there is only a moderate positive correlation between stages when people are given both sets of dilemmas. This could be a negative evaluation of Eisenberg, or Kohlberg, or both. Eisenberg found that young children were more advanced than Kohlberg's theory would suggest.

GENDER DIFFERENCES IN MORAL DEVELOPMENT: GILLIGAN'S THEORY

KEY FEATURES

Gilligan suggests that males and females show different moral orientations:

- Males base their moral judgements on *justice*.
- Females base their moral judgements on *care*.

Gilligan's Research

Gilligan (1982, see A2PKT pp.229–230) interviewed women facing real-life dilemmas. She used an opportunity sample of 29 women who were facing unplanned pregnancies and discussed with them the reasons for the choices they were making with respect to whether or not to terminate the pregnancy. On the basis of detailed clinical interviews, she proposed a new theory based on three levels of moral reasoning; at each level the justice orientation is different from the care orientation, but neither one is superior to the other one (note that the levels correspond to Kohlberg's).

Stage	Justice	Care	Response based on care orientation
1	You should always uphold moral standards and not be persuaded by others not to do so.	You should base your decisions on how they will influence your relationships.	I will have a termination so my friends won't find out I've been careless. I will not have an abortion because my mother would go mad.
2	Moral principles are very important but they should be tempered with mercy. Some account should be taken of circumstances.	It is more important to consider others, and your relationship with them, than to stick rigidly to conventional rules.	I will have an abortion because the other children will suffer if I don't. I will not have a termination because that would upset the child's father.
3	There may be occasional exceptions to rules but, generally speaking, society operates best with a set of universal laws that are obeyed by everyone.	Moral rules should be upheld in a way that values the individual and brings minimum harm to those concerned.	Whatever decision I make, it must be one that not only I, but also the important people in my life, can live with. It is not solely my decision but must involve all those affected who are old enough to appreciate the situation.

RESEARCH EVIDENCE

- Gilligan and Attanucci (1988, see A2PKT pp.229–230) interviewed 80 men and women about real-life dilemmas they had personally experienced and found that men tended to have a justice orientation and women tended more towards a care orientation, although most people showed elements of both.

EVALUATION

🙂 **The research has considerable ecological validity.** This is because it is all based on real-life situations actually being experienced or having been experienced. The interviews were lengthy and the data collected was both in-depth and insightful.

Her theory takes account of welfare for others. Although not all research supports Gilligan's ideas on gender differences (see below), she has made a valuable contribution to the research and theory of moral thinking by demonstrating that much moral thinking is based on a genuine consideration for the welfare of others. Her research has shown that moral thinking is not simply based on a justice orientation.

 The theory takes account of female attitudes. Gilligan has criticised psychologists for only investigating male attitudes and behaviour and then generalising them to women. She has put the study of women on the agenda.

 Reviews of studies have not supported the gender differences outlined by Gilligan. Contrary to the theory, research indicates that both men and women use both justice and care orientations, both showing respect for justice and individual rights as well as care and compassion. Walker, de Vries, and Trevethan (1987, see A2PKT p.227) found individual differences in the tendency to emphasise either justice or care, but these were not along gender lines.

NOTE: The information on this page is very useful for the section on gender bias (Specification 14.2).

CULTURAL DIFFERENCES IN MORAL REASONING

Theories of moral reasoning tend to assume that all cultures are similar in the way moral thinking develops but this is not necessarily the case. Research has been conducted in mainly Judaeo-Christian cultures and demonstrates *culture bias.*

In the Western world, in individualistic cultures, there is an orientation towards individual rights, whereas in societies based on collectivist ideals, there is more of a care orientation.

RESEARCH EVIDENCE

Miller et al. (1992) researched people's responses to dilemma stories in which there were two possible solutions offered, one based on care, the other on justice. For example, a person is going to a friend's wedding abroad and has to deliver the wedding rings. He needs to catch the next bus to be on time but, at the station, he has his money and train tickets stolen as well as all his credit cards. Although he pleads for help, he receives none. He then has the opportunity to steal plane tickets from a reasonably wealthy man who has left his jacket on a chair with the tickets clearly visible. Should he do that (care orientation— not letting down his friend) or should he not (justice orientation)?

Sixty per cent of participants from the US tended to choose the justice orientation on these dilemmas, whereas participants from India were overwhelmingly inclined to make judgements based on care orientation.

SO WHAT DOES THIS MEAN?

These results indicate that people from an individualistic culture base their moral decisions on justice and individual rights while those from collectivist cultures base their judgements on care of other people. Nevertheless, Berry et al. (1992, see A2PKT p.228) found that where serious moral issues are concerned, Indian and American views are fairly similar. Until more detailed research is done in other cultures, we cannot confidently know whether post-conventional morality is universal (the same in every culture) or culture specific (different in different cultures).

OVER TO YOU

1. Describe and evaluate two theories of moral development. **(24 marks)**

2. Critically consider the role of gender and culture on moral thinking. **(24 marks)**

3.(a) Describe one theory of pro-social reasoning. **(12 marks)**

  (b) Evaluate this theory in terms of other theories and/or research evidence. **(12 marks)**

QUESTIONS AND ESSAY PLANS

1(a) Outline Vygotsky's theory of cognitive development.　　　　　**(6 marks)**

(b) Outline one or more applications of Vygotsky's theory of cognitive development.　　　　　**(6 marks)**

(c) Evaluate this application/these applications of Vygotsky's theory of cognitive development.　　　　　**(12 marks)**

Part (a): Remember that this is only worth 6 marks and do not be tempted to spend too much time on it (a maximum one third of the time for the whole question). You need to carefully and precisely summarise Vygotsky's views on the importance of culture, the ZPD, scaffolding, and language. A couple of sentences on each is more than enough.

Part (b): Develop the points made in part (a) as they relate to application of the theory to education. Again, do not be tempted to write too much, as you are simply describing NOT evaluating in this section. Mention the significance of the teacher being aware of the ZPD of each individual child and of the advantages of peer tutoring.

Part (c): All of this is AO2 and is your opportunity to write more fully and to carefully develop the arguments in terms of advantages and limitations of these applications. Mention the evaluative points made on pages 107–108 but remember that it is also useful to evaluate from other perspectives. Therefore, as well as evaluating Vygotsky, you can also briefly put forward Piaget's view both in terms of similarity and differences. For example:

- Piaget argued, as Vygotsky did, that children learn through being active, not simply by being told, and that a child cannot learn a task until they have the capacity to understand the underlying concepts.

- However, there are fundamental points of disagreement in that Vygotsky placed far greater emphasis on the role of the teacher, whilst Piaget believed that if you show a child how to do something rather than giving them materials that encourage them to discover it for themselves, you may actually inhibit understanding.

- On the whole, Vygotsky's views are upheld in that children can probably benefit more than Piaget believed by being instructed. Nevertheless, it may in some part depend on the particular task.

Conclude with reference to the usefulness of Vygotsky in drawing attention to the fact that anyone who knows more than the child, not simply teachers and other adults, can greatly enhance a child's learning. Vygotsky's views on peer tutoring have added a new and important dimension to our views on a child's cognitive development.

2 "Today, a majority of psychologists believe that differences in intelligence result from a combination of heredity and environmental factors."

Discuss this statement in relation to research into the development of intelligence test performance.　　　　　**(24 marks)**

You need to be very focused on the actual question. Include only evidence from intelligence test performance, rather than just putting in evidence for genetic versus environment regardless of whether it applies to intelligence test performance. If you go off the beaten track, you will gain few marks.

Paragraph 1 Introduction

Provide a brief outline of the argument, whether intelligence is environmental or genetic. Mention that intelligence is difficult to measure and that this has traditionally been done in terms of the results of intelligence tests.

Paragraph 2

Explain that results from intelligence tests demonstrate that there are social class and racial differences in performance. Mention that, with respect to race, this has been used to argue that blacks are genetically inferior to whites. This obviously has important political implications.

Paragraph 3

Assess whether it is reasonable to assume that differences in intelligence test performance are due to genetics rather than bias inherent in intelligence test performance. Outline the main reasons why intelligence tests are biased in favour of white, middle-class, traditionally educated individuals, exploring issues such as the specific knowledge required, the approach to a testing situation (the attitude to testing), the type of language used in the questions, and so on.

Paragraph 4

Present evidence for the argument that tests are biased, e.g. Zigler et al. (1973). Note evidence from Williams (1972) on the use of less biased tests and that of Serpell (1979) comparing English and Zambian children on different types of tasks.

Paragraph 5

Mention *briefly* other evidence regarding the genetic/environment influence on intelligence, since most of it is based on measures of intelligence using conventional tests.

Paragraph 6 Conclusion

As long as we have no really adequate way of assessing intelligence other than by the use of flawed tests, which are biased towards one specific group of people, it is insensitive and dangerous, as well as grossly inaccurate, to use these test results to make statements about the relative importance of genetics versus environment. Indeed to do so provides ammunition in an intensely socially sensitive area.

Furthermore, some would argue that such a debate is pointless (you could state Hebb's argument that it is akin to trying to ascertain whether length and breadth is more important in determining area). Hence, it is futile to focus on genetics versus environment, as it is impossible, both ethically and practically, to draw any meaningful conclusions. It could be argued that it is in the best interests of society and individuals for researchers in this field to abandon this argument in favour of finding ways to maximise everyone's potential.

3 Critically consider the role of gender and culture on moral thinking.

(24 marks)

Think of this in terms of two 12-mark questions, one on gender and the other on culture, each requiring the same amounts of AO1 and AO2, describing and evaluating equally.

Paragraph 1 Introduction

Define moral behaviour and touch on the fact that as the theories are universal they don't mention differences in gender or culture.

Paragraph 2

Consider gender differences first. You need a brief overview of Kohlberg since this was Gilligan's critical starting point. Be very brief in your coverage of the theory. Criticise from the point of gender. Mention that research was done on men, the levels were drawn up on that basis, and then females were considered "inferior" because they tend to come out at level 2, conventional morality (good boy/nice girl or law and order), while men are more likely to be post-conventional (level 3).

Paragraph 3

Cover Gilligan's theory and research briefly. Emphasise that she used real-life dilemmas and detailed clinical interviews. She then asserted that men and women are different—men have a justice orientation while women are socialised into a care orientation. This care orientation comes out in Kohlberg's scheme as conventional, since it involves taking note of what others think. Evaluate Gilligan's views, mentioning both good and bad points.

Paragraph 4

Discuss cultural differences. There isn't a great deal of research on cross-cultural studies and this is the first point to make. Briefly evaluate the original research on moral development with respect to culture—that it's based on Judaeo-Christian cultures. Also mention general problems of cross-cultural research—particularly the problems of researchers inevitably not being able to appreciate cultures that are not the ones in which they were raised. This always makes cross-cultural research difficult because no researcher can make genuinely objective comparisons across cultures. Problems notwithstanding, this research is important. Outline the divide between individualistic and collectivist cultures, mentioning that although somewhat simplistic, this division is useful.

Paragraph 5

Describe the research from non-Western cultures, using examples such as Miller et al. (1992). Make reference to Berry et al. (1992) that, with respect to serious moral issues, there may be universal principles that apply rather than differences. However, without more detailed research, we simply do not know whether post-conventional morality is the same or different in different cultures.

Paragraph 6 Conclusion

Bring gender and culture together by pointing out the impossibility of a universal morality if gender and culture have an influence on the levels. On the other hand, perhaps it is possible to have a universal theory but only when more thorough research has been conducted across both genders and with a variety of different cultures.

Question 1 adapted from AQA A2 [Winter 2002] Psychology Examination Papers.
The authors are responsible for the solutions and (a) they have neither been provided nor approved by AQA and (b) they may not necessarily constitute the only possible solutions.

Developmental Psychology

SOCIAL AND PERSONALITY DEVELOPMENT

Specification 13.4

6

What's it about?

Developmental psychology focuses on the changes that occur as humans move through different life stages. You studied the first stage of development at AS in the topic "Attachments in development". In this unit we are going to focus on three other areas of development: personality, gender, and adolescence. Developmental influences include physical maturation (where development may be fixed by age), unconscious desires and instinctual drives within the psyche, and social and cultural learning. We'll consider the complex interaction of internal and external factors that determine personality. Then we'll look at the psychological and biological theories of gender development and so assess the extent to which gender is biologically determined or socially constructed. Finally, we'll consider adolescence and the evidence for and against this as a time of crisis.

What's in this unit?

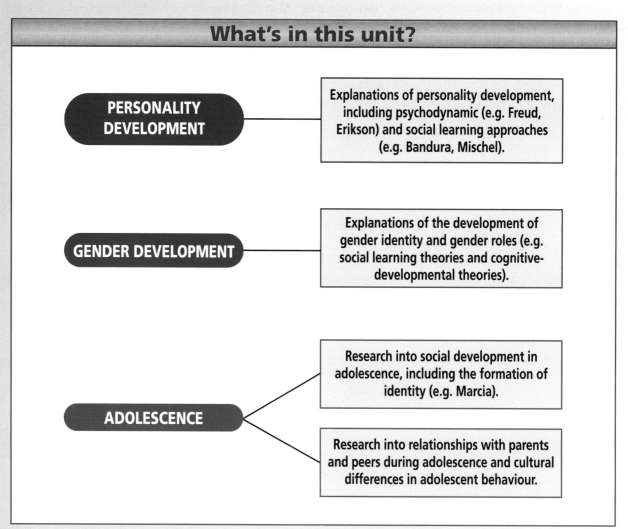

PERSONALITY DEVELOPMENT — Explanations of personality development, including psychodynamic (e.g. Freud, Erikson) and social learning approaches (e.g. Bandura, Mischel).

GENDER DEVELOPMENT — Explanations of the development of gender identity and gender roles (e.g. social learning theories and cognitive-developmental theories).

ADOLESCENCE — Research into social development in adolescence, including the formation of identity (e.g. Marcia).

Research into relationships with parents and peers during adolescence and cultural differences in adolescent behaviour.

PERSONALITY DEVELOPMENT

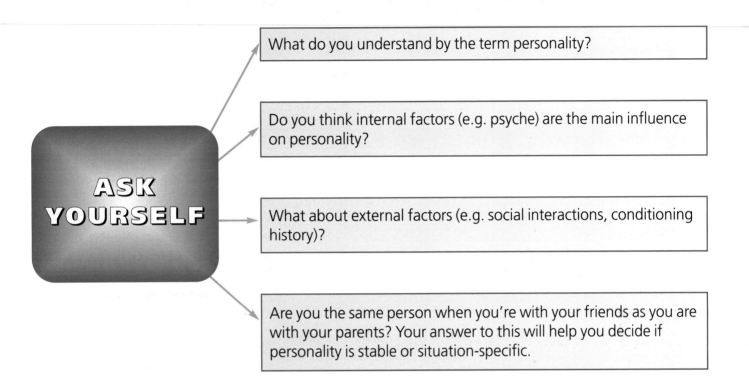

ASK YOURSELF

What do you understand by the term personality?

Do you think internal factors (e.g. psyche) are the main influence on personality?

What about external factors (e.g. social interactions, conditioning history)?

Are you the same person when you're with your friends as you are with your parents? Your answer to this will help you decide if personality is stable or situation-specific.

WHAT YOU NEED TO KNOW

THE PSYCHODYNAMIC APPROACH

- Psychodynamic theories of personality, e.g. Freud and Erikson. These explanations focus on the internal psyche as the determinant of personality.

SOCIAL LEARNING APPROACHES

- Social approaches to personality, e.g. Bandura and Mischel. These explanations focus on the interaction between the individual and their environment as the explanation of personality, as people are both a product of, and creator of, their environment.

Freud's psychodynamic theory and Bandura's social learning theory are covered in depth, and the other theories are described so that you have enough information to achieve breadth and can use them as counter-perspectives.

To read up on personality development, refer to pages 239–257 of A2PKT.

THE PSYCHODYNAMIC APPROACH

Freud's Psychoanalytic Theory

According to Freud, *personality* is made up of different levels of awareness and so is both conscious and unconscious. Personality develops out of *childhood conflicts* that arise within the psyche and between instinctual drives (aggressive and sexual) and early experience (the extent to which these desires were gratified). These conflicts are repressed into the unconscious to protect the individual from emotional threat. The unconscious mind influences personality and behaviour to a large extent. The libido (sexual energy) is the most important motivating force according to Freud, and this refers to all forms of pleasurable sensations, *not* just sex.

THE STRUCTURE OF THE PERSONALITY

Freud's metaphorical concept of the three structures of the mind or psyche:

The Id
The *id* acts on the pleasure principle because it expects immediate satisfaction of innate sexual (the life instinct—Eros) and aggressive (the death instinct—Thanatos) instincts. It is located in the unconscious and is present from birth.

The Ego
The *ego* balances the demands of the id and superego and the external demands of society. It acts on the reality principle and is the "self" because it is the conscious part of the mind and develops during the first 2 years of life.

The Superego
The *superego* acts on the morality principle. It is the conscience and ego ideal and develops from 5 years onwards, once the child has learnt a sense of right and wrong through socialisation.

Freud's three levels of consciousness
These can be represented as an iceberg, where the majority, the *unconscious*, is below surface level, the *preconscious* is just under the surface level and so information can be raised into the *conscious*, the tip of the iceberg, above surface level.

Conscious: The thoughts, emotions, and desires we are currently aware of.

Preconscious: Information that can be brought into conscious awareness, as it is accessible in memory.

Unconscious: Innate drives and instincts (e.g. food, sex) and information that has been repressed due to its emotional threat and therefore is difficult to access and bring into conscious awareness.

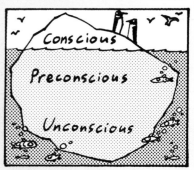

DEFENCE MECHANISMS

Conflicts arise frequently between the id, ego, and superego, and the ego tries hard to resolve these. To protect itself from the anxiety or guilt caused by these conflicts the ego uses defence mechanisms, i.e. barriers that prevent the individual from becoming overwhelmed by the impulses of the id. The id, ego, and superego fight to control our behaviour; this and the consequent defence mechanisms shape adult personality.

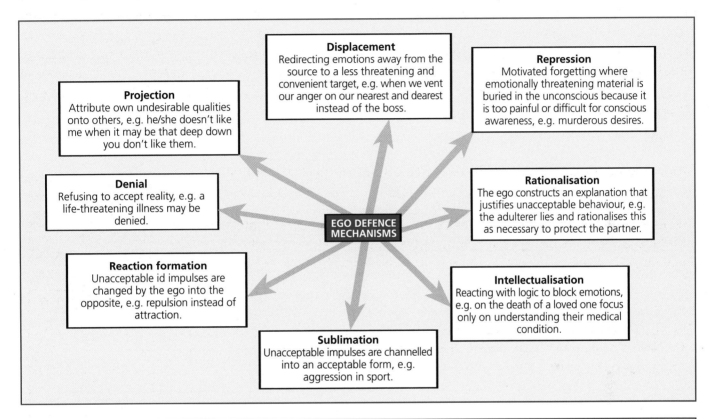

Displacement
Redirecting emotions away from the source to a less threatening and convenient target, e.g. when we vent our anger on our nearest and dearest instead of the boss.

Repression
Motivated forgetting where emotionally threatening material is buried in the unconscious because it is too painful or difficult for conscious awareness, e.g. murderous desires.

Projection
Attribute own undesirable qualities onto others, e.g. he/she doesn't like me when it may be that deep down you don't like them.

Denial
Refusing to accept reality, e.g. a life-threatening illness may be denied.

Rationalisation
The ego constructs an explanation that justifies unacceptable behaviour, e.g. the adulterer lies and rationalises this as necessary to protect the partner.

EGO DEFENCE MECHANISMS

Reaction formation
Unacceptable id impulses are changed by the ego into the opposite, e.g. repulsion instead of attraction.

Intellectualisation
Reacting with logic to block emotions, e.g. on the death of a loved one focus only on understanding their medical condition.

Sublimation
Unacceptable impulses are channelled into an acceptable form, e.g. aggression in sport.

Psychosexual Development

Stage	Age	Key points
Oral	0–18 months	Satisfaction is derived from the mouth, e.g. eating, sucking, etc. Weaning can cause conflict.
Anal	18–36 months	Satisfaction is derived from the anal region. Toilet training can cause conflict.
Phallic	3–6 years	The genitals are a key source of satisfaction. The Oedipus complex occurs, where the boy desires his mother and fears castration from the father who he sees as his "love rival". Girls desire their father during this stage and experience penis envy, where they blame their mother for the lack of a penis. Penis envy is substituted by desire for a child. Identification with the same-sex parent resolves the conflict. Jung reinterpreted this stage for girls with the Electra complex, which mirrors the Oedipus.
Latency	6 years–puberty	Sexual desires are strongly repressed and so libidinous desires are reduced.
Genital	Puberty+	Satisfaction is derived from the genitals and is the basis for mature and adult expressions of love.

(To remember the order of these stages—**OAPLG: Old Age Pensioners Love Greens.** Or, even better, make up your own one!)

Thus, Freud suggests a *stage theory* of personality development. Development is driven by the libido (sexual energy) of the id. Problems or excessive pleasure at any of the stages can lead to *fixation* where the individual's pleasure is rooted within a stage as the libido energy is attached to it or *regression* can occur to the preferred psychosexual stage. The phallic stage is the most important stage of psychosexual development and so is thought to have the greatest influence on adult development.

PERSONALITY IS AN OUTCOME OF MANY INFLUENCES

Development is driven by the libido (sexual energy) of the id

The id, ego, and superego conflict in their attempts to control behaviour

Unresolved conflicts between the id, ego, and superego lead to defence mechanisms

The consequent unconscious motivations stunt psychosexual development due to fixation in childhood and regression in adulthood to the stage of childhood fixation

This manifests in personality types and disorders

Personality Types

Fixation	Personality type	Characteristics
Oral stage	Oral receptive personality	Very trusting, dependent on others
	Oral aggressive personality	Aggressive and dominating
Anal stage	Anal receptive personality	Very generous and giving
	Anal retentive personality	Mean, stubborn, obsessively tidy
Phallic stage	Phallic personality type	Self-assured, vain, impulsive
Genital stage	Genital personality type	Well-adjusted, mature, able to love and be loved

RESEARCH EVIDENCE FOR

- Little Hans case study (see A2PKT p.376). This is the only research evidence Freud provided that involved a child! Freud only met Hans twice and so the case study was mostly based on interviews and observations by the boy's father, a member of Freud's psychoanalytic society. It supports psychosexual development as Hans did have a preoccupation with his penis from age 3½, e.g. he asked his mother if she would like to put her finger on it, and experienced castration anxiety after she told him it would be cut off if he didn't stop playing with it. He also recalled a dream of two giraffes where he took away a crumpled one and sat on it which made the big giraffe cry out. This was interpreted as his desire for his mother and fear of his father's reaction.

- Anna O is another well-known case study (see A2PKT p.240). She underwent hypnosis with Freud to treat hysterical symptoms. Under hypnosis, symptoms were traced to early childhood experiences and her father's sickness and death. Re-experience of these during hypnosis enabled her to express the emotions she had repressed at the time and this cured some of the hysterical symptoms.

- Self-analysis. Freud used his own experience as a source of empirical data and set aside half an hour each day for self-analysis. He rarely accepted the validity of a hypothesis if he could not relate it to his own behaviour.

- Research on repression came up at AS as part of the topic Human Memory. For example, Myers and Brewin (1994, see A2PKT p.244) support the validity of repression as they showed that people do repress anxiety-provoking material. *Perceptual defence*, the concept that things are likely to be ignored if they are unpleasant or emotionally threatening, supports this idea.

RESEARCH EVIDENCE AGAINST

- Bowlby (1973, see A2PKT p.376) provided an alternative psychodynamic explanation based on his attachment theory. Hans' mother would threaten to leave the family in order to discipline Hans and so Bowlby suggested that Hans experienced separation anxiety rather than Oedipal conflicts. Bowlby's theory of attachment is strongly supported and so is a persuasive alternative explanation.

- Fromm (1970) suggested that Hans' mother was the source of his anxiety, not his father. According to Fromm, the mother had fantasies about her son and caused his castration anxiety. So Freud's key evidence isn't entirely consistent with the Oedipal theory and therefore casts doubt on the validity of psychosexual development.

- Counter-perspectives contradict Freud, e.g. Erikson (1959, see A2PKT pp.245–248), a neo-Freudian, rejected Freud's emphasis on sexual development and concentrated on the role of social factors in ego development. Social learning theories suggest that personality development is a more active process than either of these stage theories suggest, as the child engages and interacts with the environment rather than progressing through predetermined stages. Social learning theory accounts for the ever-changing nature of personality, whereas Freud presents it as fixed.

- The social learning approach contradicts the psychodynamic *stage* approach, as according to Bandura (see A2PKT pp.248–252) personality is the result of the individual's interaction with the environment, which means development is person-specific and so challenges generic stages.

EVALUATION

🙂 **Significant and influential.** Freud's theories have had an enormous impact on psychology and influenced much further research into the dynamics of the mind.

🙁 **Era-dependent and context-bound.** Freud's emphasis on sex may be due to the repressiveness of the Victorian era. This is unlikely to be the same in the permissive society of many cultures today, and so temporal validity may be limited.

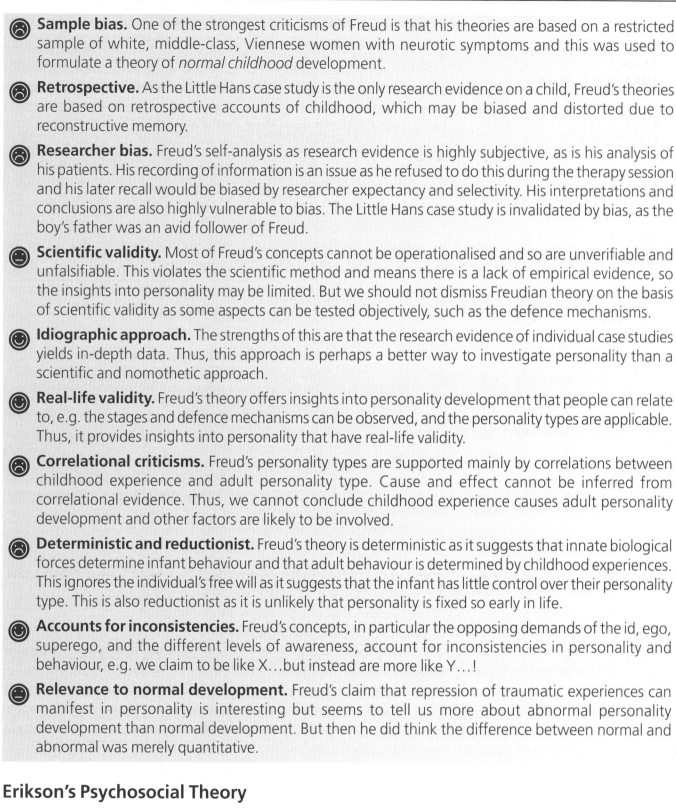

Sample bias. One of the strongest criticisms of Freud is that his theories are based on a restricted sample of white, middle-class, Viennese women with neurotic symptoms and this was used to formulate a theory of *normal childhood* development.

Retrospective. As the Little Hans case study is the only research evidence on a child, Freud's theories are based on retrospective accounts of childhood, which may be biased and distorted due to reconstructive memory.

Researcher bias. Freud's self-analysis as research evidence is highly subjective, as is his analysis of his patients. His recording of information is an issue as he refused to do this during the therapy session and his later recall would be biased by researcher expectancy and selectivity. His interpretations and conclusions are also highly vulnerable to bias. The Little Hans case study is invalidated by bias, as the boy's father was an avid follower of Freud.

Scientific validity. Most of Freud's concepts cannot be operationalised and so are unverifiable and unfalsifiable. This violates the scientific method and means there is a lack of empirical evidence, so the insights into personality may be limited. But we should not dismiss Freudian theory on the basis of scientific validity as some aspects can be tested objectively, such as the defence mechanisms.

Idiographic approach. The strengths of this are that the research evidence of individual case studies yields in-depth data. Thus, this approach is perhaps a better way to investigate personality than a scientific and nomothetic approach.

Real-life validity. Freud's theory offers insights into personality development that people can relate to, e.g. the stages and defence mechanisms can be observed, and the personality types are applicable. Thus, it provides insights into personality that have real-life validity.

Correlational criticisms. Freud's personality types are supported mainly by correlations between childhood experience and adult personality type. Cause and effect cannot be inferred from correlational evidence. Thus, we cannot conclude childhood experience causes adult personality development and other factors are likely to be involved.

Deterministic and reductionist. Freud's theory is deterministic as it suggests that innate biological forces determine infant behaviour and that adult behaviour is determined by childhood experiences. This ignores the individual's free will as it suggests that the infant has little control over their personality type. This is also reductionist as it is unlikely that personality is fixed so early in life.

Accounts for inconsistencies. Freud's concepts, in particular the opposing demands of the id, ego, superego, and the different levels of awareness, account for inconsistencies in personality and behaviour, e.g. we claim to be like X…but instead are more like Y…!

Relevance to normal development. Freud's claim that repression of traumatic experiences can manifest in personality is interesting but seems to tell us more about abnormal personality development than normal development. But then he did think the difference between normal and abnormal was merely quantitative.

Erikson's Psychosocial Theory

Erikson is a neo-Freudian because his work is heavily influenced by psychoanalysis but is distinct from it, as he did not agree with Freud's emphasis on the sexual and aggressive drives. As the name of the theory suggests, Erikson focuses on social factors. Like Freud's it is a stage theory and a specific conflict (i.e. life crisis) characterises each stage. He suggests that it is the individual's navigation of life stages and resolution of the crises within these that determines ego development and thus personality.

Erikson's Psychosocial Theory

Stage 1
INFANCY 0–1 year → *Life crisis:*
Trust vs. mistrust in self and others

Stage 2
TODDLER 2–3 years → *Life crisis:*
Autonomy (independence) vs. shame and doubt

Stage 3
PRE-SCHOOL 4–5 years → *Life crisis:*
Initiative vs. guilt

Stage 4
CHILDHOOD 6–12 years → *Life crisis:*
Industry vs. inferiority

Stage 5
ADOLESCENCE 13–19 years → *Life crisis:*
Identity vs. role confusion

Stage 6
EARLY ADULTHOOD 20–30 years → *Life crisis:*
Intimacy vs. isolation

Stage 7
MIDDLE ADULTHOOD 30–60 years → *Life crisis:*
Generativity (productivity) vs. stagnation

Stage 8
OLD AGE 60+ years → *Life crisis:*
Integrity vs. despair

SOCIAL LEARNING APPROACHES

According to social learning approaches, personality develops from social experiences and interactions.

Social Learning Theory

Bandura (1977, 1986, see A2PKT pp.248–250) expanded upon traditional learning theories, classical, and operant conditioning (see chapter 12 on Approaches) as his theory takes into account the role of *cognition* in behavioural responses to environmental stimuli. Conditioning accounts for direct learning only as, according to this, all behaviour is a result of learned associations and reinforcement, and cognition plays no role in these stimulus–response bonds. This suggests that personality development is passive as it is merely a response to environmental programming. Bandura felt this was oversimplistic as it fails to account for the *active interaction* between the child and the environment. He proposed that learning can be indirect and that cognitive factors are involved in observational learning and vicarious reinforcement.

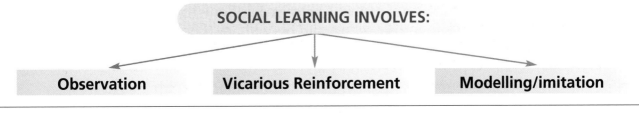

SOCIAL LEARNING INVOLVES:

| Observation | Vicarious Reinforcement | Modelling/imitation |

Modelling—A four-step process			
Attention	**Retention**	**Reproduction**	**Motivation**
The model must command attention for observational learning to take place.	The model must be remembered and recalled.	Imitation requires personal skills, otherwise we could all sing well and play football!	This depends on past, promised (incentives), and vicarious reinforcement and punishment.

Modelling is also called observational learning as we learn from observing the *consequences* (vicarious reinforcement or punishment) of other people's (role models) behaviour and this generates expectations. Thus, if we see certain behaviours being rewarded we are more likely to imitate them and if we see certain behaviours being punished we are likely to avoid that type of behaviour. Role models include parents, older children, and public figures.

Social learning influences *reciprocal determinism* and *self-efficacy* and both of these shape personality.

RECIPROCAL DETERMINISM

Bandura rejected the traditional learning theories' claim that behaviour is shaped solely by external factors (i.e. the environment) as deterministic and reductionist (oversimplified). The individual is a product of, and a creator of, their environment, i.e. the situation affects behaviour and behaviour affects the situation and other people, which in turn affect behaviour. He proposed that an interaction of the individual's behaviour, psychological factors, and the environment shape personality.

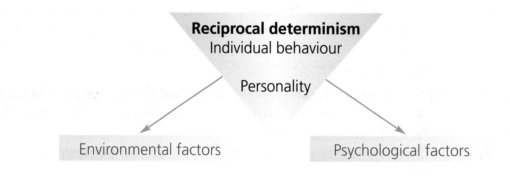

The individual's personality is a consequence of psychological abilities, which influence social learning and these determine how the individual chooses to interact with the environment, which determines future social learning.

SELF-EFFICACY

This is the individual's self-belief in his/her own effectiveness. The individual exerts control over self-efficacy through self-regulation, i.e. we monitor our behaviour and judge whether it is satisfactory through comparison with others. The consequence of this is perceived self-efficacy, which will be rewarding or punishing in itself and may influence further self-reward or self-punishment.

So, reinforcement/punishment can be *vicarious*, *direct* (operant conditioning), or *self-generated* (if we feel good or bad about the particular behaviour), and this is fundamental to personality development as this influences reciprocal determinism, i.e. how the individual interacts with the environment.

Bandura concluded that personality was not fixed—people possess more and more different "selves" as they experience different situations, due to reciprocal determinism. Personality is dynamic, not stable, as characteristics change with experience.

RESEARCH EVIDENCE FOR

- Bandura's Bobo doll studies (Bandura, Ross, & Ross, 1961; Bandura, 1965, see A2PKT pp.76–77 and 249) support the power of observational learning as in this infamous research Bandura showed a film of an adult beating up an inflatable doll, "Bobo", to three groups of nursery school children. Each group observed a different outcome to the aggressive behaviour: one group saw the adult receive sweets, the second saw her told off, and the third, the control condition, saw neither a reward nor a punishment. The children were then observed at play—those in the reward and control conditions were equally aggressive to the doll.

- Harter and Monsour (1992, see A2PKT p.252) support the idea of many "selves" as they compared children of 12, 14, and 16 years and found that when asked to describe themselves with parents, friends, and at school, the older children reported more differences, which suggested they had developed many selves.

- Mischel's (1968, see A2PKT pp.252–253) situationalism approach expands and supports Bandura's concept that personality differs in accordance with the situation.

RESEARCH EVIDENCE AGAINST

- Cumberbatch (1990, see A2PKT p.77) argues that there is intrinsic pleasure in knocking down a Bobo doll, which acts as a confounding variable, as children who did not witness an aggressive role model also showed aggressive behaviour. Aggression may be due to the nature of the toy rather than observational learning and this undermines validity.

- The psychometric approach to personality contradicts the concept that personality changes depend on the context. Trait theories of personality such as those of Eysenck, Allport, Cattell, and Kelly suggest that personality is relatively fixed and unchanging.

- Research on genetic inheritance shows consistent patterns of personality in families, which also contradicts the concept that personality is inconsistent.

- Erikson and Freud take a much more developmental approach to personality than Bandura and so a key weakness of social learning theory is that it doesn't provide enough insight into the development of personality.

EVALUATION

 Accounts for cognitive and social factors. A key strength of social learning theory is that it takes into account cognitive and social factors, which are ignored in traditional learning theories.

Active process. It takes into account that personality is an active process as the child engages with the environment (reciprocal determinism) rather than the passive processes suggested by psychodynamic and conditioning theories.

Reductionism and determinism. It is less reductionist and deterministic than traditional learning theories and so is a more realistic explanation of the complexity of personality as it places responsibility on the individual for their own behaviour.

 Explanatory power. Bandura's theory lacks explanatory power, as he does not explain in enough detail how children's personalities change during the course of development.

SITUATIONALISM

Mischel and Peake (1982, see A2PKT p.253) suggest that the "consistency paradox" leads to the misperception that people are consistent across situations and so have a stable personality. This is due to a cognitive bias called the fundamental attribution error, which is our tendency to minimise the influence of the situation and exaggerate dispositional influences because this simplification helps us to better

understand others' behaviour. Mischel believes this is not true—personality is not consistent because there is a great deal of inconsistency in people's behaviour across situations. He called this inconsistency *behavioural specificity*. This means the individual's behaviour is specific to certain situations because it depends on the reinforcement received. Mischel supported behavioural specificity with research evidence that found no correlation between friends, family, and unknown observers' ratings of participants' behaviour.

Mischel also explained individual differences as he identified a number of person variables (see figure on right).

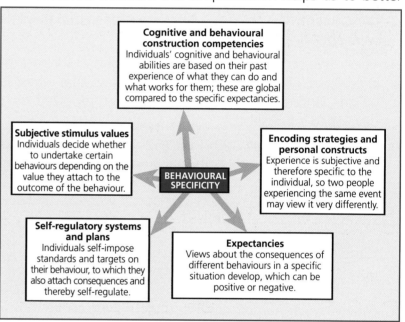

Cognitive and behavioural construction competencies
Individuals' cognitive and behavioural abilities are based on their past experience of what they can do and what works for them; these are global compared to the specific expectancies.

Subjective stimulus values
Individuals decide whether to undertake certain behaviours depending on the value they attach to the outcome of the behaviour.

BEHAVIOURAL SPECIFICITY

Encoding strategies and personal constructs
Experience is subjective and therefore specific to the individual, so two people experiencing the same event may view it very differently.

Self-regulatory systems and plans
Individuals self-impose standards and targets on their behaviour, to which they also attach consequences and thereby self-regulate.

Expectancies
Views about the consequences of different behaviours in a specific situation develop, which can be positive or negative.

SO WHAT DOES THIS MEAN?

The validity of Freud's theory is questionable yet it is difficult to disregard because some aspects are not only plausible but also observable, e.g. the stages of psychosexual development and some of the defence mechanisms. But unconscious instincts and motivations shaping personality is a fairly passive portrayal of personality development and so lacks mundane realism, as it does not account for the flexibility and dynamism of personality. Social learning theory, with its focus on the active reciprocal relationship between the individual and the environment, does account for this. A multi-perspective combining the two approaches and biological influences will yield the most insight into personality development as this will account for the psyche, internal and external factors, and the interaction of these factors.

OVER TO YOU

1. **Discuss psychodynamic and social learning explanations of personality development.**

   (24 marks)

GENDER DEVELOPMENT

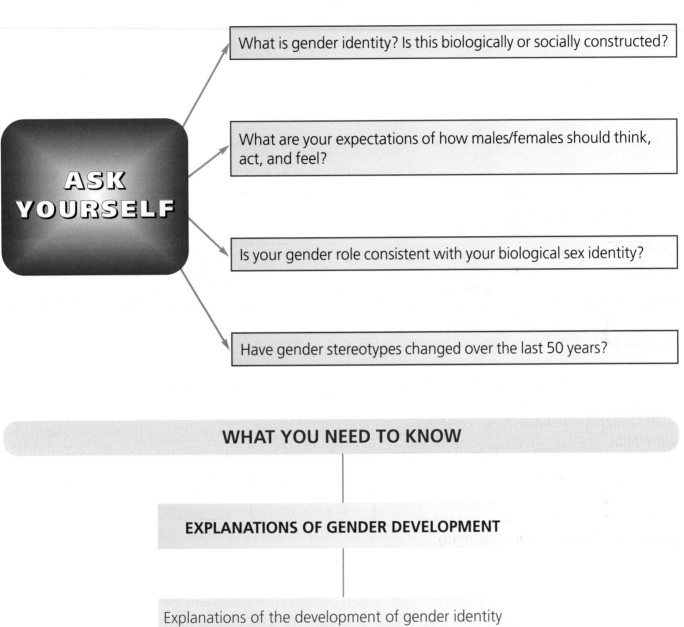

ASK YOURSELF

What is gender identity? Is this biologically or socially constructed?

What are your expectations of how males/females should think, act, and feel?

Is your gender role consistent with your biological sex identity?

Have gender stereotypes changed over the last 50 years?

WHAT YOU NEED TO KNOW

EXPLANATIONS OF GENDER DEVELOPMENT

Explanations of the development of gender identity and gender roles:

- Cognitive-developmental theory (Kohlberg, 1966)
- Social learning theories (Bandura, 1977, 1986)
- Biosocial theory (Money & Ehrhardt, 1972)

Kohlberg's cognitive-developmental theory and biosocial theory are covered in depth, and the other theories are described so that you have enough information to achieve breadth and can use them as counter-perspectives.

To read up on gender development, refer to pages 257–274 of A2PKT.

EXPLANATIONS OF GENDER DEVELOPMENT

Cognitive-developmental Theory

According to Kohlberg (1966), an understanding of gender develops over time and *gender role* develops from *gender identity*. Children attend to same-sex role models and find it rewarding to emulate them once they have developed a consistent gender identity. This occurs in stages and is an active process of cognitive structuring and maturation.

Basic gender identity/gender labelling (2–3½ years)
Prior to age 2 children are not very aware of gender but at this age they begin to categorise themselves and others based on this dimension, e.g. "I'm a big girl/boy now". Children are aware of gender identity but do not see it as fixed. They believe it is possible to change gender as they judge it on superficial characteristics, e.g. women have long hair and so if a boy grew long hair then his gender would change.

Gender stability (3½–4½ years)
Children perceive gender to be stable over time, i.e. girls will become women and boys will become men, but it is not yet stable over situations, as children believe gender can change depending on clothes worn or gender inappropriate behaviour.

Gender consistency/constancy (4½–7 years)
Children realise that gender is stable over time and situations. They no longer base gender on superficial characteristics as they realise that it is underlying and permanent. At this stage Kohlberg claims the child internalises their own gender identity and as a consequence becomes much more focused on same-sex models, and so gender role develops.

RESEARCH EVIDENCE FOR

- Kohlberg (1966, see A2PKT pp.263–264) tested his theory by providing children with pictures and asking if gender would alter with changes to superficial characteristics such as hair or clothes. He found that it was only at about 5 years that children recognised the constancy of gender.

- Cross-cultural research suggests that children do progress through the three stages (Munroe, Shimmin, & Munroe, 1984, see A2PKT p.264).

- Research shows that children high in gender consistency attend more to a same-sex model than those lower in gender consistency, which shows that this concept plays a crucial role in gender development (Slaby & Frey, 1975, see A2PKT p.264).

- Research on the effect of TV advertisements (e.g. Ruble, Balaban, & Cooper, 1981, see A2PKT p.264) supports the validity of gender consistency as it showed that children's attitudes and behaviour was affected by adverts for toys for "boys" and "girls", and that this effect was greater for those with high gender consistency.

- According to Piaget (see A2PKT pp.173–174), *conservation* is an important aspect of cognitive development. This is when the child realises that changing the appearance of an object does not change its mass. Piaget tested this with the same amount of liquid in two differently shaped glasses. This occurs at about the same age as gender consistency and so provides construct validity, which supports Kohlberg.

RESEARCH EVIDENCE AGAINST

- Research that asks children about *themselves* shows that children aged 3 know that their gender will be the same when they grow up, which shows that gender stability and gender constancy may occur earlier than Kohlberg suggested, and so invalidates the stages.

- Children show gender stability at an earlier age if they play with gender-type toys (an indicator of gender identity and role development). This suggests that the child's early learning environment is an important factor that may be able to override cognitive development (Weinraub et al., 1984).

- Parental attitudes are also highly influential, particularly those of fathers, as a positive correlation between fathers' attitudes and behaviours and child preference for gender-type toys has been found, especially in boys (Weinraub et al., 1984). This suggests that social learning may be more influential than cognitive development and so challenges Kohlberg's cognitive theory.

- Social learning theory contradicts the direction of effect predicted by Kohlberg, that children attend to same-sex models only once gender identity has developed. According to social learning theory, gender identity is the outcome of attending to role models.

- Money and Ehrhardt's research (1972, see A2PKT p.268) on gender reassignment contradicts age 3½ as the beginning of gender stability. They believed that gender reassignment was possible if it was done before 3 years of age. But the problems shown by "Brenda" suggest that gender stability and gender constancy had occurred earlier.

EVALUATION

- **Significant and influential.** Kohlberg's research provided significant insights into the role of cognition in gender development and generated much further research.

- **Face validity.** Children do seem to develop through the three stages and so the theory has face validity despite some of the details being incorrect.

- **Timing.** The research evidence against Kohlberg questions the timing of the stages and this is a significant weakness of his theory. Most children show gender typical behaviour before the age of 2 years.

- **Two-directional not one.** Children show gender role behaviour before the development of gender constancy (4½ years). Thus, gender role is not simply the outcome of gender identity as predicted by Kohlberg. The relationship is two-directional, not one-directional, as he predicted.

- **Underemphasis on social context and overemphasis on the individual.** Kohlberg's focus on the individual's cognitive development means the social context is ignored. This is highly influential as the research evidence against shows the importance of external factors such as parental attitudes, and so is a key limitation.

- **Mundane realism and ecological validity.** The use of pictures in Kohlberg's study lacks mundane realism and may have biased the findings. The research showing that children show gender stability before the age of 3½ years if asked about themselves supports this criticism and so questions the ecological validity of the research.

😐 **Counter-perspectives.** Gender is not just socially constructed as the biosocial theory demonstrates. Kohlberg's theory is more descriptive than explanatory as it doesn't explain how gender cognition develops. Gender-schema theory provides more insight into this, but also lacks explanatory power. Social learning theory demonstrates the importance of external factors, such as rewards and punishments, which are ignored by Kohlberg and may account for the *why* in gender identity and role development.

Gender-schema Theory

This is an extension of Kohlberg's theory as it provides more insight into the active interaction between cognitive and social processes. According to Martin and Halverson (1987, see A2PKT p.265) children have developed a basic gender identity from the age of 2–3 years. They then construct *gender schemas—* organised beliefs about gender-typical behaviour.

Examples of gender schemas

Ingroup/outgroup schemas. This enables the child to distinguish between the behaviours and roles of males and females. Based on this, children develop a sense of gender-typical behaviours, such as which toys and activities are suitable for boys and girls.

Which of these are "boys' toys", which are "girls' toys", and which are gender-neutral?

Own-gender schemas. This contains information on how to behave in gender-stereotypical ways. Information on gender-consistent behaviour is assimilated into their own gender role.

The schemas are used to organise and process incoming information. This shows that children are not passive recipients in development—they actively engage with, select, and internalise information that helps them successfully enact their gender role. This occurs as soon as the child can distinguish male from female and therefore *before* gender constancy is achieved, as predicted by Kohlberg.

Social Learning Theory

According to Bandura (1977, 1986, see A2PKT pp.260–263) *social factors* are the key influence as, according to social learning theory, society shapes gender development. Gender identity and role are based on two key learning processes: direct tuition and social learning.

DIRECT TUITION

This involves learning through reinforcement and punishment (operant conditioning). According to this, children are rewarded for gender-appropriate behaviour and punished for gender-inappropriate behaviour. Parents and society deliver these and this leads to gender identity and gender role development.

SOCIAL LEARNING

This includes observational learning, vicarious reinforcement, and imitation of role models. The media, especially TV, is a key source of observational learning.

Social learning theory explains the development of gender stereotypes, which influence gender identity and gender role.

Comparing and contrasting cognitive-developmental theories and social learning theory		
	Cognitive-developmental	**Social learning theory**
Similarities	Account for development as an active process (except direct tuition). Development is an interaction between the child and the environment	
Differences	Emphasis on child Rewards are internal (self-imposed) Gender cognition gradually develops Accounts for general beliefs	Emphasis on environment Rewards are external (society) Gender learning is the same at any age Accounts for specific behaviours only

Biosocial Theory

Biological influences on gender identity include genetic differences as males and females share 45 out of 46 chromosomes and differ on one, the "Y"/"X" that determines sex-identity and is inherited from the father. Sex hormones are another influence as these determine genitalia and the development of secondary sexual characteristics at puberty, which are the biological basis of adult gender identity. But it is difficult to separate out the influence of nature and nurture because, as the psychological explanations suggest, boys and girls may be treated very differently from the day they are born. Consequently, the biosocial approach focuses on the interaction of biological and social factors. For example, early maturers may be treated differently to late maturers and so biological and social factors interact.

Research evidence is based primarily on rare cases of gender abnormality, where there is a conflict between sex-identity (biological) and gender identity (psychological). Testicular feminising syndrome (chromosomal males have female-looking genitalia because of insensitivity to testosterone) and adrenogenital syndrome (chromosomal girls have male-looking genitalia because of high levels of testosterone due to abnormal enzyme activity) have resulted in boys being raised as girls and vice versa, which offers insights into the role of biological predisposition (nature) and socialisation (nurture).

RESEARCH EVIDENCE FOR BIOLOGICAL FACTORS

- Due to a rare mutant gene, four children in the Batista family were born with the biological appearance of girls, but developed male genitals at puberty due to increases in testosterone. All four then lived as males and were accepted into the community as such. This physical change supports the role of biological factors in gender development (Imperato-McGinley et al., 1974, see A2PKT p.269).
- Money and Ehrhardt's (1972, see A2PKT p.268) study of male twins. One of the twin boys was raised as a girl due to a failed circumcision. Money and Ehrhardt believed gender reassignment was possible if it was within a critical period before 3 years of age. Brenda, as the boy was named, preferred "girls'" toys and was the "fussy little mother", and so seemed to support the influence of socialisation over biology. However, follow-up research found that Brenda suffered psychiatric disturbance and reverted to a male gender role at adolescence. This is strong evidence for biological factors.
- Brain-scanning techniques have identified gender differences in the brain, especially in areas related to sexual and reproductive behaviours such as the hypothalamus. Male hormones masculinise the brain during prenatal development and this influences hemisphere dominance and behaviour (Geschwind & Galaburda, 1985, see A2PKT p.268). Exposure of female mice to male hormones led to masculinisation and male-typical behaviour.

- Recent research on the hormone oxytocin, the "love and friendship" hormone, has found that women produce more of it and it is enhanced by oestrogen, whereas men produce less of it and it is inhibited by testosterone (Taylor, 2000). This has been linked to gender differences in friendships and nurturing behaviour and so is further support for the effect of biological factors on gender-specific behaviours.

- Sociobiological explanations suggest that genetic predisposition determines gender differences due to anisogamy, the difference in the size of the sexual gametes, which impacts on behaviour (see Chapter 7, Evolutionary Explanations of Human Behaviour).

- Cross-cultural studies (e.g. Williams & Best, 1982, see A2PKT p.271) show remarkably consistent gender stereotypes in otherwise very different cultures. Universality supports the role of biological factors in gender identity and role.

RESEARCH EVIDENCE AGAINST, I.E. SOCIAL FACTORS

- A case study of a woman with testicular feminising syndrome, Mrs DW, who had been brought up as female and only realised she was biologically male after consulting a doctor when she failed to fall pregnant. The fact that Mrs DW chose to remain a woman, despite being genetically male, seems to support the role of socialisation (reared as a girl). However, as Mrs DW did not respond to testosterone, we cannot be sure if her behaviour is more due to this abnormality in biology rather than social factors (Goldwyn, 1979, see A2PKT p.268).

- Mead's New Guinea study (1935, see A2PKT pp.270–271) identified a tribe, the Tchambuli, where the males cared for the children and the household. They gossiped and discussed how to look pretty, whilst the females were assertive and took responsibility for trade and the running of the village. This complete role-reversal of traditional Western gender roles supports the role of sociocultural factors in gender development.

- Changes in gender roles over time also demonstrate the influence of socialisation over biology, as change is inconsistent with a biological basis.

EVALUATION

- **Face validity.** It makes sense that biology influences behaviour, and research evidence does support this face validity.

- **Extrapolation.** The research findings on the masculinisation of the brain in mice must be accepted cautiously due to the issue of extrapolation.

- **Sample bias and generalisability.** The case study on Mrs DW lacks generalisability, as does Money and Ehrhardt's research, particularly as evidence for normal gender development.

- **Ethnocentrism.** Mead's study is criticised on the grounds of ethnocentrism. It has been suggested that she exaggerated differences and minimised similarities. In later writings she changed her position from ethnocentrism to cultural relativism. She recognised that some behaviours are innate and universal, e.g. males were more aggressive and went to war in each of the three tribes she studied, although these behaviours may be expressed differently across cultures.

- **Reductionism and determinism.** Research on genetic predisposition and hormones can be criticised for innate and physiological determinism, as this ignores the ability of the individual to control his or her own behaviour. A solely biological focus is reductionist as this tries to reduce a complex phenomenon to one factor.

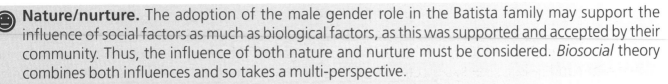

🙂 **Nature/nurture.** The adoption of the male gender role in the Batista family may support the influence of social factors as much as biological factors, as this was supported and accepted by their community. Thus, the influence of both nature and nurture must be considered. *Biosocial* theory combines both influences and so takes a multi-perspective.

🙁 **Ethical issues.** In cases of gender abnormality, gender is assigned often without consent, which has led to problems later when the wrong gender has been assigned. Money and Ehrhardt can be criticised for deception as they were aware of problems in the gender reassignment of Brenda but did not disclose them.

SO WHAT DOES THIS MEAN?

A reciprocal relationship between the child and the environment is fundamental to gender identity and gender role development, as suggested by the psychological theories. If we accept that gender is largely determined by environmental influences then the theoretical implications are that gender development will change in accordance with changes in society and so any research into gender identity and gender role lacks temporal validity. However, whilst there has been change, there is also remarkable consistency in gender roles across cultures, e.g. males are more aggressive and instrumental in every culture and females tend to be more nurturing and expressive, and this suggests that gender is biologically driven (Barry, Bacon, & Child, 1957, see A2PKT p.271). A multi-perspective that accounts for the interaction of biology, learning, and cognition, and so nature and nurture, offers the most insight into gender identity and role development.

OVER TO YOU

1. Describe and evaluate one or more explanations of gender identity and gender role development.

(24 marks)

ADOLESCENCE

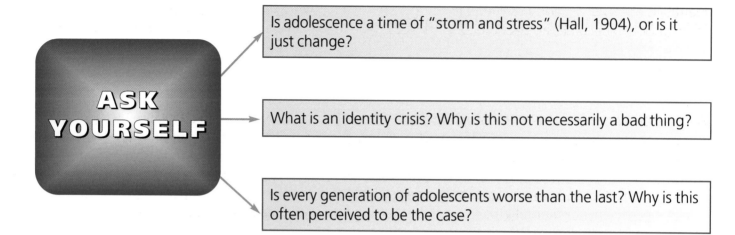

ASK YOURSELF

Is adolescence a time of "storm and stress" (Hall, 1904), or is it just change?

What is an identity crisis? Why is this not necessarily a bad thing?

Is every generation of adolescents worse than the last? Why is this often perceived to be the case?

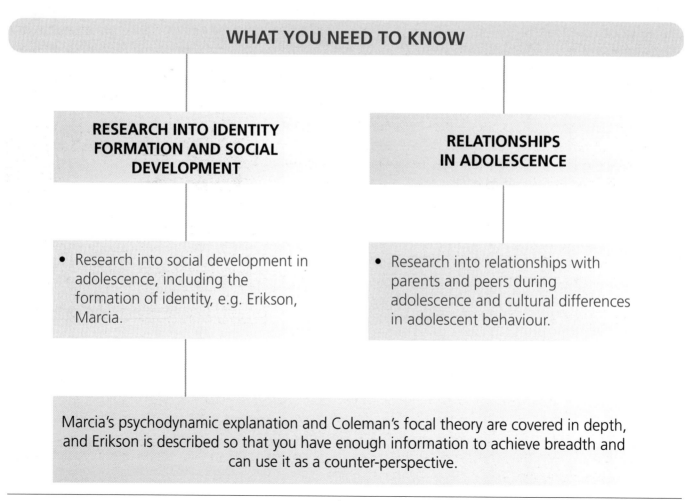

WHAT YOU NEED TO KNOW

RESEARCH INTO IDENTITY FORMATION AND SOCIAL DEVELOPMENT

- Research into social development in adolescence, including the formation of identity, e.g. Erikson, Marcia.

RELATIONSHIPS IN ADOLESCENCE

- Research into relationships with parents and peers during adolescence and cultural differences in adolescent behaviour.

Marcia's psychodynamic explanation and Coleman's focal theory are covered in depth, and Erikson is described so that you have enough information to achieve breadth and can use it as a counter-perspective.

To read up on adolescence, refer to pages 279–293 of A2PKT.

RESEARCH INTO IDENTITY FORMATION AND SOCIAL DEVELOPMENT

Identity is one's perception of self and tends to be based on physical attributes and personal characteristics in childhood. It becomes more complex in adolescence and so is an important aspect of social development.

The Psychoanalytic Approach

ERIKSON'S PSYCHOSOCIAL THEORY

As covered under personality development, Erikson (1950, 1968, 1969, see A2PKT pp.276–280) takes a stage approach to development (see earlier in this chapter) and proposed that a crisis characterised each stage. He was heavily influenced by Freud but focused on social rather than sexual factors. He suggests eight different stages and crises across the life span. Stage 5 is adolescence, and the life crisis is identity vs. role confusion, and it is the equivalent of Freud's genital stage. He introduced the term *identity diffusion* to refer to the strong sense of uncertainty adolescents have about their identity. Erikson identified four aspects to this uncertainty:

1. *Intimacy*—fear of commitment as this may result in a loss of identity.
2. *Diffusion of time*—disbelief that time will bring change and fear that it might.
3. *Diffusion of industry*—a lack of concentration or too much concentration on one activity.
4. *Negative identity*—a scornful and snobbish hostility to the role offered by family and community.

Adolescents experience an identity crisis because they do not know who they are, who they will become, nor in which direction they want their life to go. Major life decisions need to be made, which add to the stress and anxiety caused by the uncertainty. Erikson believes that the crisis should not be resolved too quickly, as *premature foreclosure* may result in an identity crisis in later life. Consequently, he recommends a *psychosocial moratorium* (now known as the "gap year"!), which means delaying the onset of adulthood so that the individual has time to try out different attitudes, roles, beliefs, and occupations before making his or her life choices. He believes this is the best way for the individual to gain a true sense of self.

Erikson proposed that an identity crisis is a normal part of development and is a prerequisite to the formation of a stable identity. He has contributed to the widely-held belief that adolescence is a time of stress and uncertainty, which can lead to high drama. It's important to note that his theory was based on his *observations* of emotionally disturbed adolescents undergoing therapy.

MARCIA'S IDENTITY THEORY

Influenced by Erikson, Marcia (1966, 1980, see A2PKT pp.280–284) also focused on adolescence as a time of identity crisis. He expanded upon what he sees as an oversimplified explanation—he believes that there are different reasons why a stable identity is not achieved. He also introduced more precise methods for assessing identity diffusion and identity formation, which have enabled his theory to be tested empirically. His theory centres on the four statuses of identity diffusion, foreclosure, moratorium, and identity achievement.

Marcia assumed that the individual would move from a low identity status (diffusion and foreclosure) to a high identity status (moratorium and identity achievement) as a result of pressure to assume an adult identity. He differs from Erikson because he does not see these four statuses as stages and so not all individuals pass through each status. However, he believed, like Erikson, that a moratorium is needed for successful identity achievement and that the identity crisis must be resolved before adulthood if the individual is to cope with this and be successful.

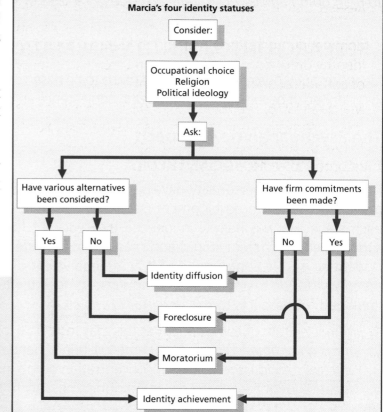

RESEARCH EVIDENCE FOR

- Marcia used a semi-structured interview to question adolescents' occupational choice, religion, and political ideology. He proposed the four statuses based on his findings.

- Marcia's findings suggest that it is important to distinguish which of the four aspects of identity development is experienced as those in the moratorium felt much more positive than those in the diffusion and foreclosure statuses, and this supports the validity of the statuses.

- Meilman (1979, see A2PKT pp.281–282) supports the four statuses in his replication of Marcia's semi-structured interview as he found evidence of all four in his study of 12- to 24-year-old males, and that the statuses were related to age. For example, the young men in his sample aged 12–18 were more likely to have a diffusion or foreclosure identity status, whilst those over 18 were more likely to have identity achievement. This supports the reliability and validity of Marcia's research and theory.

- Waterman (1982) found that diffusion and foreclosure were most common during adolescence in a sample of 11- to 17-year-olds. This supports ecological validity as it shows that it can be applied to real life.

RESEARCH EVIDENCE AGAINST

- Not everyone experiences an identity crisis and not everyone achieves a stable identity by the end of adolescence. Meilman's (1979, see A2PKT pp.281–282) research found that many in their early 20s had failed to achieve a stable identity. This shows that identity confusion does not necessarily end at adolescence. Few individuals were in the moratorium status, which suggests that not everyone experiences identity crisis and achievement.

- Archer (1982) criticised Marcia's linking together of occupational choice, religion, and political ideology as oversimplified, as only 5% of adolescents had the same identity status in all four areas. Thus, Marcia's theory is reductionist and lacks discrimination, as identity is more complex than the theory implies. This means validity is questionable.

- Munro and Adams (1977, see A2PKT p.283) found that college students were more likely to be in the moratorium period than their peers in full-time work. This shows the importance of sociocultural factors, which Marcia did not consider.

- Research on parenting style shows that this can affect identity formation. Waterman (1982, see A2PKT p.284) found that affectionate parenting is linked to identity achievement and moratorium, domineering parenting is linked to identity foreclosure, and aloof and distant parenting is linked to identity diffusion. Thus, Marcia can be criticised for too much of a focus on the individual and a lack of consideration of the wider social context.

- Marcia's (1976, see A2PKT p.283) later research revealed a key omission in Erikson's, and his own, theory. They assumed that, once achieved, a stable sense of identity is unlikely to be lost. But Marcia's follow-up research showed that some of the adolescents who had achieved a stable sense of identity returned to earlier identity statuses.

EVALUATION

Realism. Marcia's approach to identity is more flexible than Erikson's, who tends to see it as all or nothing, i.e. identity achievement vs. diffusion. Marcia's representation of the concepts first identified by Erikson as different identity statuses is more realistic because it is more representative of real-life identity formation.

Androcentric and eurocentric. Marcia's (and Erikson's) research was conducted on mainly Western (eurocentric) males (androcentric) and so generalisability is questionable as it may not be representative of other social groups. It displays the usual gender bias of using the male as the standard of normality.

Interview weaknesses. Marcia's use of the semi-structured interview means that the evidence on identity formation lacks reliability and validity. Interviewer bias and participant reactivity may have led to demand characteristics where the participants say what they think the interviewer wants to hear rather than the truth. This means the research evidence provides only weak empirical support for Marcia's theory.

Reductionism. The four statuses, like any classification system, can be criticised as being oversimplified because it is unlikely that they account for individual differences.

Descriptive rather than explanatory. Marcia *describes* four identity statuses rather than explaining how they arise and how the individual progresses from one to another. Consequently, his theory lacks explanatory power, as it covers *what* happens but not *why*.

Temporal validity. The semi-structured interviews provide only a snapshot of real life; they don't tell us how adolescents develop and how identity can change over time.

Nomothetic and cross-sectional vs. longitudinal and idiographic. Marcia has taken a nomothetic and cross-sectional approach as he suggests a generalisable process of identity formation and investigates an individual at one point in time. Whilst such an approach may be practical, it can be argued that it is not the best approach. A longitudinal and idiographic approach, which charts the individual's identity formation over time, may provide more valid evidence.

The Social Approach

COLEMAN'S FOCAL THEORY

Coleman (1974, see A2PKT pp.284–285) contradicts the psychoanalytic view that identity crisis is a normal part of adolescence as he does not consider crisis to be a requisite of healthy development. He suggests that the majority of adolescents do not experience crisis because they are able to focus on and resolve problems as they occur, hence the term *focal theory*. Those that do experience crisis will have additional external pressures. Thus, he agrees with the idea that it is a time of *change* but not that it is inevitably a period of "storm and stress" (Hall, 1904, see A2PKT p.284).

RESEARCH EVIDENCE FOR

- Coleman and Hendry (1990, see A2PKT pp.284–285) support focal theory with evidence from a large-scale study of interviews with boys and girls aged 11–17 years. Questioning on stressful subjects, such as self-image, career choices, and peer, sexual, and parental relationships revealed a distribution curve where worries about the different subjects peaked at different ages. This supports the concept that problems are dealt with and, to a large extent, resolved before the next issue arises, e.g. peer relationship concerns peak before occupational choice concerns.

- Rutter et al.'s (1976, see A2PKT p.275) Isle of Wight study supports focal theory as this showed that whilst young adolescents reported feelings of inner turmoil, severe disturbances could be traced to psychiatric problems in *childhood*. Thus, the problems existed before adolescence. In cases where problems did first appear in adolescence, family conflict tended to be the stressor that triggered these, which supports the social approach's emphasis on external pressures.

- Research on cross-cultural differences (see A2PKT pp.287–289) supports Coleman's focus on the social group as the key determinant of adolescence.

- Research on good parental relationships (e.g. Ryan & Lynch, 1989, see A2PKT p.286) supports Coleman's claim that adolescence need not be a time of stress.

RESEARCH EVIDENCE AGAINST

- Biological explanations of development predict that we all follow a fairly universal pattern. Therefore adolescence is biologically constructed, contradicting a social focus.

- Freud's approach can be contrasted with the social approach, as he believes adolescent crisis is more a consequence of early childhood conflicts than current external pressures.

- Research showing the wide range of individual variations contradicts the sociological emphasis on the social group and the lack of emphasis on the individual.

EVALUATION

- 😊 **High population validity.** The sample size was large in Coleman and Hendry's and in Rutter et al.'s research, which increases confidence in the generalisability of the findings.

- 😊 **Face validity.** Many individuals clearly do cope with adolescence without serious disturbance and so it does make sense that adolescence is a time of change but not necessarily of crisis. Certainly Coleman's emphasis on the external pressures at adolescence is integral to our common understanding of adolescence.

- ☹ **Self-report.** Participant and researcher effects may have biased the research.

- ☹ **Understanding of "crisis".** The term may not have been used to mean the same thing. Erikson and Marcia's understanding of it as a normal and healthy event suggests that they view it differently to Coleman, who seems to see it more as a psychological breakdown.

RELATIONSHIPS IN ADOLESCENCE

Socialisation refers to the process by which we learn the norms and values of our culture. Parents and peers are the key influences in this and the accepted view is that parental influence declines as peer influence increases.

Relationships With Parents

Relationships with parents are often perceived to deteriorate in adolescence and to become characterised by conflict and psychological distance.

RESEARCH EVIDENCE FOR CONFLICT

- Different approaches offer insights into why conflict may occur. For example, cognitive-developmental theories can explain conflict as the development of thoughts and opinions due to attainment of the formal operations stage of cognitive development. The sociological approach focuses on external pressures, such as the peer group, as a source of conflict in the home. The psychoanalytic approach links conflict to the adolescent's inner crisis and striving for independence. The evolutionary theory explains conflict as competition for resources. The humanistic perspective links conflict to a lack of unconditional positive regard and self-esteem.
- Smetana (1988, see A2PKT p.286) classified disputes into two types: (1) adolescent domains, e.g. time of getting up and going to bed, and (2) parental domains, e.g. not clearing up after a party, stealing. The latter were regarded as legitimate areas that the parent could exercise control over. Disputes arise when the parent tries to exercise control of adolescent domain issues.
- Conflict with parents is most likely if they feel their child has become involved with the "wrong crowd" (a deviant peer group), according to Dishion et al. (1991).

RESEARCH EVIDENCE AGAINST CONFLICT

- Cross-cultural research found that 91% of adolescents did not hold a grudge against their parents, and did not feel that their parents were ashamed of them. This contradicts the idea of conflict and shows that adolescents may be happy with their home situation (Offer et al., 1988, see A2PKT p.286).
- Conflict within the household is *not exclusive to adolescence* as we tend to conflict with the people we share a house with at any age. This is an important part of social life through which we learn to negotiate and compromise and so maintain a relationship despite the conflict (Durkin, 1977).

EVALUATION

- **Face validity.** Conflict with parents has face validity because it is commonly experienced during adolescence. But it may be that these conflicts are relatively minor and so their existence is not as defining of adolescence as early research suggests.
- **Criticisms of self-report.** The research evidence against conflict may be biased by the social desirability effect, whereby the participant wants to present him- or herself in the best light and so negates any problems within the parental relationship. Or demand characteristics may cause a biased response. Self-report is highly vulnerable to such researcher and participant effects, and this invalidates the research.

Relationships With Peers

Peer influence increases during adolescence. This is fairly indisputable and part of healthy development, as we need to function outside the family as an adult. Hence, there is a plethora of evidence for this.

RESEARCH EVIDENCE FOR

- Tests using Asch's paradigm to test conformity show that it peaks at 11–13 years (Costanzo & Shaw, 1966, see A2PKT p.288).

- Berndt (1979; see A2PKT p.288) found that conformity to adults' suggestions decreased with age, whereas conformity to the peer group increased.

- *Group socialisation theory* (Harris, 1997, see A2PKT p.288) claims that the peer group is far more influential than the parents and that, as long as adequate care is received, it would not matter who the parents were as the adolescents' behaviour is determined by the peer group. Harris claims that it is better to come from a bad family in a good neighbourhood than come from a good family in a bad neighbourhood!

- The peer group provides the adolescent with security and self-confidence outside the family and so is an important bridge between childhood and adulthood (Steinberg & Silverberg, 1986).

- Peer conformity is most likely a prerequisite of healthy development given that we all have a need for affiliation (Argyle, 1994).

- During mid-adolescence groups of friends normally form cliques, which give the members a sense of belonging outside the family (Rubin et al., 1998). As adolescence progresses the cliques are based on couples rather than individuals.

- Changes in relationships during adolescence support the concept that adolescence is a time of transition. The emphasis in relationships changes from platonic to sexual in late adolescence and this is often a time when cliques dissolve as love relationships form.

RESEARCH EVIDENCE AGAINST

- Humans are capable of multiple attachments and so an increase in attachment to peers does not necessarily decrease parental ties.

- Research evidence on parenting style suggests that the peer group is more influential in children of authoritarian parents than democratic parents, which suggests that peer influence may be limited by good parenting (Fuligni & Eccles, 1993, see A2PKT p.288).

- Parents and peers have different areas of influence; parental influence is likely to be stronger for issues such as education and career choices.

EVALUATION

- 😊 **Strong research evidence.** The amount and variety of research on the peer group provides indisputable evidence of its influence at adolescence.

- 😞 **Researcher bias.** Harris' group socialisation theory is controversial as it is difficult to accept that individual parents don't matter. This is of course a subjective viewpoint and so may lack validity.

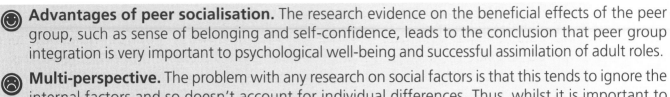

☺ **Advantages of peer socialisation.** The research evidence on the beneficial effects of the peer group, such as sense of belonging and self-confidence, leads to the conclusion that peer group integration is very important to psychological well-being and successful assimilation of adult roles.

☹ **Multi-perspective.** The problem with any research on social factors is that this tends to ignore the internal factors and so doesn't account for individual differences. Thus, whilst it is important to recognise the importance of social factors, a multi-perspective is needed to fully understand adolescent relationships.

Cultural Differences

Socialisation is a culturally relative process as the research evidence on cultural differences in adolescent behaviour demonstrates.

RESEARCH EVIDENCE FOR

- The individualistic (USA and Europe) vs. collectivist (Asia and China) dimension shows that different cultures have very different constructs of self. For example, individualistic cultures have an independent construct where sense of self is based on individual attributes and is egocentric, i.e. self-centred; and collectivist cultures have interdependent constructs where sense of self is based on the collective, i.e. how the individual fits as part of the group (Markus & Kitayama, 1991, see A2PKT p.289). These differences show that adolescence is culturally constructed.

- Some collectivist cultures discourage peer relationships to maintain the tie to the family, whereas in individualistic cultures the emphasis on independence means the family has less influence over peer relationships.

- Collectivist cultures with clear rites of passage often do not have a clearly identifiable period of adolescence. Mead (1928) reports that the transition from childhood to adulthood can be swift and is usually marked by a ritual that provides guidance on the adult role and identity. This suggests that adolescence is a cultural construction that results from individualistic cultures' educational and career structure. This provides the young person with so many options and freedom of choice that crisis often occurs. In the collectivist culture the young person is more acquiescent to parental guidance—this often involves "following in the father's footsteps" and is seen as a natural progression.

- The concept of adolescence is relatively new. According to Shaffer (1993, see A2PKT p.289), it is an "invention" of the twentieth century. The concept of the teenager is even more recent as this developed in the 1950s. This shows that adolescence is socially constructed and therefore a product of time and context, which reinforces the idea that it is culturally specific.

- Sub-cultural differences in identity formation during adolescence provide further support that this is culturally constructed. Adolescents from ethnic minorities tend to take longer to achieve identity formation. This makes sense because it is probably harder to carve out an identity if the ethnic identity deviates greatly from the dominant majority.

- The delinquent sub-culture is further evidence of cultural differences. Hargreaves' (1967, see A2PKT p.290) research on sub-cultures in a school population of 14- to 15-year-old boys in north-east England revealed that the delinquent sub-culture tends to comprise low achievers, and status and popularity are gained from anti-social behaviour rather than academic achievement. The sub-culture provided a sense of success and acceptance that was not available to the boys within the mainstream culture. The growing phenomenon of underachieving boys shows that the delinquent sub-culture is not necessarily based on lack of ability. It has appeal to students who could do well within the mainstream school culture if they had the motivation to do so. This shows that the cultural context is critical in adolescent identity formation because it is culture that constructs the deviant and nondeviant routes to this.

- Cross-cultural differences in attitudes to education exist. Stevenson et al. (1986) found that students in Asian cultures spend more time at school and complete more work. There is a strong belief in the long-term benefits of hard work and a high value placed on education. As a result, a more positive attitude to education exists than in Western cultures.

RESEARCH EVIDENCE AGAINST

- Barry, Bacon, and Child (1957, see A2PKT p.271) found a high level of cross-cultural similarity in the socialisation pressures experienced by boys and girls. Achievement and self-reliance were encouraged more in boys, and obedience, responsibility, and nurturance were encouraged more in girls, in both individualistic and collectivist cultures.
- Offer et al.'s (1988, see A2PKT p.286) study on the positive relationships adolescents had with their parents was conducted in individualistic and collectivist cultures and shows that there is also similarity across cultures.

EVALUATION

- **Strong research evidence.** The amount and variety of research on cultural differences and differences within the same cultures over time provides indisputable evidence that adolescence is culturally rather than biologically constructed.
- **Ethnocentrism.** Cross-cultural research is often biased because of the researcher's own cultural viewpoint, which invalidates the findings and interpretations. The Western norm is often imposed on other cultures, which is culturally biased.
- **Linguistic difficulties.** Research across cultures relies on translation, which can be a source of bias, as meanings can get lost in the translation. Other cultures' understanding of adolescence may also differ.

SO WHAT DOES THIS MEAN?

Adolescence has yielded much contradictory research, for example on the one hand the psychoanalytical approach presents it as a time of crisis and as a prerequisite of normal identity formation, but on the other hand the social approach rejects the inevitability of crisis or the necessity of this to health and well-being. Certainly, there is some merit in taking the middle ground here and concluding that experience of crisis is very much subject to individual differences. This is supported by the vast differences in adolescence across cultures. It doesn't even exist in some, and many argue it didn't exist in our own culture until it became illegal to employ children. Adolescence developed for those who were no longer considered adult (i.e. old enough to work), nor a child. This means that much of the research we have on adolescence and the adolescents' relationships (to parents and peers) is limited to a restricted Western population. Also, temporal validity is questionable as the construction of adolescence is dynamic. Puberty is beginning earlier and adolescence may be lasting longer as increasingly children live at home into their late 20s. To conclude, if we accept that adolescence is a time of psychological turmoil for some, then some of the responsibility for alleviating this must be placed on society, given that research evidence suggests that it is a cultural rather than a biological construction.

OVER TO YOU

1. Discuss research into social development in adolescence, including the formation of identity. **(24 marks)**

2. Discuss research into relationships with parents and peers during adolescence and cultural differences in adolescent behaviour. **(24 marks)**

Question 1 adapted from AQA A2 [Summer 2002] Psychology Examination Papers.

QUESTIONS AND ESSAY PLANS

Definition of personality: Personality is relatively stable and unchanging over time as it is an internal and underlying aspect of the individual, which gives rise to individually specific characteristics and behaviour that distinguish the individual from others.

Definition of gender identity: Social awareness of being male or female and incorporation of that into self-identity.

Definition of gender roles: Expectations of how each gender should think, feel, and behave.

Definition of adolescence: Adolescence is a period of transition between childhood and adulthood, which can range from 10 to 21 years. This stage of development is when the individual undergoes dramatic biological, social, and psychological changes.

1 Discuss psychodynamic and social learning explanations of personality development. (24 marks)

Paragraph 1

Define personality: Personality is relatively stable and unchanging over time as it is an internal and underlying aspect of the individual. Describe how the explanations have opposing focuses, as the psychodynamic explanation considers the internal psyche and innate biological processes, whilst the social learning explanation focuses mainly on external factors.

Paragraph 2

Describe Freud's stage theory, making sure that you include the structure of the personality; link this to the three levels of consciousness. Identify the defence mechanisms and summarise the stages of psychosexual development. Explain that early childhood conflicts and the consequent unconscious motivations, in particular the libido, determine personality development.

Paragraph 3

Use research evidence for (Little Hans, Anna O, Freud's self-analysis) and against (Bowlby, 1973, and Fromm, 1970) to discuss the validity of the psychodynamic approach. Then discuss Erikson's (1959) counter-perspective. Note that Erikson both supports and challenges Freud. Give an overall evaluation of the psychodynamic approach, e.g. retrospective; only one case study on a child; sample and researcher bias and so questionable scientific validity; era-dependent, context-bound, and reductionist. But it is a highly influential theory. Give an informed conclusion on how well you think it accounts for personality development.

Paragraph 4

Introduce social learning theory as a counter-perspective to psychoanalytic theory. Consider the differences, i.e. psychoanalytic theory is passive, whereas social learning theory is an active process. Psychoanalytic focuses on the individual's internal psyche, whereas social learning theory takes into account the interaction between the child and the environment (reciprocal determinism). Describe the four-step process in social learning: attention, retention, reproduction, and motivation. Emphasise the role of reinforcement—direct, vicarious, and self-generated—in shaping personality and explain how this is not fixed, as reciprocal determinism means we are different in different situations.

Paragraph 5

Discuss the research evidence for social learning theory, such as Bandura's Bobo doll studies (Bandura et al., 1961, Bandura, 1965), and give Cumberbatch's (1990) criticisms. Assess the concept of many selves using Harter and Monsour (1992), James (1890), and Mischel's (1968) situationalism as evidence for, and the psychometric approach and genetic research as evidence against. Use the psychodynamic approach as a counter-perspective to social learning theory as it takes a more developmental approach than social learning theory. Discuss the strengths and weaknesses of social learning theory, e.g. it accounts for cognition and development as an active process; less reductionist and deterministic. Conclude how well you think it accounts for personality development.

Paragraph 6

Assess the real-life validity of both explanations and use the multi-perspective to conclude.

2 Describe and evaluate one or more explanations of gender identity and gender role development. (24 marks)

Paragraph 1

Define gender identity: social awareness of being male or female and incorporation of that into self-identity, and gender role: expectations of how each gender should think, feel, and behave. Explain that explanations take into account the effect of cognition, social learning, and biosocial factors. Consider that to explain gender identity and gender role development it is necessary to understand gender differences.

Paragraph 2

Describe Kohlberg's (1966) cognitive-developmental theory, i.e. the three stages, basic gender identity, gender stability, and gender consistency/constancy. Consider the research evidence for Kohlberg's theory, including his own research, and research on the effect of gender consistency, such as paying more attention to TV adverts, which supports the validity of this stage of development. Use Piaget to support construct validity and consider face validity. Explain that, according to this theory, gender identity develops as a consequence of cognitive maturation and that gender role develops from a consistent gender identity.

Paragraph 3

Then consider the criticisms, the main one being that children seem to have a basic gender identity much earlier than Kohlberg suggested. Use research to support this, e.g. research that asks children about themselves, and Money and Ehrhardt's (1972) research on gender reassignment. Criticise the lack of consideration given to the social context, as research on parental attitudes shows the importance of this, and so this is a significant weakness. Use social learning theory as a counter-perspective as it takes into account the interaction of cognitive and social processes, and has greater explanatory power than Kohlberg's theory as it explains *why*, not just *how*, i.e. rewards and punishments. Also question the direction of effect as Kohlberg predicts gender role develops from a consistent gender identity, whereas social learning theory claims gender identity is the result of observing and imitating gender role models. Conclude how well you think it accounts for gender development based on the fact that it does account for general beliefs about gender.

Paragraph 4

Introduce the biosocial approach as a counter-perspective. Outline the biological influences on gender such as genetic inheritance and hormones, and consider the evidence for, e.g. gender abnormality case studies, brain scanning techniques, oxytocin, and sociobiological explanations. Emphasise that universality in gender roles across cultures supports the influence of biological factors.

Paragraph 5

Consider the evidence against biological factors, e.g. Mrs DW (Goldwyn, 1979), Mead's (1935) research on the Tchambuli tribe (note problems of ethnocentrism—much of her data was secondhand and she had a political agenda), and changes in gender role over time. Use the criticisms (face validity, extrapolation, generalisability, reductionism, determinism, and nature/nurture) to assess the validity of biological factors. Conclude that a lack of validity reduces the meaningfulness of the research and limits understanding of the role of biological and social factors.

Paragraph 6

Essentially gender identity and role development involve an interaction of biological and psychosocial factors and so a multi-perspective is needed to account for nature and nurture.

3 Discuss research into social development in adolescence, including the formation of identity. (24 marks)

Paragraph 1

Define adolescence: Adolescence is a period of transition between childhood and adulthood, which can range from 10–21. This stage of development is when the individual undergoes dramatic biological, social, and psychological changes. Explain the concept identity, i.e. one's perception of self, and how this becomes increasingly complex at adolescence.

Paragraph 2

Outline Erikson's (1950, 1968, 1969) psychosocial theory of identity formation, including key concepts such as identity diffusion, premature foreclosure, and psychosocial moratorium. Introduce Marcia's (1966, 1980) theory as a more elaborate version of Erikson's and describe the key points, e.g. the four statuses, and explain that this differs from Erikson because these are not stages and can be tested empirically. Explain that, according to the psychoanalytical approach, identity crisis is a normal and necessary part of the development of a stable identity.

Paragraph 3

Consider the research evidence for Marcia's theory, including his own research, Meilman's (1979), and Waterman's (1982). Then consider the evidence against, e.g. not everyone experiences an identity crisis; Marcia's theory is oversimplified as the individual may have different statuses for different aspects of identity (Archer, 1982); and doesn't account for sociocultural factors (Munro & Adams, 1977) such as parenting styles (Waterman, 1982). Evaluate Marcia's theory, e.g. realism, sample bias, interview weaknesses, reductionism, descriptive rather than explanatory, temporal validity. Consider that a longitudinal and idiographic approach may be preferable to a nomothetic and cross-sectional one. A key weakness is that neither Erikson nor Marcia recognised that identity formation could regress. That is, identity achievement can be attained and then lost.

Paragraph 4

Compare and contrast the social approach with the psychoanalytic approach and describe Coleman's (1974) focal theory. Use Coleman and Hendry's (1990) and Rutter et al.'s (1976) research as support. Then use the research on cross-cultural differences in adolescence to support the sociological approach. Conclude that, according to this theory, adolescence is a time of change but not necessarily of crisis.

Paragraph 5

Consider the evidence against the social approach, e.g. biological influences, the psychoanalytic approach, and individual differences. Then evaluate the validity and consider the different interpretations of the concept crisis.

Paragraph 6

Assess the real-life validity of both approaches and use the multi-perspective to conclude.

4 Discuss research into relationships with parents and peers during adolescence and cultural differences in adolescent behaviour.   (24 marks)

Paragraph 1

Define adolescence: Adolescence is a period of transition between childhood and adulthood, which can range from 10–21 years. This stage of development is when the individual undergoes dramatic biological, social, and psychological changes. Identify common preconceptions about adolescent relationships such as conflicts with parents and the increasing influence of peers. Then explain that cross-cultural differences mean that the very existence of adolescence can be questioned and suggest that this may be a socially constructed rather than a biologically determined stage in development.

Paragraph 2

Consider the research evidence for conflict in relationships with parents, e.g. the different approaches, Smetana's (1988) study on adolescent and parental domains, and Dishion et al.'s (1991) research on deviant peer groups. Then consider the evidence against, which suggests that adolescents get on well with their parents, e.g. Offer et al. (1988). Then consider that conflict is a normal part of house sharing (Durkin, 1997). Assess the research validity and make a conclusion about adolescents' relationships with parents.

Paragraph 3

Consider the research evidence for the importance of peer relationships in adolescence, e.g. research on peer conformity (Brendt, 1979, and Costanzo & Shaw, 1966), group socialisation theory (Harris, 1997), and research on cliques and how these change during the course of adolescence (Rubin et al., 1998). Then discuss the rather limited evidence against (adolescents can have multiple attachments and good parenting can counter the influence of peers), as the influence of peers is indisputable. Use the criticisms to complete this discussion, e.g. researcher bias which questions validity, the benefits of peer socialisation. Conclude that a multi-perspective is needed to fully understand adolescent relationships as this takes into account social factors and characteristics of the individual.

Paragraph 4

Present the evidence for cultural differences. Compare individualistic and collectivist cultures to show that adolescence doesn't exist in all cultures. Consider that it is historically a new concept in individualistic cultures. Then use examples of sub-cultural differences, e.g. deviant sub-cultures. Conclude that adolescence is socially constructed and therefore culturally relative.

Paragraph 5

Present the evidence against cultural differences, i.e. the biological explanations, which predict universality and are supported by Offer et al.'s (1988) study of similarity in relationships across cultures. Evaluate that there is stronger evidence for cultural differences, although there are methodological weaknesses, which limit the validity of such research. These methodological weaknesses include ethnocentric bias and the fact that other cultures' understanding of adolescence may have got lost in translation.

Paragraph 6

Conclude that there is strong evidence that adolescence is culturally relative. This suggests that the research on relationships has limited ecological and temporal validity, as it lacks generalisability to other cultures and it is difficult to predict how a socially constructed phenomenon will change over time. Changes in the parent/child relationship are evidence of this, for example the decrease in parent power and increase in child power.

Question 3 adapted from AQA A2 [Summer 2002] Psychology Examination Papers.
The authors are responsible for the solutions and (a) they have neither been provided nor approved by AQA and (b) they may not necessarily constitute the only possible solutions.

Comparative Psychology

EVOLUTIONARY EXPLANATIONS OF HUMAN BEHAVIOUR   Specification 13.5

7

What's it about?

Evolution refers to the gradual process of genetic transmission through natural selection of adaptive characteristics into the gene pool as a consequence of "survival of the fittest". This refers to reproductive success, not a physical characteristic—the "fittest" are those who have survived to reproduce. Evolutionary explanations have great explanatory power as they can account for a wide range of behaviours, even gossip, which apparently performs a vital function, as it is a source of interaction, akin to the social grooming of our evolutionary ancestors.

But are evolutionary explanations just highly creative stories? The validity (truth) of evolutionary explanations is a key issue. Explanations of human reproductive behaviour certainly make interesting reading as they account for gender differences in sexual selection, i.e. what is considered sexually attractive and how this results in different mating systems and strategies. Evolutionary explanations of mental disorders offer a new perspective on abnormality as they suggest that mental disorders may have functional purposes. Evolutionary explanations for intelligence raise questions such as, "Does size matter?" and if so, "Do males' bigger brains confer greater intelligence?" We will consider why the answer to that is a simple "No"!

What's in this unit?

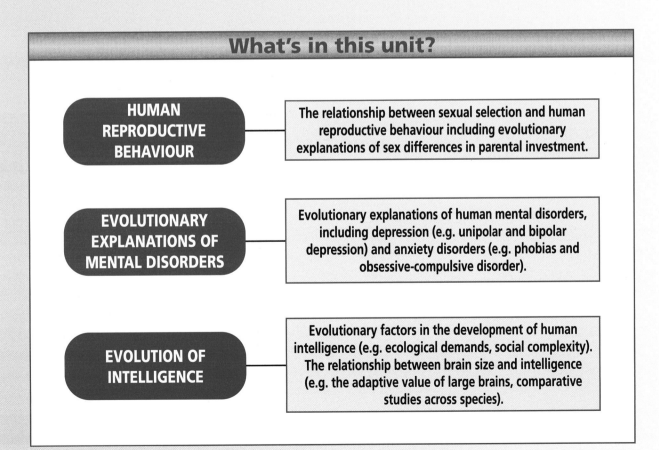

HUMAN REPRODUCTIVE BEHAVIOUR — The relationship between sexual selection and human reproductive behaviour including evolutionary explanations of sex differences in parental investment.

EVOLUTIONARY EXPLANATIONS OF MENTAL DISORDERS — Evolutionary explanations of human mental disorders, including depression (e.g. unipolar and bipolar depression) and anxiety disorders (e.g. phobias and obsessive-compulsive disorder).

EVOLUTION OF INTELLIGENCE — Evolutionary factors in the development of human intelligence (e.g. ecological demands, social complexity). The relationship between brain size and intelligence (e.g. the adaptive value of large brains, comparative studies across species).

HUMAN REPRODUCTIVE BEHAVIOUR

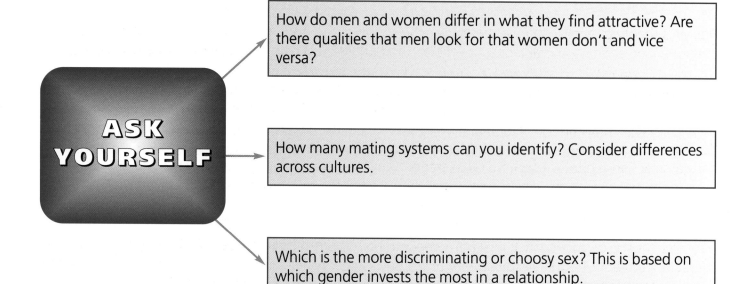

ASK YOURSELF

How do men and women differ in what they find attractive? Are there qualities that men look for that women don't and vice versa?

How many mating systems can you identify? Consider differences across cultures.

Which is the more discriminating or choosy sex? This is based on which gender invests the most in a relationship.

WHAT YOU NEED TO KNOW

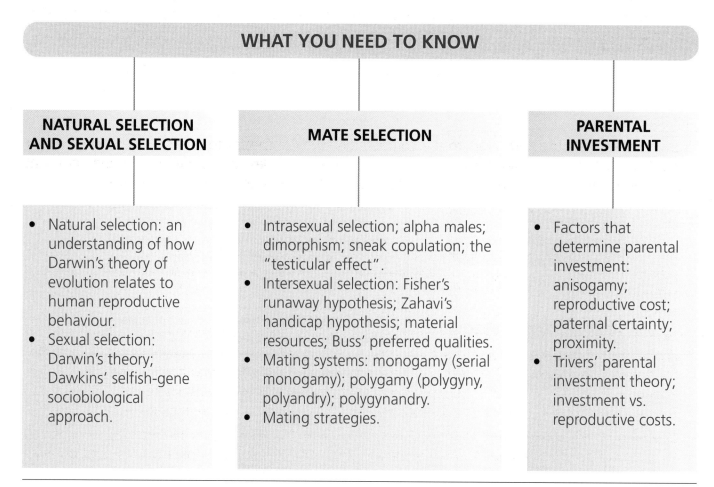

NATURAL SELECTION AND SEXUAL SELECTION

- Natural selection: an understanding of how Darwin's theory of evolution relates to human reproductive behaviour.
- Sexual selection: Darwin's theory; Dawkins' selfish-gene sociobiological approach.

MATE SELECTION

- Intrasexual selection; alpha males; dimorphism; sneak copulation; the "testicular effect".
- Intersexual selection: Fisher's runaway hypothesis; Zahavi's handicap hypothesis; material resources; Buss' preferred qualities.
- Mating systems: monogamy (serial monogamy); polygamy (polygyny, polyandry); polygynandry.
- Mating strategies.

PARENTAL INVESTMENT

- Factors that determine parental investment: anisogamy; reproductive cost; paternal certainty; proximity.
- Trivers' parental investment theory; investment vs. reproductive costs.

To read up on human reproductive behaviour, refer to pages 298–315 of A2PKT.

NATURAL SELECTION AND SEXUAL SELECTION

Natural Selection

Darwin's theory of evolution by *natural selection* suggests that the physical environment exerts selective pressure upon adaptive characteristics, which are traits (physical or behavioural) that increase the individual's *survival potential* because they enable them to better adapt to their ecological niche. Such adaptive traits differ within a species due to individual genetic variation and random mutation, which can generate further genetic variation. The adaptive characteristics are genetically transmitted (inherited) because the individual survives to reproduce and the characteristics are inherited by their offspring. This is known as "survival of the fittest", where fitness is measured by the number of genes present in the next generation. However, natural selection cannot account for characteristics that seem disadvantageous, for example, the peacock's tail and the stag's large antlers, both of which would inhibit escape from predators.

Sexual Selection

Darwin's theory of evolution by *sexual selection* (1871, see A2PKT pp.298–299) suggests that such characteristics are due to selective pressure from the social environment. This means they are selected because they increase *reproductive potential.* Features that denote reproductive fitness make the individual more attractive to the opposite sex or more able to compete and so increase the individual's chance of reproduction. Dawkins (1976) has expanded upon this in a sociobiological approach that considers further the interaction of social and biological factors as the basis of behaviour. Dawkins proposed the selfish-gene theory, which explains that fitness is based on the perpetuation of the genes, not the individual's survival. In the remainder of this subunit we consider aspects of sexual selection.

MATE SELECTION

Intrasexual Selection (the Male Strategy)

"Intra" means "within" and refers to the competition *within a species* to attract mates. The sex that invests least will compete over the sex that invests most. Thus, males compete to achieve the dominant position of the alpha male and so have exclusive access to females, the more investing sex.

RESEARCH EVIDENCE FOR

- Size *dimorphism* refers to the difference in size between the two forms, male and female. Darwin claimed this was influenced by sexual selection, as males tend to be bigger and so have greater physical strength, which is consistent with the claim that they must compete for access to females. Dimorphism is evidence of competition (intrasexual selection) and polygyny as it suggests that males fight for access to females. Dimorphism is not pronounced, which means polygyny is limited.

- *Alpha males* and *sneak copulation* are evidence of intrasexual selection. The fact that males compete for dominance is supported by nonhuman animal hierarchies, which show that less dominant males engage in secretive copulation when the alpha male is unlikely to detect such insubordination. Baboons may even work in pairs where one distracts the alpha male whilst the other engages in copulation.

- *Sperm competition theory* and the *"testicular effect"*. Short (1991) proposes that testicle size is related to the level of sperm competition. Comparing the testicle size of chimps, humans, and gorillas supported this. Body weight was controlled for and it was found that gorillas had the smallest testicles, followed by humans and chimps. This was consistent with Short's theory as gorillas are polygynous creatures, where the alpha male heads a harem, and so have little sperm competition, whereas chimps are promiscuous and so experience greater sperm competition. This supports intrasexual selection, as it is evidence of competition between males.

Intersexual Selection (the Female Strategy)

"Inter" means "between" and refers to the selection of characteristics between the genders, i.e. what they find attractive in the opposite sex. The females tend to do the choosing and their selection is accounted for by two hypotheses:

Fisher's runaway process: the "good taste" hypothesis	Zahavi's handicap hypothesis: the "good sense" hypothesis
Fisher's hypothesis (1930, see A2PKT pp.303–304) is also known as the "sexy sons" hypothesis as, according to this, the female's choice is based on desirable characteristics, as these will be inherited by her offspring. This will increase their chance of reproduction and so the survival of her genes. This becomes a runaway process, as more exaggerated versions of the characteristic are preferred, e.g. larger and larger tails in male peacocks.	According to Zahavi's hypothesis (1977, see A2PKT p.304) characteristics such as the peacock's tail are indicative of good genes because they have survived in spite of the handicap. It is also possible that such genes indicate health as only animals in good health could cope with such a handicap. Thus, such characteristics are selected because they indicate good genetic quality. Concar (1995, see A2PKT p.305) suggests that symmetry is due to good genes and so symmetry is perceived as physically attractive due to an innate sensory bias.

The female may also base selection on material resources as opposed to genetic resources. This also makes "good sense" in terms of eliciting care for her offspring but such characteristics are not inheritable.

RESEARCH EVIDENCE FOR

- Buss' (1989, see A2PKT pp.300–301) cross-cultural study of mate choice supports the "good sense" hypothesis as it shows that females are attracted to resources. Buss conducted a self-report survey across 37 cultures and found that males rated *youth* and *physical attractiveness* (indicators of health and child-bearing potential) as more important in a potential mate than females did and that females rated *resources* more highly than males did. This provides some support for evolutionary explanations as the stability and universality of the mate choice preferences may be evidence of a genetic basis.

- Personal advertisements support Buss' findings as Davis (1990, see A2PKT p.300) found gender differences in the qualities emphasised in the ads that were consistent with parental investment and sexual selection explanations. Women tended to emphasise their physical attractiveness and desire for a high-status man, whereas men tended to indicate their resources and their desire for a younger, physically attractive partner. This led Davis to conclude that women were looking for "success objects" and men for "sex objects".

- Clark and Hatfield (1989, see A2PKT p.300) support intersexual selection as it provides evidence that females are more discerning than males. In this study male and female college students were approached by confederates and asked if they would sleep with them that night. 75% of the male students accepted compared to none of the female students, which is evidence that females are more selective in their choice of partner.

- Females' promiscuity also supports the "good sense" hypothesis. According to Brown (2000, see A2PKT p.308), women are naturally promiscuous as they are genetically programmed to seek out variety as this increases reproductive potential. The adulterous female can mate with a partner with better genetic resources than her current partner.

- Research on pheromones (Kohl et al., 2002) provides further evidence for a "good sense" strategy. According to this we are attracted by pheromones (odourless chemical messengers) as these indicate genetic compatibility, i.e. that the mate has genes that are sufficiently different to our own. This also defends against incest.

RESEARCH EVIDENCE AGAINST INTRASEXUAL AND INTERSEXUAL SELECTION

- Strassberg's (1999) research on internet dating contradicts the traditional sexual stereotypes. Fictitious ads were placed, which advertised a woman as "very attractive", "passionate and sensitive", or "financially successful and ambitious". The latter received more replies than the physically attractive condition and this challenges evolutionary explanations—if mate choice preferences were coded in the genes they should be relatively stable and universal.

- Intrasexual selection and intersexual selection are not the strategy of one gender or the other. Female competitiveness is evidence of intrasexual selection. Moreover, perhaps the greatest indicator of intersexual selection is *neoteny* (child-like appearance) and as this is more pronounced in females than males we must be cautious in accepting the gender differences identified by evolutionary explanations.

- Social scientists challenge evolutionary explanations, as research on gender role socialisation may be a more valid explanation of sexual stereotypes. Social and cultural expectations may better explain the "double-standard" (i.e. promiscuity is acceptable in men but not in women) than evolved biological factors. *Social constructionism* can better account for changes and variations in behaviour, such as those found by Strassberg (1999), than the evolutionary explanations. Neoteny in females may be due to the fact that, historically, women had only their appearance to rely upon to attract a mate, as working and earning money were considered unsuitable for women. Thus, the greater female interest in beauty products and plastic surgery may be due to social factors rather than evolution.

Mating Systems

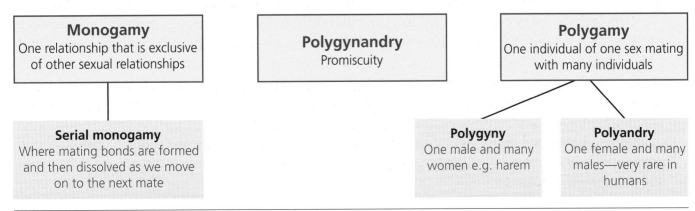

Monogamy
One relationship that is exclusive of other sexual relationships

Polygynandry
Promiscuity

Polygamy
One individual of one sex mating with many individuals

Serial monogamy
Where mating bonds are formed and then dissolved as we move on to the next mate

Polygyny
One male and many women e.g. harem

Polyandry
One female and many males—very rare in humans

Short (1991) concluded that we are not promiscuous as human testicles would be the size of tennis balls if we were as promiscuous as the chimps! But nor are we inherently monogamous. Thus, according to Short, humans are a polygynous species but this takes the form of serial monogamy, and this system is subject to adulterous liaisons from either gender.

Mating systems have been criticised because they ignore the wide variations within species. *Mating strategies* are a better approach as, according to this, the mating system can change to fit varying environmental conditions. For example, promiscuity can change to monogamy or vice versa. Humans may be naturally polygynous but if resources are limited (e.g. if the male cannot provide for numerous offspring) monogamy may be the preferred strategy. The premature birth of human babies and the need for prolonged parental care encourage monogamy. The high divorce rate is evidence that we are serial monogamists.

EVALUATION

- 🙂 **Face validity.** "Trophy wives", "gold diggers", and "sugar daddies" support the validity of the gender differences in mate choice identified by evolutionary theories.

- 🙂 **Universality.** Some human reproductive behaviour appears relatively universal. This supports evolutionary explanations as such consistency suggests a genetic basis. For example, the dilation of the eye in response to danger or an attractive mate is evidence of an evolved mechanism.

- ☹ **Lack of scientific validity.** Evolutionary theories lack empirical support; as they are post hoc, i.e. proposed after the event, we do not know they are true and so all explanations are inferences only. Also the evolutionary concept of the gene is criticised by geneticists, as complex behaviours are not coded onto the genes in the way suggested by evolutionists. The Genome Project has shown that traits are a consequence of many interlinked genes, which may be inconsistent with evolutionary accounts of human reproductive behaviour.

- ☹ **Self-report criticisms.** Buss' research can be criticised as it is subject to the researcher and participant effects that are weaknesses of self-report. Thus, participants may not answer truthfully due to evaluation apprehension or due to the social desirability effect. Furthermore, reported preferences are not necessarily representative of behaviour and so the validity of the research is questionable.

- ☹ **Researcher bias.** Buss, to some extent, magnified the gender differences and failed to highlight the many similarities between genders, e.g. the fact that kindness and intelligence were rated as equally important by both genders. This links to a criticism levelled at many evolutionary psychologists, which is that they are highly selective in their use of research evidence, which brings its validity into question.

- 🙂 **Natural experiments.** The research studies of Buss, Clark and Hatfield, and Davis are natural experiments because gender is a naturally occurring IV. Consequently, causation cannot be inferred, we cannot say that behavioural differences are caused by gender and so conclusions are limited. But they may have greater real-life validity than more controlled, artificial research.

- ☹ **Contradictory and so unverifiable and unfalsifiable.** Female promiscuity as a natural behaviour seems inconsistent with parental investment and sexual selection explanations. Surely the selection in the first place should be better? Would she risk her partner's investment in her offspring for the sake of an affair? This is another case of evolutionary explanations being used to explain any pattern of behaviour that occurs because they can be neither verified nor falsified. This has led to the criticism that they are little more than evolutionary stories, as reliability and validity are limited.

- ☹ **Ethical issues.** Feminists have challenged evolutionary theories as sexist as they give scientific legitimacy to the double standard in sexual promiscuity and support an oppressed female role and so perpetuate stereotypes and discrimination.

Extrapolation. Much of the research into evolutionary explanations in human behaviour is based on animal research and so extrapolation is an issue as there are qualitative differences between humans and animals. Cultural transmission plays a much greater role in human behaviour than animals and so the generalisability of the explanations may be limited.

Evolutionary continuum. The existence of the phylogenic tree and the fact that differences between humans and animals may be more quantitative than qualitative challenges the criticism that extrapolation is an issue.

Determinism. Evolutionary theories are considered deterministic because they suggest that genes control behaviour, which ignores the free will of the individual, i.e. their ability to control their own behaviour. Whilst evolutionary psychologists do not usually take the view that we cannot escape our genes, the theories themselves can appear deterministic.

Reductionism. Evolutionary theories are reductionist as they focus on one factor only, the gene, when other emotional, social, cognitive, behavioural, and developmental factors are highly relevant to human reproductive behaviour. They are oversimplified accounts at best, which is illustrated by the fact that relationships are not just about reproduction. Evolutionary theories cannot account for women who do not want children or for homosexual relationships. Emotions such as love are ignored.

Postmodernism and social constructionism. According to postmodernism there are no universal explanations, which questions the validity of the genetic basis of behaviour. Furthermore, behaviour is era-dependent and context-bound, as changes in gender role evidence. This contradicts evolutionary explanations as these predict that behaviour is relatively consistent across time and contexts.

Multi-perspective. Social explanations also account for gender differences in mating behaviour. Human reproductive behaviour needs to be considered as multifactorial, i.e. it results from the interaction of two or more genes with multiple environmental factors. Thus, the interaction of nature and nurture needs to be considered.

PARENTAL INVESTMENT

Factors that determine parental investment	
Factors in investment	**Evidence**
Anisogamy: This is the difference in the size of the sexual gametes, the egg and sperm.	The female egg is larger, takes longer to produce, and so has greater biological cost than the male sperm.
Reproductive cost: The female has the greater burden.	The female has the cost of gestation (carrying the baby) and lactation (providing milk).
Paternal certainty: Females have this due to internal conception, males do not.	Ridley (1993, see A2PKT pp.310–311) found that 20% of children in the UK are not the biological child of the man they assume is their father ("mommies' babies, daddies' maybes").
Proximity: The adult in closest proximity is responsible for care, which is the female due to internal conception.	Females are more likely to be left "holding the baby" whilst the male "runs away" than vice versa.

Trivers' Parental Investment Theory

Trivers (1972, see A2PKT pp.299–300) claimed that differences in parental investment determine who will be the more discerning or "choosy" sex when selecting a partner. In humans it is the female because they invest more in offspring as a result of the factors identified on the previous page. There are greater reproductive costs for the female and so the consequences of indiscriminate mating and the benefits of choosing a suitable partner are high. The male, as the less investing sex, has lower costs and higher benefits of indiscriminate mating. Consequently, the female's optimal strategy is to choose a mate who offers the best genetic or material investment in her limited number of eggs as her reproductive fitness is dependent on eliciting adequate care for the relatively few offspring she can parent. The male's optimal strategy is to impregnate as many females as possible as this will maximise his reproductive fitness and can incur few costs, given that the male's contribution to offspring can begin and end with the donation of sperm!

> According to parental investment theory, males achieve greater reproductive success through promiscuity and abandonment of young, and females achieve greater reproductive success through selectivity and nurturing of young.

EVALUATION

😊 **Face validity.** It certainly makes sense that parents would protect their genetic investment. Fellner and Marshall (1981, see A2PKT p.33) found that 86% of people reported that they would give up a kidney for their child compared to only 50% for a sibling, which shows that parents are prepared to invest more in their offspring.

😐 **Generalisability.** This is limited because parental investment explanations cannot account for broody men, women who don't want to have children, or homosexuality.

😐 **Reproduction is not the sole motivator of relationships.** Relationships are more complex and serve many more needs than just reproduction. Bromhall (2002) challenges the parental investment explanations with his claim that humans are gradually losing the urge to reproduce because the human species is now evolving into a more infantile form. This is reflected in the "child-like" appearance and behaviour of humans compared to other primates.

☹️ **Counter-perspectives.** Psychological and social factors are ignored. Psychological explanations provide alternative accounts of parental care, which may better explain the rate of change in parental behaviour than evolution, given that this is a gradual process. They may also account for love whereas the evolutionary explanations do not.

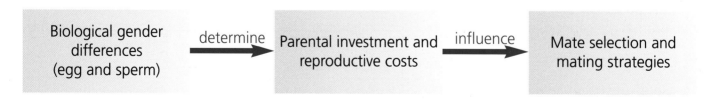

Biological gender differences (egg and sperm) — *determine* → Parental investment and reproductive costs — *influence* → Mate selection and mating strategies

SO WHAT DOES THIS MEAN?

Evolution is fact; the explanations, however, are not! Evolutionary explanations offer only a partial account of human reproductive behaviour as they are reductionist and deterministic. Individual, social, and cultural variations in human reproductive behaviour may be better explained by social explanations. But this underestimates the variety of evolutionary explanations and the fact that sociobiology does account for an interaction of genetic and cultural transmission. Thus, rather than using social constructionism to challenge evolution and vice versa, we need to accept that we are neither a blank slate, nor solely a product of our genetic predispositions. However, human reproductive strategies are highly complex behaviours and so more flexible versions of the traditional explanations need to be taken. For example, the influence of intrasexual and intersexual selection within both genders needs to be considered. Intrasexual selection in women is evident in the ambitiousness and competitiveness of females in the workplace. Evolutionary psychologists suggest that this peaks in the 20s, as this is when women are most fertile and competing for mates. Intersexual selection in males is evident in their selection of youth and physical attractiveness as desirable characteristics. In the same way that evolution lays the groundwork for early attachment, it may provide the genetic predisposition, which interacts with psychosocial factors (learning, cognition, and emotions such as love) to determine human reproductive behaviour. Thus, evolution provides the programming, and psychosocial factors determine the variations and options within this.

OVER TO YOU

1. **Outline and evaluate the relationship between sexual selection and human reproductive behaviour.** **(24 marks)**

EVOLUTIONARY EXPLANATIONS OF MENTAL DISORDERS

ASK YOURSELF

Mental disorders may be adaptive. What does this mean?

Which evolved defence mechanism do anxiety and depression link to? Clue: think back to AS, unit 2.

When was the EEA (evolutionary environment of adaptation)? Does this mean our genes have failed to keep up with changes in society (called genome lag)?

WHAT YOU NEED TO KNOW

EVOLUTIONARY EXPLANATIONS OF DEPRESSION

- Unipolar depression: genome lag; increased fitness.

EVOLUTIONARY EXPLANATIONS OF ANXIETY DISORDERS

- Phobias: Seligman's preparedness argument.
- Obsessive-compulsive disorder.

Unipolar depression and phobias will be covered in depth and bipolar depression and obsessive-compulsive disorder will also be described so that you have enough information to achieve depth and breadth. A general evaluation is given at the end of the subunit, as many of the points are generalisable, to avoid repetition.

To read up on evolutionary explanations of mental disorders, refer to pages 315–326 of A2PKT.

EVOLUTIONARY EXPLANATIONS OF DEPRESSION

Unipolar Depression

Depression is an emotional response that can have physical (loss of appetite, sleep disturbances), behavioural (social withdrawal, apathy), cognitive (pessimistic thinking and hopelessness), motivational (lack of drive, energy), and emotional (loss of pleasure, unhappiness) symptoms.

GENOME LAG OR "EXILES FROM EDEN" EXPLANATION

Social explanations can be seen as directly contradictory to evolutionary explanations or can be reinterpreted using genome lag as the reason for the increase in depression in today's society. According to this explanation, today's society is very different from the EEA (evolutionary environment of adaptation), which was the period when our current genotype was shaped by natural selection. Evolution is a slow and gradual process and so has failed to match the pace of environmental change. Hence the term genome lag as the evolution of the genome has lagged behind environmental changes. Consequently, we are still subject to evolutionary responses that were adaptive in the EEA but are less adaptive today. Freud, Jung, and many more have supported this view that we have stone-age genes and a space-age culture and that this clash of genes and culture causes psychological problems such as depression.

RESEARCH EVIDENCE FOR

- In the EEA humans would have been exposed to very few extremely attractive people. In today's society technological advances mean we are constantly exposed to images of unattainable physical perfection. This can lead to loss of self-esteem and depression, which are a direct consequence of the emphasis given to physical attractiveness in today's society (Buss, 1996).

- Kin support has declined drastically from the EEA. The family and community formed close-knit bonds in our evolutionary past. The nuclear family is in decline and the extended family is severely disrupted and this lack of kin support may be a key difference between the EEA and contemporary society and so may account for depression and other psychological disorders.

- Nesse and Williams (1995, see A2PKT p.321) suggest that developed societies are highly competitive and so create greater stress and opportunities for loss. We are exposed to images of ideal lives and material possessions that can result in feelings of inferiority, dissatisfaction, and consequently depression.

RESEARCH EVIDENCE AGAINST

- We are not perfect organisms. Natural selection did not create perfect organisms and so the psychological problems we have today may be more due to this than superficial differences between the EEA and current society.

- The differences between the EEA and modern environment have been exaggerated according to Crawford (1998). By focusing on technological advances dramatic differences can be identified but this ignores the fundamental similarities of human existence then and now, i.e. we are social beings who form relationships, have children, gossip, compete for resources and position. This does not invalidate genome lag but suggests we need to focus more clearly on the specific differences that lead to psychological disorders.

- The fact that agricultural man "replaced" hunter-gatherer man challenges the concept of the EEA and our ancestors living in harmony as the term Eden implies. This seems unlikely, as the hunter-gatherer man should have had greater reproductive fitness if this were the case.

INCREASED FITNESS

The *pleiotropy hypothesis* refers to the established fact that genes can have more than one effect. Application of this to mental disorders leads to the possibility that they persist because the genes responsible for the abnormality are also linked to desirable traits and so have been naturally selected. This is based on the assumption that if the disorder were not adaptive in some way then surely it would have been weeded out of the gene pool by now. It may be useful to be depressed as the apathy and withdrawal associated with this may aid survival (Nesse & Williams, 1995, see A2PKT p.325). For example, the impulse to hide under the bedclothes may stem from our evolutionary ancestors hiding in a cave, which could increase survival in times of bad weather. Thus, whilst the disorder itself is dysfunctional some aspects of it may be adaptive and so the genes responsible are perpetuated in the gene pool. Mental disorders are "pathological aberrations" of adaptive emotional responses (Allen, 1995).

RESEARCH EVIDENCE FOR

- Human social groups are hierarchical and so conflicts arise over position and authority. According to the *rank theory* of depression (Allen, 1995), this emotional response is adaptive when the individual has lost because accepting loss and the consequent withdrawal ends the conflict. The loser retreats and so is protected from further injury and the winner has a clear sense of victory. The individual suffers in the short-term but this is better than risking further losses and so is adaptive in the long-term. According to Allen clinical depression is a "pathological aberration" of an adaptive emotional response.

- There is evidence of a genetic basis to unipolar depression as shown by twin studies where concordance rates of between 40% (Allen, 1976, see A2PKT p.356) and 59% (Bertelsen, Harvald, & Hauge, 1977, see A2PKT p.356) have been found, and adoption studies which show that depression is common to biological relatives but not adoptive relatives (Wender et al., 1986, see A2PKT p.357).

- Depression is a relatively universal condition, as it exists across cultures, which further supports a genetic basis.

- The manic phase of *bipolar depression* (where the individual alternates between depressive and manic, i.e. euphoric, states) has been related to creativity and charismatic leadership. Winston Churchill, Abraham Lincoln, Vincent Van Gogh, and Ludwig van Beethoven are only a few of the many great leaders and artists who are said to have suffered with bipolar disorder, which offers support for this explanation.

- There is much stronger evidence of a genetic basis to bipolar than unipolar depression as the concordance rate for bipolar in MZ twins is 80% compared to 16% in DZ (Bertelsen et al., 1977, see A2PKT p.356).

- There is evidence that individuals with seasonal affective disorder suffer from severe depression during the winter months rather than the summer. Furthermore, patients with bipolar disorder are more likely to have manic phases in the spring and summer times of the year (Carroll, 1991, see A2PKT p.321). This supports the argument that there may be an adaptive value in being most active during the time of the year when there are the most hours of daylight, and "hibernating" during winter months.

RESEARCH EVIDENCE AGAINST

- Disorders may not be weeded out because they are recessive, i.e. a person may carry the gene but not exhibit the disorder, which only manifests when both parents carry recessive alleles. Thus, it is naturally selected not because of increased fitness but because it is difficult to eliminate as recessive genes do not affect the individual's reproductive fitness.

- Psychological explanations of depression may be more valid (see Psychopathology, Chapter 8).

- Social explanations challenge evolutionary explanations. For example, James (1998), the author of *Britain on the Couch,* proposes that we are facing an epidemic of depression because society manufactures psychological illness. Social and cultural factors may better explain the causes of the "psychological aberration", which transform the adaptive emotional responses to mental disorders.

EVOLUTIONARY EXPLANATIONS OF ANXIETY DISORDERS

The adaptive value of anxiety is indisputable as the arousal of the "fight or flight" response ensures that the individual is able to face environmental threats. Also, it encourages caution and reduces risk-taking behaviour, which clearly links to survival and so increased reproductive fitness.

Phobias

Phobias are irrational fears that are out of proportion to the reality of the threat provided by the fear-provoking stimulus. Whilst anxiety can be adaptive, phobias can be maladaptive.

According to the "preparedness" argument (Seligman, 1970, see A2PKT p.322), phobias are adaptive because they are a fear of things that would have been of danger in our evolutionary past, e.g. snakes, spiders, heights, strangers. The "preparedness" explanation suggests that humans have an innate predisposition to acquire the fear response through conditioning. This means humans are biologically prepared to exhibit physiological and emotional responses as defence mechanisms to environmental demands.

RESEARCH EVIDENCE FOR

- Non-random distribution of feared objects. We fear things that would have existed in our evolutionary past more than modern dangers. Or the fear of modern dangers can be linked to previous dangers, e.g. fear of flying can be linked to fear of heights.

- Fear conditioning. According to this research, we more readily associate harm with certain stimuli more than others. The non-random distribution supports this as does work on classical conditioning. For example, monkeys exposed to a videotape of other monkeys reacting fearfully to a snake will develop a phobia, whereas they do not do so for flowers or leaves (Nesse & Williams, 1996).

- Mental disorders have been linked to the normal distribution of anxiety, where those with a mental disorder are distributed at the extremely high end of an anxiety continuum due to genetic inheritance. This genetically predisposed reactivity is the basis of the "fight or flight" response and supports the "preparedness" argument.

- Fear is negatively correlated with animals' appearance. Those least like humans elicit stronger phobic responses (Bennett-Levy & Marteau, 1984, see A2PKT p.323). This suggests an evolutionary basis as we are programmed to imprint onto our own species and evade unrelated species and so supports the evolutionary explanation that phobias are due to innate predispositions.

RESEARCH EVIDENCE AGAINST

- We do fear modern dangers, e.g. public transport and driving. Of those with a phobia of driving about 50% had been involved in a car accident (Barlow & Durand, 1995, see A2PKT p.377).

- Traditional behavioural explanations alone may fully account for phobias and so contradict an evolutionary basis. The two-process theory (Mowrer, 1947, see A2PKT p.377) of phobias suggests they are acquired through classical conditioning (association of fear with a stimulus) and maintained through negative reinforcement (avoidance of the negative consequence). This contradicts evolutionary explanations as it shows that phobias are learned.

- Social learning theory provides an alternative behavioural explanation. According to this, phobias are culturally transmitted as they are learned through observation and imitation.

- A breakdown in cognitive processing has been linked to phobias—interpretations of the fear-provoking stimulus, bodily response, and emotions are maladaptive given that the fear is disproportionate to the threat. Thus, counter-perspectives provide insights that may have more relevance to the individual's current experience than explanations based on our evolutionary past.

Obsessive-compulsive Disorder

This is characterised by obsessive thinking and compulsive behaviour, where the individual experiences intrusive thoughts that lead them to perform ritualised behaviours. Such rituals often involve cleaning and checking behaviours. This supports an evolutionary basis as such cleaning is adaptive because it protects against contamination and disease, and checking behaviours can be linked to defence of resources and territory. Thus, according to evolutionary explanations, obsessive-compulsive disorder is a distortion of adaptive grooming and territorial behaviours.

EVALUATION

🙁 **Universality of mental disorders.** Depression and anxiety occur in all cultures. Whilst there may be differences in terms of how they are labelled and expressed it can be argued that they are fundamentally the same disorder, which supports a genetic basis. But just because behaviours are common does not mean that they are genetic, and evidence of a genetic basis does not necessarily validate evolutionary explanations.

🙂 **Face validity.** The linking of mental disorders to the EEA and the adaptive behaviours of our evolutionary ancestors makes sense.

🙁 **Descriptive rather than explanatory.** The explanation that mental disorders may be distorted forms of adaptive behaviour is debatable as this oversimplifies the difference between adaptive and maladaptive. Also, evolutionary explanations *describe* the environment or behaviour they are derived from rather than *explaining* how or why the distortion has occurred, and so are more descriptive than explanatory and cannot account for individual differences.

🙁 **Genetic evidence is not synonymous with an evolutionary basis.** Evolutionary explanations are not necessarily supported by genetic evidence, as the evolutionary concept of the gene and the biological concept are very different. For example, evolutionary theories see the disorders as being naturally selected because they are advantageous in some way, whereas recent gene-mapping studies focus on mutant or defective genes. This questions the evolutionary explanation of adaptive responses gone wrong and the idea that traits were once adaptive in the EEA but clash with today's society.

Instead they suggest mutant genes cause pathology, which given the biological evidence in support of such research, means that the evolutionary explanations may need to be redefined.

- **Conjecture—evolutionary stories?** Deciding what was dangerous in our evolutionary past is highly speculative. Such explanations are post hoc and so have little scientific basis.

- **Reductionist and deterministic.** Evolutionary theories are reductionist as they focus on one factor only (the gene) when other emotional, social, cognitive, behavioural, and developmental factors are highly relevant to the aetiology of mental disorders. They are oversimplified accounts at best. They are also deterministic as they suggest that the genes control behaviour, which ignores the free will of the individual.

- **Psychological explanations.** The psychological models of abnormality are counter-perspectives (see Psychopathology, Chapter 8). Moreover, they may account for why adaptive behaviours have become distorted. For example, the evolved "fight or flight" stress response may be genetically predisposed and have adaptive value. But it interacts with psychological factors such as individual differences and self perception, which may result in maladaptive anxiety or depressed responses.

- **Social learning theory has great explanatory power.** It accounts for how children learn so much so quickly and so may provide a more valid explanation of how children acquire phobias, obsessive-compulsive behaviours, and depressive responses. This doesn't necessarily invalidate evolutionary explanations, as nature and nurture are causative in mental disorders.

- **Anti-psychiatry.** Anti-psychiatrists such as Szasz, Laing, and Goffman claim that abnormality is due to "problems in living" and that madness is a "myth". Evolutionary explanations do not account for social and cultural factors, which is a key weakness.

- **Nature/nurture.** The evolutionary explanations overemphasise the role of nature and ignore nurture. It is not a question of nature *or* nurture, as indisputably an interactionist perspective must be taken. However, as the evolutionary explanations ignore nurture this is a key weakness.

- **Multi-perspective.** Evolutionary explanations need to be considered in combination with other explanations. Both biological and psychological factors interact in the aetiology of mental disorders as the compromise position of the diathesis–stress model suggests—"the genes (diathesis/nature) load the gun but the environment (stress/nurture) pulls the trigger" (Goldman, 1992).

- **Adaptive or maladaptive?** Mental disorders are often very disturbing to the patient and may severely disrupt their everyday functioning, thus we shouldn't exaggerate any adaptive value they may have. It is often unclear how some behaviour of patients with mental disorders could be classed as adaptive (e.g. self-harm, suicide). At best, the explanations lack generalisability for all types of depression and anxiety disorder.

NOTE: The increased fitness and genome lag explanations covered under depression are also applicable to anxiety disorders.

SO WHAT DOES THIS MEAN?

There is a lack of research evidence to support the evolutionary explanations of mental disorders and so it is debatable whether mental disorders are evolved defence mechanisms. The explanations are contradictory as the "Exiles from Eden" hypothesis suggests that behaviours are maladaptive, whereas other explanations suggest that mental disorders are pathological exaggerations of normal adaptive responses. This may be the wrong approach as if there is a genetic basis a defective gene may be the cause. Gene-mapping studies have identified possible defective genes in anxiety and mood disorders. This suggests that the evolutionary approach may need to focus on mutant genes rather than evolved adaptive responses. Another problem is that evolutionary explanations cannot account for the recent rise in mental disorders. Genome lag provides only a weak explanation, as there are many fundamental similarities between the EEA and current society. Thus, evolutionary explanations fail to account for mental disorders as cultural phenomena. Evolutionary explanations explain the underlying predisposition, but this is not the cause as it does not inevitably result in disorder, nor does it explain how adaptive emotional responses become maladaptive. The biological, behavioural, cognitive, and psychodynamic models of abnormality provide insight into the precipitating causes and so may be more relevant to the individual's current experience than evolutionary inheritance.

OVER TO YOU

1. **Outline and evaluate** *two* **evolutionary explanations of human mental disorders.**

(24 marks)

How frightened would you be of each of these animals? Is this consistent with Bennett-Levy and Marteau's (1984) findings?

EVOLUTION OF INTELLIGENCE

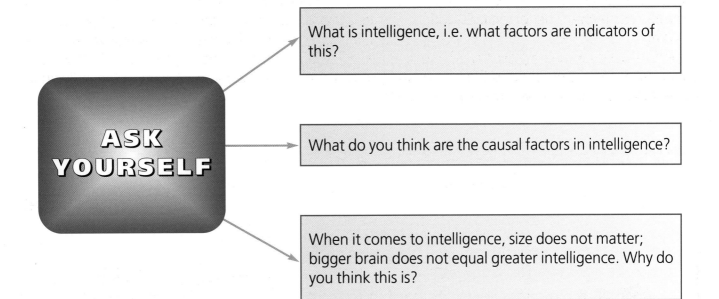

ASK YOURSELF

What is intelligence, i.e. what factors are indicators of this?

What do you think are the causal factors in intelligence?

When it comes to intelligence, size does not matter; bigger brain does not equal greater intelligence. Why do you think this is?

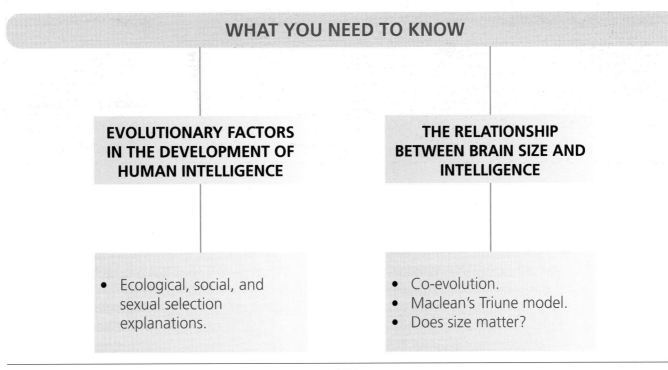

WHAT YOU NEED TO KNOW

EVOLUTIONARY FACTORS IN THE DEVELOPMENT OF HUMAN INTELLIGENCE

- Ecological, social, and sexual selection explanations.

THE RELATIONSHIP BETWEEN BRAIN SIZE AND INTELLIGENCE

- Co-evolution.
- Maclean's Triune model.
- Does size matter?

To read up on the evolution of intelligence, refer to pages 327–337 of A2PKT.

EVOLUTIONARY FACTORS IN THE DEVELOPMENT OF HUMAN INTELLIGENCE

Ecological Selection Theory

Intelligence developed in response to *environmental demands*. Foraging for food, hunting, and tool use require intelligence. Obtaining food presents a cognitive challenge as the location and variations in sources of food must be remembered. Food supplies are often unpredictable and the capture of food may require complex hunting strategies.

RESEARCH EVIDENCE FOR

- Research evidence on foraging suggests that mammals do have cognitive maps of food sources. This supports a link between intelligence and food acquisition.

- Tool use is very limited; only chimps, orang-utans, and humans routinely use tools, which can be linked to their higher intelligence. This supports the ecological theory as it suggests that intelligence is related to more complex foraging strategies.

- Milton (1988) compared howler monkeys and spider monkeys. The spider monkeys had more difficulty foraging for food as their food supply was distributed over an area 25 times larger than the howler monkeys'. The brain capacity of the spider monkeys was twice the size of the howler monkeys'. This was irrespective of weight as body size effects were controlled for.

- Humans' diet is more varied and complex than the herbivorous gorillas and orang-utans and consequently the digestive systems differ. In humans the small intestine takes up the most space, whereas in gorillas and orang-utans the colon does. This shows that the food supply exerted selective pressures on the digestive system and supports the theory that it may have done the same to the brain.

RESEARCH EVIDENCE AGAINST

- The social theory may provide a more convincing explanation of the development of human intelligence as Dunbar's (1998, see A2PKT p.333) research suggests (see Evidence for social selection theory on the next page).

- There is not a clear association between tool use and intelligence. For example, 150,000 to 300,000 years ago was a time of rapid brain growth in humans, however, tool manufacture did not show a parallel growth. Between 300,000 years ago and today human brain growth has been slight but the advancement of tools/technology has been enormous. Consequently, Wynn (1988) concluded that tool use did not exert a direct selection pressure on intelligence.

- Dunbar (1998, see A2PKT p.332) reported across 20 primate species that there was essentially no correlation between complexity of extractive foraging and the size of the neocortex.

- A key weakness of the foraging theory, as a basis on which to judge intelligence, is that animals with brains much smaller than humans' successfully use cognitive maps and hunt.

Social Selection Theory

Intelligence developed in response to the demands of *group living*. The social environment presents a cognitive challenge as a Theory of Mind is needed. That is, the individual must have self-awareness and an understanding that others' intentions, viewpoint, thoughts, and emotions are different from one's own in order to predict the behaviour of others.

RESEARCH EVIDENCE FOR

- Research on self-recognition supports the Theory of Mind. Gallup's (1971) *mirror test* involves applying a red mark to an animal's forehead. Animals with a self-concept should touch this mark when they look in the mirror. Gallup found that chimps and orang-utans reliably demonstrate self-recognition, whereas lower primates and nonprimates do not. Theory of mind develops in humans during infancy.

- Another aspect of the Theory of Mind is the ability to deceive and recognise deception in others. This is called *Machiavellian intelligence* and is adaptive as the individual has much to gain from being able to deceive and cheat others without raising suspicion. Observational evidence suggests that only the higher primates show tactical deception (Byrne, 1995). This supports the social theory that intelligence is a result of social complexity.

- Dunbar (1998, see A2PKT pp.332–334) correlated both environmental and social complexity with the size of the neocortex, the area of the brain associated with higher order thinking. No relationship was found between neocortex size and environmental complexity, whereas a strong positive correlation was found between this and group size.

- The fossil record provides evidence that the size of the human social group has increased as we have evolved over time—from *Homo sapiens* co-habiting in groups of 150, to the much larger villages and towns of agricultural man. As the social group increases, so does the need for more complex interpersonal skills, supporting the theory that intelligence is required for success and survival within the group.

RESEARCH EVIDENCE AGAINST

- There is great diversity in the social systems of primates with a Theory of Mind. Orang-utans have a Theory of Mind and are thought to be intelligent but do not live in large social groups, which challenges the social complexity theory.

- Social groups may exist without knowledge of others' minds (e.g. ants) and so intelligence is not inextricably linked to social living as the Theory of Mind and the Machiavellian hypothesis suggest.

- Given that many apes do live in social groups, much larger brains should be found in apes and monkeys if intelligence had a social origin. The EQ for primates is 2.34 and the EQ for humans is 7; the proportion of the cortex to the rest of the brain is 50% in primates and 80% in humans. Therefore we would expect primates' brains to be 2–3 times bigger if group living was the main factor in the development of intelligence.

EVALUATION OF ECOLOGICAL AND SOCIAL THEORY

- **Face validity.** Both ecological theory and social theory make sense as both food acquisition and living in groups do present cognitive demands and do enhance survival and reproductive potential.

However, Dunbar's (1998, see A2PKT pp.333–334) research presents strong evidence that social factors drove the evolution of intelligence.

☹ **Anthropomorphic measures of intelligence.** There are great difficulties in measuring and interpreting animal intelligence. Consider the difficulty we have in creating a culturally fair test of IQ in humans to appreciate the even greater difficulty of devising a species-fair test of intelligence across animals and humans. Thus, the research evidence may lack validity as the measures of intelligence may lack accuracy.

☹ **Cause and effect.** The research evidence on ecological and social factors identifies associations, which do not indicate cause and effect. Consequently, conclusions are limited to "links" rather than causes.

☹ **Direction of the effect.** Cannot establish which came first, varied diet or intelligence; large social groups or intelligence; it may be that better diet and group living were consequences of the development of intelligence. In which case what caused intelligence in the first place is not clearly established.

☹ **A chance mutation.** Human intelligence may be the result of a chance mutation that resulted in bipedalism and so freed our hands to forage and create tools. Brain size and intelligence would be a consequence of better diet.

Sexual selection

As discussed earlier in this unit, according to this, intelligence is a courtship display that has been selected in accordance with the "good taste" hypothesis. Females, as the "choosy" sex, have selected intelligence as a sexy trait that will increase the probability that their sons will reproduce and so perpetuate their genes. A runaway process leads to more and more exaggerated versions of the trait being preferred, i.e. greater and greater intelligence. Females evolved intelligence in order to decode and appreciate the males' intelligence.

RESEARCH EVIDENCE FOR

- Miller (1996, see A2PKT p.335) uses self-report surveys of qualities looked for in a partner as evidence—intelligence usually appears in the top five.

- Miller (1998, see A2PKT p.335) claims that males' greater contribution to the arts, music, and literature supports the validity of intelligence as a male courtship display.

- Sexual selection accounts better for the rapid increase in the size of the human brain. In the last 3 million years it has trebled in size and this is something the other explanations have difficulty explaining. Also, the male brain is bigger than the female brain, even when body weight is controlled for.

RESEARCH EVIDENCE AGAINST

- The first section in this chapter reveals that many factors are involved in physical attraction besides intelligence. Youth, physical attractiveness, and resources were rated above intelligence, which casts doubt on the strength of the selective pressure on intelligence.

EVALUATION

 Androcentric bias. The claim that females' intelligence is an outcome of the males' is clearly gender biased and so raises ethical implications.

 The role of social factors. The greater quantity of male contributions to the arts can be explained by social factors such as the female role in society, given that such contributions would have been deemed unfitting for women in previous eras. Women who did contribute wrote under male pseudonyms to gain credibility.

 Does size matter? The next section will consider the correlation between brain size and intelligence. There is of course a link between intelligence and brain size but there are also other factors to consider, such as organisation, which means that total size is not an indicator of total intelligence.

> **NOTE:** The methodological criticisms of the evolutionary theories covered previously, such as lack of scientific validity, the fact that they are unverifiable and unfalsifiable, post hoc, etc. can apply. Theoretical criticisms such as reductionism and determinism can also be applied to the explanations of the development of intelligence.

OVER TO YOU

1. **Critically consider evolutionary factors in the development of human intelligence.**

(24 marks)

THE RELATIONSHIP BETWEEN BRAIN SIZE AND INTELLIGENCE

RESEARCH EVIDENCE FOR

- **Co-evolution.** This refers to when two characteristics evolve in tandem. Analogies have been drawn where the brain growth is the "hardware" and the mental abilities the "software", and consequently they are interdependent. This suggests that there is a positive correlation between brain size and intelligence.

- **The Triune Model.** According to MacLean (1970), the brain consists of three main sections:

  - **The Reptilian core.** Inherited from our reptile-like ancestors, all animals have this primitive core, which is responsible for basic drives and simple behaviour.

  - **Old mammalian (limbic system)—the mid-section.** This area of the brain is concerned with fighting, feeding, self-preservation, sociability, attachments, and parental care. It integrates sensory perception with bodily functions.

  - **The neocortex—outer layer.** The cortex is found only in mammals and is responsible for higher order mental processes. The cortex is the outer layer of the cerebral hemispheres and is known as the grey matter compared to the white matter of the hemispheres. The cortex is only 2 millimetres thick and has a bumpy, folded appearance. These folds mean that the actual area of the cortex is large.

The Triune model shows the increasing growth and sophistication of the brain in animals higher up the phylogenic tree. It provides research evidence for a relationship between brain size and intelligence.

MEASURES OF BRAIN SIZE

The question of whether size is a clear indicator of intelligence has been researched extensively through comparative studies. Initially, crude measures of gross brain size were compared. However, measures of brain size are oversimplistic as the elephant's brain is four times the size of a human's and some species of whale have brains five times human size, which is explained by their greater body mass. The ratio of brain size to body mass was thought to be a better indicator. However, using this criterion the mouse outclasses the human with a relative brain to body size of 3% compared to 2% for humans.

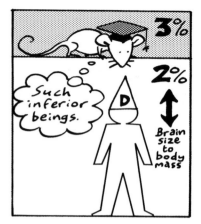

ENCEPHALISATION QUOTIENT (EQ)

Consequently, the encephalisation quotient (EQ) was introduced. This is the calculation of the brain size relative to body mass compared to what would be expected for a mammal of similar body size. An allometric line (in this case, allometry equals the relationship between the size of a mammal and the size of its brain) can be constructed on a graph where those above the line have a positive encephalisation showing the brain size is greater than that expected of an animal of its body mass. Humans lie well above the allometric line as we have a high EQ—the human brain is twice the size expected for an ape of similar size. A chimp devotes only 8% of its basal metabolic rate (i.e. number of calories when resting) to maintaining the brain, whereas humans devote 22%.

FOSSIL RECORDS

The fossil records suggest that the human brain underwent rapid expansion about 2 million years ago, as *Australopithecines* possessed normal size brains for body mass whereas *Homo sapiens* possess brains twice the size. Thus, the *Australopithecines*' brain size falls on the allometric line, whereas the *Homo*

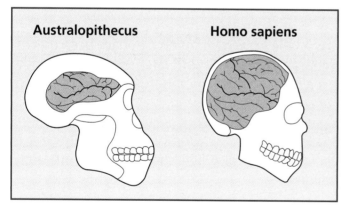

sapiens' lies above it, showing a positive encephalisation of 2.95. Seven million years ago our ancestors had a brain that was only about 400 cubic centimetres (cc). Brain size didn't change much for millions of years after that, but by 2.5 millions years ago with *Homo habilis* the brain size had almost doubled to about 700 cc. *Homo habilis* then evolved into *Homo erectus* who had a brain size of about 1000cc. Over the past 500,000 years, human brain size increased again and is now about 1350cc (Stewart, 1997, see A2PKT p.328).

The fact that the human brain has grown to a size that incurs great costs (such as the dangers of child-birth and an extended period of parental care, as the human infant is now born at an earlier stage in development because the brain is larger) suggests that large brains must have adaptive value so that the benefits outweigh the costs. This supports the argument that larger brains are linked to intelligence.

COMPARATIVE STUDIES

Comparative studies support a relationship between brain size and intelligence by comparing animals' performance on different tasks. Rumbaugh, Savage-Rumbaugh, and Washburn (1996, see A2PKT p.328) found that larger-brained primates (gorilla and chimpanzee) were able to transfer learning from one task to another whereas smaller-brained primates were not.

BRAIN SIZE AND IQ

A correlational analysis of brain size and IQ in a quota sample of college students showing a good spread of IQ scores found that high IQ students had larger brains than low IQ students. A correlation of .51 between IQ and brain:body weight ratio was recorded (Willerman, Schultz, Rutledge, & Bigler, 1991, see A2PKT p.329).

RESEARCH EVIDENCE AGAINST

- The size of the human brain is not solely genetic as it is also influenced by environment. Lucas, Morley, Cole, Lister, and Leeson (1992, see A2PKT p.329) found that babies fed on breast milk had higher IQs in later life, which shows that intelligence is not just due to our evolved brain size but also diet and nutrition.

- This applies not just to size but to brain specialisation and localisation. As the Triune model shows, the cortex is a specialised area of the brain found only in mammals. It is the seat of higher order mental functions and so is linked to thought, language, perception, attention, and intelligence. The *frontal cortex* in humans is significantly larger than that of other mammals (see A2PKT p.328). This shows that it is not overall brain size that is significant but particular specialised areas of the brain.

- Brain organisation appears to be just as influential as size. This explains why although men have bigger brains they do not have higher IQs. A post-mortem examination of Albert Einstein's brain found that the neurons in the prefrontal cortex were more tightly packed. This supports the idea that brain localisation (the organisation of the brain whereby different regions relate to different functions) is more important than size.

EVALUATION

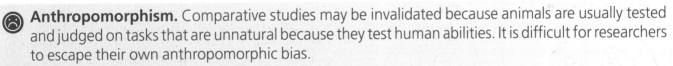

Anthropomorphism. Comparative studies may be invalidated because animals are usually tested and judged on tasks that are unnatural because they test human abilities. It is difficult for researchers to escape their own anthropomorphic bias.

Reductionism. Intelligence is extremely complex and so there is unlikely to be a simple relationship between this and the EQ.

Correlational criticisms. The research evidences an association only between brain size and intelligence. Thus, cause and effect cannot be inferred and so conclusions are limited to association rather than causation. Furthermore, the correlation quotient of .51 is only a moderate correlation. Another weakness is that correlations are reductionist because they only analyse two factors when in reality the relationship is likely to be multifactorial, as supported by the identification of factors such as nurture and organisation.

Direction of effect. Utilisation versus atrophy. Use it or lose it! The direction of effect is difficult to establish, e.g. was Einstein's prefrontal cortex the cause or effect of his intellectual powers?

Sample bias. The college students in Willerman et al.'s (1991) research are a restricted sample and therefore unrepresentative, and so population validity is constrained.

Validity of IQ tests. As these are culturally biased their meaningfulness as a measure of intelligence is reduced, so providing only weak support to the relationship between brain size and intelligence.

SO WHAT DOES THIS MEAN?

The factors in the development of human intelligence thus far offer no conclusive explanation for why human brains grew so large. A combination of ecological, social, and sexual factors seems the most comprehensive account and so a multi-perspective needs to be taken. Particular weight needs to be given to social factors, given Dunbar's (1998) research and sexual selection, since a runaway process can best account for the dramatic increase in human brain size. However, these factors do not effectively pinpoint the origin of intelligence. The mutant gene that led to bipedalism may be the origin, and so the development of intelligence needs to be traced back to this. The co-evolution of brain size and mental abilities may be in part due to a chance mutation. There is evidence to support co-evolution as brain size and intelligence are related. However, other factors are involved in the association. The human brain is highly complex and more organised than any other animal's and this may be equally, if not more, relevant than size.

It seems likely that environmental and then social complexity are the earliest origins of human intelligence, however, these do not account for why the human brain is more advanced, at least according to EQ measures! Thus, social and ecological factors must interact with later factors, more specific to humans, such as sexual selection, language, bipedalism, and the ability to control fire.

OVER TO YOU

1. **Critically consider the relationship between brain size and human intelligence.**

(24 marks)

Adapted from AQA A2 [Winter 2002] Psychology Examination Papers.

QUESTIONS AND ESSAY PLANS

Definition of intelligence: Intelligence is a collection of mental abilities, which include problem solving, memory, reasoning, language, etc.

The development of human intelligence: Such abilities enable us to adapt to the demands of the environment and so increase survival and reproductive fitness.

1 Outline and evaluate evolutionary explanations for human reproductive behaviour. **(24 marks)**

OR   Outline and evaluate the relationship between sexual selection and human reproductive behaviour. **(24 marks)**

The questions are similar and so the essay plan can be adapted to either; just make sure you tailor your link sentences to the question.

Paragraph 1 Introduction

Define evolution. State that the theory originated with Darwin and outline his theory of sexual selection, which expanded on his theory of natural selection to account for the peacock's tail. Then explain how Darwin's theory has been modified by sociobiologists, such as Dawkins, who have attempted to explain social behaviour using evolutionary processes. Many insights are offered by sociobiologists into reproductive behaviour but their main weakness is that they do not account for nurture and so offer one-dimensional explanations for reproductive behaviour when of course there are valid social explanations for reproductive behaviour.

Paragraph 2

Describe anisogamy, i.e. the different size of the gametes, and how this determines parental investment, which results in different mating strategies. The man's main concern is to spread his genes and the woman's is to nurture the limited number of offspring she can produce. Outline intrasexual selection (the male strategy) and give evidence for dimorphism, the testicular effect, and sneak copulation. Then outline intersexual selection (the female strategy) and give evidence for the "good taste" and "good sense" hypotheses. Assess that this sex difference in preferred mating strategies is oversimplified as in reality women compete between themselves. Perhaps the greatest indicator of intersexual selection is neoteny (child-like appearance)—this is more evident in females as males have selected it. Also, social explanations may be the real reason for the gender differences in mating strategy as socialisation into the traditional gender roles may explain when men "do" and women "don't", i.e. the double-standard. The evidence that this is the case is the changing norms in mating behaviour, which suggests that human reproductive behaviour is socially constructed.

Paragraph 3

Research that has tested for evidence of sexual selection in mating behaviour: Buss (1989), Davis (1990, and Strassberg, 1999, which contradicts this), and Clark and Hatfield (1989). Criticise the research; there are many criticisms of Buss, e.g. he exaggerated differences and gave little emphasis to consistencies between genders such as the fact that kindness and intelligence were rated as most important by males and females. Also, the findings are self-report, and so may not be representative of actual behaviour. This limits the support the research provides to evolutionary explanations and so casts doubt on their validity.

Paragraph 4

Discuss whether sexual differences in sexual selection are translated into mating strategies, e.g. polygyny is the most common mating strategy but is expressed as serial monogamy. But evidence against sexual selection shaping mating systems is that both genders can be serial polygamists, whereas the explanations predict monogamy for females. Consider whether polygamy is the natural behaviour of both genders as it ensures genetic variation, i.e. are we programmed to seek out variety? Present the evidence that this is the optimal strategy for males. Ridley's research on paternal certainty suggests it may be common in women as 20% of children mistakenly thought the man they lived with was their biological father. Polygamy is the most common mating strategy across cultures and perhaps females are just as likely to engage in this but may do so without detection. Divorce and thus serial polygamy provide more valid evidence. However, if evolutionary explanations are valid then behaviour should be fairly universal and consistent over time. In fact there is much variation in mating systems within and between populations and over time. Evolutionary explanations try to account for this with their claim that mating strategy is a better term, as this will change depending on the environment. However, this isn't very convincing given that there is such great variation and so social factors may provide a more valid account of human sexual behaviour as changes in social constructions could explain mating strategy preferences better. Social explanations may account for monogamous males, whereas evolutionary explanations struggle to do so.

Paragraph 5

Present the generic evaluations of evolutionary explanations, i.e. the ones that work in any essay, e.g. reductionism, determinism, scientific validity, unfalsifiable or verifiable. They are often modified to account for inconsistencies with some new adaptive explanation. They have been criticised as evolutionary stories because they cannot be tested as they are conjecture, and post hoc (made up after the event). They are also selective in the behaviours they choose to explain, ignoring the ones they cannot explain or that clearly have better alternative explanations. And of course they ignore nurture. You must elaborate each of these and relate each clearly to why it consequently may not account for human reproductive behaviour.

Paragraph 6 Conclusion

You may be asked to weigh up "the extent they explain/offer insights…"

Weigh up pros and cons of the explanations. Use the postmodern critique and social constructionism to do this, e.g. no universal truth, need a multiperspective as sexual selection only accounts for one level of reproductive behaviour when it exists at different levels, e.g. behavioural, cognitive, unconscious, which are ignored in the explanations. Reproductive behaviour is seen as synonymous with relationships by the evolutionary perspective when of course this is not the case as it ignores love, which may be a more valid reason for sexual behaviour than reproduction. Also, it is a situated account as to some extent it is a product of the time and context when explanations were biased towards nature as the reason for behaviour. Evolution is enjoying a resurgence in popularity in the current context and so we must be careful not to be influenced and draw unbiased conclusions. Social explanations may offer more insight into the variation and flexibility evident in reproductive behaviour. A multi-perspective is needed to gain the most insight into human reproductive behaviour. In the same way that evolution lays the groundwork for early attachment, it may provide the genetic predisposition, which interacts with psychosocial factors (learning, cognition, and emotions such as love) to determine human reproductive behaviour. Thus, evolution provides the programming and psychosocial factors determine the variations and options within this.

2(a) Describe sex differences in parental investment. (12 marks)

Note that (a) is AO1 only so should have no evaluation.

Paragraph 1

Describe Trivers' (1972) parental investment theory, which is based on anisogamy, reproductive cost, paternal certainty, and proximity. Anisogamy shapes reproductive cost, i.e. the balance between effort (time and resources) and reproductive success. According to this, "males' donation to childrearing may begin and end with the donation of sperm". Females have relatively few eggs and so mate with one partner and devote more energy to the survival of their offspring. Males have many sperm and so do not provide extra care. Reproductive success for males lies in a high number of partners who may be left to care for the offspring.

Paragraph 2

Explain how the adult in closest proximity is responsible for care and of course, given that internal fertilisation takes place in humans, this is the female. Thus, the male can "run away" and the female is left "holding the baby". This is also linked to the order of gamete release hypothesis. The male releases his first and so may not care what happens next.

Paragraph 3

"Mommies' babies, daddies' maybes"—describe Ridley's research on paternal certainty (1993).

(b) Assess the contribution of evolutionary explanations to our understanding of these sex differences in parental investment. (12 marks)

Note that (b) is AO2 only so should have no description.

Paragraph 1

To some extent the evolutionary theories seem to be correct. It's true that traditionally women have been left holding the baby and single-parent and divorced families are more likely to be headed by a female. Research statistics demonstrate that even when the man does stay to care the woman does most of the work (Oakley, 1974). The facts of internal fertilisation and long gestation do explain why the female is more likely to care for the baby. The evolutionary concepts have inspired further theory, e.g. Bowlby, 1951, which supports their validity. Evidence that adults are programmed to care (i.e. this behaviour is innate) is explained by Bowlby as he claims that we cannot ignore the social releasers used by children to elicit care, e.g. we can't bear to hear a baby cry. Bowlby also implied a sex difference as he said that the main caregiver would usually be the mother. But evidence against is that humans tend to share the care of their offspring and so the differences may be exaggerated. The evolutionary explanations suggest that when resources are limited, and because the human infant requires prolonged care, monogamy is favoured—but is it? This is another case of evolutionary explanations being used to explain any pattern of behaviour and doesn't really account for the individual differences in parenting.

Paragraph 2

Evolutionary explanations of parental investment lack explanatory power, as they do not account for broody men or women who don't want children. Relationships are more complex and serve many more needs than just reproduction. Bromhall (2002) challenges the parental investment explanations with his claim that humans are gradually losing the urge to reproduce because the human species is now evolving into a more infantile form. This is reflected in the "child-like" appearance and behaviour of humans compared to other primates. There are other explanations for parental care, e.g. other explanations of attachment, learning explanations, and Freud's theory, and the gender differences may be better explained by social explanations, e.g. gender role socialisation. Females are expected to be nurturing. Furthermore, there is much more of a stigma if a woman abandons her child than the man, which is nothing to do with the size of the gametes but the socially constructed norms and values. Of the explanations anisogamy may be the weakest, as it is certainly more plausible that the fact that the female carries the child leads to her being more likely to care for it, as of course this provides time for her to become attached. If she becomes pregnant and decides to keep the baby then she has no choice but to make some sort of commitment to it at least for 9 months, whereas the male has none of this. Thus, the proximity hypothesis appears right, but is it? The explanation is descriptive not explanatory as it describes what is fact—the woman has to bear the baby—but it does not mean that this behaviour is genetically predisposed.

Paragraph 3

The generic criticisms: e.g. reductionism, determinism, scientific validity, unfalsifiable or verifiable. They are often modified to account for inconsistencies with some new adaptive explanations, which some call evolutionary stories because they cannot be tested, as they are post hoc (made up after the event). They are also selective in the behaviours they choose to explain, ignoring the ones they can't or which have clearly better alternative explanations. And of course it ignores nurture. You must elaborate each of these and relate each clearly to why they consequently may not account for parental investment. The evolutionary explanations provide insight into only one aspect of parental investment and ignore the complex psychological and social factors involved in this, such as the intense emotions that characterise the attachment bond. Thus, a multi-perspective provides more insight into sex differences in parental investment than evolutionary explanations, as this can account for the interaction of genetic programming with other factors.

3 Outline and evaluate evolutionary explanations of human mental disorders.

(24 marks)

Be selective—decide which two areas of content you are going to write about in depth and do the rest in less depth so your answer achieves breadth and depth.

Paragraph 1 Introduction

Define evolution and identify two explanations, e.g. genome lag and innate preparedness (Seligman, 1970).

Paragraph 2

Describe genome lag including the following: the environment of evolutionary adaptation (EEA) means that genes which conferred adaptive traits in the EEA have not yet been eliminated by the process of natural selection as this is a passive and gradual process. The traits predisposed by the genes may be less adaptive in the current environment but the gene(s) may not affect reproductive success and so remain(s) in the gene pool, e.g. the "fight or flight" response is seen as an evolutionary defence mechanism better suited to the environment of our evolutionary ancestors. This explanation has been used to explain depression and anxiety. A problem with genome lag is that the environment may not be sufficiently different today to the EEA to make any sense. It's reductionist, i.e. oversimplified. Use the evolutionary stress response as the basis of anxiety disorders to illustrate this, as physiological reactivity may be to some extent genetically predisposed, but this is modified by psychological factors such as individual differences and self-perception. Genome lag of course does not account for psychological factors.

Paragraph 3

According to increased fitness, genes can have more than one effect. Application of this to mental disorders leads to the possibility that they persist because the genes responsible for the abnormality are also linked to desirable traits and so have been naturally selected. Thus, mental disorders are pathological aberrations of adaptive emotional responses. Use the rank theory of depression and the creativity explanation of bipolar disorder to illustrate increased fitness. The problem with this explanation is that it underestimates the differences between adaptive and maladaptive. Also, even if this is accepted as a valid explanation this just shifts the question of what causes mental disorders to what causes the psychological aberrations. The biological and psychological models offer insights into possible causes that the evolutionary explanations do not. The evolutionary explanations only account for the individual's underlying vulnerability and fail to account for the factors that trigger the underlying vulnerability. The fact that evolutionary explanations ignore social and cultural factors means that they explain psychopathology solely in terms of the individual, when anti-psychiatrists suggest that "sick society" may be causal.

Paragraph 4

Seligman (1970) suggested we are biologically prepared to fear dangerous stimuli and this is used to explain phobias. A phobia is defined as an irrational fear that is out of proportion to the danger presented by the stimuli. The normal distribution of anxiety supports the preparedness argument. Evidence to support this is Nesse and Williams' (1995) research where they conditioned the fear response in monkeys. Evidence in support includes the nonrandom distribution of phobias and Bennett-Levy and Marteau's (1984) research on phobias. But evidence against is that there are counter-perspectives, which may offer more valid insights into mental disorders, in particular the cognitive approach, Mowrer's (1947) two-process theory, and social learning theory. Behavioural explanations can account for the fact that people are phobic of modern-day dangers. This is another example of evolutionary psychologists' selectivity in choice of evidence. Also it presumes that all behaviour is adaptive, which may well be a misperception.

Paragraph 5

Obsessive-compulsive disorder can also be explained from an evolutionary perspective as the compulsive behaviours may be distortions of grooming and territory rituals. The explanations have face validity, in particular the use of the normal distribution curve to account for individual differences in physiological reactivity and how this may underpin mental disorders. But this is descriptive not explanatory, it's difficult to test empirically, and does not fully account for individual differences.

Paragraph 6 Conclusion

Recent gene-mapping research into defective genes questions the evolutionary explanation of adaptive responses gone wrong and the idea that traits were once adaptive in the EEA but clash with today's society. Instead they suggest pathology is caused by mutant genes and so the evolutionary explanations may need to be redefined. Generic criticisms: e.g. reductionism, determinism, scientific validity, unfalsifiable or verifiable. They are often modified to account for inconsistencies with some new adaptive explanation, which some call evolutionary stories, because they cannot be tested as they are conjecture and post hoc (made up after the event). They are also selective in the behaviours they choose to explain ignoring the ones they can't or which have clearly better alternative explanations. And of course it ignores nurture. Conclude why the explanations do not account for mental disorders. Evolutionary explanations explain the underlying predisposition, but this is not the cause as it does not inevitably result in disorder, nor does it explain how adaptive emotional responses become maladaptive. A multi-perspective is needed such as the diathesis–stress model, which accounts for more than one level of explanation and for the interaction of predisposing and precipitating factors.

4 Critically consider evolutionary factors in the development of human intelligence.

(24 marks)

Consider how to structure the material in the plan. Ecological and social have been organised together as both can be assessed using Dunbar's (1998) research evidence.

Paragraph 1 Introduction

Define evolution and intelligence.

Paragraph 2

Outline the ecological explanations including foraging and tool use. Outline the social explanation including the Theory of Mind and Gallup's (1971) research using the mirror test and Machiavellian intelligence as support. Use Dunbar's (1998) research on the correlation between the neocortex and intelligence to support social as the more valid theory.

Paragraph 3

Consider the face validity of both explanations. Both ecological theory and social theory make sense as both food acquisition and living in groups present cognitive demands and enhance survival and reproductive potential. However, Dunbar's (1998) research presents compelling evidence that social factors drove the evolution of intelligence.

Paragraph 4

Outline and evaluate sexual selection as an explanation of the development of human intelligence, including evidence that it is a result of intersexual selection and so has evolved as a runaway process because it is used by males as a courtship display. Consider that sexual selection does account for the rapid increase in human brain size. Use Miller's (1996, 1998) evidence as support and evaluate the alpha bias (exaggerates the differences between the genders) and possible social explanations for the findings. Also consider that there are many factors in human attraction that may limit the selective pressure on intelligence.

Paragraph 5

There are great difficulties in measuring and interpreting animal intelligence. Consider the difficulty we have in creating a culturally-fair test of IQ in humans to appreciate the even greater difficulty in devising a species-fair test of intelligence across animals and humans. Thus, the research evidence may lack validity as the measures of intelligence may lack accuracy due to anthropomorphism. The research evidence on ecological and social factors is correlational and so identifies associations, which do not indicate cause and effect. Consequently, conclusions are limited to "links" rather than causes. The direction of the effect can't be established as it's not clear which came first—varied and better diet or intelligence; large social groups or intelligence—as it may be that better diet and group living were consequences of the development of intelligence. In which case what caused the intelligence in the first place is not clearly established.

Paragraph 6 Conclusion

Human intelligence may be the result of a chance mutation that resulted in bipedalism and so freed our hands to forage and create tools. Brain size and intelligence would be a consequence of better diet. Generic criticisms: e.g. reductionism, determinism, scientific validity, unfalsifiable or verifiable, and are often modified to account for inconsistencies with some new adaptive explanation which some call evolutionary stories because they cannot be tested as they are post hoc (made up after the event). They are also selective in the behaviours they choose to explain, ignoring the ones they can't or which have clearly better alternative explanations. A multi-perspective is needed, as the factors in the development of human intelligence identified thus far offer no conclusive explanation for why human brains grew so large. A combination of ecological, social, and sexual factors seems the most comprehensive account. However, these factors do not effectively pinpoint the origin of intelligence. The mutant gene that led to bipedalism may be the origin and so the development of intelligence needs to be traced back to this.

5 Critically consider the relationship between brain size and human intelligence. (24 marks)

Note the term "relationship". This immediately means correlational criticisms will be relevant as AO2.

Paragraph 1 Introduction

Explain what is meant by intelligence and explain co-evolution and how this has resulted in growth of the brain according to the Triune model.

Paragraph 2

Outline the comparative studies that provide evidence for a relationship between brain size and intelligence, focusing on the gross brain size, brain:body ratio, and then the EQ and how this places humans above the allometric line, and also the fossil records that evidence the evolution of this EQ. Evaluate the measures as reductionist as they do not account for the complexity of intelligence.

Paragraph 3

Comparative studies support a relationship between brain size and intelligence by comparing animals' performance on different tasks. Rumbaugh et al. (1996) found that larger-brained primates (gorilla and chimpanzee) were able to transfer learning from one task to another, whereas smaller-brained primates could not. This suggests that larger brains do confer greater intelligence. However, the comparative studies may be invalidated because animals are usually tested and judged on tasks that are unnatural because they are designed to test human abilities. It is difficult for researchers to escape their own anthropomorphic bias.

Paragraph 4

Consider the correlation between IQ and brain size, .51 (Willerman et al., 1991) and assess that it is only a moderate correlation and other factors are involved. Also, the research had methodological weaknesses including sample bias and the validity of the IQ test. The evolutionary explanation that intelligence is determined by genetically predisposed brain size ignores the role of nurture. Intelligence is in part due to genetic inheritance but is also a consequence of nutritional and social factors such as levels of stimulation. Thus, intelligence is a consequence of nature and nurture, not just nature, as Lucas et al.'s (1992) research on the importance of nutrition supports. The evolutionary explanation provides a reductionist and deterministic account of intelligence.

Paragraph 5

Consider the gender differences in brain size, e.g. Gall (1822) argued men's brains were bigger and therefore they were more intelligent. On his death his brain was measured and was smaller than the average woman's! Does bigger mean better? No, because organisation is more important. Intelligence is not determined solely by size but by brain specialisation and localisation. Evidence for this is the fact that the frontal cortex in humans is significantly larger than in other mammals; gender differences; and the post-mortem examination of Albert Einstein's brain. However, the direction of effect is not clear, as brain organisation could be a consequence of high intelligence rather than a cause. To establish brain organisation as a causal factor further research needs to take a prospective and longitudinal approach, where brain organisation and intelligence need to be charted throughout childhood.

Paragraph 6 Conclusion

It is oversimplistic to consider brain size as the only influence on intelligence. The research evidence is correlational. Thus, cause and effect cannot be inferred and so conclusions are limited to association rather than causation. Another weakness is that correlations are reductionist because they only analyse two factors when in reality the relationship between brain size and intelligence is likely to be multifactorial, as the identification of other factors such as nurture and organisation supports. The evolutionary explanation that brain size and intelligence are related is subject to the usual criticisms. The evolutionary perspective lacks scientific validity, is unfalsifiable or verifiable and is difficult to test because it is post hoc (made up after the event). Conclude that co-evolution is supported but needs to be expanded upon because the human brain is highly complex and more organised than in other animals and this may be equally, if not more, relevant than size. There is consequently not a direct relationship between size and intelligence as there are other factors that mediate in the association.

Question 5 adapted from AQA A2 [Winter 2002] Psychology Examination Papers.
The authors are responsible for the solutions and (a) they have neither been provided nor approved by AQA and (b) they may not necessarily constitute the only possible solutions.

Individual Differences

PSYCHOPATHOLOGY Specification 14.1

What's it about?

Psychopathology refers to the scientific study of abnormality, which includes nature (characteristics/symptoms) and aetiology (causes/explanations). Early psychiatrists such as Kraepelin (1856–1926) and Bleuler (1857–1939) shaped the direction of the modern approach to mental illness, where different types of mental illness are diagnosed and classified according to specific symptoms. Kraepelin and Bleuler favoured a somatogenic approach where physical explanations of disorder are sought and this is known as the medical model of abnormality. The behavioural, cognitive, psychodynamic, and humanistic models take a psychogenic approach as they identify psychological causes of mental illness. You will be familiar with the models of abnormality from this topic at AS level, so try to recall what factors are likely to be implicated by the different models. However, questioning whether mental illness is due to nature or nurture is invalid as mental illness is caused by a complex interaction of multiple factors; we will therefore consider schizophrenia, depression, and phobic disorders using a multidimensional approach.

What's in this unit?

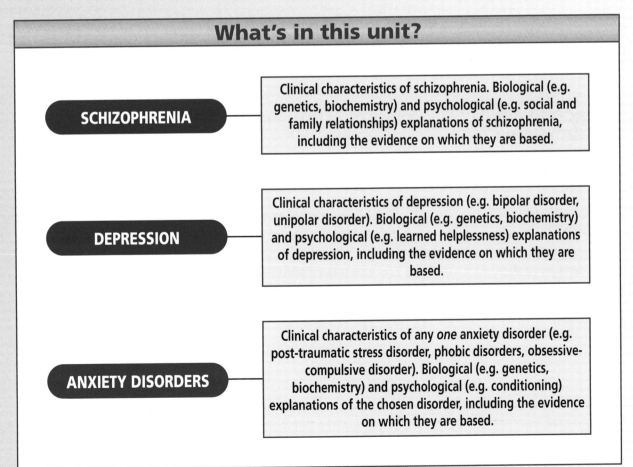

SCHIZOPHRENIA

Clinical characteristics of schizophrenia. Biological (e.g. genetics, biochemistry) and psychological (e.g. social and family relationships) explanations of schizophrenia, including the evidence on which they are based.

DEPRESSION

Clinical characteristics of depression (e.g. bipolar disorder, unipolar disorder). Biological (e.g. genetics, biochemistry) and psychological (e.g. learned helplessness) explanations of depression, including the evidence on which they are based.

ANXIETY DISORDERS

Clinical characteristics of any *one* anxiety disorder (e.g. post-traumatic stress disorder, phobic disorders, obsessive-compulsive disorder). Biological (e.g. genetics, biochemistry) and psychological (e.g. conditioning) explanations of the chosen disorder, including the evidence on which they are based.

SCHIZOPHRENIA

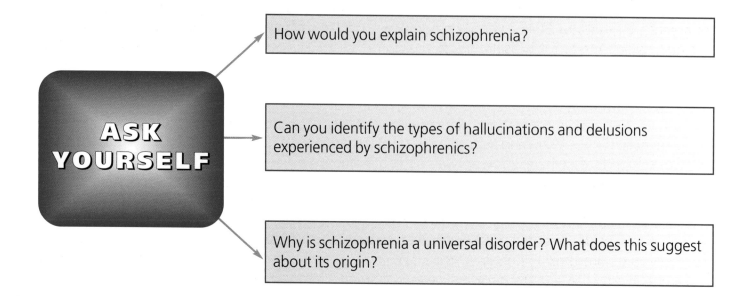

ASK YOURSELF

How would you explain schizophrenia?

Can you identify the types of hallucinations and delusions experienced by schizophrenics?

Why is schizophrenia a universal disorder? What does this suggest about its origin?

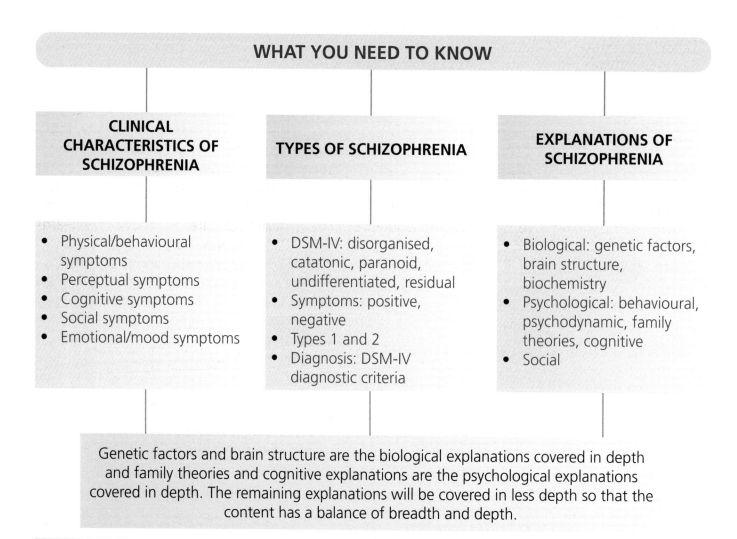

WHAT YOU NEED TO KNOW

CLINICAL CHARACTERISTICS OF SCHIZOPHRENIA

- Physical/behavioural symptoms
- Perceptual symptoms
- Cognitive symptoms
- Social symptoms
- Emotional/mood symptoms

TYPES OF SCHIZOPHRENIA

- DSM-IV: disorganised, catatonic, paranoid, undifferentiated, residual
- Symptoms: positive, negative
- Types 1 and 2
- Diagnosis: DSM-IV diagnostic criteria

EXPLANATIONS OF SCHIZOPHRENIA

- Biological: genetic factors, brain structure, biochemistry
- Psychological: behavioural, psychodynamic, family theories, cognitive
- Social

Genetic factors and brain structure are the biological explanations covered in depth and family theories and cognitive explanations are the psychological explanations covered in depth. The remaining explanations will be covered in less depth so that the content has a balance of breadth and depth.

To read up on schizophrenia, refer to pages 341–355 of A2PKT.

Schizophrenia is a psychotic disorder as it often involves a loss of contact with reality (sufferers cannot distinguish between inner experience and external reality) and a lack of self-insight (sufferers do not realise or accept that they are ill). It is based on two Greek words: *schizo* meaning "split" and *phren* meaning "mind", which refers to the splitting of the normal associations between mental processes such as perception, cognition, and emotion.

CLINICAL CHARACTERISTICS OF SCHIZOPHRENIA

Physical/Behavioural Symptoms
Schizophrenics may experience psychomotor poverty and in extreme cases catatonia, when awkward postures are assumed and the schizophrenic remains motionless in this position for hours at a time. They can exhibit "waxy flexibility" where their body can be manipulated into different positions. Schizophrenics may fall into a catatonic stupor where they lie motionless and appear unaware of their surroundings but are fully conscious throughout. Or increased motor activity can occur, such as stereotypy, purposeless, and repetitive movement. Disorganised, chaotic, and bizarre behaviour can be linked to other symptoms, e.g. covering up all the windows with black paper as a result of cognitive disturbance.

Perceptual Symptoms
Hallucinations: auditory hallucinations are most common, where the schizophrenic hears voices that are often abusive or offer a critical running commentary on their behaviour. Visual, smell, and taste hallucinations may also be experienced but are less common.

Cognitive Symptoms
Thought disorders include *delusions* and *thought interference*. Delusions of grandeur, persecution, paranoia, and control (sometimes known as alien control symptoms as the schizophrenic believes that their behaviour is under external control) can occur, which can develop during the course of the illness into an increasingly complex web of delusion. Thought insertion (belief that ideas are being planted in their mind), withdrawal (belief that thoughts are being removed from their mind), and broadcasting (belief that others can "tune into" their thoughts) can occur—these are collectively known as thought interference symptoms. Cognitive impairments include intellectual deficits in learning and memory. Most evident are the language impairments such as repeating sounds (echolalia), inventing words (neologisms), jumbled speech (word salad), and nonsensical rhyming (clang associations). The speech is characterised by incoherence and abrupt changes of topic due to cognitive distractibility (inability to maintain a train of thought).

Social Symptoms
Schizophrenics usually show social withdrawal and may always have lacked social skills. They have little interest in social interactions and do not gain pleasure from them, and so may be aloof, reclusive, and emotionally distant even before the onset of the disorder.

Emotional/Mood Symptoms
Symptoms can include a lack of emotion (emotional blunting) or inappropriate affect (e.g. giggling when told of a bereavement). One third of patients suffer depressive symptoms and one in eight patients meet the criteria for a mood disorder as well as schizophrenia and so tend to be diagnosed with *schizo-affective disorder*. Apathy, and a lack of drive, interest, personal care, and hygiene are common and can be linked to the depressed state.

TYPES OF SCHIZOPHRENIA

DSM-IV (*Diagnostic and Statistical Manual*, Volume 4, see A2PKT pp.342–343) identifies five types of schizophrenia: disorganised, catatonic, paranoid, undifferentiated, and residual. However, a more recent typology is presented in the table of symptoms below. This is based on the results of statistical analysis, which showed that these symptoms tend to cluster together (Liddle, 1987). However, most patients show a range of the symptoms during the course of their illness so these are not separate varieties of schizophrenia.

LIDDLE'S (1987) CORE SYMPTOMS OF SCHIZOPHRENIA		
Reality distortion	**Disorganisation**	**Poverty**
Hallucinations	Thought disorder	Lack of emotion
Delusions	Language disturbances	Apathy, lack of motivation
Thought interference	Psychomotor disturbances	Cognitive impairments
	Inappropriate affect	Psychomotor poverty
		Social withdrawal

Type 1 and Type 2 Classifications

Another common classification is into the *positive symptoms* (hallucinations, delusions, thought disturbances) of Type 1 schizophrenia and the *negative symptoms* (lack of interest, emotion, motivation, social withdrawal) of Type 2.

Schizophrenia is usually an episodic illness as it consists of periods of acute disturbance (positive symptoms) interspersed with periods of better functioning (negative symptoms). Schizophrenics may show both positive and negative symptoms, which contradicts the reductionist typology. However, the acute phase often resembles Type 1 and the chronic phase often resembles Type 2.

Diagnosis of Schizophrenia

The DSM-IV diagnostic criteria are:

1. Two or more of the symptoms identified above for a period of over 1 month. One symptom only is needed if the delusions are bizarre or if the hallucination is critical and abusive of the individual's behaviour.
2. The disturbance must be evident over a significant period of time, at least 6 months, including 1 month of pronounced symptoms.
3. The symptoms must have led to a failure to function in social and occupational roles.

EXPLANATIONS OF SCHIZOPHRENIA

Biological Explanations

GENETIC FACTORS

The fact that schizophrenia tends to run in families led to the inference that it has a genetic basis. According to the genetic hypothesis, the more closely related the family member to the schizophrenic the greater their chance of developing the disorder. Concordance rates, which show the percentage of family members developing schizophrenia, are investigated as research evidence. The comparison is the 1% probability of schizophrenia in someone selected at random.

RESEARCH EVIDENCE FOR

- *Twin studies.* Gottesman's (1991, see A2PKT p.345) analysis of twin studies revealed 48% concordance for monozygotic (MZ; identical) twins and only 17% for dizygotic (DZ; fraternal) twins. Gottesman also reported that the concordance rate for identical twins brought up apart was very similar to that for identical twins brought up together—this suggests that the high concordance rate for identical twins is not due to them being treated in a very similar way within the family.

- *Family studies* show that the risk of developing schizophrenia is greater for those more closely related to the schizophrenic. If both parents have schizophrenia there is a 46% chance, with one schizophrenic parent there is a 16% chance, and it is 8% if a sibling has schizophrenia (Gottesman, 1991, see A2PKT pp.345–346). Also, there is a 17% chance of developing schizophrenia in families where the identical twin of one parent has schizophrenia, which shows the influence of genes over nurture.

- *Adoption studies.* Tienari's study (1991, see A2PKT p.346) showed that 10.3% of adopted children who had a schizophrenic mother developed schizophrenia in adulthood, compared with only 1.1% of adopted children who did not have a schizophrenic mother. This supports the importance of genetic factors and is evidence against the role of nurture.

- *Gene-mapping studies.* A gene located on chromosome 5 has been linked to schizophrenia in a small number of extended families where a number of family members had the disorder (Sherrington et al., 1988).

RESEARCH EVIDENCE AGAINST

- The higher concordance rate in MZ twins may be due to the fact that MZ twins tend to be treated more similarly than DZ twins and so nurture may explain the concordance rates rather than nature (Loehlin & Nichols, 1976, see A2PKT P.204).

- Whilst Gottesman's (1991, see A2PKT p.345) finding that the concordance rates are similar for twins reared apart and together supports nature, critics have argued that the twins did not spend all of their childhood apart. Some were raised by close relatives and went to the same school and so did share a very similar environment (Kamin, 1977).

- The fact that concordance rates increase with genetic relatedness may be explained by the fact that this is because they are also likely to spend more time together, which means environmental factors may be influential.

- Fewer than 50% of children where both parents have schizophrenia develop the disorder, which is evidence against a direct genetic link.

- Further research into the gene on chromosome 5 has failed to replicate Sherrington's et al.'s (1988) findings and so reliability is low. Validity is questionable as the findings may be only representative of the original sample (Kennedy et al., 1988).

- The research evidence on psychological factors can be used as evidence against genetics, see below.

EVALUATION

 Twin studies provide strong genetic evidence. As the MZ twins are genetically identical whilst DZ twins are no more alike than ordinary siblings this supports the involvement of genetic factors. If these were not important, and instead nurture was the key determinant, then there should be no difference in the concordance rates between MZ and DZ twins.

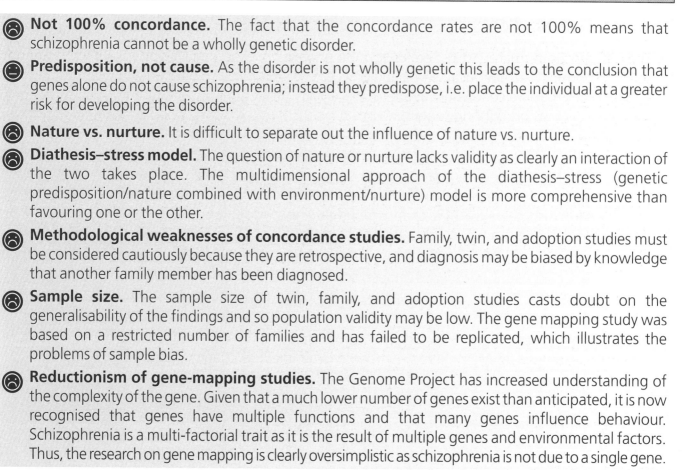

☹ **Not 100% concordance.** The fact that the concordance rates are not 100% means that schizophrenia cannot be a wholly genetic disorder.

😐 **Predisposition, not cause.** As the disorder is not wholly genetic this leads to the conclusion that genes alone do not cause schizophrenia; instead they predispose, i.e. place the individual at a greater risk for developing the disorder.

☹ **Nature vs. nurture.** It is difficult to separate out the influence of nature vs. nurture.

☹ **Diathesis–stress model.** The question of nature or nurture lacks validity as clearly an interaction of the two takes place. The multidimensional approach of the diathesis–stress (genetic predisposition/nature combined with environment/nurture) model is more comprehensive than favouring one or the other.

☹ **Methodological weaknesses of concordance studies.** Family, twin, and adoption studies must be considered cautiously because they are retrospective, and diagnosis may be biased by knowledge that another family member has been diagnosed.

☹ **Sample size.** The sample size of twin, family, and adoption studies casts doubt on the generalisability of the findings and so population validity may be low. The gene mapping study was based on a restricted number of families and has failed to be replicated, which illustrates the problems of sample bias.

☹ **Reductionism of gene-mapping studies.** The Genome Project has increased understanding of the complexity of the gene. Given that a much lower number of genes exist than anticipated, it is now recognised that genes have multiple functions and that many genes influence behaviour. Schizophrenia is a multi-factorial trait as it is the result of multiple genes and environmental factors. Thus, the research on gene mapping is clearly oversimplistic as schizophrenia is not due to a single gene.

BRAIN STRUCTURE

Schizophrenics have smaller brains and *enlarged ventricles* (fluid-filled cavities due to brain cell loss) in comparison to people without schizophrenia. The frontal lobes, temporal lobes, and hypothalamus may also be affected. The *neurodevelopmental hypothesis* suggests that schizophrenia is due to abnormal brain development, which is latent in the individual and triggered by brain maturation (Murray et al., 1988) during early adulthood.

RESEARCH EVIDENCE FOR

- MRIs (magnetic resonance imaging) showed that in MZ twins where one had schizophrenia and the other didn't, the schizophrenic twin had more enlarged ventricles and a reduced anterior hypothalamus (Suddath, Christison, Torrey, Casanova, & Weinberger, 1990, see A2PKT p.348).

- Post-mortem studies have shown disturbances in the temporal and frontal lobes, which have been linked to the negative symptoms.

- Schizophrenics' brains have lower rates of activity in the prefrontal cortex than the brains of non-schizophrenic controls (Buchsbaum, Kessler, King, Johnson, & Cappelletti, 1984).

- People with schizophrenia show abnormality in cognitive, behavioural, social, and emotional development many years before the onset of the disorder, which is consistent with the neurodevelopmental hypothesis. Parents' home movies of pre-schizophrenic children support this (Walker et al., 1994, see A2PKT p.349).

RESEARCH EVIDENCE AGAINST

- The differences in the MZ twins' brains show that genetics or neurodevelopmental factors are not solely responsible, as only environmental factors can account for such differences.

- Research shows that enlarged ventricles are found in non-schizophrenics, which contradicts this as a physical cause. Brain scans are not used as diagnostic tools because there is no consistent brain dysfunction, which reliably predicts schizophrenia.

- Brain abnormality may be caused by difficulties during pregnancy and at birth as high levels of such complications occur in schizophrenic patients (Done et al, 1992).

- Schizophrenia has been linked to viral infection as exposure of the mother to the influenza virus, particularly during the middle stages of pregnancy, increases the risk of schizophrenia in the child (Bar et al., 1990). Viral infection may also affect the newborn in a similar way, as people with schizophrenia are more often born during the winter months.

EVALUATION

- **Reliability.** There is a lack of consistency in the nature of brain abnormalities across different research studies, which clouds the exact nature of brain dysfunction in schizophrenics.

- **Cause and effect.** Causation cannot be inferred as associations only have been identified. The brain dysfunction may be a symptom of the disorder rather than a cause, as the plasticity (flexibility) of the brain means that it may change as a result of abnormality. Further research is needed for conclusive insights into the direction of the effect.

- **Nature or nurture.** The brain abnormality, to some extent, is due to genetic factors but as the brains of the MZ twins (one with schizophrenia and one without) differed considerably then nature must interact with nurture.

- **Diathesis–stress model.** Individuals may be predisposed (the diathesis) to brain dysfunction and so the neurodevelopmental hypothesis is correct. But the brain abnormality does not necessarily result in schizophrenia as this depends on the interaction of the diathesis with environmental factors. This accounts for the lack of consistency in the findings on brain dysfunction and the fact that the abnormality differs across MZ twins who share the same genes.

- **Generalisability.** Brain dysfunction is linked to negative symptoms only.

BIOCHEMISTRY

Genetic factors may lead to imbalances in the brain chemicals (neurotransmitters). According to the *dopamine hypothesis* of schizophrenia, excess levels of dopamine or an oversensitivity of the brain neurons to dopamine, is the cause of the disorder. There is strong empirical support for the role of dopamine as increasing dopamine function with drugs produces symptoms that are similar to those experienced by schizophrenics, and antipsychotic drugs work by blocking dopamine receptors. However, the drugs do not work for all patients and whilst they block the dopamine receptors immediately, symptom relief takes days or weeks, which shows there is not a direct link between dopamine and schizophrenia. The dopamine hypothesis is oversimplistic and can be criticised for using the treatment aetiology fallacy, that the cure is not necessarily the cause. Dopamine does not account for the variety of schizophrenic symptoms and seems more relevant to the positive symptoms. Currently the interaction of dopamine with other neurotransmitters (serotonin and glutamate) is being investigated and the biochemical basis of schizophrenia is likely to be highly complex. Further research is needed to see if biochemical imbalance is a cause, effect, or merely a correlate of schizophrenia.

Psychological Explanations

BEHAVIOURAL APPROACH

The principles of operant conditioning are used to explain the schizophrenic's bizarre behaviour. The behavioural explanation claims that abnormality is learned dysfunctional behaviour. Punishment may lead the child to withdraw and consequently they are labelled as "odd". The bizarre behaviour is rewarded with attention and this positive reinforcement encourages them to conform to the label according to Scheff's (1966) labelling theory. Consequently, more exaggerated versions of the disorder are displayed and so schizophrenia develops. Whilst this has some face validity it lacks conviction as a causal explanation. It is probably more relevant to the maintenance rather than the cause of the disorder as it does not explain how the bizarre behaviour originates or account for the severity of the disturbance. Genetic and cognitive explanations may better account for the severity of schizophrenia, and these are ignored as the behavioural explanation is reductionist and environmentally deterministic, only accounting for nurture.

PSYCHODYNAMIC APPROACH

The trauma caused by unresolved conflict between the id, ego, and superego is repressed into the unconscious and this causes regression to an earlier stage of psychosexual development, according to Freud. The schizophrenic regresses to an early part of the oral stage called primary narcissism where the ego had not separated from the id. The ego is the rational part of the mind, which is usually involved in reality testing, and so the lack of ego development results in egotism and a loss of contact with reality, which, in combination with strong sexual impulses, results in schizophrenia. The theory is speculative because it is impossible to test empirically concepts such as the unconscious, ego, regression, etc., and so there is lack of research evidence. Whist there is some face validity in assuming that the schizophrenic experiences inner turmoil, this may not necessarily be due to primary narcissism or strong sexual impulses. Freud's research is dated as it was conducted in the Victorian era and so may lack temporal validity. He used his own patients, upper-class Viennese hysterical women, as the sample and so population validity may be low. Thus, his research may have little relevance to schizophrenics today, as the research may be era-dependent and context bound. Also the psychodynamic emphasis on the past means current problems are often neglected.

FAMILY THEORIES

According to family theories, schizophrenia is a consequence of maladaptive behaviour and poor communication within the family.

RESEARCH EVIDENCE FOR FAMILY THEORIES

- The term *schizophrenogenic mother* was used by Fromm-Reichmann (1948) to describe a parent who was cold, domineering, and manipulative, creating a high level of conflict within the family. This causes the child to be distrustful and resentful of others and can manifest as schizophrenia.

- *Double-bind communication is* destructive and ambiguous interpersonal communication where the parent sends the child mixed messages and places them in a no-win situation. For example, assurances of love in a tone of voice that suggests the opposite. It is suggested that this explains the confused thinking of the schizophrenic (Bateson, Jackson, Haley, & Weakland, 1956, see A2PKT p.350).

- Lidz et al. (1958) introduced the terms *schism* to describe relationships where the parents are emotionally distant from one another and *skew* to describe a marriage where one partner is dominant and the other submissive. He proposed that such dysfunction could psychologically damage the child and so lead to schizophrenia.

- The anti-psychiatrist Laing (1971) claimed that schizophrenia was the sane response to a dysfunctional family environment. The disorder helped the individual and the family to cope with the maladaptive family unit.

RESEARCH EVIDENCE AGAINST FAMILY THEORIES

- *EE (expressed emotion)* refers to the criticism, hostility, and emotional over-involvement directed at the schizophrenic by family members. High EE has been well supported as a factor in relapse (i.e. a factor in *maintenance* rather than *cause*) as individuals are four times more likely to relapse if EE is high (Kavanagh, 1992, see A2PKT p.350).

- Patterns of communication are no different from those of parents of non-schizophrenics (Liem, 1974).

- Mischler and Waxler (1968, see A2PKT p.350) found significant differences in the way mothers spoke to their schizophrenic daughters compared to their normal daughters, which suggests that dysfunctional communication may be a result of living with the schizophrenic rather than the cause of the disorder.

- The biological explanations challenge environmental causes.

EVALUATION

- 🙁 **Ethical implications.** There are serious ethical concerns in blaming the family, particularly as there is little evidence upon which to base this. Gender bias is also an issue as the mother tends to be blamed the most, which means such research is highly socially sensitive. It is questionable whether the ends justify the means.

- 🙁 **Lack of evidence.** There is little research evidence that schizophrenic families are different and there is research evidence that dysfunctional communication characterises all family interactions to some extent. See if you can think of a time when you experienced a double-bind.

- 🙁 **Lack of explanatory power.** Given that communication may be similar in schizophrenic and non-schizophrenic families, the theories lack explanatory power—they don't account for the varied expression and severity of the disorder.

- 🙁 **Explains maintenance rather than cause.** The research on EE provides compelling evidence that family dynamics influence the maintenance rather than cause schizophrenia.

- 😐 **Multidimensional approach.** Not all siblings develop schizophrenia, which challenges the family environment as a cause, although different family members will have their own micro-environment. But it is more likely that this can be explained by differences in genetic vulnerability, cognition, and unconscious motivations, so a multidimensional approach is needed.

COGNITIVE APPROACH

A breakdown in the information-processing system results in faulty thinking, i.e. cognitive distortion. Recent research suggests that schizophrenic symptoms may be due to a lack of self-monitoring, and consequently thoughts and ideas are attributed to external sources such as hallucinations, or result in delusions because the individual does not realise that they are self-generated.

RESEARCH EVIDENCE FOR

- Frith (1992, see A2PKT p.352) suggests that positive symptoms are a result of the schizophrenics' inability to monitor their own cognition and behaviour.
- PET scans show underactivity in the frontal lobe of the brain, which is linked to self-monitoring and so provides biological support for this explanation.

RESEARCH EVIDENCE AGAINST

- The research into brain structural abnormality did not identify such dysfunctions and so there is a need for further research to link together the cognitive and biological explanations.

EVALUATION

- **Generalisability.** The self-monitoring explanation accounts for the positive symptoms but not the negative symptoms.
- **Scientific validity.** Research on self-monitoring employs the experimental method and so has scientific validity.
- **Artificiality.** The research, being experimental, lacks mundane realism and so may lack generalisability to the schizophrenic symptoms.
- **Cause or effect?** It is not clear whether the cognitive dysfunction is a cause or effect of the disorder. Prospective and longitudinal research where children at risk for schizophrenia are assessed over time or by self-monitoring is necessary to establish the direction of the effect.

Social Factors

Stressful life events may trigger schizophrenia as Day et al. (1987, see A2PKT pp.351–352) found a high number of stressful life events in the weeks leading up to the onset of schizophrenia in a study carried out cross-culturally. Many patients' illnesses do follow a major life event but this is not a clear-cut relationship because life events are not a prerequisite. They are more strongly linked to relapse than onset and may be due to genetic inheritance (innate differences in physiological reactivity) and so a multi-perspective is needed.

Summary

The factors in schizophrenia can be organised into those that create a vulnerability (*predisposing*), those that trigger the disorder (*precipitating*), and those that maintain it (*perpetuating*):

- Predisposing: genetics, neurodevelopmental hypothesis, dysfunctional family dynamics.
- Precipitating: life events, family conflict, biochemistry.
- Perpetuating: expressed emotion, faulty cognition, reinforcement.

This organisation is not absolute as certain factors in schizophrenia may be predisposing, precipitating, *and* perpetuating.

SO WHAT DOES THIS MEAN?

Genetics (the diathesis) may predispose neurodevelopmental abnormality, which may lead to problems in self-monitoring, i.e. cognitive dysfunction. However, the genetic factors and brain dysfunction are in a sense not the cause as they constitute vulnerability but do not necessarily give rise to schizophrenia. It is the predisposing factors or psychological triggers that explain why one individual develops schizophrenia and the other doesn't. The multidimensional approach of the diathesis–stress model provides the most insight into schizophrenia. But further research is needed to investigate the interaction of multiple biological (nature) and social/psychological (nurture) factors, e.g. the effect of environmental factors on the neurodevelopmental brain abnormality and how this links to cognitive dysfunction. More consideration needs to be given to the different types of schizophrenia and to which factors cause which symptoms in order to comprehensively account for the varied expression and complexity of the disorder. To conclude, schizophrenia is to some extent the best understood of the mental disorders, as there is strong evidence of a biological basis, but understanding is still limited compared to that of many physical illnesses.

OVER TO YOU

1.(a) Outline the clinical characteristics of schizophrenia. **(10 marks)**

(b) Outline one explanation of schizophrenia and evaluate using research studies and/or alternative explanations. **(20 marks)**

2. "Schizophrenia appears to be an abnormality in brain development that arises from mainly genetic, but also environmental factors" (Harrison). Discuss research into the causes of schizophrenia. **(30 marks)**

DEPRESSION

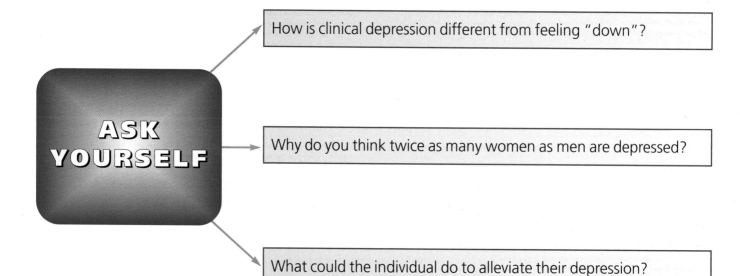

ASK YOURSELF

How is clinical depression different from feeling "down"?

Why do you think twice as many women as men are depressed?

What could the individual do to alleviate their depression?

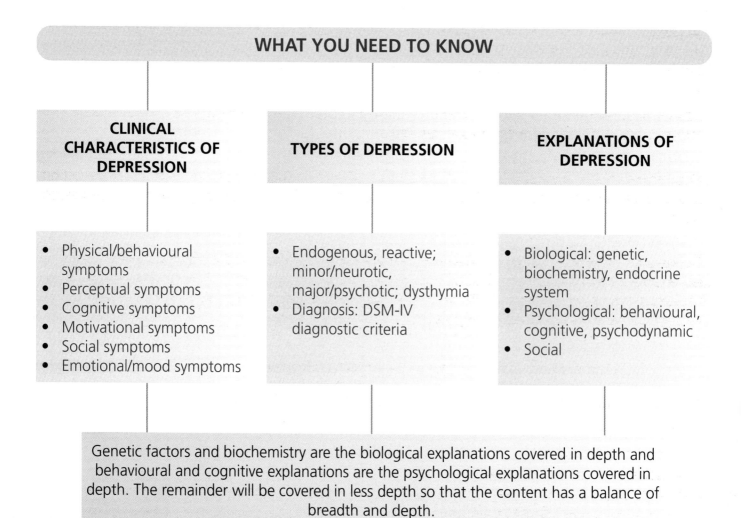

WHAT YOU NEED TO KNOW

CLINICAL CHARACTERISTICS OF DEPRESSION

- Physical/behavioural symptoms
- Perceptual symptoms
- Cognitive symptoms
- Motivational symptoms
- Social symptoms
- Emotional/mood symptoms

TYPES OF DEPRESSION

- Endogenous, reactive; minor/neurotic, major/psychotic; dysthymia
- Diagnosis: DSM-IV diagnostic criteria

EXPLANATIONS OF DEPRESSION

- Biological: genetic, biochemistry, endocrine system
- Psychological: behavioural, cognitive, psychodynamic
- Social

Genetic factors and biochemistry are the biological explanations covered in depth and behavioural and cognitive explanations are the psychological explanations covered in depth. The remainder will be covered in less depth so that the content has a balance of breadth and depth.

To read up on depression, refer to pages 355–370 of A2PKT.

Mood disorders are characterised by disturbances of affect (mood), which can be in the direction of depression or elation. This is distinguished from normal mood variations by the *duration* and *degree of disturbance*. Depression is an emotional response that can have physical, behavioural, perceptual, cognitive, motivational, social, and emotional symptoms.

CLINICAL CHARACTERISTICS OF DEPRESSION

Physical/Behavioural Symptoms
Appetite is usually reduced, but can increase (comfort eating) and tends to be unhealthy. *Sleep disturbances* occur. Insomnia tends to be most common with problems in falling asleep and early morning waking. Hypersomnia can also occur which is excessive sleeping and may be an attempt to escape reality. Sleep disturbances result in tiredness and feelings of lethargy (loss of energy) or restlessness. *Sex drive* is usually reduced.

Perceptual Symptoms
Auditory hallucinations may occur, which are extreme forms of self-critical delusions as the hallucinations often involve voices that are abusive and critical of the depressive.

Cognitive Symptoms
Depressives have slow, muddled thinking and difficulty in making decisions. Thinking is pessimistic, negative, and in severe cases suicidal. A negative self-concept can lead to faulty thinking where the individual is overly critical of him- or herself—this can develop into delusions.

Motivational Symptoms
Depressives show a lack of interest (*apathy*) in their appearance, work, home, and others. There is also reduced activity due to their lack of interest and energy.

Social Symptoms
Depressives usually show *social withdrawal* because they do not gain pleasure from social interaction and may feel they have nothing to contribute and do not want people to see them in their depressed state.

Emotional/Mood Symptoms
Depressives show low mood, unhappiness, anguish, and are often on the verge of tears. They may experience *anhedonia*, which refers to a loss of pleasure in activities previously enjoyed. *Diurnal mood variations* may occur where the mood changes throughout the day, being particularly low in the morning and improving a little as the day progresses.

TYPES OF DEPRESSION

Depression is the main symptom of a range of mood disorders, which include:

- Major depression (unipolar)
- Manic depression (bipolar)
- Seasonal affective disorder (SAD)
- Premenstrual syndrome (PMS)
- Postpartum depression (PPD)

Major depression can be divided into different types:

- *Endogenous*—caused by factors within the person.
- *Reactive*—caused by factors external to the person, such as stressful life events; this is the type that people are most likely to experience.

Although a useful distinction, this can be difficult to apply as the depression may be due to internal and external factors. In clinical practice a distinction is often made between minor, neurotic illness, and major, psychotic illness. The former is used when there is mood disturbance only and the latter is used when there are also severe cognitive and perceptual distortions, such as delusions and hallucinations. Dysthymia is a type of depression that persists over time (months even years) but is less severe. Major depression tends to be episodic. However, there is no clear dividing line between minor and major depression and so it is not always possible to use these labels.

Diagnosis of Depression

According to DSM-IV, diagnosis of major depression requires five of the physical, perceptual, behavioural, cognitive, social, and emotional symptoms to persist over a minimum period of 2 weeks.

EXPLANATIONS OF DEPRESSION

Biological Explanations

GENETIC FACTORS

Family, twin, and adoption studies suggest the involvement of genetic factors. The prevalence of depression in the random population (10% for men and 20% for women) is the baseline against which the concordance rates can be compared.

RESEARCH EVIDENCE FOR

- Allen (1976, see A2PKT p.356) reported a mean concordance rate of 40% for MZ twins compared to 11% for DZ twins. The high ratio supports the role of genetic factors.

- Gershon (1990, see A2PKT pp.356–357) reviewed the findings from a number of family studies and found that depression runs in families, as the rate of depression was two to three times higher in first degree relatives of depressives compared to the general population.

- Adoption studies have shown that the biological parents of adopted children who develop depression were eight times more likely than the adopted parents to have suffered with depression, which suggests the role of nature over nurture (Wender, Kety, Rosenthal, Schulsinger, Ortmann, & Lunde, 1986, see A2PKT p.357).

- McGuffin et al. (1996, see A2PKT p.356) found a concordance rate of 46% for identical twins compared to 20% for fraternal twins. Bertelsen, Harvald, and Hauge (1977) found a concordance rate for major depression of 59% for identical twins and of 30% for fraternal twins. For bipolar disorder, the concordance rate was 80% for identical twins and 16% for fraternal twins.

- Craddock and Jones (1999, see A2PKT p.356) found with bipolar disorder that the concordance rate was 40% for identical twins compared to between 5% and 10% for fraternal twins, siblings, and other close relatives.

RESEARCH EVIDENCE AGAINST

- The higher concordance rate found for MZ twins may be due to nurture as they are likely to experience a more similar environment than DZ twins since they tend to be treated the same.
- The depression may be culturally rather than genetically transmitted as the family members may observe and imitate depressive behaviour as predicted by social learning theory.
- The research evidence for psychological factors can be used as evidence against genetics, see page 212.

EVALUATION

Nature vs. nurture. It is difficult to separate out the influence of nature and nurture. Whilst the twin studies provide strong evidence for the role of genetic factors and the adoption studies point to the role of nature over nurture this is not conclusive.

Sample size. The samples in such studies are very small and so generalisability and population validity is constrained.

Diathesis–stress model. Genes alone do not determine who will develop depression—they only create vulnerability. Thus, they are not a direct cause as other factors must trigger the disorder. Evidence for this is that the concordance rates are not 100%, which shows that depression is due to an interaction of genetic and other factors.

BIOCHEMISTRY

The monoamine hypothesis suggests that depression is due to abnormal levels of neurotransmitters in the monoamine group. This was expanded upon with the *permissive amine theory* (Kety, 1975, see A2PKT p.358), which proposes that the level of noradrenaline and dopamine are controlled by serotonin. When serotonin is low the levels of noradrenaline fluctuate wildly; low levels are associated with depression and high levels with mania. The low levels of serotonin may be genetically inherited.

RESEARCH EVIDENCE FOR

- The three neurotransmitters—serotonin, dopamine, and noradrenaline—are part of the monoamine group and play a role in normal arousal and mood.
- By-product compounds of the enzymes that act upon noradrenaline and serotonin were lower than normal in the urine of depressives (Teuting, Rosen, & Hirschfeld, 1981, see A2PKT p.358).
- Antidepressant drugs such as the monoamine oxidase inhibitors (MAOIs) increase the levels of noradrenaline and serotonin and alleviate the symptoms of depression, which supports the influence of the biochemicals on mood. Similarly, SSRIs inhibit the re-uptake of serotonin and the resulting increase in the level of serotonin is linked to improved mood.
- Post-mortem studies of patients who committed suicide show reduced levels of serotonin and an increased number of serotonin receptor sites.

RESEARCH EVIDENCE AGAINST

- Abnormalities in serotonin function continue after recovery from depression, which suggests that there is not a clear-cut link between this and depression (Deakin & Graeff, 1991).

- Antidepressant drugs do not work for all patients. Also, the drugs increase the levels of the biochemicals immediately but can take weeks before they alleviate the depression, which further challenges a direct link between the neurotransmitters and depression.

- The research evidence on psychological factors can be used as evidence against.

EVALUATION

 Cause, effect, or correlate. It is difficult to establish whether the low levels of neurotransmitters cause depression, are an effect of having the disorder, or are merely associated. Causation cannot be inferred as associations only have been identified.

Treatment aetiology fallacy. The success of antidepressant drugs as a treatment does not necessarily mean the biochemicals are the cause of the depression in the first place. MacLeod (1998, see A2PKT p.359) described this as the treatment aetiology fallacy and used headaches as an example. Aspirin works well as a treatment but this doesn't mean the headache was due to an absence of aspirin.

Reductionist and deterministic. Biological explanations are reductionist as they focus on only one factor and at present our understanding of biochemistry is oversimplified. This means other biological factors, such as hormones, and psychological factors are ignored. The biological explanations are also deterministic because they ignore the individual's ability to control their own behaviour.

ENDOCRINE SYSTEM

Cortisol produced during the body's response to stress has been linked to depression, as levels of cortisol tend to be elevated in depressed patients. However, this lacks explanatory power, as it does not explain why one individual develops depression and another develops an anxiety disorder, as cortisol levels are also high in other mental disorders. This could be genetically determined as physiological reactivity may be inherited.

Psychological Explanations

BEHAVIOURAL APPROACH

According to this approach, depression is due to maladaptive learning. The principles of operant conditioning have been applied to explain depression using reinforcement and punishment.

RESEARCH EVIDENCE FOR

- Lewinsohn (1974, see A2PKT pp.362–363) suggests that depression is due to a reduction in positive reinforcement as a consequence of some form of loss, e.g. redundancy, relationship breakdown. Also, once depressed, the individual may receive positive reinforcement such as sympathy and attention.

- Learned helplessness occurs when an individual is placed in a no-win situation. When the individual associates a lack of control with a situation, e.g. when punishment is seen as unavoidable, passive, helpless behaviour is shown. Seligman (1975, see A2PKT p.363) tested his theory by exposing dogs to electric shocks they could not avoid. When they were then given the opportunity to avoid the shocks by jumping over a barrier the dogs did not learn to do this, whereas dogs not exposed to unavoidable shocks readily learned to avoid them. Seligman generalised this to depression in humans. Stressful experiences may be experienced as unavoidable and uncontrollable and so result in learned helplessness, which leads to depression.

RESEARCH EVIDENCE AGAINST

- Many people suffer loss without becoming depressed, which the theory on reinforcement reduction cannot explain.

- Research into the role of cognitive factors in depression suggests that self-perception and faulty thinking may be more influential than learned helplessness and may account for why this develops. Abramson, Seligman, and Teasdale (1978, see A2PKT pp.363–364) have expanded upon Seligman's theory of learned helplessness with the *attribution model*, which does account for cognition, see overleaf.

EVALUATION

Reductionist. The behavioural explanations are greatly oversimplified as they focus on only one factor, the environment. This focus on the external means internal factors that may be more influential, such as biological and cognitive, are ignored.

Environmentally deterministic. The behavioural explanations are deterministic as they suggest that behaviour is controlled by the environment, which ignores the individual's ability to control their own behaviour.

Ignores nature. The behavioural explanations overemphasise nurture and ignore nature.

Extrapolation. The generalisability of Seligman's research is an issue as there are qualitative differences between humans and animals.

Face validity. The symptoms in depression do appear similar to the responses shown by Seligman's dogs and so the behavioural explanations do have face validity.

Ecological validity. Seligman's research lacks mundane realism and so may not be generalisable to real-life settings and so may lack ecological validity.

Population validity. Learned helplessness as an explanation of the development of depression may be more relevant to certain types of people, e.g. those who lack social skills and so have limited emotional support.

Cause or effect? Causation cannot be inferred as associations only have been identified. The lack of reinforcement experienced in social interactions or the tendency to feel helpless may be a consequence of being depressed rather than a cause. Consequently, the behavioural explanations may be more relevant to the maintenance than the onset of depression.

COGNITIVE APPROACH

Cognitive dysfunction in attributional style (Abramson et al.'s attribution model) and view of self, the world, and the future (Beck's cognitive triad) have been linked to the development of depression. Negative schemas develop during childhood as a consequence of critical interpersonal experiences, and are activated when the individual experiences similar situations in later life.

RESEARCH EVIDENCE FOR

- Abramson et al. (1978, see A2PKT pp.363–364) developed Seligman's work with the attribution model, which considers how people respond to failure. Individuals susceptible to depression attribute failure to *internal* (my own fault), *stable* (things will never change), and *global* (applies the failure to a wide range of situations, e.g. "I'm rubbish at everything") causes. Such thinking is more negative and self-critical than attributing experience to external, unstable, and specific causes. This suggests that aversive stimuli on its own doesn't cause learned helplessness and depression, as this is dependent on how the individual *thinks*. Hence, the attribution model supports the role of cognitive factors and improves upon the original learned helplessness theory.

- Beck and Clark (1988, see A2PKT pp.364–365) proposed the cognitive triad, which is the individual's thoughts about *self*, *world*, and *future*. The more negative and therefore the more *hopeless* the cognition, the greater the risk of depression. Beck also identified errors in logic or cognitive biases, such as magnification, minimisation, and personalisation, where weaknesses are exaggerated and strengths under-emphasised. Polarised thinking is another bias, which is also known as black and white thinking. For example, depressives often set themselves unattainable standards such as, "I must be liked by everybody; if not I'm unlovable".

- A prospective study by Nolen-Hoeksma, Girgus, and Seligman (1992, see A2PKT pp.365–366) investigated thinking before the onset of depression. They found that a negative attributional style predicted the onset of depression in response to stressful life events, so supporting the role of negative thinking as a risk factor in depression.

RESEARCH EVIDENCE AGAINST

- Lewinsohn, Steimetz, Larsen, and Franklin (1981, see A2PKT p.365) found that negative thinking did not precede depression in their prospective study. They concluded that people who suffered with depression were not more likely to have negative cognitions and so the direction of causality may be that depression causes the negative thinking rather than vice versa.

EVALUATION

- **Face validity.** Depressive people do have the negative cognitions described by Abramson and Beck and so there is a high level of face validity.

- **Success of cognitive treatments.** Cognitive behavioural therapy (CBT) has been found to be as effective as antidepressants (Elkin et al., 1985), which supports the role of cognitive factors in depression. But the cure does not necessarily indicate the cause, as the treatment aetiology fallacy states.

- **Self-report criticisms.** Research into cognitive factors relies on self-report, e.g. the Beck Depression Inventory (Beck, 1967, see A2PKT p.365). The self-report method yields subjective data as it's vulnerable to bias and distortion as a consequence of researcher effects and participant reactivity and so may lack validity.

- **Lack of reliability.** The prospective research is inconsistent and so we cannot be sure if negative cognitions cause or are a consequence of depression.

- **Cause or effect?** The evidence is not convincing that negative cognitions precede the disorder but nor has this been disproved. Therefore, conclusions are limited. It may be that the relationship is curvilinear, i.e. negative thinking predisposes depression and depression increases negative thinking.

- **Descriptive not explanatory.** The research may describe the nature of depressives' thoughts rather than explain the development of depression if negative cognition is a consequence, not a cause, of depression. If it is a cause then it is not clear what causes the negative cognitions in the first place.

- **Multidimensional approach.** To account fully for depression it is necessary to consider how cognition interacts with other approaches. For example, faulty thinking could be due to an interaction of biological and social factors.

PSYCHODYNAMIC APPROACH

According to Freud we are victims of our feelings, as repression and displacement are defence mechanisms in response to *actual loss* (death of a loved one) and *symbolic loss* (loss of status) that enable us to cope with the emotional turmoil, but can result in depression. Individuals with excessive dependence on others for self-esteem as a consequence of oral fixation are particularly vulnerable and unable to cope with loss. Anger at the loss is displaced onto the self, which affects self-esteem and causes the individual to re-experience loss that occurred in childhood. Freud believed the superego (or conscience) is dominant in the depressed person and this explains the excessive guilt experienced by many depressives. In contrast, the manic phase occurs when the individual's ego, or rational mind, asserts itself and he/she feels in control. Thus, this approach has face validity as even if a psychodynamic approach is not favoured it is widely accepted that childhood experience can predispose the individual to mental illness in adulthood. However, early loss does not consistently predict depression. Also, as usual, the key weakness is that Freud's theory lacks empirical support and so is neither verifiable nor falsifiable.

Social Factors

Depression is often preceded by a high number of stressful life events. Interviews of depressed women showed that 61% of the depressed women had experienced at least one very stressful life event compared to only 19% of the non-depressed women. Social support was identified as a variable that protected against depression, as only 10% of women with a close friend became depressed compared to 37% of those without an intimate friend (Brown & Harris, 1978, see A2PKT p.366). However, as you may remember from studying stress at AS, we are only as stressed as we think ourselves to be. Thus, the critical mediating factor may be self-perception, which suggests that cognitive factors predispose the individual to depression. This partly accounts for why people can experience very similar stressful situations and some become depressed whereas others don't. However, to account fully for such variation the interaction of biological predisposing factors (innate physiological reactivity) and environmental factors (stress) needs to be considered.

James (1998), the author of *Britain on the Couch*, proposed another social explanation. He suggests that we are facing an epidemic of depression as society manufactures psychological illness because we are exposed to unrealistically high standards of living against which we cannot measure up and so are left with a sense of failure. This is particularly so if the individual has a high level of perfectionism. This has a high level of face validity and further supports the role of cognitive factors. A key strength is that it accounts for the influence of society rather than just the individual in the development of depression.

> **NOTE:** The evolutionary explanations can also be used, so see Chapter 7, Evolutionary Explanations of Human Behaviour.

Summary

The factors in depression can be organised into those that create a vulnerability (*predisposing*), those that trigger the disorder (*precipitating*), and those that maintain it (*perpetuating*):

- Predisposing: genetics, early childhood experience of loss, negative thinking and self-criticism.
- Precipitating: life events, family conflict, adult experience of loss, biochemistry, ideal standards of society.
- Perpetuating: faulty cognition, reinforcement.

SO WHAT DOES THIS MEAN?

Statistics show that women are two to three times more likely to suffer with depression than men, which may be best explained by differences in gender socialisation. Thus, more consideration needs to be given to the role of the "sick society" rather than just the "sick individual" and how the two interact, for example nature (the innate characteristics of the individual, e.g. heightened physiological reactivity and so high levels of cortisol) creates nurture (experience of the environment as threatening). It is likely that there are multiple causes and effects as depression is a multifaceted disorder that exists at biological, behavioural, cognitive, social, emotional, and unconscious levels. Thus, a multidimensional approach such as the diathesis–stress model is needed, as at present understanding is limited as to how the many predisposing, precipitating, and perpetuating factors interact and how these differ depending on the type of depression.

OVER TO YOU

1. **"There are many different kinds of depression. For example, unipolar and bipolar, endogenous and reactive."**

   Discuss explanations for depression, including the evidence on which they are based.

   (30 marks)

2. **Describe and evaluate the possible contribution of psychological (e.g. social) and/or biological (e.g. genetic) factors to depression.**

   (30 marks)

ANXIETY DISORDERS

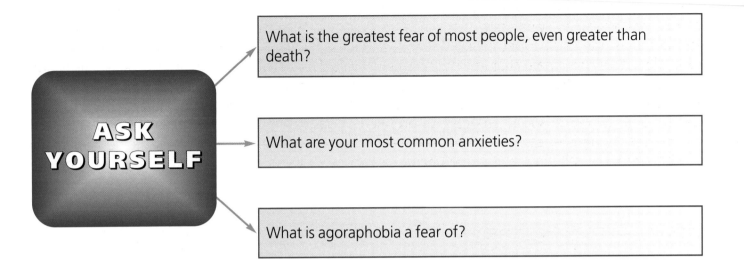

ASK YOURSELF

What is the greatest fear of most people, even greater than death?

What are your most common anxieties?

What is agoraphobia a fear of?

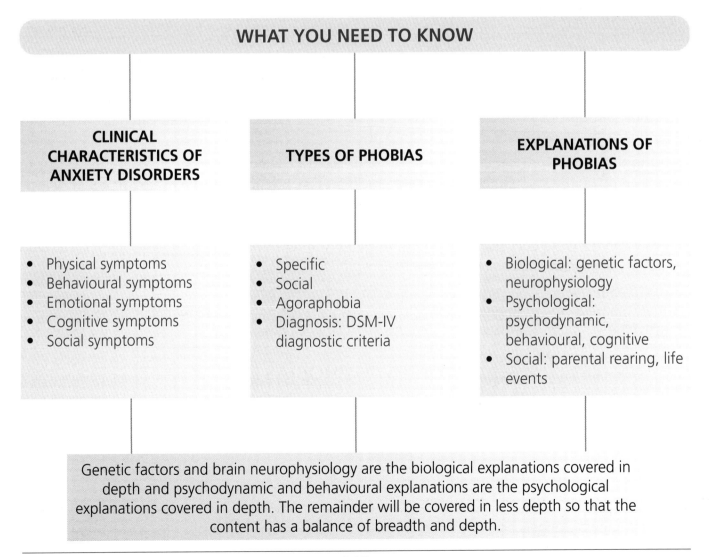

WHAT YOU NEED TO KNOW

CLINICAL CHARACTERISTICS OF ANXIETY DISORDERS

- Physical symptoms
- Behavioural symptoms
- Emotional symptoms
- Cognitive symptoms
- Social symptoms

TYPES OF PHOBIAS

- Specific
- Social
- Agoraphobia
- Diagnosis: DSM-IV diagnostic criteria

EXPLANATIONS OF PHOBIAS

- Biological: genetic factors, neurophysiology
- Psychological: psychodynamic, behavioural, cognitive
- Social: parental rearing, life events

Genetic factors and brain neurophysiology are the biological explanations covered in depth and psychodynamic and behavioural explanations are the psychological explanations covered in depth. The remainder will be covered in less depth so that the content has a balance of breadth and depth.

To read up on anxiety disorders, refer to pages 370–384 of A2PKT.

NOTE: As stated in the Specification, you need to know the clinical characteristics of *one* anxiety disorder, including the biological and psychological explanations for it, and the evidence on which these explanations are based; we are using phobias as our example.

PHOBIAS

Phobias are a form of anxiety disorder where the adaptive emotional response has become chronic and disabling. They consist of irrational fears that are out of proportion to the reality of the threat provided by the fear-provoking stimulus.

CLINICAL CHARACTERISTICS OF ANXIETY DISORDERS

Physical Symptoms
The immediate physical symptoms are the body's response to stress. However, this is heightened and can result in breathlessness and tightness in the chest, hyperventilation (increased breathing), and palpitations (increased heart rate). Hyperventilation increases carbon dioxide and this can lead to light-headedness, "pins and needles", and even painful muscle contractions. Muscle tension can lead to headaches and aching and stiffness, particularly in the back, neck, and shoulders.

Behavioural Symptoms
Avoidance behaviour is shown as the individual usually avoids the feared object, which can greatly restrict their everyday behaviour. Anxiety often results in restless, "jumpy" behaviour, where the individual has difficulty relaxing and doing nothing. A startle response is often common where the individual is easily unnerved.

Emotional Symptoms
Anxiety is accompanied by a feeling of dread. The individual is frightened and distressed and may feel he or she is about to die or lose control of their bodily functions.

Cognitive Symptoms
Anxiety can decrease concentration and so decrease the person's ability to perform complex tasks. Reduced cognitive capacity can inhibit workplace functioning.

Social Symptoms
Anxiety may reduce the individual's ability to cope with social settings and so inhibit personal and social functioning.

TYPES OF PHOBIAS

The main categories of phobia are specific phobia, social phobia, and agoraphobia. The latter usually causes more disturbances to the individual's daily life than specific phobias, which are more easily avoided.

Specific Phobia

This is the phobia of a specific object, which usually fall into four main subtypes:

1. Animal type.
2. Environmental dangers type.

3. Blood-injection-injury type.
4. Situational type (planes, lifts, enclosed spaces).

A fifth, "other type" is an umbrella type that covers any specific phobia that does not fall into the four main types. The prevalence is 4–7% of the population.

Social Phobia

Social phobia is a fear of social situations due to self-consciousness of own behaviour and fear of others' reactions. This can be *generalised*, where the individual suffers social anxiety in most situations, or *specific*, where the individual fears a particular situation, such as public speaking. The prevalence is 1–2% of the population.

Agoraphobia

This is the fear of open or public places, which can include open or closed spaces, public transport, or crowds. It is very rare on its own as it is co-morbid with panic disorder. The panic disorder usually occurs first and then the individual avoids open or public places so as not to have a panic attack, and thus the agoraphobia develops. Approximately 50% of all phobics suffer with agoraphobia with panic disorder. The prevalence is 2–3% of the population.

Diagnosis of Phobias

The DSM-IV diagnostic criteria are:

1. Marked and persistent fear of a specific object or situation.
2. Exposure to the fear-provoking stimulus produces a rapid anxiety response.
3. The individual recognises that the fear experienced is excessive.
4. The phobic stimulus is either avoided or responded to with great anxiety.
5. The phobic reactions interfere significantly with the individual's working or social life, or there is marked distress about the phobia.

EXPLANATIONS OF PHOBIAS

Biological Explanations

GENETIC FACTORS

Family, twin, and adoption studies suggest the involvement of genetic factors. The evidence is strongest for agoraphobia, least for specific phobia, and falls in the middle for social phobia. The concordance rates can be compared with the prevalence rates for the random population given above.

RESEARCH EVIDENCE FOR

- **Agoraphobia.** A twin study found concordance rates of 31% for MZ compared to 0% for DZ for agoraphobia (Torgersen, 1983, see A2PKT p.374). Close relatives of agoraphobics were more likely to be suffering from agoraphobia than relatives of nonagoraphobics (Harris, Noyes, Crowe, & Chaudhry, 1983, see A2PKT p.374).
- **Specific phobias.** 31% of relatives of individuals with specific phobia also had a phobia (Fyer et al., 1990, see A2PKT p.374). Ost (1989, see A2PKT p.374) found that 64% of blood phobics had a relative who was also blood phobic.

- **Social phobia.** Social phobics are extremely introverted (Stemberger, Turner, & Beidel, 1995) and as personality is partly genetically determined then this supports the influence of genetic factors.

RESEARCH EVIDENCE AGAINST

- Skre, Onstad, Torgersen, Lygren, and Kringlen (1993, see A2PKT p.374) found that the concordance rate for social phobia was similar in MZ and DZ twins, which challenges the role of genetic factors.
- The psychological explanations covered below provide counterperspectives. In particular, social learning theory provides a persuasive explanation as phobias may run in families because the phobic behaviour is imitated and so learned, rather than because it is inherited.

EVALUATION

- **Not 100% concordance.** The concordance rates are moderate apart from the finding on blood phobics, which suggests that genetic factors may predispose but do not cause phobias. However, the lack of genetic evidence means that this is not conclusive.
- **Nature vs. nurture.** Do concordance rates reflect nature or are they really due to nurture? The phobia could be culturally rather than genetically transmitted.
- **Biologically deterministic.** The suggestion that the genes determine phobias is deterministic as this ignores the individual's ability to control their own behaviour.
- **Sample size.** The samples in such studies are very small and so generalisability and population validity may be limited, which means the findings may not be representative of other populations.
- **Methodological weaknesses of concordance studies.** Family, twin, and adoption studies must be considered cautiously because they are retrospective and diagnosis may be biased by knowledge that another family member has been diagnosed.

NEUROPHYSIOLOGY

The stress response and biochemistry have been linked to the development of phobic disorders.

RESEARCH EVIDENCE FOR

- Individuals with phobias may have inherited a high level of *physiological reactivity*, i.e. the stress response is greater than the norm. This reactivity may predispose the individual to phobic disorder because they may be more easily aroused by stimuli.
- The neurotransmitters serotonin and noradrenaline have been implicated in the physiological reactivity.
- Lader and Mathews (1968, see A2PKT p.375) found that agoraphobics and social phobics do have higher levels of arousal.

RESEARCH EVIDENCE AGAINST

- A natural experiment that tested for a difference between agoraphobic patients and normal controls found no significant difference in physiological reactivity when they were exposed to biological challenges. This suggests the disorder was due to how the patients perceived the threat and so implicates *cognitive* rather than physiological factors.

- Social learning theory provides an alternative behavioural explanation. According to this, phobias are culturally transmitted as they are learned through observation and imitation. Social learning theory has great explanatory power. It accounts for how children learn so much so quickly and so may provide a more valid explanation of how children acquire phobias. This doesn't necessarily invalidate biological explanations, as nature and nurture are causative in mental disorders.

- Anti-psychiatrists such as Szasz, Laing, and Goffman claim that abnormality is due to "problems in living" and that madness is a "myth". Biological explanations do not account for social and cultural factors, which is a key weakness.

EVALUATION

 Cause or effect. It is not clear whether high arousal is causative or if the phobia leads to high arousal. It may be a curvilinear relationship. Causation cannot be inferred as associations only have been identified.

 Reductionism. The neurophysiological research is reductionist as only one factor is considered, whereas the psychological perspectives show that cognition and social learning may be more influential.

Lack of research evidence. There is a lack of research evidence on the role of neurotransmitters. But it is likely that the biochemical basis of phobias is much more complex and involves more neurotransmitters than is currently understood.

Multi-perspective. Biological explanations need to be considered in combination with other explanations. Both biological and psychological factors interact in the aetiology of anxiety disorder as the compromise position of the diathesis–stress model suggests—"the genes (diathesis/nature) load the gun but the environment (stress/nurture) pulls the trigger" (Goldman, 1992).

Psychological Explanations

PSYCHODYNAMIC APPROACH

Freud proposed that anxiety results when id impulses or sexual (libidinous) desires are repressed into the unconscious. Repressing and therefore denying wish-fulfilment of whatever it is we know we shouldn't do creates tension that is expressed as anxiety. Phobias develop when psychic energy, as a consequence of conflict and fixation at one of the psychosexual stages of development, becomes attached to a specific object as a way of coping with the conflict and that object then comes to *symbolise* the conflict.

RESEARCH EVIDENCE FOR

- Freud, as evidence for his theory, offered the case study of Little Hans' phobia of horses (see A2PKT p.376). According to Freud, Hans feared horses because they resembled his father; their black muzzles and blinkers looked like his father's moustache and glasses. He feared his father because of castration anxiety as a result of his Oedipal conflict and displaced this onto horses.

RESEARCH EVIDENCE AGAINST

- Behavioural explanations can provide a simpler and more convincing account of the phobia as a conditioned fear response, as Hans' phobia developed after he witnessed a serious accident involving a horse and cart moving at high speed.

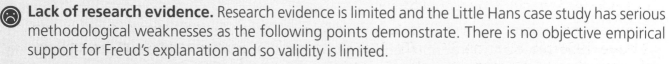

- Fromm (1970) suggested that Hans' mother was the source of his anxiety, not the father. The mother, according to Fromm, had fantasies about her son and caused his castration anxiety, and so Freud's key evidence isn't entirely consistent with the Oedipal theory, which casts doubt on the validity of this as an explanation of phobia.

EVALUATION

 Face validity. It makes sense that we feel anxious when we give in to unacceptable desires, but these are not necessarily a consequence of unconscious conflicts.

Lack of research evidence. Research evidence is limited and the Little Hans case study has serious methodological weaknesses as the following points demonstrate. There is no objective empirical support for Freud's explanation and so validity is limited.

Researcher bias. Freud only met Little Hans twice and so most of his information came from the boy's father who was an ardent supporter of Freud's work. This brings into question the validity of the research, as researcher expectancy and bias in interpretations mean that the truth of the research is questionable.

Generalisability. Case studies have limited generalisability and so population validity is questionable, which means the findings may not be representative of other populations.

BEHAVIOURAL APPROACH

The behavioural approach uses the principles of classical conditioning (learned associations) and operant conditioning (learned consequences) to explain the development of phobias. Bandura (1986, see A2PKT p.379) expanded on the traditional learning theories with modelling or observational learning, which offers another explanation of phobia development.

RESEARCH EVIDENCE FOR

- The conditioning of a phobia in Albert (an 11-month-old boy) by Watson and Rayner (1920, see A2PKT p.378) using the principles of classical conditioning. They induced fear of a rat (neutral stimulus) by repeated pair associations of it with a loud noise (unconditioned stimulus). Albert automatically feared the loud noise (unconditioned response) and quickly learned to fear (conditioned response) the rat (conditioned stimulus). This showed that a phobia could develop through association of a previously neutral stimulus with a fear-provoking stimulus.

- As predicted by the behavioural principle of generalisation the phobia can then be generalised to similar objects. For example, Albert generalised his fear to other furry white objects including cotton wool and Santa Claus' beard.

- Mowrer's (1947, see A2PKT pp.377–378) two-process theory expanded upon the traditional explanation as, according to this, the phobia is acquired through classical conditioning and maintained by operant conditioning as avoidance of the feared object is negatively reinforcing and so stamps in the phobia.

- 50% of people being treated by Barlow and Durand (1995, see A2PKT pp.377–378) for driving phobia recalled a traumatic incident that triggered the phobia so supporting classical conditioning. Similarly, nearly everybody they were treating for choking phobia linked this to an experience of choking.

- Bandura (1986, see A2PKT p.379) proposed that phobias could also be developed through observational learning, modelling, and direct reinforcement.
- Evidence of modelling was found in monkeys who developed snake phobia by observing another monkey's fearful reaction to a snake (Mineka, Davidson, Cook, & Kuir, 1984, see A2PKT p.379).

RESEARCH EVIDENCE AGAINST

- According to the principles of classical conditioning the association is extinguished if the bonds cease. Thus, the phobia should not persist over time, although Mowrer's (1947, see A2PKT pp.377–378) expanded explanation can account for this.
- Phobias of neutral stimuli cannot be as easily conditioned as the Albert experiment suggests (Davison & Neale, 1996, see A2PKT pp.377–378). Attempts to condition phobias of neutral stimuli using electric shocks in the laboratory have had little success.
- Approximately half of all phobics cannot recall a highly unpleasant experience with the feared object (Keuthen, 1980, see A2PKT p.379).
- DiNardo et al. (1988, see A2PKT pp.378–379) reported that 50% of dog phobics had had an unpleasant encounter but about 50% of normal controls had also had such experiences and did not develop a phobia. Behaviourism ignores cognitive factors and so cannot account for this individual variation, which is probably due to the patients' perception and interpretation and so implicates *cognitive* rather than behavioural factors.
- Menzies and Clarke's (1994, see A2PKT p.379) analysis of existing research found that there are only a few well-documented cases where social learning had clearly led to phobia.

EVALUATION

 Ethical issues. Protection of participants was clearly an ethical issue in the Albert study, which the researchers acknowledged but felt was justifiable because children experience fearful situations in daily life. However, whether the ends justify the means is debatable.

 Face validity. Learning from experience and social learning theory do make sense and the latter is particularly convincing as children do imitate their parents' responses and parents do reinforce fear responses, e.g. of traffic.

 Reliability. The research evidence on whether phobias result from a traumatic experience, and so classical conditioning, is very inconsistent and so lacks reliability. Also, attempts to replicate Watson and Rayner's research have been unsuccessful. This casts doubt on the validity of the explanation and shows that not all phobias can be explained by conditioning.

Retrospective. The fact that unpleasant experiences of the phobic object are not identified could be due to poor recall as retrospective data is subject to error. Or the memory could have been repressed if it was particularly traumatic, which supports the validity of conditioning as an explanation, as it may be that frightening experiences have initiated the phobia but that these are not remembered.

Reductionism. Behavioural explanations are oversimplified because they only account for learning and ignore other important factors such as cognition and biological preparedness.

Environmental determinism. The behavioural explanations are deterministic because they suggest that behaviour is controlled by the environment, which ignores the individual's ability to control their own behaviour.

Nature vs. nurture. Behavioural explanations account for nurture only as, according to these, behaviour is solely a product of learning as we are born as a blank slate (*tabula rasa*). They ignore nature, which is a significant weakness as the evolutionary explanation suggests certain objects are more likely to be conditioned than others.

 Multidimensional approach. As not all phobias can be explained by conditioning and social learning, other processes must be involved, such as biological preparedness as suggested by the evolutionary approach. So to understand phobias an interaction of different factors must be considered.

COGNITIVE APPROACH

The cognitive approach suggests that cognitive biases underpin phobias. According to Beck and Emery (1985, see A2PKT p.380), anxious people employ vulnerability schemas (or cognitive biases), which means they are more likely to perceive stimuli as threatening and harmful to themselves. This has face validity as it does account for the high level of anxiety reported by phobics and it makes sense that people with anxiety disorder find the world a threatening place. But it is descriptive rather than explanatory. It describes the thought patterns experienced rather than explaining how or why they developed in the first place. Furthermore, it is not clear whether these precede or follow the disorder so cause and effect is an issue. Clark's (1986, see A2PKT p.380) cognitive theory of panic disorder suggests a cognitive bias towards bodily sensations. This means they are over vigilant to changes in their body sensations and exaggerate the danger of them, e.g. increased heart rate could be life threatening. This increases anxiety, which increases the catastrophic thoughts, and so a vicious circle develops. This is relevant to agoraphobics who also tend to suffer with panic disorder and may offer insight into the other phobic disorders.

Social Factors

Parental rearing styles high in control and overprotection and low in affection have been linked to social phobia and agoraphobia. This is concurrent with the social learning theory that anxiety disorders are learned through cultural transmission. However, accounts of parental styles are retrospective and so may lack validity and research is correlational so this cannot be inferred as a cause of phobias.

A high number of life events has been reported in the months preceding an anxiety disorder. Kleiner and Marshall (1987, see A2PKT p.382) report that 84% of agoraphobics suffered family problems in the months prior to onset. Finlay-Jones and Brown (1981, see A2PKT p.382) report a difference in the types of life events experienced by anxiety disorder patients compared to depressed patients. Anxiety disorders tended to be preceded by life events involving danger such as injury or illness, whereas depression tended to be preceded by life events involving loss, such as divorce or redundancy. This research is also correlational and so cause and effect cannot be inferred. It is based on retrospective self-report, and so internal validity may be reduced due to bias and distorted recall.

NOTE: The evolutionary explanations can also be used, so see Chapter 7, as biological preparedness is a key explanation. It is a counterperspective against the traditional conditioning explanation as it is evidence against the neutrality of the feared stimulus and so may explain why replications failed to condition phobias to neutral stimuli.

Summary

The factors in phobias can be organised into those that create a vulnerability (*predisposing*), those that trigger the disorder (*precipitating*), and those that maintain it (*perpetuating*):

- Predisposing: genetics, neurophysiology, biological preparedness, early childhood conflicts, cognitive biases.
- Precipitating: life events, family conflict.
- Perpetuating: faulty cognition, negative reinforcement of avoidance behaviour, physiological reactivity.

SO WHAT DOES THIS MEAN?

Not all family members develop the same disorder, and so it may be misleading to assume that genetic factors are specific to a single type of phobia, or even mental disorder. Genetic vulnerability may be more general than that (Kendler et al., 1995, see A2PKT p.375). Genes alone cannot explain why different types of phobia develop. Therefore, genetic factors do not account for individual differences in susceptibility to different types of phobias.

The physiological and psychological explanations offer a wide range of insights into the basis of phobic disorders. Given the variety of types of disorder, a multidimensional approach, such as the diathesis–stress model, must be taken in order to account for the influence of nature (genetic predisposition, neurophysiology, and biochemistry) and nurture (conditioning, social learning, and stress). Physiological reactivity and consequently temperament are genetically predisposed and this may influence biochemistry, social learning, and cognitive biases. Further research is needed to understand how the various biological and psychological factors interact.

OVER TO YOU

1. **Compare and contrast two explanations of one anxiety disorder.** **(30 marks)**

QUESTIONS AND ESSAY PLANS

The key focus in this unit is synopticity so make sure you refer to the different methodologies, approaches, issues, and debates. Note the different types of question and be prepared to answer the different types of question for each of the three disorders.

1(a) Outline the clinical characteristics of schizophrenia. (10 marks)

The question is divided in terms of AO1 and AO2, where (a) is AO1 and in (b) AO1 = 5 marks and AO2 = 15 marks.

Paragraph 1

Explain what schizophrenia is: schizophrenia is a psychotic disorder as it often involves a loss of contact with reality (cannot distinguish between inner experience and external reality) and a lack of self-insight (do not realise or accept that they are ill). It is based on two Greek words—*schizo* meaning "split" and *phren* meaning "mind", which refer to the splitting of the normal associations between mental processes such as perception, cognition, and emotion.

Paragraph 2

Then identify the physical, perceptual, behavioural, cognitive, social, and emotional symptoms, how these are diagnosed, and how they can manifest as different types of schizophrenia.

1(b) Outline one explanation of schizophrenia and evaluate using research studies and/or alternative explanations. (20 marks)

You have to be selective in which ONE explanation you choose to describe and make sure that you use alternatives as evaluation rather than merely describing them.

Paragraph 1

Begin by stating that the biological model proposes a genetic basis (this is a predisposition that is triggered at adolescence) for schizophrenia and how the genes may be responsible for biochemical imbalances and abnormal brain structure. Don't spend long on this as it is only worth 5 marks.

Paragraph 2

Evaluation is research evidence, i.e. research that supports a genetic basis, e.g. Gottesman (1991), Tienari (1991), Sherrington et al. (1988). Focus on findings and conclusions only, to avoid AO1 description and to maintain an AO2 focus. Then evaluate using the research evidence against and criticisms, including the methodological weaknesses. This must be covered in depth.

Paragraph 3

The dopamine hypothesis and enlarged ventricles may be evidence of genetic abnormality. But does the gene cause them? Cause and effect is difficult to determine, although the neurodevelopment hypothesis suggests that brain structure abnormality precedes the onset of the disorder, which supports a genetic basis. But it is difficult to separate this out, as the disorder itself will affect the brain structure. This should be covered in less depth.

> **LINK SENTENCE:** The main weakness of the gene as an explanation for schizophrenia is that this ignores the role of nurture and so alternative psychological explanations offer insights that the genetic explanation does not. *You need a link sentence like this to ensure that your content on the alternative explanations is RELATED to the question.*

Paragraph 4

The role of nurture is supported by behavioural, social, psychodynamic, and cognitive explanations. These illustrate the reductionism and determinism of the biological explanation. Explain these criticisms with some research evidence from the counterperspectives (psychological models) to back it up—but not a lot, as this content must be AO2.

Paragraph 5

Consider how the biological and psychological explanations need to interact, e.g. a genetic basis for faulty cognition, e.g. the self-monitoring explanation. Cover this as the second in-depth content.

Paragraph 6

Do we need to identify different interactions for the different types of schizophrenia? Consider the need for a multidimensional approach, which accounts for different levels of causation, which means one explanation alone is not comprehensive. The tendency to exaggerate the importance of a biological explanation ignores the valid psychological explanations. The diathesis–stress model suggests a compromise position—explain this and evaluate that the strength of this is that it accounts for nature *and* nurture. More emphasis needs to be placed on such interactive explanations of schizophrenia as the success of combined treatments of the disorder suggests. Treating it at more than one level is more effective because it exists at more than one level. Furthermore, the biological explanations are limited because they take a nomothetic approach (universal focused). Whilst this is useful in identifying generalisable causes, such universal explanations may have limited relevance to individual cases. An idiographic approach (individual focused) may be better able to explain how the different factors interact and so give rise to different forms of the disorder.

2 "There are many different kinds of depression, for example, unipolar and bipolar, endogenous, and reactive."

Discuss explanations for depression, including the evidence on which they are based. (30 marks)

You need to make sure that your answer addresses the quote, i.e. consider the need to explain the different types of depression.

Paragraph 1

Depression belongs to the category mood disorders, which are characterised by disturbances of affect (mood). These can be in the direction of depression or elation and are distinguished from normal mood variations by the duration and degree of disturbance. Use the quote, i.e. show you understand unipolar, bipolar, endogenous, and reactive. Perhaps identify other types, e.g. PMS, PPD, and consider that explanations may vary for these different types of depression.

Paragraph 2

The biological model suggests a genetic basis, which means that different genes may predispose different types of depression. Give the evidence for unipolar depression, e.g. Allen (1976), Gershon (1990), and Wender et al. (1986), and then evaluate using the research evidence against and the criticisms. The evidence for bipolar is stronger as concordance rates are higher, which supports the idea that the different types of depression are predisposed by different genes. But question whether this is a cause as an individual may have the predisposition but never develop the disorder. Cover this in depth. Use the evolutionary explanations as further evidence of a genetic basis.

Paragraph 3

The genes may result in biochemical imbalances. Outline Kety's (1975) permissive amine theory. Give the research evidence for this based on the biochemical compounds found in depressives' urine and the action of antidepressants. Use the research evidence against as evaluation—they do not work for everybody and take time to relieve the symptoms. Criticise using the treatment aetiology fallacy and the issue of cause and effect. Cover this in less depth.

Paragraph 4

Hormonal explanations have also been suggested. Explain the evidence on cortisol. PMS and PPD also support fluctuating hormone levels as a cause of depression. Statistics on female mental hospital admissions support this, as 41% were admitted on the first day or within a day of starting their period. Women are two to three times more likely to be diagnosed as depressed as men, which may be due to the role of hormones. However, postmodernists argue that PMS is in part socially constructed and the diagnosis of depression in more women than men is due to social factors and gender bias rather than biological factors. Consider the generalisability of the hormone explanation. Is it more relevant to PMS and PPD than other types of depression?

LINK SENTENCE: The biological explanations and research evidence have many weaknesses and so lack conviction as a comprehensive explanation. They are reductionist and deterministic—explain why. They ignore the role of nurture and so it is necessary to consider the psychological explanations to gain a fuller understanding of depression. *You need a link sentence like this to ensure that your content on the alternative explanations is RELATED to the questions.*

Paragraph 5

Outline the behavioural explanation including Lewinsohn's (1974) and Seligman's (1975) research. Cover this in less depth and evaluate that these may be an effect rather than a cause of being depressed. Consider the reductionism and determinism of behavioural explanations and use the role of cognitive factors to illustrate this, i.e. it is not learned helplessness that causes depression but the perceptions and interpretations that lead to learned helplessness.

Paragraph 6

Outline Abramson et al.'s (1978) attribution model and Beck and Clark's (1988) cognitive triad and errors in logic. Cover this in depth, so consider fully the research evidence for and against and the criticisms. Research does show that emotion and cognition are interrelated and that the influence is bi-directional as they influence each other, which lends some support to a cognitive basis to depression. But it also supports the criticism that cognitive dysfunction is a result of the depression. Conclude that cognition is likely to be a predisposing factor but a key limitation is that it is more descriptive than explanatory as this doesn't explain how or why the faulty cognition developed. Is this a result of experience of learned helplessness or is there a biological basis to this, or a social basis as suggested by James (1998) in his claim, "society manufactures depression"?

Paragraph 7

Discuss Freud's explanation and consider it as a possible cause of faulty cognitions. We may be victims of our feelings, which determine our cognition. The influence of social experiences is supported by the research on life events. Consider the methodological weaknesses of Freud's and the life events research.

Paragraph 8

Consider whether the different explanations are more relevant to the different types of disorder, for example, the greater role of biological factors in endogenous depression and the greater role of life events in reactive depression. Then assess whether such a classification is possible, as it is oversimplistic and ignores the fact that depression is likely to be due to an interaction of internal and external factors. For example, three times as many women are likely to be diagnosed with depression as men, which may be a form of reactive depression to their role in society or it may be due to biological differences. We need to consider "sick society" not just the " sick individual". Thus, a multidimensional approach such as the diathesis–stress model is needed, as at present understanding is limited as to how the many predisposing, precipitating, and perpetuating factors interact and how these differ depending on the type of depression. Thus, an idiographic (individual focused) rather than a nomothetic (universal focused) approach may be preferable. Whilst a nomothetic approach is useful in identifying generalisable causes, such universal explanations may have limited relevance to individual cases. An idiographic approach may be better able to explain how the different factors interact and so give rise to different forms of the disorder.

3 Compare and contrast two explanations of one anxiety disorder.   (30 marks)

To gain marks on this question you need to identify similarities (comparison) and differences (contrast). In doing so you will describe and evaluate but will NOT gain marks unless this is supporting the compare and contrast.

Paragraph 1

Begin by focusing on the fundamental differences between the biological and behavioural explanations. The biological approach focuses on the role of inheritance and so nature; the behavioural approach claims that phobias are a result of maladaptive learning from the environment and so focuses on nurture. Thus, they are on opposite sides of the nature/nurture debate and focus on opposing factors, as the biological focuses on internal factors, whereas the behavioural approach focuses on external factors to explain phobias. Define phobia: phobias are irrational fears that are out of proportion to the reality of the threat provided by the fear-provoking stimulus. They are a form of anxiety disorder where the adaptive emotional response has become chronic and disabling.

Paragraph 2

Discuss the differences in the biological and behavioural explanations of phobias. For example, the biological claims that they are inherited and so genetically transmitted, whereas the behavioural claims that they are culturally transmitted. Outline the classical conditioning explanation of acquisition and how this is supported by research evidence of traumatic experiences triggering the phobias. Then explain that social learning theory provides a more complex account.

Paragraph 3

Consider the similarity in their approach to research as both the biological and behavioural explanations employ the experimental method, as they are concerned with observable and measurable phenomena and consequently ignore the subjective experience of the individual. Given that they take a scientific approach they are both supported by research evidence. For example, the biological approach is supported by…describe the twin, family, and adoption studies and neurophysiology. Then describe the laboratory research on phobias conducted by behavioural psychologists such as Watson and Rayner's (1920) conditioning of Albert.

Paragraph 4

Evaluate that the research evidence for both explanations have similar methodological weaknesses. For example, the focus on the observable and measurable phenomena means both approaches may have identified symptoms rather than underlying causes. Another example is bias—the concordance studies may be biased if it is known another family member has been diagnosed with mental illness. Watson and Rayner's (1920) study may also have been subject to bias, which is supported by the fact that later attempts to condition phobias in the laboratory have been unsuccessful. Explain that reliability is an issue for both biological and behavioural explanations as there are inconsistencies in the genetic evidence on phobias and the behavioural approach has problems of replication and a lack of consistency in the research on whether phobias result from a traumatic experience.

Paragraph 5

Thus, the research evidence is limited for both, but perhaps genetic factors more so…explain. The above criticisms mean that both biological and behavioural explanations are inconclusive because validity is questionable as a result of the methodological flaws. Furthermore, both are challenged by contradictory research. Consider that they are both challenged by the role of cognitive factors.

Paragraph 6

Other perspectives offer support for both explanations. Explain that the evolutionary perspective supports a genetic basis and the research on social factors supports the social learning theory strand of behaviourism.

Paragraph 7

The validity of the biological and behavioural explanations is supported to some extent by the success of their treatments. Discuss the different approaches taken to treatment by the biological and behavioural approaches, i.e. anti-anxiety drugs vs. systematic desensitisation. Then criticise using the treatment aetiology fallacy and explain what this means. Evaluate both approaches as reductionist and deterministic and explain why. Distinguish between them in terms of the type of determinism, biological vs. environmental.

Paragraph 8

The explanations are supported by contrary evidence, as evidence of genetic factors is the universality of phobias, whereas evidence of learning is the variability in the prevalence of phobias. Neither of which is clearly established, which leads to the conclusion that neither explanation is comprehensive on its own. They contrast because the biological explanation suggests predisposing factors, whereas the behavioural explanation suggests that classical conditioning and social learning are precipitating factors. Both lack explanatory power and so other processes must be involved. Hence, both explanations need to be incorporated into a multidimensional approach to phobias. Both approaches are nomothetic as they try to identify universal explanations for disorder. Whilst a nomothetic approach is useful in identifying generalisable causes, such universal explanations may have limited relevance to individual cases. Thus, to conclude, both the biological and behavioural explanations need to be integrated with the alternative explanations in an idiographic approach, as this may be better able to explain how the different factors interact and so give rise to different forms of the disorder.

Individual Differences

TREATING MENTAL DISORDERS
Specification 14.1

What's it about?

There is a large variety of ways in which mental disorders can be treated. These can be classified into biological (also known as somatic), behavioural, cognitive, and psychodynamic therapies. Biological treatments arise from the medical model of abnormality, that is, the belief that disorders are caused by physical problems. Biological therapies therefore involve the direct manipulation of body processes by, for example, drugs, electricity, or surgery. Behavioural treatments are based on the belief that mental disorders involve maladaptive learning. Behavioural therapies involve techniques for learning better ways of functioning. Cognitive therapies derive from the belief that some mental disorders arise from attitudes and beliefs that prevent the sufferer from functioning effectively. Treatments based on this approach involve replacing irrational and self-defeating attitudes with more realistic and adaptive ones. Finally, psychodynamic therapies are rooted in the belief that the unconscious mind of sufferers contains extreme conflicts and anxiety and that therapy must uncover the sources of these conflicts.

As you can appreciate, these treatments differ greatly from one another. Some are more effective with certain conditions than others; some work better with certain individuals. In this unit we will consider what is involved in the actual treatments together with their effectiveness and application. We will also pay attention to a very important aspect of such therapies, the ethical implications of their use.

What's in this unit?

BIOLOGICAL (SOMATIC) THERAPIES	Chemotherapy, ECT, and psychosurgery. Issues surrounding the use of such therapies (e.g. appropriateness and effectiveness).
BEHAVIOURAL THERAPIES	Behavioural therapies, including those based on classical (e.g. flooding) and operant (e.g. token economies) conditioning. Issues surrounding the use of such therapies (e.g. appropriateness and effectiveness).
ALTERNATIVES TO BIOLOGICAL AND BEHAVIOURAL THERAPIES	Therapies derived from *either* the psychodynamic (e.g. psychoanalysis, psychodrama) *or* cognitive-behavioural (e.g. rational-emotive therapy, stress inoculation therapy) models of abnormality. Issues surrounding the use of such therapies (e.g. appropriateness and effectiveness).

BIOLOGICAL (SOMATIC) THERAPIES

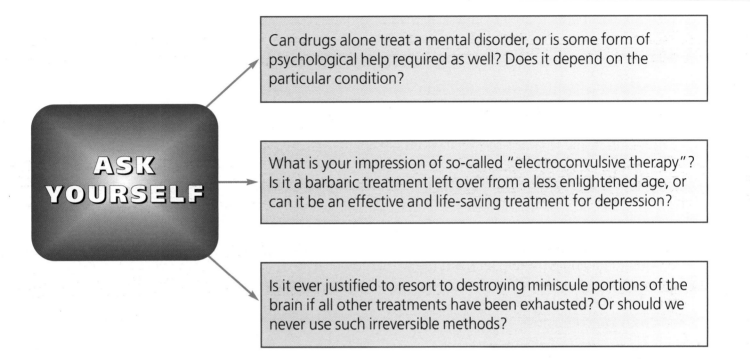

ASK YOURSELF

Can drugs alone treat a mental disorder, or is some form of psychological help required as well? Does it depend on the particular condition?

What is your impression of so-called "electroconvulsive therapy"? Is it a barbaric treatment left over from a less enlightened age, or can it be an effective and life-saving treatment for depression?

Is it ever justified to resort to destroying miniscule portions of the brain if all other treatments have been exhausted? Or should we never use such irreversible methods?

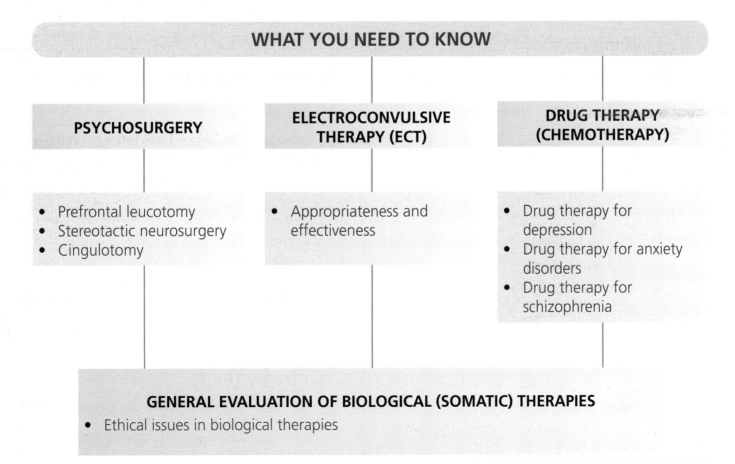

WHAT YOU NEED TO KNOW

PSYCHOSURGERY

- Prefrontal leucotomy
- Stereotactic neurosurgery
- Cingulotomy

ELECTROCONVULSIVE THERAPY (ECT)

- Appropriateness and effectiveness

DRUG THERAPY (CHEMOTHERAPY)

- Drug therapy for depression
- Drug therapy for anxiety disorders
- Drug therapy for schizophrenia

GENERAL EVALUATION OF BIOLOGICAL (SOMATIC) THERAPIES

- Ethical issues in biological therapies

To read up on biological (somatic) therapies, refer to pages 389–405 of A2PKT.

The biological (biomedical) approach is based on the assumption that the causes of mental disorders are biological so treatments should be physical, involving the direct manipulation of body processes.

PSYCHOSURGERY

WHAT IS IT?

Psychosurgery involves severing (cutting) or otherwise disabling areas of the brain to treat psychological and behavioural disorders. Early surgery, pioneered by Moniz (see A2PKT p.389), was an operation known as a frontal lobotomy that left patients extremely apathetic and intellectually impaired. Many patients died as a result.

Modern methods bear no comparison and only destroy very minute amounts of tissue. They include:

- *Prefrontal leucotomy*—this involves drilling two holes, one either side of the skull, into which needles are inserted to sever specific nerve fibres.
- *Stereotactic neurosurgery*—this involves a very small hole being drilled and a very fine electrode inserted. Computer imaging is used to pinpoint the exact region to be destroyed by an electric current.
- *Cingulotomy* is an example of stereotactic neurosurgery. It involves cutting the cingulate gyrus, a part of the brain involved in emotion. It is performed to alleviate major depression, chronic anxiety states, and obsessive-compulsive disorder (OCD).

APPROPRIATENESS AND EFFECTIVENESS

- Psychosurgery is a treatment of last resort and is very rarely used. There were fewer than 25 operations recorded in Britain in 2000.
- Cosgrove et al. (1996, see A2PKT p.392) report an improvement rate of 33% on 34 patients with cingulotomies operated on from 1991 to 1995.
- Cosgrove et al. (2000) estimated a success rate of psychosurgery of 50–67% for obsessive-compulsive disorder and 55–78% for major depression and bipolar disorder. They also reported few adverse side effects.
- One negative aspect is that there is a lack of knowledge about how the procedures work and what the exact effect on emotion is.

SO WHAT DOES THIS MEAN?

Psychosurgery can be effective if performed precisely on the right patients. Because of its irreversibility, it is only used after all other options have been exhausted. In Britain it requires a patient's consent and the opinion of a second doctor. The major ethical concern of psychosurgery is the irreversibility of the procedure. The organisation MIND is pioneering an alternative biological treatment for intractable obsessive-compulsive disorder that involves stimulation of the brain but no destruction. As yet it's too early to tell if this will be a viable alternative.

ELECTROCONVULSIVE THERAPY (ECT)

WHAT IS IT?

ECT involves a brief application of electricity (70–130 volts) to the brain in order to induce a seizure. Before treatment, the patient is anaesthetised and given a muscle relaxant. Electrodes are attached to the head and the current passed through for a second or less. This induces a seizure lasting no longer than 2 minutes. Patients regain consciousness about 15 minutes later and have no memory of events immediately prior to treatment. This is done two to three times a week for 1–4 weeks and may be repeated if the patient relapses.

APPROPRIATENESS AND EFFECTIVENESS

- ECT is mainly used for severe depression but is occasionally used for acute mania and certain forms of schizophrenia.
- Fink (1985, see A2PKT pp.392–393) reported a success rate of 60% in depressive-psychotic patients.
- Sackheim, Nordlie, and Gur (1993, see A2PKT p.393) found a high level of relapse within a year.
- Ng et al. (2000), in a supportive review, reported a 50% drop in depression scores after treatment and full recovery from any memory loss.
- Papolos (1997) argues that ECT offers a higher rate of success for depression than any other treatment with a drastically reduced risk of suicide.
- ECT appears to work more quickly and be more effective than antidepressants. Janicak et al. (1985, see A2PKT p.393) found an 80% success rate for ECT and a 64% success rate for antidepressants in a sample of severely depressed patients. Gagne et al. (2000), in a 2-year follow-up study, reported that 93% of patients who had ECT and antidepressants were free of symptoms compared with 52% on antidepressants alone.
- It is very controversial because of the side effects, mainly memory loss. It also carries with it a negative attitude from the days when it was dangerous, painful, and was probably used as a punishment in some dubious institutions.
- It is uncertain why it works. It probably changes levels of noradrenaline and serotonin in the brain, thereby reducing depression. For some people this effect is permanent, in others it is temporary.

SO WHAT DOES THIS MEAN?

ECT remains a controversial treatment associated with punishment and permanent damage. A new treatment, transcranial magnetic brain stimulation, which is painless, safe, and does not induce seizures, offers a promising alternative to ECT for the treatment of depression.

DRUG THERAPY (CHEMOTHERAPY)

WHAT IS IT?

The use of drugs to treat mental disorders also has a controversial history, the main concerns being the potential for addiction, the side effects and, more fundamentally, that people are being fobbed-off with a drug when their need is for some psychological help. Nevertheless, drugs can be of great help in alleviating symptoms.

Depression

- *Monoamine oxidase inhibitors (MAOIs)* and *tricyclics* work by offsetting the shortage of monoamines, which include the neurotransmitters serotonin, noradrenaline, and dopamine, thought to be responsible for some forms of depression. They both effectively increase levels of serotonin and noradrenaline. Tricyclics do this by preventing reuptake of noradrenaline and serotonin. MAOIs work by preventing the enzyme monamine oxidase from deactivating these neurotransmitters.

- *Selective serotonin reuptake inhibitors (SSRIs)* (e.g. Prozac) inhibit the uptake of serotonin. These were hailed as entirely safe because they could not lead to dependence but Harriman (2001) reports that they lead to an increase in suicide rates in the early stages of treatment.

- *Lithium carbonate* is used for the treatment of bipolar disorder (manic depression). Gerbino, Oleshansky, and Gershon (1978, see A2PKT p.395) report a reduction of manic and depressive episodes in 80% of patients. It can, however, have lethal side effects and Jefferson et al. (1989) comment that it needs to be carefully monitored or it can threaten life. Despite this, the alleviation of the disorder and the reduction in suicide rates among people with the disorder has led to this drug being described as a "true medical miracle" (Comer 1992).

Even if used only temporarily, antidepressants can be of great benefit as they reduce the potential for suicide. They should, however, be combined with, or substituted by, psychological therapies as soon as possible. With lithium carbonate, it is a different story. It is recommended that this be taken continuously throughout life since discontinuing the drug can result in even more serious symptoms.

Anxiety Disorders

- *Barbiturates* were the earliest treatments, but these are highly addictive and have side effects of slurred speech and lack of coordination.
- *Benzodiazepines* (trade names Valium, Librium) were introduced in the 1960s. They were more precise with fewer side effects, although they did cause drowsiness, which could be severe. However, they resulted in such severe physical and psychological dependence that they are now rarely prescribed for regular use. They can, nevertheless, be useful for short-term use in very stressful situations.
- *Buspirone* is the most recent drug to be introduced and appears not to have the side effects of lethargy and sleepiness, but further research is required to assess its effectiveness.

These drugs cope with the symptoms, not the underlying cause. Once patients come off the drugs, they tend to relapse into a state of anxiety, so any remission is temporary.

Schizophrenia

- *Neuroleptic drugs* including the *phenothiazines* are the oldest class of drugs used for schizophrenia, but they only work on about 70% of patients and have serious side effects. These include severe shaking and spasms of jerky movements. They may have an irreversible effect in 10–20% of patients. These unpleasant side effects cause up to 75% of patients to stop taking the drugs within 2 years, so injected long-lasting antipsychotic drugs are sometimes used.
- *Clozapine* has partly replaced these and is equally or more effective overall (Rosenhack et al., 1999). However, it can cause a fatal blood disorder in 1–2% of patients.
- *Olanzapine* and *risperidone* are even more recent, with fewer side effects and at least as much effectiveness (Wirshing et al., 1999).

Antipsychotic drugs are an essential treatment for schizophrenia. Unfortunately not all patients respond to these drugs and, even for those who do, the drugs alone are not always sufficient. However, especially combined with psychotherapy, they can help many patients lead a reasonably normal life.

APPROPRIATENESS AND EFFECTIVENESS OF DRUG THERAPY

- Drugs treat the symptoms, not the underlying cause.
- Most of them have side effects. These range from moderate to very severe, even life-threatening.
- There are problems with compliance. Some patients do not take their drugs. In some cases this has led to tragic consequences.
- They are not effective with everyone. This applies to many conditions, including schizophrenia in which a fairly large percentage of patients do not respond to drugs.
- They allow many people to live normal lives. They do, in some cases, make people capable of resuming a reasonably normal life. This applies, for example, to those with bipolar disorder taking lithium carbonate.
- They can save lives by preventing suicide. This is particularly true of antidepressants.
- They can sometimes greatly improve the quality of life.
- An ethical consideration is that drugs remove responsibility from the patient. They put all the power into the hands of doctors and psychiatrists.

GENERAL EVALUATION OF BIOLOGICAL (SOMATIC) THERAPIES

For more general information on ethical issues and evaluating therapies, please see A2PKT pp.399–402.

☺ **Most somatic therapies have proved effective.** Biological therapies have been shown to reduce symptoms fairly quickly, thereby making sufferers better able to benefit from psychological therapies (obviously this does not apply to psychosurgery which is intended as a permanent treatment).

☹ **They all have side effects.** Some of these can be serious and dangerous.

☹ **They reduce symptoms but do not effect a cure.**

☺ **They are particularly useful for certain patients.** This applies to people who cannot express their feelings (and who therefore cannot fully benefit from some psychological therapies), and for those who need very fast treatment for fear of serious harm to themselves or others.

☹ **They are inappropriate for some conditions.** For example, there are no effective somatic therapies for eating disorders. This may be because such disorders are primarily caused by social and cultural factors.

Ethical Issues in Biological Therapies

The biological model of mental disorders removes responsibility from the patient and places it on faulty functioning of the body. With respect to ethics, this means that no blame is attached to the individual, but on the negative side it means that the patient is not empowered to help him- or herself. All responsibility is taken away and placed in the hands of the health professionals.

There is also the ethical issue that the patient may feel it is the condition that is being treated rather than them as an individual. They may feel that they are being dismissed with "a packet of pills", with no real consideration given for the intense misery they are experiencing.

SO WHAT DOES THIS MEAN?

Biological therapies are an indispensable means of treatment that can alleviate suffering and save lives but they should never be the sole method of therapy. The most effective treatment for mental disorders is a combination of psychological and biological therapy. Sometimes somatic therapy can be used in the short term in order to improve the patient's state of mind sufficiently for psychological treatment to be effective. This applies particularly to depression and anxiety disorders. Other conditions, such as schizophrenia and bipolar disorder, may require a lifetime of medication.

OVER TO YOU

1. Discuss the use of any two biological (somatic) therapies in the treatment of mental disorders. **(30 marks)**

2. Discuss issues surrounding the use of biological (somatic) therapies. **(30 marks)**

BEHAVIOURAL THERAPIES

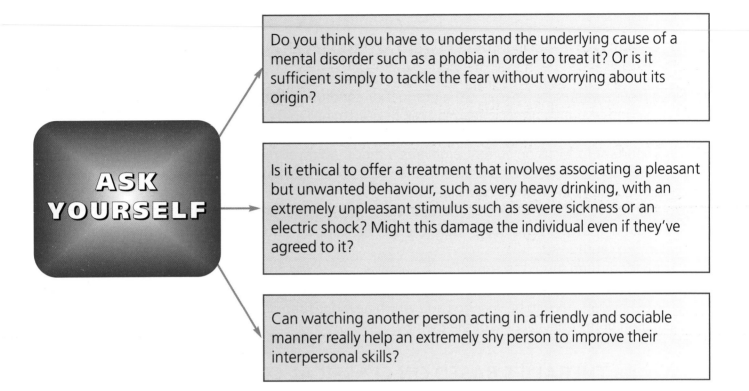

ASK YOURSELF

Do you think you have to understand the underlying cause of a mental disorder such as a phobia in order to treat it? Or is it sufficient simply to tackle the fear without worrying about its origin?

Is it ethical to offer a treatment that involves associating a pleasant but unwanted behaviour, such as very heavy drinking, with an extremely unpleasant stimulus such as severe sickness or an electric shock? Might this damage the individual even if they've agreed to it?

Can watching another person acting in a friendly and sociable manner really help an extremely shy person to improve their interpersonal skills?

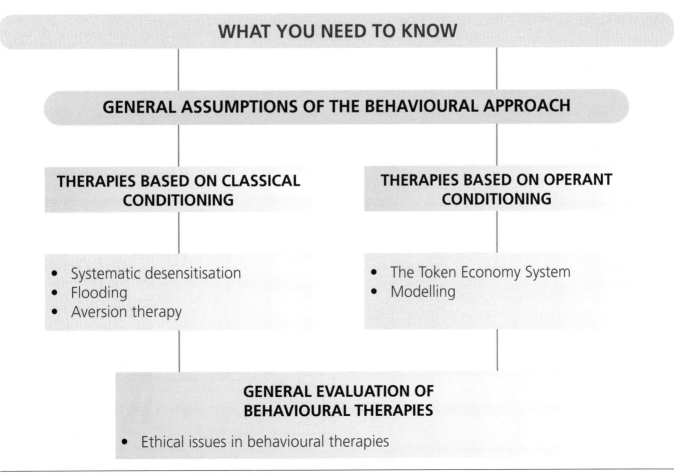

WHAT YOU NEED TO KNOW

GENERAL ASSUMPTIONS OF THE BEHAVIOURAL APPROACH

THERAPIES BASED ON CLASSICAL CONDITIONING

- Systematic desensitisation
- Flooding
- Aversion therapy

THERAPIES BASED ON OPERANT CONDITIONING

- The Token Economy System
- Modelling

GENERAL EVALUATION OF BEHAVIOURAL THERAPIES

- Ethical issues in behavioural therapies

To read up on behavioural therapies, refer to pages 405–413 of A2PKT.

GENERAL ASSUMPTIONS OF BEHAVIOURAL THERAPIES

- Maladaptive behaviours are learned, so they can be unlearned.
- Since this unwanted behaviour is the product of conditioning, the principles of conditioning (both classical and operant) and social learning can be used to help patients replace this unwanted behaviour with more appropriate responses.
- It is important to focus on current problems rather than dwell on past experiences. The behavioural approach acknowledges that problems may have been caused by earlier experiences, but this is considered irrelevant in effecting a cure.
- The emphasis should be on observable behaviour, rather than on biology, thinking, or emotions.
- The main aim of therapy should therefore be the removal of any symptoms without concern for underlying causes.
- The methods used should be scientific. This applies both to the application of the therapy itself and the way in which its effectiveness is measured. After examining the patient, the therapist outlines precisely what behaviours need to be changed and which new ones should be learned. This is then used in the evaluation of the effectiveness of the therapy.

THERAPIES BASED ON CLASSICAL CONDITIONING

Classical conditioning involves learning by association. These methods of therapy are based on unlearning old, maladaptive associations and learning more adaptive ones. Usually this involves learning not to associate certain stimuli with extreme fear.

Systematic Desensitisation

WHAT IS IT?

This method, designed to treat phobias, was introduced by Wolpe (1958, see A2PKT pp.407–408). It aims to gradually and systematically reduce the fear response to the phobic object or situation—hence the name. It is based on *counterconditioning* (counteracting previous conditioning). The underlying principle is that of *reciprocal inhibition*, that it is impossible for a person to experience extreme fear at the same time as being relaxed (one reaction inhibits the other). Therefore if a phobic can learn to be relaxed in the presence of the feared object, then the fear will be overcome. The procedure is in three stages:

1. Training in deep muscle relaxation.
2. The building up of a hierarchy of feared stimuli by the patient with the assistance of the therapist, from the least to the most fearful. For example, with a spider phobic, you may start with a picture of a spider, gradually working up, perhaps to a toy one, then a live one confined to a deep dish, eventually progressing to a reasonably large, live, unconfined spider.

3. Imagining each stimulus from the least frightening to the most frightening while relaxing. Each new stimulus in the hierarchy is not introduced until the patient is relaxed with the last one.

A modified version of systematic desensitisation, named the "in vivo" version, uses the actual feared stimulus, for example, a real spider, again in a hierarchical way. Craske et al. (1992), amongst others, believes this is a much more effective method than simply imagining the feared stimulus.

APPROPRIATENESS AND EFFECTIVENESS

- Unlike some other behavioural techniques, the patient does not have to experience intense fear and, importantly, feels in control of the situation.
- It has a high success rate with simple phobias such as fear of birds or other creatures.
- It is also useful, although less successful, with obsessive-compulsive disorder, having a 50% success rate (Sue et al., 1990).
- Some therapists believe that the most effective means of using systematic desensitisation is a combination of imagined and in vivo exposure. This combination is very successful.
- It has the secondary usefulness of teaching people how to relax, a skill that can usefully be transferred to other situations.

Flooding

WHAT IS IT?

Flooding involves introducing the patient to a feared stimulus in its most extreme form for a prolonged period of time. The underlying principle is that the physiological responses of extreme fear cannot be maintained for a prolonged period, so the fear eventually subsides and *extinction* has occurred. Under normal circumstances extinction is prevented from taking place because the patient flees as fast as possible from any terrifying stimulus and then is strongly reinforced in this action by the intense relief they get (running away acts as a powerful negative reinforcer).

Flooding can be used for obsessive-compulsive disorder as well as for phobias. For example, someone with a hand-washing obsession may be forced to touch something they regard as dirty and then not be allowed to wash their hands for several hours.

Although they are both based on classical conditioning, flooding and systematic desensitisation differ in that flooding deliberately induces huge amounts of anxiety, whereas systematic desensitisation tries to prevent intense fear occurring.

APPROPRIATENESS AND EFFECTIVENESS

- It is a very quick method of treatment and therefore capable of alleviating suffering in a very short time, as well as being economical.
- It cannot be used on those who have heart conditions or other conditions that may yield them incapable of withstanding intense fear.
- Some people think it unethical to cause people so much suffering.
- Flooding causes so much fear that the individual may refuse to go on and the reinforcement they obtain from leaving the programme and escaping the intense fear will then make the condition even more difficult to treat.
- Marks (1987) argues that it is more successful than systematic desensitisation for treatment of phobias.

Aversion Therapy

WHAT IS IT?

Aversion therapy is a method used to eliminate pleasurable but maladaptive behaviour such as alcoholism. The principle underlying it is the use of classical conditioning to pair the undesirable behaviour with a very unpleasant (noxious) stimulus. For example, an alcoholic would be given alcohol and a strong emetic to make them violently sick. (Aversion therapy in this form is an example of the use of classical conditioning but it can also be applied using operant conditioning. In this case the alcoholic would be given an implant or similar that would cause sickness whenever alcohol was drunk. This then becomes a punishment for voluntary behaviour. Be careful to make the distinction and only describe the first method if you are discussing the use of *classical* conditioning to change problem behaviour.)

APPROPRIATENESS AND EFFECTIVENESS

- Since the treatment is unpleasant, the drop-out rate is high.
- The changes in behaviour do not always generalise to real life, especially as in ordinary situations the individual knows that no noxious stimulus will be given.
- It only gets rid of a behaviour, it does not help the individual learn more appropriate behaviour (such as how to cope with social situations involving alcohol) so it is rarely used as a sole means of treatment.
- The person being treated may become angry and resentful even if they agreed to it in the first place.
- Many therapists believe it is wrong to use very unpleasant stimuli that cause pain or discomfort.

THERAPIES BASED ON OPERANT CONDITIONING

Operant conditioning involves learning by the consequences of voluntary actions. In therapy, this involves reinforcing appropriate behaviour whilst not reinforcing (and occasionally even punishing) inappropriate behaviour.

The Token Economy System

WHAT IS IT?

The system of token economy is based on the principle of providing reinforcement for desired behaviour. Secondary reinforcement is used in the form of tokens that can be exchanged for such primary reinforcers as cigarettes, television watching, confectionery, and additional leisure time. It is used with problem children and schizophrenics, amongst others. The therapist makes a careful appraisal of all the behaviours that are to be reinforced and the people operating the system are carefully trained to recognise exactly which behaviours are to be reinforced. They are requested to be vigilant in reinforcing every example of such behaviour and not to inadvertently reinforce undesirable behaviour (e.g. by paying the person attention for "misbehaving"). A classic study of the use of the token economy system was that of Ayllon and Azrin (1968, see A2PKT pp.409–410), who used it to improve the behaviour of long-stay female schizophrenic patients.

APPROPRIATENESS AND EFFECTIVENESS

- The token economy system works best in institutions in which behaviour can be carefully monitored and there is control over the reinforcement contingencies.

- However, the improvements do not necessarily generalise to behaviour outside the institution.

- The system is limited. It is not effective in encouraging complex behaviours such as language.

- There are ethical concerns. It can be viewed as taking all power away from the patient and giving too much power to others, some of whom are not even therapists. It therefore has the potential for abuse.

Modelling

WHAT IS IT?

Modelling involves learning by vicarious rather than direct reinforcement and is based on social learning theory as well as operant conditioning. Vicarious reinforcement involves seeing another person being reinforced. Patients watch another person behaving in a certain way and learn by observation and reinforcement. Modelling can be used to learn a variety of behaviours. For example, a phobic person may watch the therapist calmly dealing with the feared stimulus; films have also been used to help people overcome sexual problems.

Modelling has been particularly useful in *social skills training*. Goddard and Cross (1987, see A2PKT p.411) used modelling to demonstrate to disruptive children how to deal with bullying, how to apologise, and how to listen.

Modelling is most effective if the model is similar to the patient and is rewarded for the behaviour. It is useful to use a commentary so that the benefits of actions can be emphasised. It is then important to ask the patient to repeat the behaviour soon after watching the model and to positively reinforce any appropriate behaviour.

APPROPRIATENESS AND EFFECTIVENESS

- Modelling is an easy, painless, and relatively stress-free method of treatment.

- It is an appropriate method of treatment for a variety of conditions.

- It is particularly useful in treating those who lack social skills and are poor in interpersonal communication. These are conditions that do not easily lend themselves to other treatments.

GENERAL EVALUATION OF BEHAVIOURAL THERAPIES

For more general information on ethical issues and evaluating therapies, please see A2PKT pp.399–402.

 They are based on proven underlying scientific principles. The principles of conditioning on which the therapies are based have been demonstrated many times in the laboratory and therefore have scientific validity.

 They are an economical method of treatment. Since most behavioural treatments require only a short period of time, they are not costly.

 They only tackle immediate symptoms and do not deal with underlying problems. Many therapists from other approaches, especially those from a psychodynamic orientation, argue that behavioural approaches provide people with little insight into their condition or its underlying causes. Nevertheless, many behavioural therapists offer encouragement and counselling as an integral part of treatment. This then introduces a confounding variable—is it the behavioural treatment or the attention and encouragement of the therapist that is responsible for any improvement?

There is a danger of symptom substitution. Because the underlying causes are not addressed, the symptoms may appear in a different form. This is the argument proposed from the psychodynamic approach, although some studies indicate that this does not necessarily occur (e.g. Lang & Lazonik, 1963).

 Any improvement may not generalise to the real world. Since treatment is carried out in the therapist's room, any improvements may not be maintained when the patient is in an ordinary, everyday situation. In fairness, many behaviour therapists start treatment inside but then take the patient into an appropriate part of their real-world environment (for example, taking a worm phobic into the garden).

Ethical Issues in Behavioural Therapies

The main ethical issue with behavioural treatments is that they can be seen to treat patients in a rather mechanistic way that does not take full account of their feelings. The therapist has a great deal of control and the patient has very little. In addition, some forms of treatment (such as aversion therapy) involve the use of unpleasant and even painful stimuli, while others (such as the token economy) may be subject to abuse of power by those administering the tokens. On the positive side, the general approach does absolve individuals of blame for their condition and offer treatments that mean they can regain control over their lives.

SO WHAT DOES THIS MEAN?

As with all therapies, behavioural ones are better with some conditions than with others. They work very well with conditions in which it is possible to pinpoint exactly what behaviours need to be changed, such as simple phobias (phobias of very specific things or events). They are, however, less successful with conditions that have vague and ill-defined symptoms, such as generalised anxiety disorder (in which people have a constant feeling of anxiety that is not focused on anything in particular). With conditions like schizophrenia, behavioural approaches can never offer anything even approaching a cure but they can be used to help make schizophrenics' behaviour more acceptable in a social sense, leading to an improved environment for all. In addition, techniques based on operant conditioning are particularly useful in treating disruptive behaviour in children. In sum, behavioural therapies are a relatively quick, easy, and inexpensive method of successfully treating a limited number of conditions.

OVER TO YOU

1. **Critically consider issues surrounding the use of operant conditioning in the treatment of mental disorders.** **(30 marks)**

2. **Distinguish between those behavioural therapies based on classical conditioning and those based on operant conditioning.** **(30 marks)**

3. **Compare and contrast therapies derived from the biological (somatic) and behavioural models of abnormality in the treatment of mental disorders (AQA-A June 2002).** **(30 marks)**

ALTERNATIVES TO BIOLOGICAL AND BEHAVIOURAL THERAPIES

ASK YOURSELF

Do you think that some conditions, especially depression, can be caused by unrealistic expectations that an individual has of themselves? If so, what kinds of expectation might these be?

Do you think it is possible to treat some mental disorders simply by getting the patient to examine their attitudes closely and attempting to change them, without any other treatment being necessary?

What advantages might this have over treating someone solely with drugs or other biological therapies?

Is it necessary to have insight into the unconscious mind in order to effect a full and lasting treatment of mental disorders?

WHAT YOU NEED TO KNOW

COGNITIVE AND COGNITIVE-BEHAVIOURAL THERAPIES
- Rational-emotive therapy
- Beck's cognitive therapy
- General evaluation of cognitive-behavioural therapies
- Ethical issues in cognitive-behavioural therapies

PSYCHODYNAMIC THERAPIES
- Psychoanalysis
- Ego analysis
- General evaluation of psychodynamic therapies
- Ethical implications of the psychodynamic approach

COMPARISONS BETWEEN THERAPIES
- Research on meta-analysis

ETHICAL ISSUES IN THERAPIES
- Informed consent
- Confidentiality

GENERAL ISSUES IN EVALUATING THERAPIES

To read up on alternatives to biological and behavioural therapies, refer to pages 414–431 of A2PKT.

> **EXAM ADVICE:** Note that in this section, you can do *either* cognitive-behavioural *or* psychodynamic therapies. We have covered both in this text to provide you with choice, but it's worth noting that you will only be required to know one of these two types of therapy.

COGNITIVE AND COGNITIVE-BEHAVIOURAL THERAPIES

The Difference between Cognitive and Cognitive-behavioural Therapies

Cognitive therapy is based on the assumption that certain attitudes and beliefs create and compound psychological disorders and it is therefore necessary for patients to undergo *cognitive restructuring*: changing the irrational, self-defeating thoughts and attitudes for more realistic and adaptive ones.

Cognitive-behavioural therapy (CBT) is a more recent innovation, brought about by the recognition that behaviour also needed to be changed alongside alterations in thinking. Note that the first therapy discussed below, Rational Emotive Therapy, recently had its name changed to Rational-Emotive Behavioural Therapy when it started tackling behaviour as well as irrational and self-defeating beliefs. As Kendall and Hammen (1998, see A2PKT p.416) point out, thoughts, behaviour, and feelings are all interrelated. Therefore, it is desirable to change both the client's cognitive processes and their behaviour. The therapies discussed below operate by changing both thoughts and behaviours, and have been referred to as both cognitive and cognitive-behavioural therapies since in essence any clear distinction is inappropriate.

Cognitive-behavioural therapy is used predominantly for conditions such as depression and some anxiety disorders.

Rational-Emotive Therapy (RET)

WHAT IS IT?

Rational-emotive therapy (RET), now renamed rational-emotive behavioural therapy (REBT), is a therapy for depression and anxiety devised by Albert Ellis (1962, see A2PKT pp.414–415). He proposes that many problems are created by irrational and self-defeating beliefs that put unreasonable demands on the individual holding them. Ellis particularly focuses on how self-defeating attitudes cause problems when something unpleasant happens. The ABC model, as it is called, can be illustrated thus.

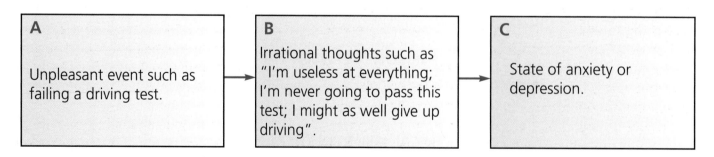

A	B	C
Unpleasant event such as failing a driving test.	Irrational thoughts such as "I'm useless at everything; I'm never going to pass this test; I might as well give up driving".	State of anxiety or depression.

The therapy is designed to replace the beliefs in B with a new belief system called D, a dispute belief system that allows the person to interpret what happens to them in ways that are more realistic and positive. The emphasis is on less self-criticism and more positive action. In our example, that could be: "It's my first test and I did some of it well; lots of people fail the first time and become good drivers. Even if I have to take the test a couple more times, I'll be OK in the end".

The first part of the therapy, which can be quite confrontational, aims to persuade the patient that their beliefs are irrational, that they are the cause of their emotional turmoil, and that they need to be challenged. The behavioural part of the therapy is that patients are given homework assignments that make them face up to how damaging their beliefs are in everyday life.

In this way, the patient is taught to replace these irrational beliefs with more rational ones that provide them with positive self-worth and a more emotionally satisfying and fulfilling life. The eventual goal is a full acceptance of these new, rational beliefs.

In his original theory, Ellis produced a list of commonly held irrational thoughts that cause problems, such as "I must be loved by everyone"; "I must be thoroughly competent at everything". More recently he has moved to a general concept of "demandingness", an impossibly demanding belief system that people impose on themselves that causes problems of anxiety and depression that the therapy is designed to address.

APPROPRIATENESS AND EFFECTIVENESS

- REBT appears most effective with people who are riddled with guilt and who make high demands on themselves (Brandsma, Maultsby, & Welsh, 1978, see A2PKT p.415).
- It has been useful in treating people who are antisocial and who have excessive anger.
- Although it has reasonable success with social anxiety and agoraphobia, it is not as effective for these conditions as behavioural methods such as systematic desensitisation.
- Interestingly, it can help people with no particular problems cope better with everyday stress.
- It is not a method that is suitable for conditions involving severe thought disorders, such as schizophrenia.
- In terms of ethics, this approach does try to convince people that they are capable of changing their lives for the better, that they are in control, and that they are the main determinant of their own destiny.

Beck's Cognitive Therapy

WHAT IS IT?

Beck's therapy is mainly designed for depression but has been used for anxiety disorders. Beck, like Ellis, argues that depression is related to irrational thinking and that the aim of therapy is to replace negative thoughts with more realistic and positive ones. Beck believes that depressives have negative attitudes towards the self, the world, and the future, referred to as a *negative cognitive triad*. They view themselves as worthless, stupid, unattractive, and helpless; the world as a cold and insensitive place; and the future as hopeless. Therapy consists of challenging these attitudes by making the individual examine the objective evidence on which their beliefs are based, thus making them recognise that they are faulty. The therapist engages the patient in a process rather like a scientific investigation, focusing on cognitive biases, questioning the evidence on which their beliefs are based.

The behavioural part then comes into play. Beck (1976, see A2PKT p.417) instructs his patients to monitor and log their thought processes between therapy sessions. Homework assignments are provided that require patients to adopt new behaviours they previously found extremely difficult or impossible, such as walking into a room full of strangers, or initiating a conversation. Patients are asked to anticipate how difficult they think they will find this and then compare it to how they actually felt. Since they have usually been pessimistic, their ability to cope better than they thought they could speeds up the therapeutic process.

APPROPRIATENESS AND EFFECTIVENESS

- Many studies have demonstrated that Beck's cognitive therapy is effective for depression (e.g. Wilson et al., 1983).

- A meta-analysis of therapies for depression showed that Beck's achieved greater short-term improvement than any other numerous therapies, such as drugs and behavioural treatments (Dobson, 1989, see A2PKT p.419).

- It appears to be better than drug therapy at preventing future episodes of depression (Hollon et al., 1996).

- Elkin et al. (1985), in a study for the National Institute for Mental Health, did find Beck's therapy effective for depression but *not* more effective than drug therapy.

- Beck's therapy has also been effective in treating panic disorder, generalised anxiety disorder, social phobia, and bulimia nervosa (Chambless et al., 1996, for the APA—the American Psychological Association).

General Evaluation of Cognitive-behavioural Therapies

☺ **They take full account of the individual's attitudes and feelings.** No matter how distorted the patient's view is, it is given full consideration.

☹ **Ellis' approach makes too many generalisations.** Ellis' therapy assumes that the same irrational beliefs underlie most mental disorders and this is not necessarily the case.

☺ **Ellis' approach is effective.** Engels, Garnefski, and Diekstra (1993, see A2PKT p.418) surveyed 28 studies of RET and found it more effective than systematic desensitisation and far better than no treatment.

☺ **Beck's view differentiates more clearly.** It takes account of the fact that specific irrational beliefs are associated with each disorder.

☺ **They both emphasise choice.** They emphasise that people's minds can be set free and that their thinking can be altered in a way that provides positive psychological change.

Ethical Issues in Cognitive-behavioural Therapies

This approach offers patients a greater degree of control over their own behaviour than does either the biological or the behavioural approach. By following the instructions provided by the therapist, patients feel empowered to help themselves. These therapies also involve a reduction in self-criticism, an increase in self-esteem, and a more positive approach to life in general.

On the negative side, the underlying assumptions of this approach may be seen as blaming the individual for his or her maladaptive thinking and it is necessary for the therapist to emphasise that the blame lies with childhood experience rather than with the patient. Ellis tends to use terms such as irrational or nutty to describe people's feelings (this is not true of Beck) and although this is done humorously, it might cause offence. Finally, on a rather different note, it is also necessary to consider whether the cognitions causing problems are genuinely faulty or are a rational response to dreadful living conditions and/or experiences. If this is the case, attempts to change attitudes may be seen as rather callous when the only way to deal with the disorder is to make changes to the circumstances of people's lives.

SO WHAT DOES THIS MEAN?

Cognitive-behavioural therapies are principally used for depression but can be useful for other anxiety-based conditions. They are not, however, appropriate for psychotic conditions in which insight into the unrealistic nature of beliefs and attitudes is not possible. Because they require an analysis by the patient of their life situation, it is generally assumed that they are best suited to fairly intelligent individuals (Whisman, 1993), although not all researchers have found this to be the case (Haaga et al., 1991). After treatment, people do appear to have a change in attitudes. However, these changes have also been shown in those treated with drugs alone, so they may be the consequence of any treatment for depression. One reason why cognitive-behavioural therapies may be useful in the long term is that such therapies appear to enable people suffering from depression to acquire new cognitive and behavioural skills that they can use after therapy has terminated.

PSYCHODYNAMIC THERAPIES

Psychodynamic therapies are based on the work of Freud and attempt to deal with problems in the unconscious mind. We will consider psychoanalysis, the original therapy used by Freud, and ego analysis, a later variation introduced by neo-Freudians in the 1940s and 1950s.

Psychoanalysis

WHAT IS IT?

Psychoanalysis is a long-term procedure that uses various techniques to uncover repressed memories, fears, and conflicts. Behavioural disorders are believed to be *symbolic expressions* of unconscious conflicts between the id, ego, and superego. When this conflict is excessive, defence mechanisms become overused, seriously distorting reality and leading to self-defeating behaviour. Before people can effectively resolve their problems, they need to become aware of the sources of these problems. The purpose of psychoanalysis is to uncover these hidden, deep-seated sources of conflict and thereby gain insight. There are several techniques by which this can be done, including the following:

- *Free association*—the patient relaxes comfortably and says literally anything that comes to mind, no matter how personal or embarrassing. Interpretations of this material by the analyst provide insight into the unconscious and, eventually, the type of defence mechanism being used. Because the patient's unconscious mind attempts to block unacceptable motives, the analyst can use any evidence of "resistance" (such as hesitation in free association) to help reveal unconscious conflicts. The analyst makes a careful note of hesitations, the mind going "blank" or upset, and analyses the words or incident associated with this "blocking" until the conflict can be revealed. This is known as *analysis of resistance*.
- *Dream analysis*—the analyst uncovers the disguised meanings of the dream and thereby provides the patient with insight into the motives and feelings that are causing anxiety. Freud's dream theory is covered in Biological Rhythms, Sleep, and Dreaming (Chapter 4).
- *Transference*—as therapy progresses, the clients redirect the feelings they had for their parents onto the analyst, thereby re-enacting early conflicts. In a sense, what is happening is that the patient is recreating an earlier neurosis that, in a therapeutic environment, can be resolved.

Classical psychoanalysis is not used a great deal nowadays, possibly because it is a very long-term and intense therapy, taking about five sessions a week for several years. Psychoanalytic psychotherapy is a reduced version, taking about two sessions a week for up to 5 years. The principle is the same but there may be some giving of information to the patient by the therapist rather than waiting for findings to emerge.

APPROPRIATENESS AND EFFECTIVENESS

- H.J. Eysenck (1952, see A2PKT p.424) conducted a review of the effectiveness of psychoanalysis and concluded that it was not an effective treatment. He estimated that 72% of patients who received no treatment over a period of 2 years made a recovery (called *spontaneous remission*) compared to only 44% of those who received psychoanalysis. However, this review has been criticised for being very flawed. First, Eysenck counted patients who withdrew from treatment as failures for psychoanalysis. If these were removed from the statistics, the recovery rate was 66%. Second, it was believed that many of the patients who received psychoanalysis were suffering from more severe disorders than were the untreated individuals.

- Bergin (1971, see A2PKT p.424) reassessed the findings using different criteria for recovery and considered that the recovery rate for those receiving treatment was 83%.

Ego Analysis

WHAT IS IT?

Ego analysis was developed after Freud's death by a group of neo-Freudians including Karen Horney, Anna Freud, and Erik Erikson. Ego analysts believe that people are not totally at the mercy of the instinctual urges of the id but can select a time and means of satisfying them. They place greater emphasis on the ego rather than the id, believing that people are able to control their environment rather than it controlling them. A basic assumption of ego analysis is that people have a set of ego functions that are conscious and present at birth. These ego functions are capable of controlling both the id and the external environment and, importantly, have energies and gratifications of their own. Herein lies an important difference between ego analysts and Freud. Whereas Freud believed that society inevitably presented people with problems by trying to control their instinctual urges, ego analysts believe that society can be a source of fulfilment by providing gratification of ego functions.

The therapy involves the use of strategies such as *ego support* and *ego building* to strengthen the ego so that patients can cope better with any problems. The therapist identifies any areas in which the patient is functioning successfully and then helps them to use these skills in problem areas. Most of the techniques involved in psychoanalysis are used, but there is much greater emphasis on the patient's current social and interpersonal problems rather than on their childhood experiences.

APPROPRIATENESS AND EFFECTIVENESS

- Sloane et al. (1975, see A2PKT p.424) conducted a detailed study comparing ego analysis with behavioural therapy or no treatment on patients mainly suffering from anxiety disorders. They found that both ego analysis and behaviour therapy produced an improvement rate of 80%, compared with a 48% improvement rate for a control group on a waiting list for treatment. However, at 8 months there was no difference between the three groups because the controls had improved, indicating that ego analysis is equally as effective as behavioural therapy but neither is, in the long term, more effective for these conditions than no therapy—they simply work more quickly.

General Evaluation of Psychodynamic Therapies

 Psychodynamic therapies work better with some people than others. Sloane et al. (1975, see A2PKT p.424) report that it is best suited to well-educated people of middle and upper socioeconomic classes who have anxiety disorders rather than psychotic behaviour. Luborsky and Spence (1978, see A2PKT pp.424–425) point out that the reason such therapies are more suited to the better educated is because in order to be effective they require considerable verbal skills.

 Psychodynamic therapies work better on some conditions than others. They are most suited to the treatment of anxiety disorders, depression, and some sexual disorders but are less effective for the treatment of psychotic conditions such as schizophrenia in which insight is unlikely to develop (Luborsky and Spence, 1978, see A2PKT pp.424–425).

Classic psychoanalysis has been extended in several ways by modern psychodynamic therapies. Therapies such as ego analysis, brief psychodynamic therapy, and group psychodynamic therapy have enabled the treatment of children and groups, and over a shorter period of time.

Ethical Implications of the Psychodynamic Approach

Classic psychoanalysis placed great emphasis on the influence of adverse childhood experiences in causing adult problems, so on the positive side, it strongly implies that children should be treated with compassion and understanding and their basic needs should not be neglected. The approach also points to the possible dangers of sexually repressive attitudes within society. However, it also implies that a great deal of blame can be laid at the feet of parents whose children grow into seriously troubled adults. A further ethical problem with the Freudian view of humanity is that it is an extremely pessimistic one, seeing people as constantly at the mercy of the selfish instinctual urges of the id. The ego analysis approach, however, is a much more positive one in its belief that we all have the power to control our environments and can gain considerable pleasure in our social lives by the satisfaction of ego functions.

SO WHAT DOES THIS MEAN?

Davison and Neale (2001) point out that there is conflicting evidence as to whether psychoanalysis yields any greater improvements than do the mere passage of time or talking things over with health professionals such as the family doctor. This is not to say that this type of therapy is not useful, just that clear evidence is lacking. This is hardly surprising given the likely huge range in quality of such therapy, especially when compared to such tightly structured ones as behavioural therapy. One of the greatest problems of classic psychoanalysis is the considerable amount of time such therapy takes and therefore its considerable expense. This does not apply to most of the more recent variations, which are much briefer in duration.

With respect to all classes of therapy, it is not possible to say that any one group is overall more successful than another and it would not be productive to unreservedly reject or accept any such group. Rather what is necessary is to find the treatment and therapist best suited to each individual case, taking account of their condition, circumstances, and personal characteristics.

OVER TO YOU

1. **Discuss the use of two therapies that are derived from either the psychodynamic or cognitive-behavioural models of abnormality.** **(30 marks)**
2. **"One of the greatest problems for any patient suffering from mental disorder is the question of how to choose the best and most appropriate therapy."**
   Distinguish between any *two* types of therapies for mental disorders. **(30 marks)**

GENERAL ISSUES IN THERAPY

COMPARISONS BETWEEN THERAPIES

One of the most important points when choosing a therapy is to be able to compare the effectiveness of each method of treatment. Such comparisons are not easy to make for obvious reasons—no two patients are ever going to be exactly alike in the severity of their condition nor in the actual symptoms shown. Rarely are therapies offered in their "pure" form: therapists change their techniques to meet a particular challenge. Furthermore, patients are often, quite rightly, given a choice in their treatment, so there are issues of commitment to consider. Nevertheless, we can learn from large-scale reviews comparing different methods by means of a statistical technique known as meta-analysis. Meta-analysis involves a thorough literature search, the translating of results into a common format, and then the averaging out of the results from many studies.

Smith, Glass, and Miller (1980, see A2PKT p.411) meta-analysed 475 psychotherapy outcome studies involving more than 25,000 patients. This showed that:

- Any treatment is better than no treatment; the treated patients were found to be better off than almost 80% of untreated patients.
- Different therapies were equally effective.
- The beliefs and preferences of the therapists were important in determining effectiveness.

In another meta-analysis, Lambert et al. (1986) found that:

- Factors common to all therapies, namely warmth, trust, and encouragement, lead to significant and lasting improvement on a wide range of anxiety and mood disorders.
- The positive effects of psychotherapy last many months following the end of treatment (note that this does not include biological therapies).
- There is a great variation in the improvement of individual patients, so using "average" improvement scores can be misleading.

Research on Meta-analysis

Matt and Navarro (1997, see A2PKT p.427) analysed 63 meta-analyses of the effects of therapy. The main findings were as follows:

- From 28 of these providing relevant data, 75% of patients improved more than untreated controls.
- From 10 particular studies, it was found that 57% of placebo control patients (who had had general encouragement but no specific therapy) improved more than untreated controls. However, 75% of patients receiving specific treatment did better than placebo controls. This indicates that specific effects are greater than the common effects of warmth, etc.
- Generally, cognitive and behavioural treatments were better than client-based ones, i.e. psychodynamic and humanistic. However, because there was no standardisation, the outcome measures used are not objective.

However, the negative evaluations below apply to this review.

EVALUATION OF META-ANALYSIS

It is impossible to be totally objective. In general, there is disagreement among therapists as to the judgements made. Different reviewers reading the same research papers reach different conclusions. Ultimately someone has to judge which outcomes are good and which are bad and then someone else can criticise this judgement. There simply are no objective standards.

There are deficiencies in research. The process of meta-analysis has uncovered deficiencies in research, for example, inadequate reporting of precise outcomes, and outcomes judged by people who knew what treatment was used (therefore giving potential for bias).

Long-term benefit. Having pointed to the deficiencies in research and reporting, meta-analysis may lead to an improvement in research practices and standards of publication (Kazdin, 1986).

SO WHAT DOES THIS MEAN?

Common factors such as warmth, acceptance and empathy on behalf of the therapist appear to be quite important in determining the outcome of therapy. Despite Matt and Navarro's (1997, see A2PKT p.427) contention that specific therapies are four times more effective than these common factors, Strupp (1996, see A2PKT p.400) estimates that the success of therapies may depend on factors other than the distinct characteristics of the therapy. This alone shows that there is as yet no agreement on the success of therapies. Perhaps meta-analysis is not necessarily the way forward and what is required is a case study approach in which patients' own views can be taken into account rather than relying on notes from second-hand observation. The case study approach may not provide us with quantitative data and convenient statistics but would avoid inaccurate generalisations and give a more sensitive picture of what individual patients may require from therapy.

ETHICAL ISSUES IN THERAPIES

There are important ethical issues that need to be considered in therapy, regardless of the type of treatment given.

Informed Consent

In an ideal world, all patients would be given sufficient information to give fully informed consent before treatment was administered. This would include information about:

- All the treatments available.
- The probability of success of each treatment.
- The possible side effects.
- The right to terminate treatment and the possible effects of this.

However, there are several reasons why this may not happen:

- The therapists may not have detailed information on the success rates of all treatments.
- Any one treatment may work well with some patients but cause problems with others.
- The patient may not remember the information. Irwin et al. (1985, see A2PKT p.401) found that 75% of patients forgot important information.
- Many people, such as young children, people with learning difficulties, and schizophrenics, cannot give such consent. In this case it must be sought from parents or legal guardians.
- Patients may feel an exaggerated respect for the therapist and make their judgement on this rather than on the information given.
- If patients do not give consent, it may cost them their lives. Some people argue that it is unethical *not* to oblige them to have treatment under these circumstances because they are not in a frame of mind to fully appreciate the consequences. This is a particularly difficult ethical dilemma.

Confidentiality

Confidentiality with regard to sensitive information is necessary to establish trust between the patient and therapist. However, MacLeod (1998, see A2PKT p.402) argues that complete confidentiality is unusual and rarely necessary since the best treatment is obtained when several therapists discuss the case. Problems can arise, however, when information is disclosed to *outside* organisations. Confidentiality may not be maintained if the therapist believes the patient is likely to kill or harm someone. In particular, the therapist has a legal obligation to disclose information under the following two specific circumstances:

- If the information is relevant to terrorism.
- If the information is relevant to the welfare of children.

GENERAL ISSUES IN EVALUATING THERAPIES

In assessing a treatment, the most important question to ask is "Does it work?" Unfortunately this is a difficult question to answer for various reasons.

- **There is no agreed definition of "cure" or "improvement".** Therapists from different perspectives view the goal of therapy differently. The behavioural therapist aims to change behaviour; the psychoanalyst tries to uncover the unconscious; and the cognitive-behavioural therapist attempts to change attitudes. Ideally it should be possible to obtain physiological, behavioural, and self-report measures to assess improvement but this is rarely the case.

- **Short-term follow-up does not measure long-term effects.** If patients recover soon after treatment this does not mean they will not relapse. Long-term follow-ups are required but are not always conducted

- **Benefits may not be due to therapy alone.** They may, at least in part, be caused by other factors such as the particular therapist or the expectations of the patient.

- **There is great variety in the severity and nature of symptoms.** This makes assessment of improvements rather difficult.

- **Effectiveness of therapies depends on the skills of the therapist as well as the therapy itself.** Again, this makes it difficult to assess the treatment independently from the therapist's skills.

- **Random control trials are rare.** Usually patients are a self-selected sample who have opted for a particular treatment. This makes comparison between different treatments very difficult. A more satisfactory method sometimes employed is to compare the treatment group with a waiting list of similar patients.

- **Some types of therapy work better with some people than others.** This means that measures of improvement are not necessarily generalisable to the population of people with the disorder.

- **People often exaggerate their initial symptoms and their improvement (the hello–goodbye effect).** This means that the degree of effectiveness of treatment may be enhanced.

NOTE: These considerations are important in assessing the effectiveness of *any* type of therapy. Bear this in mind when answering exam questions.

QUESTIONS AND ESSAY PLANS

In all of these essays bear in mind the synoptic criteria that are assessed here. This means that the questions are assessing your knowledge of psychology as a whole, not just the specific topic. Read Chapter 1 of A2PKT and Chapter 1 of this book, Preparing for the Exam, in order to appreciate exactly which criteria you need to fulfil in order to gain maximum marks.

1 Discuss issues surrounding the use of biological (somatic) therapies. **(30 marks)**

In this essay it is useful to cover all three forms of biological treatment. After the introduction, follow the format for each of the three with one paragraph of description of the treatment (in reasonable detail as there are a lot of AO1 marks), then a paragraph on appropriateness and effectiveness, followed by a paragraph along the lines of "So what does this mean?", in which ethical issues are addressed and there is a general summing up. Conclude by covering appropriateness, effectiveness, and ethical issues common to biological therapies as a whole.

Paragraph 1 Introduction

Outline the assumptions of the medical model, on which biological therapies are based. Mention that all these treatments involve direct manipulation of body processes and that you will discuss psychosurgery, drug treatment, and electro-convulsive therapy (ECT).

Paragraph 2

Psychosurgery. Describe what it involves, including prefrontal leucotomy, stereotactic neurosurgery, and cingulotomy. Discuss the appropriateness and effectiveness of these treatments, paying attention to them being a last resort. Provide research support for your arguments, especially recent research (e.g. Cosgrove et al., 2000). Sum up this part by mentioning ethical concerns due to irreversibility, and therefore how few operations are done. Discuss the need for fully informed consent, etc., the concerns of MIND, and the possible new alternative for obsessive-compulsive disorder.

Paragraph 3

Describe what is involved in ECT nowadays, including the length of treatment. Discuss the appropriateness and effectiveness of ECT, supporting your arguments with as much research as possible. Mention why it is such a controversial treatment.

Paragraph 4

Discuss ethical issues and the modern alternative of transcranial brain stimulation (appropriate to this essay as it is biological).

Paragraph 5

Describe the drug therapies available for depression, anxiety disorders, and schizophrenia. Keep it reasonably brief for each one, as there's a lot to cover.

Paragraph 6

Discuss appropriateness and effectiveness of drug treatments. Discuss ethical issues, including the problems of *not* using drugs but also the problem of using them without other help—

of the individual perhaps feeling that only their condition, rather than them as a person, is being treated.

Paragraph 7

Do a general evaluation of somatic therapies.

Paragraph 8 Conclusion

Do a general summing up, mentioning the fact that somatic treatments, especially drugs, are indispensable in the treatment of mental disorders but on their own can never provide a total cure.

2 Distinguish between those behavioural therapies based on classical conditioning and those based on operant conditioning. (30 marks)

The AO1 marks in this essay come from describing the treatments based on classical conditioning (CC) and those based on operant conditioning (OC). The AO2 marks are derived from distinguishing between the two and this is far more difficult than the description. Be careful not to spend too much time on the description as this may prevent you getting good AO2 marks.

Paragraph 1 Introduction

Outline the principles involved in all behaviour therapies and distinguish between those based on classical conditioning and those based on operant conditioning.

Paragraph 2

Outline the principles involved in therapies based on classical conditioning, and *briefly* describe what is involved in systematic desensitisation, flooding, and aversion therapy. Make sure it is brief, with the emphasis on the principles of classical conditioning. Do the same for therapies based on operant conditioning, i.e. the token economy system and modelling.

Paragraph 3

Outline the distinction (and similarity) in terms of principles involved. In terms of similarity, both types of therapies are based on learning principles, so they emphasise the need for unlearning maladaptive behaviour and replacing it with more adaptive ways of functioning. The emphasis is on treating observable behaviour, with scant if any attention made to cognitions (thinking) and certainly not the unconscious mind. In terms of distinctiveness, therapies based on classical conditioning work on *learning by association* while those based on operant conditioning work on the principle of *learning by consequences.* Outline how these work using one therapy each—for example, in systematic desensitisation used to treat phobias, you are replacing association of the object (or event) and fear with association of the object (or event) and relaxation. In the token economy system you are reinforcing certain behaviour, so the patient is being reinforced for voluntary behaviour—quite a different principle.

Paragraph 4

Outline the distinction (and similarity) in terms of effectiveness and type of disorders they treat: both types of therapy are reasonably effective but are used for quite different types of mental disorder. Classical conditioning is used for disorders such as phobias in which the problem behaviours, through learning, are now involuntary (the fear is not something the patient can choose not to show), whereas operant conditioning works on voluntary behaviour (a patient can choose to cooperate in order to gain tokens). This distinction is not, however, always clear-cut because modelling can be used to prevent phobias. Nevertheless, operant conditioning is more appropriate for acquiring behaviour that was previously difficult to attain, such as social skills, whereas classical conditioning cannot be used for this type of training.

Paragraph 5

Outline the distinction (and similarity) in terms of applicability to different patients. This relates back to the type of disorders being treating but has other implications. Both types of therapy require the cooperation of the patient, but in rather different ways. You could impose flooding and aversion therapy on an individual (although for ethical reasons you obviously should not) but with operant conditioning the patient can choose not to cooperate at all. Because the behaviour to be acquired is voluntary, it requires considerable cooperation on the part of the patient who must not be half-hearted towards it. Both methods are appropriate for use with children but operant conditioning is especially appropriate, perhaps because children are used to having their behaviour controlled by others. The appropriateness of these therapies for treating children makes them distinct from a lot of other therapies (especially many forms of cognitive and psychodynamic therapies).

Paragraph 6

Outline the distinction (and similarity) in terms of research support. Both types of therapy are well supported by controlled research studies. Since changes in observable behaviour are being measured it is possible to get a reasonably objective measure of any improvements, possibly more so than when measuring changes in attitudes or feelings, as with other approaches.

Paragraph 7

Consider distinction in terms of ethics. Both types of therapy can be accused of taking a rather mechanistic view of humans but distinctions can be made in terms of the types of control that patients and therapists have. In general, therapists have greater control in operant conditioning therapies. In operant conditioning the therapist (or other authority figure) is dispensing rewards (and sometimes punishments) so they have considerable power, but the client also has some since there is an element of choice in how much they cooperate. In classical conditioning, the patient is not so controlled by the therapist. This is especially the case in systematic desensitisation in which the patients build the initial hierarchy and do not move from one stage to another until they are ready. Nevertheless, since their responses are not voluntary, in some ways they have less control over the situation as a whole and their own progress than those undergoing therapies based on operant conditioning.

Paragraph 8 Conclusion

Summarise the main points—that there are obvious similarities because both types of therapies are based on learning principles, and this makes them both distinct from other forms of therapy. They are also different in a number of ways, in the types of conditions they can be applied to, the types of patient they can treat, and the ethical issues that need to be addressed.

3 Discuss the use of two therapies that are derived from the psychodynamic or cognitive-behavioural models of abnormality. (30 marks)

In this essay we will deal with the cognitive-behavioural models. As you have to discuss them you will need a description of each of them followed by an evaluation in terms of effectiveness and appropriateness. You need then to look at a general evaluation of cognitive therapies, comparing them with other therapies. Last, but certainly not least, consider ethical issues.

Paragraph 1 Introduction

Define what is meant by cognitive-behavioural therapy. Say which two models you will cover—in our case Ellis' rational-emotive behavioural therapy (REBT; 1962) and Beck's (1976) cognitive therapy.

Paragraph 2

Describe rational-emotive behavioural therapy (REBT), mentioning that it has changed its name from rational-emotive therapy (RET) first, in response to aiming to make more specific changes to behaviour, and second, to encompass the change from a concentration on a set of irrational beliefs to the concept of "demandingness". This ensures your essay is up to date.

Paragraph 3

Evaluate this specific therapy in terms of appropriateness and effectiveness.

Paragraph 4

Describe Beck's cognitive therapy. Note that it is less confrontational than Ellis'.

Paragraph 5

Evaluate this specific therapy in terms of appropriateness and effectiveness.

Paragraph 6

Now do a general evaluation of cognitive-behavioural therapies. Emphasise that they take full account of people's feelings but also tackle behavioural consequences, so in a sense you have "the best of both worlds" when comparing them to behavioural or humanistic/psychodynamic therapies. Like all therapies, they are limited and reductionist in that they lay great emphasis on thoughts and beliefs above other factors such as biology or the importance of early experience. Nevertheless, they are relatively quick without ignoring the patient's need to have his/her opinions and feelings fully acknowledged. You could make mention of the results of meta-analysis—that cognitive-behavioural therapies, according to Matt and Navarro (1997), are more effective than humanistic and psychodynamic therapies. Do, however, acknowledge the problems inherent in such meta-analyses.

Paragraph 7

Consider the ethical issues involved in cognitive-behavioural therapies—the empowerment of the individual, the likely reduction in self-criticism and increase in self-esteem likely to result from it, but also the confrontational nature of some approaches.

Paragraph 8 Conclusion

Conclude along the lines of "So what does this mean?" (see page 249) Cognitive-behavioural therapies are best suited to depression and anxiety-based conditions and to fairly intelligent individuals who are capable of gaining insight into their condition. Their long-term effectiveness may be due to the therapy helping patients to acquire life-long skills for effective coping.

Perspectives

What's it about?

The same issues appear across most areas of psychology: *ethics*, *gender*, and *culture*. You have already studied ethics as part of the AS topic "Social Influence". How many ethical guidelines can you recall? Use these to assess whether Zimbardo's, Milgram's, and Asch's research should have taken place. Next consider how many studies using non-human animals you can recall from your AS studies, e.g. what did Selye, Brady, and Harlow research? You have considered the issue of cultural relativism in the definitions of abnormality. What does ethnocentrism mean and why was Ainsworth and Bell's Strange Situation research ethnocentric? Gender bias is another issue that you will have come across at AS. For example, how did Bowlby's research influence the role of women? How have women been stereotyped in the research into gender differences in stress?

What's in this unit?

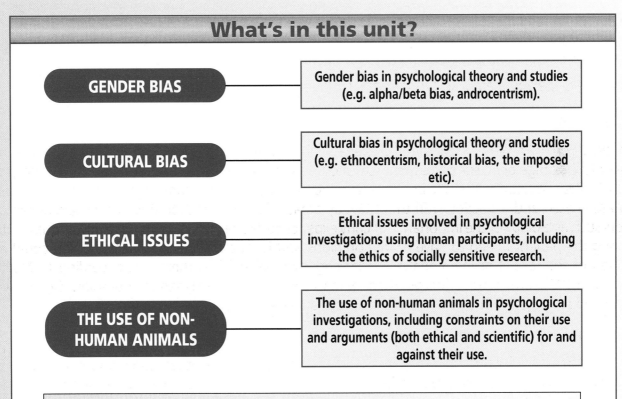

GENDER BIAS	Gender bias in psychological theory and studies (e.g. alpha/beta bias, androcentrism).
CULTURAL BIAS	Cultural bias in psychological theory and studies (e.g. ethnocentrism, historical bias, the imposed etic).
ETHICAL ISSUES	Ethical issues involved in psychological investigations using human participants, including the ethics of socially sensitive research.
THE USE OF NON-HUMAN ANIMALS	The use of non-human animals in psychological investigations, including constraints on their use and arguments (both ethical and scientific) for and against their use.

Bias refers to the systematic distortion of a person's or society's views. This has led to bias in psychological research as the dominant subcultural group—western, white, middle-class, American (WWMCA) male—has been used as the standard against which other subgroups have been measured. Consequently, psychological research contains many examples of gender and cultural bias. Such research has social consequences and so the studies in this section also have implications as socially sensitive research.

GENDER BIAS

To read up on gender bias, refer to pages 435–442 of A2PKT.

THEORETICAL BIAS

Alpha and Beta Bias

- *Alpha bias* refers to research that exaggerates the differences between the genders, e.g. sociobiology, which assumes innate differences.

- *Beta bias* refers to research that minimises or ignores gender differences, e.g. research that has used male participants (androcentric samples) and assumed that the findings apply equally well to women, such as Asch's (1955, see A2PKT p.439) research on conformity, Milgram's (1963, see A2PKT pp.451–452) research on obedience, and Kohlberg's (1963, see A2PKT pp.438–439) theory of moral development.

METHODOLOGICAL BIAS

- *Formulation of the research question.* This shows evidence of bias because traditionally issues that did not concern men were not investigated and so androcentric bias (bias towards male concerns) influenced what were considered suitable research interests. Also consider the tendency to investigate causes of abnormality as internal for women, i.e. their hormones cause PMS, but external for men, i.e. socialisation and upbringing cause aggression.

- *Selection of participants.* Androcentric samples such as those in Milgram's, Asch's, and Kohlberg's research are guilty of beta bias, as findings based on men are considered generalisable to women and so ignore gender differences.

- *Interpretation and use of results.* Results have often been interpreted as evidence of female inferiority, e.g. Freud and Kohlberg, and so used to perpetuate discrimination.

- *Publishing of research.* This may be biased as traditionally editors have been predominantly male and so research that failed to find expected gender differences is less likely to have been published.

- *Research methods.* It is claimed that the traditional scientific method shows gender bias, as the experimental context disadvantages women because men usually dominate it. Also quantitative data can easily be manipulated, e.g. "scientific" research has led to women being pathologised as more easily depressed than men. Feminists favour qualitative methods (interviews, observations, case studies) over quantitative (experiments, correlational analysis, closed questionnaires), as they believe that qualitative methods are better able to identify valid gender differences.

- *Research approaches.* The nomothetic approach (which seeks to identify universal explanations of behaviour) is more subject to beta bias, and the idiographic approach (which assumes everyone is different) is more susceptible to alpha bias.

THEORETICAL EXAMPLES

Example of Alpha Bias

Freud (see A2PKT p.435) claimed, "Anatomy is destiny" and based his theories around boys' fear of castration and girls' "penis envy", the key elements of the Oedipus/Electra conflicts, which occur during the phallic stage of psychosexual development, and which he claimed result in gender differences. Freud argued that these gender differences in psychosexual development result in female moral inferiority, because girls do not identify as strongly with their same-sex parent as they have less to fear than boys because they have already been "castrated". His theory focused mainly on the Oedipus complex, which is experienced by boys—further evidence of gender bias. Freud generalised the Oedipus complex to women by saying that there was a similar process; Jung developed this into the Electra complex. These gender-biased views have not been supported, as certainly there is no evidence that women are morally inferior to men.

Example of Beta Bias

Erikson's (1968, see A2PKT p.439) theory of development across the lifespan is an example of beta bias as his research was based on androcentric samples. Kohlberg's (1963, see A2PKT pp.438–439) theory of moral development was based on the assumption that there would be minimal differences (beta bias) between men and women in terms of moral development. Consequently, he used an all-male sample as representative of males and females. He concluded that men were at a higher level of moral development than women when he went on to use the test on women and found differences between women's and men's morality. His results show gender bias as it is now accepted that there are only small, if any, differences in moral reasoning between men and women. This is a clear-cut example of androcentric bias—the male norm is used as the standard and when females differ from this they are classed as inferior.

RESEARCH EXAMPLES

An Example of Alpha Bias

Research such as Buss' (1989, see A2PKT p.301) on evolutionary explanations of mating behaviour show alpha bias as he overemphasised the different factors prioritised by men and women in prospective partners, and underemphasised the similar factors that both genders preferred.

An Example of Beta Bias

The studies of conformity such as Asch (1955, see A2PKT p.439) and Perrin and Spencer (1980, see A2PKT p.439) both used androcentric samples and so are guilty of androcentric bias.

Rosenthal (1966, see A2PKT p.438) suggests that the majority of research is guilty of beta bias, as even studies that use male and female participants tend to disregard gender differences, i.e. they do not analyse the data to see if there are significant sex differences. Rosenthal found that male experimenters treat female participants differently from male participants, e.g. they tend to smile more at females, and so concluded that: "Male and female participants may, psychologically, simply not be in the same experiment at all." Research that aims to, and does, establish gender differences may be a result of beta bias, i.e. differential treatment in the research process, rather than the phenomenon being investigated. This is particularly so as the majority of researchers/academics are male.

FEMINISTS AND THE STATUS QUO

Feminists argue that gender differences have been distorted to maintain the status quo of male power. This is supported by the many examples of male dominance in society, and in psychological research it is evident in the disproportionate number of male compared to female researchers, and in research such as Bowlby's that encourages gender stereotypes. Male-dominated universities may fail to appoint female academics. This was particularly true traditionally and accounts for why past research is dominated by male concerns and mainly male psychologists. Female psychologists did contribute to the development of the subject and so their largely invisible role in the textbooks is further evidence of gender bias.

Feminists aim to redress this imbalance by revising the "facts" about gender. The aim is to establish the real gender differences from the gender stereotypes. They reject many of the biological causes identified in the past as they feel that these are better explained by social causes, and so gender differences are not inevitable. For example, the greater diagnosis of depression in women may be due to gender bias in diagnosis, but there are also valid biological and social explanations (see A2PKT pp.359–361, and 366–368). Gender differences in diagnosis show alpha bias, as the biological (hormones) and social (sex-role stereotypes) factors tend to be exaggerated and bias the process of assessment and diagnosis.

Feminists study women as normal human beings as opposed to the past approach, which tested how they differed and were deficient to the male norm, or restricted them to the one-dimensional role of nurturers of children and men. The increasing number of female psychologists has led to women being studied in their own right and female experiences, never previously studied, have been researched, such as female sexuality, pregnancy, the dual burden of working and childcare, sexual abuse, rape, prostitution, sexual negotiation, and many more. Feminists have reviewed the literature on gender differences and concluded that where sex differences exist they are so close to zero that they are insignificant (Maccoby & Jacklin, 1974, see A2PKT p.436). Differences between individuals are greater than those between genders, which means that variation is greater within than between genders.

SO WHAT DOES THIS MEAN?

Psychological research faces real difficulty in distinguishing between actual and distorted gender differences. The fact that it is not always clear whether these are innate or socially constructed or to what extent they are an interaction of the two makes the research process yet more complex. As the review of the traditional research in psychology shows, too much of it has been weakened by gender bias. Feminists have successfully highlighted this and, by researching women in their own right, addressed the imbalance of the male norm being the standard against which all behaviour is judged. Further research needs to be open to possible gender differences, as these should not be disregarded if beta bias is to be avoided. If found, these need to be accepted as differences, not deficiencies, as a gender-free approach is needed, which avoids sexist and stereotyped concepts. The extent of the actual difference needs to be determined, not ignored (beta bias) or exaggerated (alpha bias) and should be used to increase equality rather than used as a basis for discrimination.

OVER TO YOU

1. **Describe gender biases in psychological research and assess how these biases may have influenced research.**

(30 marks)

CULTURAL BIAS

To read up on cultural bias, refer to pages 443–451 of A2PKT.

THEORETICAL BIAS

- *Individualistic vs. collectivist.* Psychologists distinguish between individualistic and collectivist cultures, in that individualistic ones emphasise the needs of the individual, whereas collectivist ones emphasise the needs of the group. Western cultures are high in individualism and Eastern cultures are high in collectivism. However, this is an oversimplification because it ignores the variation within a culture, e.g. subcultural variation. Thus, cross-cultural comparisons may lack validity.

- *Ethnocentrism.* This is when the views of one's own group or culture bias assumptions and judgement, e.g. when assumptions about one's own culture are considered generalisable to other cultures, when this is often not the case.

- *Eurocentrism.* Nobles (1976, see A2PKT p.445) criticises European psychologists' approach as Eurocentric because a view of human behaviour is presented that is based on one type of culture and is not representative of other cultures. The Eurocentric approach is based on concepts such as "survival of the fittest". The use of this as a standard against which to assess the African self-concept amounts to scientific colonialism and has resulted in oppression.

METHODOLOGICAL BIAS

- *Etic constructs.* Etic constructs are universal, e.g. an attempt to establish a universal explanation. An *imposed etic* is when a theory developed in one's own culture is used to study other cultures, and so an emic is mistakenly assumed to be an etic. This is often based on the mistaken view that culture doesn't matter, which leads to the assumption that an explanation developed in one culture is universally applicable. For an example, review Ainsworth and Bell's (1970) Strange Situation covered at AS Psychology, as this is an imposed etic.

- *Emic constructs.* Emic constructs are specific and so vary from one culture to another. These tend to have been ignored or have been misinterpreted due to biases in cross-cultural research. Research that does consider cultural differences takes a viewpoint called *cultural relativism*. An example is Cole, Gay, Glick, and Sharp's (1971, see A2PKT pp.446–447) research into intelligence, which investigated how objects were sorted into groups. Western cultures organised by categories, whereas the African Kpelle culture organised by functional groups, i.e. whether the objects were used together. This suggests that intelligence has different meanings across cultures.

- *Biases in cross-cultural research.* These include: the researcher's ethnocentrism, as it is difficult to disregard one's own cultural view; translation errors, as accurate meaning can get lost in the translation of instructions and responses and data may be little more than second-hand accounts after translation; the trust between the researcher and participants, which may be affected by cultural differences and so result in data that lacks validity.

- *Racial bias.* This has been identified in a well-known psychology textbook (by Atkinson, Atkinson, Smith, & Bem, 1993)—Owusu-Bempah and Howitt (1994, see A2PKT p.449) claim that the textbook does not specify which African tribes have been studied, which is, to say the least, insensitive. Describing cultures as "primitive" and "underdeveloped" perpetuates cultural stereotypes and so is guilty of racial bias.

- *Formulation of the research question.* Ethnocentrism and Eurocentrism, outlined above, may bias questions.

- *Selection of participants.* Research samples tend to be ethnocentric because over 90% of psychological research has been conducted on Western, white, middle-class Americans. Fewer than 5% of participants tested are other than white.

- *Interpretation and use of results.* The biases in cross-cultural research mean that there is a high probability of erroneous interpretations being made. Results may be used to perpetuate racial discrimination, such as H. J. Eysenck's (1981, see A2PKT pp.212–213) research on racial differences in IQ.

RESEARCH EXAMPLES

Examples of Imposed Etics

PERSONALITY TESTS

Tests of personality in other cultures have usually used Western-derived tests and so these are imposed etics. Research has proven that personality structures differ across cultures, e.g. Kuo-shu Yang and Bond (1990, see A2PKT p.447) found little similarity between the Big Five (extraversion, agreeableness, emotional stability, culture, and conscientiousness) personality factors of Cattell's 16 PF test and those identified by an analysis of personality descriptions in Chinese newspapers (social orientation, expressiveness, competence, self-control, and optimism). Thus, using Western personality tests to assess personality in other cultures is an imposed etic.

THE STRANGE SITUATION

Ainsworth and Bell's (1970) Strange Situation is an imposed etic as it is an ethnocentric (culturally biased) measure because it has been derived in one culture—the USA—and so is representative of that culture only. Cross-cultural comparisons of attachment lack validity, for example, replications of the Strange Situation have found greater incidence of anxious-resistant attachment type in Japan and China compared to Western cultures. However, this does not mean that these cultures have a greater rate of insecure attachments as the nature of attachment is culturally relative but the Strange Situation does not account for this. Thus, attachment is not expressed in the same way in all cultures and so the Strange Situation's indicators of attachment type may lack generalisability.

DSM-IV AND ICD-10

Methods used to diagnose (DSM-IV and ICD-10) and treat mental disorders are also imposed etics, which result in cultural bias in diagnosis. For example, Blake (1973) found that psychiatrists were more likely to use the diagnosis of schizophrenia, in a standardised case study, if the patient was described as African-American rather than as white.

GENDER DEVELOPMENT IN NEW GUINEA

Mead's (1935, see A2PKT p.448) research on gender development in New Guinea is another example of an imposed etic because she used her standards of masculine and feminine behaviour to judge the three tribes she investigated. She concluded that the Mundugumor exhibited masculine characteristics because both males and females were aggressive, and that the Arapesh exhibited feminine qualities because both males and females were warm, emotional, and nonaggressive (the men even took to their beds during childbirth!). She reported a sex role reversal in the Tchambuli, where the males cared for the household, gossiped, and discussed how to look pretty, whilst the females were assertive and took responsibility for trade and the running of the village. However, Mead's research is ethnocentric, and much of her data was secondhand and so meanings may have got lost in translation. This cultural bias undermines the validity of the research.

IQ Tests

H. J. Eysenck (1981, see A2PKT p.462) investigated cultural differences in IQ and claimed that the lower achievement of African Americans on IQ tests was due to innate differences in ability. Goddard (1913, see A2PKT p.462) issued IQ tests to immigrants as they entered America. He argued that 87% of Russians, 83% of Jews, 80% of Hungarians, and 79% of Italians were "feeble-minded". These findings were used politically to support a eugenics policy of restricted immigration. This is an emic approach, as it is an attempt to identify cultural differences. It is evidence of cultural bias because the IQ tests were ethnocentric and so imposed etics.

Examples of Emics

An example of an emic approach is cross-cultural research that takes a viewpoint known as cultural relativism. According to this, behaviour can only be understood when it is considered in the context from which it originates. Berry (1974, see A2PKT p.446) rejected a universal (etic) approach to intelligence as he felt that intelligent behaviour differed (an emic approach) in accordance with the demands of the culture—cultural relativism. Cole et al.'s (1971, see A2PKT pp.446–447) research, discussed previously as an example of an emic construct, used this approach. Another example is cross-cultural differences in eating disorders. Lee, Hsu, and Wing's (1992) research showed that eating disorders are very rare in Chinese populations, which suggests that views of "thin/fat" are culturally determined.

THE CHANGING PICTURE

Attitudes to other cultures have fortunately changed and there is a reduction in racism today. The highlighting of cultural bias, whether through imposed etics or lack of cross-cultural research, has been addressed and the situation is changing. Recent research is addressing the cultural imbalance but more research into cultural differences is needed to redress this fully.

The difficulty lies in the pervasiveness of culturally-biased research; most psychological research has been conducted by Americans and Europeans on themselves. Furthermore, there are difficulties in researching other cultures as it often comes across as, "strange people from strange countries doing strange things" (Banyard, 1999). The language used is further evidence of cultural bias as the word "tribe" is not used to refer to social groups in Europe or America, yet is used to describe groups in Africa. This shows the pervasiveness of ethnocentrism as it exists in research that tries to address the cultural imbalance. Thus, although such patronisation is on the decline, complacency should not set in, as this issue has certainly not been eradicated.

Nowadays, psychologists acknowledge that differences across cultures are not indicative of one culture being superior to another. Although attempts to better understand differences are oversimplified, e.g. the individualistic/collectivistic distinction, they at least recognise that cultures differ from each other in major ways.

HISTORICAL BIAS

A further consideration is that all research is a product of the time and context it originates in. Many psychologists assume that their findings apply to past, present, and future societies—this assumption shows historical bias.

Freud's research illustrates this as it is considered to be era-dependent and context-bound—his key concept of repression may be more representative of the Victorian era than today's more permissive society. However, this view is culturally biased, as not all societies today are as permissive as Western cultures. Another example of historical bias is the change in attitudes to homosexuality (see A2PKT pp.464–465). Homosexuality was classified as a mental disorder until the APA removed it from its list of disorders in 1973. This reflected changing attitudes in society as, up until the 1960s, homosexuality had been a prosecutable offence. Psychological research into homosexuality at this time reflected the view that homosexuality was a mental illness. Morin (1977, see A2PKT p.463) found that 70% of research on homosexuality between 1967 and 1974 researched homosexuality as an illness that needed to be "cured".

The above examples show that the relationship between culture and psychological knowledge is bi-directional as they influence each other. Psychological knowledge and culture are symbiotic, which means that both are dependent on each other and so develop together. Therefore, psychological knowledge is likely to have limited temporal validity (generalisability to other time periods) as all research is a product of its time (era-dependent) and context (context-bound), and to assume otherwise is to show historical bias.

SO WHAT DOES THIS MEAN?

Unfortunately ethnocentrism and cultural bias have not been fully addressed. Institutionalised racism and a lack of tolerance in wider society can still appear in research, but subtler and less overt forms make it harder to detect. For example, the racial bias reported in the Atkinson et al. textbook is indefensible, as a textbook should be educating and therefore aim to reduce racial bias. An approach based on cultural relativism provides the means to resolve cultural bias, as such an approach accounts for the differences between cultures rather than trying to provide universal etics. However, this is still too reductionist as it ignores the variation within a culture and certainly within a country, which is usually made up of many subcultures. Thus, future research needs to address subcultural and cultural variations and accept and tolerate differences as differences rather than deficiencies.

OVER TO YOU

1. **Discuss the extent to which cultural bias is a problem in psychological research.**

   (30 marks)

2. **"Some psychological theories are derived from research studies which used only American male participants but nevertheless the theory is claimed to apply to all human beings."**

   Discuss the extent to which psychological theories are biased in terms of gender and culture.

   (30 marks)

ETHICAL ISSUES

To read up on ethical issues, refer to pages 451–469 of A2PKT.

Ethical issues arise in the implementing of research when there is conflict between how the research should be carried out and the methodological consequences of observing this. The ethical issues raised by psychological research led to the introduction of ethical guidelines. The British Psychological Society (BPS) Ethical Guidelines for Research with Human Participants is a code of conduct that gives guidance on the design and implementation of research. The guidelines focus on the need to treat participants with respect and how to avoid harm and distress.

The following section is a summary of the ethical guidelines and the ethical issues of social influence research.

ETHICAL GUIDELINES

Deception

ETHICAL ISSUES

Milgram's participants were deceived because they were told the experiment was a test of memory and learning. Similarly Asch's participants were deceived because they were told the experiment was a test of visual perception. Deception is an issue because it is often considered necessary to avoid demand characteristics, which would invalidate the findings, and so it may be used because it is practical. This means that participants are tested without a full knowledge of the nature and purpose of the research, which is an issue because they might not have consented had they not been deceived.

ETHICAL GUIDELINES

Deception of the participants should be avoided wherever possible. Information should not be deliberately withheld and nor should the participants be misled without extremely strong scientific or medical justifications. Deception should only be used when alternative procedures, which do not involve deception, have been fully considered and rejected as unfeasible by independent advisors. Also, participants should be fully informed at the earliest possible stage and should be consulted in advance as to how deception would be received.

Informed Consent

ETHICAL ISSUES

Studies that have involved deception lead to the related issue of informed consent. Participants may have consented to the research, but this is not informed consent if they have been deceived. Even in studies such as Zimbardo's where participants were briefed in advance it is difficult to be sure if the true nature of the study was grasped and, thus, consent may not be fully informed. This is an issue because participants might not have consented had they known the true nature and purpose of the research, and may suffer distress as a consequence.

ETHICAL GUIDELINES

Participants' agreement to take part in research should be based on their full knowledge of the nature and purpose of the research. Thus, they should be made aware of any tasks required of them and their rights as a participant, i.e. right to withdraw and right to confidentiality. If the participant is a child (under 16 years) or impaired adult, consent must be gained from the parent or from those *in loco parentis*. If informed consent is not gained at the outset then the safeguards needed for such a deception would be as detailed above in the deception guideline.

Protection of Participants from Psychological Harm

ETHICAL ISSUES

Asch's study raises this issue because at best his participants experienced embarrassment and for some this discomfort may have been more severe depending on their level of social anxiety. Milgram's and Zimbardo's studies demonstrate a more clear lack of protection because of the evident suffering of the participants, e.g. sweating, trembling, and seizures in Milgram's study, and crying, screaming, and depression in Zimbardo's study. The issue is that participants should have been protected from this distress, particularly as it is debatable whether the ends (findings) justify the means (distress).

ETHICAL GUIDELINES

Participants should be protected from harm, such as distress, ridicule, or loss of self-esteem. The risk of harm during the research study should be no greater than that experienced in everyday life. Measures must be taken to support participants who have experienced psychological harm. If there is the potential for harm then independent approval must be sought, the participants must be advised, and informed consent gained.

Confidentiality

ETHICAL ISSUES

Confidentiality is an issue because the participant may disclose personal information, which they would prefer others not to know. When information is not kept confidential, and when the participant's anonymity is not guaranteed, issues arise. For example, in Milgram's and Zimbardo's studies film footage was shown that the participants may have preferred not to have seen.

ETHICAL GUIDELINES

In accordance with the Data Protection Act, information disclosed during the research process is confidential and if the research is published the anonymity of the participant should be protected. If either of these is likely to be compromised then the participants' agreement must be sought in advance.

Debrief

ETHICAL ISSUES

If deception and a lack of informed consent have occurred, then the debrief provides a way to *resolve* these issues. However, issues will arise if the debrief does not effectively address these issues and if the debrief fails to relieve any distress caused by the research.

ETHICAL GUIDELINES

At the end of a study the researcher should provide detailed information about the research and answer any questions the participants may have. They should also monitor the participants for unforeseen negative effects and it is their responsibility to provide active intervention if necessary.

Right to Withdraw

ETHICAL ISSUES

This issue arises if the participants are prevented from leaving a study. For example, many of Zimbardo's "prisoners" asked to be released, as the study was not what they had expected—one even asked for parole—yet they were not granted this. In Milgram's research, withdrawal was discouraged by the experimenter's insistence that the participants continue. Whilst withdrawal was not physically prevented it was difficult psychologically for the participants to exercise their right to withdraw.

ETHICAL GUIDELINES

Participants' right to withdraw must be clearly communicated at the outset of the research. Also, the participant has the right to withdraw their consent retrospectively, and consequently their data must be destroyed.

RESOLVING ETHICAL ISSUES

The Ethical Guidelines

The ethical guidelines do successfully impose some restraint by setting out clear restrictions. However, they lack legislative power, i.e. are not enforceable by law and so are too easily disregarded. The penalty for unjustified breach of the guidelines is disbarment from the BPS, which is not severe enough, and has limited censure because such a penalty can only be applied to BPS members. The fact that the ethical guidelines differ across cultures, and breaches can be justified, means that there are no universal ethical truths, which reduces their influence. *Charter status* (a professional status conferred by the BPS since 1987) is an effective restraint for those working in the public sector, as the removal of this as a consequence of ethical breaches would limit work opportunities. The guidelines are limited because they do not give any direct guidance on socially sensitive issues. They account for "how" the research should be carried out, but not "what" research, and "should" the research be carried out. Consequently the guidelines are classed as a managerial ethic as their focus is limited to the participants being researched, which means they lack a social ethic, as they do not consider the wider social implications of the research.

Ethical Committees

Ethical committees try to enforce the guidelines but the same criticisms can be applied to them as the guidelines—they lack censure and legislative power. They may also be biased if the research has financial or status benefits for the organisation the ethical committee serves. This is particularly so given the increasing commercialism of psychology. Furthermore, there is a lack of consistency as there are not enough ethical committees and judgements are not necessarily standardised.

The Cost–Benefit Analysis (Aronson, 1992)

This should be conducted at the outset of any research investigation and involves weighing up whether the ends justify the means. It involves considering "how" the research should be carried out, "what" it intends to find out, and whether it "should" take place. This involves a dilemma—with the participants vs. society.

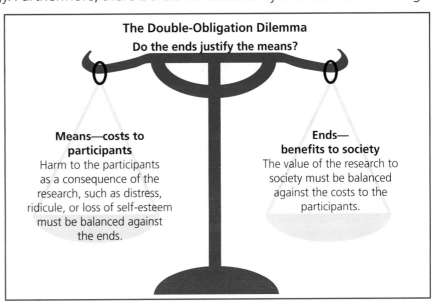

The Double-Obligation Dilemma
Do the ends justify the means?

Means—costs to participants
Harm to the participants as a consequence of the research, such as distress, ridicule, or loss of self-esteem must be balanced against the ends.

Ends— benefits to society
The value of the research to society must be balanced against the costs to the participants.

EVALUATION

☺ **Effective safeguard.** The cost–benefit analysis is an effective restraint that should precede all research.

☹ **It is difficult to predict outcomes.** The outcomes of the research are not always clear at the outset. This was the case with Milgram's research where it was predicted that 3% or less would go to the maximum 450 volts, when in fact 65% did.

☹ **Quantification is difficult.** The costs and benefits are not objective and so can be difficult to measure and weigh up.

☹ **The cost–benefit analysis is vulnerable to researcher bias and value judgements.** The subjectivity of the analysis means judgements may be value laden, i.e. biased.

☹ **Society favoured over the participants.** The individual's rights tend to be ignored in favour of the utilitarian concerns of society.

😐 **The decision is a moral dilemma.** The guidelines were supposed to take away the moral responsibility from the individual researcher, but the cost–benefit analysis is more a moral than an ethical dilemma.

SOCIALLY SENSITIVE RESEARCH

Research is socially sensitive when it has social consequences for the participants or the group they represent. Research is also socially sensitive if it discriminates or encourages prejudice.

Five Key Concerns of Socially Sensitive Research

1. *Implications.* Controversial research may be subject to gender or culture bias. For example, research on cultural differences in IQ can legitimise or perpetuate discrimination, and so the implications must be considered carefully. But research should not be avoided just because it is controversial.

2. *Uses.* Research findings can be used to the benefit or detriment of humankind. Consideration needs to be given to the possible uses of research and what would happen if it were used for the wrong purpose, e.g. the issue of human cloning.

3. *Public policy.* This concerns the amount of influence the research has on the government, e.g. Burt (1955) influenced governmental policy as his research on IQ led to the introduction of the 11-plus examination.

4. *The validity of the research.* Research can never be objective and value free (Howitt, 1991). This means to some extent researcher bias and subjectivity reduces the validity of the research. This of course is a serious problem because often this has been ignored and the research has been taken as truth in spite of the lack of validity, e.g. Burt's (1955, see A2PKT p.458) research on IQ.

5. *The availability of the findings.* Research findings should be freely available to prevent exploitation. However, given the increasing commercialism of psychology this is not always the case. This is a concern because this increases the potential for misuse or may limit the positive application of the research.

Research Examples

RACE-RELATED RESEARCH

H. J. Eysenck (1981, see A2PKT p.212) investigated cultural differences in IQ and claimed that the lower achievement of African Americans on IQ tests was due to innate differences in ability. This is better explained by the cultural bias of the IQ test, which was based on Western, white, middle-class knowledge and understanding.

Goddard (1913, see A2PKT p.462) issued IQ tests to immigrants as they entered America. His findings claimed that 87% of Russians, 83% of Jews, 80% of Hungarians, and 79% of Italians were "feeble-minded". This can be better explained by the fact that the immigrants were expected to answer the test in English but had limited command of the language.

"ALTERNATIVE" SEXUALITY

Kitzinger and Coyle (1995, see A2PKT p.464) claim that research on homosexuality can be organised into different phases, the first two of which show:

1. *Heterosexual bias.* This is the assumption that heterosexuality is superior and more natural than homosexuality.

2. *Liberal humanism.* Although in this phase of research equality was recognised, the research still raised ethical issues because homosexual relationships were compared against heterosexual norms. Aspects in the homosexual relationships that did not fit with heterosexual relationships were either ignored or pathologised.

3. *Liberal humanism plus.* This approach minimises ethical issues by recognising the differences in relationships, i.e. it does not attempt to assess homosexual relationships using the heterosexual standard.

Morin (1977, see A2PKT p.463) offers further evidence for a heterosexual bias—his review of studies on homosexuality published between 1967 and 1974 showed that a high percentage of them (70%) investigated whether homosexuals were mentally ill.

RESEARCH THAT INFLUENCED SOCIAL POLICY

Burt (1955, see A2PKT p.458) investigated 53 pairs of identical twins separated at birth and concluded that there was an 80% concordance for IQ, which led to his conclusion that IQ was innate. The social consequence of this was the 11-plus examination, which determined whether children experienced grammar, secondary modern, or tertiary education. The implications of this research were great, particularly as the validity of it is highly questionable as Burt made up some of his data. Thus, the most significant ethical issue is the fact that it influenced governmental policy.

Bowlby's (1953) maternal deprivation hypothesis had social consequences as this claimed that any separation of the child from the mother could result in permanent maladjustment. This message was advanced by the WHO (World Health Organisation) who lauded Bowlby as the "wise man of the Western world". This was because the political agenda at the time was to encourage women to stay at home and thus leave the jobs that they had carried out during World War 2 to the men returning home.

Arguments For and Against Socially Sensitive Research

Arguments For

- Attempts have been made to resolve ethical issues, see below.

- Ethical committees do reject more socially sensitive research than other types of research, and so socially sensitive research today does face stringent scrutiny (Ceci, Peters, & Plotkin, 1985, see A2PKT p.460).

- According to Scarr (1988, see A2PKT p.460), there is a need for more socially sensitive research as this can be used to help underrepresented people.

- A greater understanding of differences in gender, culture, and sexuality may open our eyes to diversity and so reduce prejudice and encourage acceptance.

- The researcher has a responsibility to society (social obligation) to advance scientific understanding.

- It is not always possible to predict the outcomes of research and so the effects may not be known until the research is completed. Although this means there is an element of risk, a lack of predictability should not prevent research. Nor should the fact that it is controversial.

- Socially sensitive research has benefited society through constructive application of psychological knowledge. For example, research into eyewitness testimony (EWT) has informed the judicial process. In 1973 74% of 350 cases were found guilty based on EWT alone—a serious issue because there have been cases where innocent people were found guilty. Research evidence that EWT is easily distorted and therefore unreliable has led to less emphasis being given to it and defendants can no longer be found guilty based on EWT alone. Thus, research into EWT has had serious social consequences as it has reduced the risk of innocent people being found guilty.

- Over 90% of the research in psychology textbooks was conducted on Western, white, middle-class Americans, usually male. This means the standard of assessment against which others are judged is ethnocentric and often androcentric. The past research failed to consider individual, social, and cultural diversity. The situation is changing as recent research is addressing this imbalance, but more research into gender and cultural differences and "alternative" relationships is needed to fully redress the balance.

Against

- Research has been used to exploit and manipulate, and has influenced social policy despite a lack of validity, e.g. Burt's research on IQ.

- Research has perpetuated discrimination and has been used to justify socially constructed stereotypes, e.g. H. J. Eysenck's research on race-related differences in IQ.

- Research has been used as justification for social control. For example, in America between 1910 and 1920 certain American states passed laws to enforce the sterilisation of certain types of people deemed unworthy of children, such as those low in intelligence, epileptics, drug or alcohol addicts, criminals, and people with mental illness. Psychologists supported such policies with psychological research and this supports the argument against socially sensitive research given that historically it has been used for discriminatory purposes.

- Socially sensitive issues have not been resolved. It is difficult to regulate psychological research. The psychological societies and ethical committees lack legislative power and censure and so cannot prevent indefensible research being carried out. Sieber and Stanley's (1988, see A2PKT p.458) guidance may be disregarded and cost–benefit analyses may be biased, i.e. the same weaknesses exist for socially sensitive research as research using human participants.

Resolving Socially Sensitive Issues

Sieber and Stanley (1988, see A2PKT p.458) issued guidance to help resolve ethical issues.

THE RESEARCH QUESTION

Simply asking certain questions can pose ethical issues and so this needs to be considered cautiously, e.g. the question of whether there is a genetic basis to homosexuality assumes a role for genetic factors.

THE CONDUCT OF THE RESEARCH AND TREATMENT OF THE PARTICIPANTS

This, of course, is the managerial ethic provided by the BPS ethical guidelines.

THE INSTITUTIONAL CONTEXT

The institutional context poses ethical issues because it may affect the research findings, as Yale University did in Milgram's (1963, see A2PKT pp.451–452) research. Also the institution may be very selective in accepting research findings, depending on whether they will be of benefit or not. Hence, undesirable research findings may be buried and desirable findings promoted, which is why there is a concern about the availability of the findings. Findings may be concealed if the institution hopes to gain financially by doing so. Also, prestigious institutions may have undue influence and may exploit their position.

INTERPRETATION AND APPLICATION

The potential implications and uses of the research need to be fully considered, particularly if the application is predictable.

SO WHAT DOES THIS MEAN?

Research can be used for advantage or exploitation. Issues include "how", "what", and "should", and the implications and uses of the findings. The ethical guidelines, cost–benefit analysis, and guidance on socially sensitive research are not enforceable, as they lack censure and legislative power. Hence, the responsibility lies with the individual psychologist to guard against discrimination and to account for individual, social, and cultural diversity. It is worth noting that the worst cases of ethical breaches occurred in very different times and contexts, when there was less awareness of ethnocentrism and discrimination. Thus, it is less likely that such research would be carried out today, but this assumption may be guilty of ethnocentric bias, as it may be that bias and discrimination are all the more destructive and pervasive today, if concealed for the sake of social acceptability. Thus, as the structures put in place to resolve ethical issues are not effective enough and as the individual cannot necessarily be trusted, the answer may be an external audit, where one centralised statutory regulatory body controls the ethical committees, and all research *must* pass though an ethical committee. This would provide a more consistent safeguard and a means of limiting, but not preventing, research—to avoid research is not the answer, as this negates the social responsibility of the psychologist.

OVER TO YOU

1.(a) Outline the ethical issues that arise in socially sensitive psychological research. **(15 marks)**

  (b) Assess how effectively psychologists have dealt with such issues. **(15 marks)**

2. Describe and evaluate the ethical problems faced by psychologists when carrying out socially sensitive research. **(30 marks)**

THE USE OF NON-HUMAN ANIMALS

To read up on the use of non-human animals, refer to pages 469–480 of A2PKT.

SAFEGUARDS FOR NON-HUMAN PARTICIPANTS

The Animals (Scientific Procedures) Act (1986)

This is legislation that protects animals and so noncompliance results in prosecution. It provides guidance on:

- *Ethical considerations.* Do the ends justify the means? Alternatives to using animals should be considered.
- *Species.* Investigators must have a good knowledge of the species being used, and if the research is likely to cause pain or discomfort they should do the research on those species that are likely to suffer the least.
- *Number of animals.* Studies should use the smallest number of animals possible.
- *Endangered species.* These should not be used in research unless as an attempt at conservation.
- *Caging and social environment.* This should take into account the social behaviour of the species so as to avoid overcrowding and isolation if this is not the norm.
- *Motivation.* The experimenter should consider the animal's normal eating and drinking habits and its metabolic requirements. Research involving deprivation should take into account that what constitutes deprivation will differ depending on the species.
- *Aversive stimuli and stressful procedures.* These are illegal in the UK unless the experimenter has a Home Office Licence. Alternatives to aversive stimuli should be considered; if not, possible suffering should be kept to a minimum and the ends (scientific contribution) must outweigh the costs.

The British Psychological Society Guidelines (1985)

These guidelines (see A2PKT p.478) cover similar issues to the Animals Act, e.g. legislation, choice of species, number of animals, procedures, procurement of animals, housing and animal care, final disposal of animals, animals in psychology teaching, the use of animals for therapeutic purposes, and how to obtain further information about the care and use of animals in research.

Bateson's Decision Cube

According to Bateson (1986, see A2PKT p.477), three main criteria need to be considered before undertaking animal research:

1. The *quality* of the research, which is assessed by the funding agency.
2. The amount of animal *suffering*, which can be assessed from the animal's behaviour and any signs of stress.
3. Likelihood of *benefit*, which can be judged by the researcher and funding agency.

Research is justified when quality is high, suffering is low, and there is a high probability of benefit.

THE USE OF NON-HUMAN ANIMALS *(continued)*

EVALUATION

 Value judgements. The effectiveness of Bateson's decision cube depends on the accuracy of the assessments of quality, suffering, and benefit. These may be biased and subjective.

Quantification is difficult. It can be difficult to quantify the quality, suffering, and benefit.

Era-dependent and context-bound. Assessments may change over time and vary across cultures and individuals, and so the cube is neither universal nor objective.

RESEARCH EXAMPLES

Drugs

Animals are routinely used in experimental tests of drugs. For example, the drug heparin, essential for kidney dialysis treatment, was extracted from animal tissue and then tested for safety on animals.

Research Involving Electric Shocks

Seligman et al. (1969) exposed dogs to unavoidable electric shocks. He then presented a signal before each shock that enabled the dogs to avoid the shocks if they responded to it by jumping over a barrier. The dogs did not learn to do this; instead they showed apathetic and passive behaviour, which Seligman called *learned helplessness*. In comparison dogs not exposed to the unavoidable shocks first did learn to avoid the shocks. This research has been extrapolated to depression in humans and so has made a significant contribution to psychological knowledge. However, extrapolation is an issue and so generalisability may be limited, which consequently questions the justifiability of the research.

Brady (1958) exposed monkeys yoked together in pairs to electric shocks. One, the "executive" monkey, was able to control the shocks by pressing a lever on hearing a bell; the other monkey had no control over the shocks. The "executive" monkeys developed ulcers and eventually died. The research was stopped because it was so unethical and, although it was supposed to cast light on the relationship between stress and illness, extrapolation and mundane realism may limit generalisability.

Research Involving Physical Harm

Research into the biological basis of anxiety has involved lesions being made in the septo-hippocampal system of animals. The effect of these lesions was very similar to that of anti-anxiety drugs and so it was concluded that the septo-hippocampal system is involved in anxiety. Research such as this would be justified on medical grounds but is it justified ethically and morally?

Another study looked at the genetic basis of anxiety (Eysenck & Broadhurst, 1964, see A2PKT p.471). Rats were bred to be either reactive or nonreactive to loud noise and bright lights. The reactive rats were also more anxious than the nonreactive ones. The value of this research is that it suggests that individual differences in anxiety may have a genetic basis. However, the key ethical issue is protection as rats were being bred to suffer.

Deprivation Research

A study of maternal deprivation (Harlow, 1959) tested the basis of attachment. Infant rhesus monkeys were taken from their real mother and provided with two substitute mothers. Both were made of wire and one had a feeding bottle attached to it and the other was covered in cloth. When the infant monkey was frightened it was the cloth mother it sought comfort from. The research provides important insights into the nature of attachment but it could be argued that the findings were transparent.

276

A study of social deprivation isolated monkeys for the first few months of life (Harlow & Mears, 1979, see A2PKT p.471). This had serious consequences for their social behaviour because when placed with other isolated monkeys high levels of aggression were shown. This maladjustment continued into adulthood, as they did not develop normal sexual behaviour. These severe effects need to be weighed against the "value" of such research in showing the possible effects of early deprivation.

Sleep deprivation research such as Jouvet's (1967, see A2PKT p.148) and Rechtschaffen et al.'s (1983, see A2PKT p.147) resulted in death, which raises the issue of whether the ends justify the means.

Arguments For and Against Research Using Animals

ARGUMENTS FOR

- **Utilitarian argument.** Singer (1975) states that research should only be carried out if it is for the "greater good" and if "happiness for the greatest number" will result.

- **Moral obligation.** We have a moral obligation to advance understanding for human good. According to Gray (1991, see A2PKT p.474), "we owe a special duty to members of our own species". He believes that animal suffering is justifiable if it is for scientific and medical purposes and if it enables us to avoid human suffering.

- **Continuity argument.** According to Darwin's (1859, see A2PKT p.475) theory of evolution, we have evolved from animals as supported by the similarity in basic physiology and the nervous system of nearly all mammals. The phylogenic tree represents an evolutionary continuum, which means that the differences between humans and animals are quantitative not qualitative. This means that comparisons are valid and so research on animals yields genuine insights.

- **Scientific and practical arguments.** Animals can be used when human participants would not be legally permitted, such as the study into anxiety involving lesions. Animals have shorter breeding cycles, which enable genetic inheritance to be studied, such as the study on the reactivity of rats to stimuli. Laboratory experiments have a high level of control and so cause and effect can be inferred and findings are less likely to be biased by participant reactivity. Also research methods have adapted to changing views on animal research as a much greater percentage of research is now field studies, 46% according to Cuthill's (1991, see A2PKT p.469) review, and the number of laboratory experiments being conducted has halved.

- **Research contributions and practical applications.** Animal research has given insights into vital areas of medicine including diseases, drug treatments, organ transplants, surgical techniques, and cloning. Most of what we know about the brain, nervous, and sensory systems is based on animal research. Behaviourism (classical and operant conditioning) is based on animal research, and conditioning techniques have been usefully applied within therapeutic contexts. Thus, animal research does make an important contribution, although this comes at a high cost in terms of animal suffering. However, some research has beneficial effects and very little cost, e.g. pigeons were trained using operant conditioning to detect life-rafts because their vision is superior to human vision—their detection rate was 85% compared to 50% for helicopter crews. Thus, animal research can be of great value and with relatively few negative effects for the animals themselves.

- **Safeguards provide protection.** It can be argued that the safeguards in place do provide adequate limitations, as the Animals Act, the ethical guidelines, and the Home Office restrictions are effective and among the strictest in the world. They ensure that animals are humanely treated and that alternatives are considered. The dramatic reduction in the use of animals in psychological research over the last 15 years is evidence that the safeguards are working.

- **Cost–benefit analysis.** This is a further safeguard that is a legal requirement of the Animals Act. It is used to weigh up whether the ends justify the means at the outset of the research process. Thus, this is a further restraint, which ensures that research must be of value (theoretical and practical applications) if it is to be justified.

ARGUMENTS AGAINST

- **Utilitarian argument and speciesism.** Singer (1991, 2005, see A2PKT pp.474–475) is strongly opposed to any research on animals that could not also be conducted on humans. He believes in the equality of all species and so is against the view that animals should be used because they are more expendable. According to Singer this is *speciesism*, which is akin to racism, as human interests are not more important than those of other species and to think so is prejudiced and discriminatory.

- **Animal rights argument.** According to this argument all animals have rights to be treated with respect and not harmed. Thus, according to Regan, animal research is not justifiable under any conditions. Making research more humane, using more naturalistic methods, decreasing the number, and using safeguards such as the cost–benefit analysis, do not justify the indefensible.

- **Moral obligation.** The argument against Gray's (1991, see A2PKT p.474) moral obligation is that this is speciesism; human interests should not be elevated above those of other species. We have a moral obligation to protect other species.

- **Continuity/discontinuity argument.** Another perspective to the continuity argument is that if animals are so closely related and are capable of emotions then using them poses a serious ethical dilemma. Opposing this is the discontinuity argument of humanistic psychologists. According to this, humans are qualitatively different from other species and so extrapolation from animals to humans is an issue. This means research on animals provides very limited insights into human behaviour as findings are not necessarily generalisable.

- **Scientific arguments.** Research on animals is often repetitive and transparent, i.e. addresses problems where the answer is self-evident. The value of such research is further questioned by the scientific weaknesses of the research—research conducted in the laboratory is artificial and so lacks mundane realism, and may therefore have limited generalisability to real-life situations, so lacking ecological validity. Extrapolation may also reduce the validity of the research. Furthermore, generalisations between animals and humans are guilty of anthropomorphism, which is when animals are mistakenly attributed with human qualities, which also reduces the validity of the findings. Furthermore, field studies may be preferable to the laboratory but still disturb animals' natural behaviour patterns, which may limit the value of the research.

- **Criticisms of research contributions.** Medical advances have been delayed and confused because results from non-human experiments do not transfer to human patients. Different evolutionary pressures have led to subtle differences in physiology, which mean the effects of medical treatment on one species does not predict their effect on another species. The stress caused by the laboratory conditions acts as a confounding variable and so reduces validity. Results are often conflicting and so reliability and validity are questionable, reducing the value of the research contribution. Validity has implications for whether the study is justified, as results that lack value do not justify the means.

- **Criticisms of the safeguards.** A key weakness is enforceability, as it may be that unethical research is carried out but just not detected.

- *Cost–benefit analysis.* This may be biased by value judgements that favour the contribution of the research to society over the animals. According to critics of the pro-animal research lobby, researchers tend to overemphasise the benefits and underemphasise the suffering. Costs and benefits are often difficult to predict at the outset and so judgements may lack accuracy. The costs involve assessing the level of suffering likely to be experienced; however, this is very difficult to do, as animal distress is difficult to determine because assessment relies on indirect measures.

THE CHANGING PICTURE

People's attitudes to animal research depend on the nature of the research, as research for medical purposes is considered more justifiable than the use of animals to test cosmetics (Furnham & Pinder, 1990, see A2PKT p.473). Views on animal research tend to be very mixed but overall seem less supportive than previously (Mukerjee, 1985). This is because moral codes depend on "human psychology" (Herzog, 1988, see A2PKT p.473) and so judgements are clouded by subjectivity and change over time. Society's views on animal research have changed and this is reflected in the decline in the number of studies being conducted. Thomas and Blackman (1991, see A2PKT p.472) report that the number of research studies dropped by more than 50% between 1977 and 1989, a reduction that is likely to have continued. The "three Rs" (replacement, reduction, refinement) reflect the prevailing attitude that animal research must be kept to a minimum, and is an approach that has helped to further reduce the number of animals used in research.

SO WHAT DOES THIS MEAN?

The pro-animal research lobby criticises the selectivity of the animal rights movement as they only draw attention to the most vivid cases of animal suffering and ignore the majority of studies where animals are treated humanely. However, those who favour the utilitarian argument and animal rights criticise the pro-animal research movement on the grounds of speciesism and because they downplay or conceal the suffering inherent in the research. Thus, the use of animals is extremely contentious; we would not have the knowledge we have today without animal research but it has come at a high cost. Fortunately, due to advances in technology, there is a decreasing need for animal research; for example, the increased use of brain scanners has reduced the number of animal studies. However, the fact that alternatives to animal research (cell and tissue cultures and computer modelling) are not always practical and may not yield the same results as testing drugs/procedures on live animals, means that non-human research is still necessary for medical advancement. The situation for animals in research today has greatly improved but this is not enough for some, and too much for others who strongly believe that human advancement justifies animal suffering. Animal rights activists and those who favour speciesism, and so animal research, have opposing views that will never be reconcilable.

OVER TO YOU

1. **Critically consider the arguments for and against the use of non-human animals in psychological research.** **(30 marks)**

2.(a) **Outline how the issues raised by research using non-human participants have been dealt with.** **(10 marks)**

   (b) **Discuss the use of non-human animals in psychological research.** **(20 marks)**

QUESTIONS AND ESSAY PLANS

1 Describe gender biases in psychological research and assess how these biases may have influenced research. (30 marks)

Unpack the question—note that the AO1 marks require a focus on psychological research and that the AO2 marks require an assessment of the influence of gender bias.

Paragraph 1 Introduction

Define bias and describe alpha and beta bias as sources of theoretical bias.

Paragraph 2

Describe the methodological biases including question formulation, selection of participants, interpretation and use of results, research methods and approaches, etc.

Paragraph 3

Describe the theoretical examples of bias, e.g. Freud and Kohlberg (1963). These will be relevant as theory and research studies are credited as psychological research. Describe the research examples of bias, e.g. Buss' (1989) research on human relationships, the conformity studies, and Rosenthal's (1966) criticism of research.

Paragraph 4

Consider that the gender differences in research may be the result of not considering the differential treatment of the participants rather than valid gender differences. Thus, the truth and meaningfulness of such research is questionable—beta bias may have reduced internal validity due to the confounding effect of the relationship between the researcher and participants. Consider the consequences of alpha and beta bias. The exaggeration and minimising of gender differences have clouded the real gender differences and perpetuated discrimination. Such biases have resulted in research that legitimises gender stereotypes, e.g. evolutionary explanations of the double standard in sexual relationships.

Paragraph 5

Discuss how the methodological biases have influenced the research process. In particular consider how research in the past was dominated by male concerns and that research was only published if it supported the status quo of male power, according to the feminists. Bowlby's (1953) research, which discouraged working mothers, can be used to support this. Also, it has been suggested that girls consistently outperformed boys on the 11-plus, but more boys gained entrance to grammar school, which is further evidence of gender bias.

Paragraph 6

Consider the consequences of the male norm as the standard against which females are judged as deficient. Use Freud's research to illustrate this. This has also resulted in the perpetuation of gender stereotypes and has influenced further research to investigate "abnormal female behaviour".

Paragraph 7

Consider how feminists have addressed the gender bias. Explain that a review by Maccoby and Jacklin (1974) of the research on gender differences has revealed very few significant differences and so feminists have rejected many of the biological causes traditionally cited and instead have proposed social causes. Research on PMS or the greater likelihood of women to be diagnosed with depression can be used to support this, as can gender bias in the diagnosis of mental disorders. Gender differences in diagnosis show alpha bias, as biological (hormones) and social (sex-role stereotypes) factors tend to be exaggerated and so bias the process of assessment and diagnosis. Thus, the gender bias in past research has been the impetus for changes in the nature of research.

Paragraph 8 Conclusion

Conclude that negating gender differences is a beta bias. The extent of the actual difference needs to be determined, not ignored (beta bias) or exaggerated (alpha bias), and should be used to increase equality rather than used as a basis for discrimination.

2 Discuss the extent to which cultural bias is a problem in psychological research. (30 marks)

Paragraph 1 Introduction

Define bias and identify the issues of individualism vs. collectivism, ethnocentrism, and Eurocentrism, and explain what they mean.

Paragraph 2

Outline the methodological sources of cultural bias such as emic and etic constructs, and give evidence to illustrate, such as research on personality, attachments, and intelligence, which are examples of imposed etics. Then consider cultural relativism as an emic approach and use Cole et al.'s (1971) research to illustrate this.

Paragraph 3

Outline further methodological sources of cultural bias such as the formulation of the question, selection of participants, and interpretation and use of results, H. J. Eysenck's (1981) and Goddard's (1913) research are evidence of these issues.

Paragraph 4

Assess the extent to which this is a problem in psychological research by considering the amount of ethnocentric research, i.e. over 90% of research has been conducted on Western, white, middle-class American samples.

Paragraph 5

Discuss how cross-cultural research is not only limited but also culturally biased as ethnocentrism, translation, and the trust between researcher and participants can all reduce the validity of the research. Use Mead's (1935) research and Ainsworth and Bell's (1970) Strange Situation to illustrate this.

Paragraph 6

Discuss the racial biases in psychological research, e.g. the language used to describe different cultures and the portrayal of them as "strange people from strange countries doing strange things" (Banyard, 1999). Owusu-Bempah and Howitt (1994) claim that the Atkinson et al. (1993) textbook does not specify which African tribes have been studied, which is, to say the least, insensitive. Describing cultures as "primitive" and "underdeveloped" perpetuates cultural stereotypes and so is guilty of racial bias. The use of the word "tribe" is an issue, as it is not used to refer to different Western populations. Consider the changing nature of the problem. Racial bias and patronising approaches are less likely today. So discuss the extent to which the problem has been addressed and the future potential of an approach based on cultural relativism.

Paragraph 7

Consider that all research is a product of the time and context it originates in and that therefore all research shows historical bias, which cannot be prevented. Freud's research illustrates this as it is considered to be era-dependent and context-bound. Also, use the change in attitudes to homosexuality to develop your discussion of historical bias.

Paragraph 8 Conclusion

Assess the extent to which cultural bias has been a problem in the past and to what extent it still exists today. Conclude that considering cultural differences introduces a new bias as this ignores subcultural variations, which need to be investigated further in future research.

3(a) Outline the ethical issues that arise in socially sensitive psychological research. (15 marks)

Always answer parted questions separately and focus on how the AO1 and AO2 marks have been split.

Paragraph 1 Introduction

Explain that socially sensitive research has social consequences for the participants or the group of people represented by the participants. Outline the five key concerns: implications, uses, public policy, the validity of the research, and the availability of the findings.

Paragraph 2

Outline research examples that illustrate these issues, e.g. race-related research and research on "alternative" sexuality. Outline research that has affected social policy such as Burt's (1955) and Bowlby's (1953) and how the validity of such research is questioned. Burt's data was criticised and Bowlby's findings were assimilated into social policy because they suited the political agenda.

Paragraph 3

Outline the lack of consideration given to individual, social, and cultural diversity in psychological research and illustrate using examples of gender and culture bias.

3(b) Assess how effectively psychologists have dealt with such issues. (15 marks)

Paragraph 4

Sieber and Stanley (1988) have provided explicit guidance on socially sensitive research because the ethical guidelines fail to do so, as they advise on "how" (managerial ethic), not "what", and "should", and so lack a social ethic. The cost–benefit analysis requires the researcher to stop and think about the consequences of the research and so ensures that serious thought is given to the possible research outcomes, and that the issues of "what" and "should" are addressed. This is a strength, as it ensures to some extent that there is sufficient consideration within the research process and that ethically dubious research conducted in the past such as H. J. Eysenck's (1981) and Goddard's (1913) research on IQ would not be considered justifiable today.

Paragraph 5

However, Sieber and Stanley's guidance lacks censure as it has no legislative power and therefore is not enforceable, partly because detection is also an issue. The ethical guidelines that Sieber and Stanley advise the researcher to observe also lack sanctioning power because rogue psychologists found guilty of breaching the Code of Conduct can be expelled from the BPS, but this does not stop them from continuing in private practice. Furthermore, transgressions can be justified and so it is too easy to disregard the guidelines.

Paragraph 6

The cost–benefit analysis also fails to fully resolve ethical issues because it is not always possible to predict outcomes, as Milgram's (1963) research illustrates. In the pilot study it was predicted that only complete psychopaths would go up to 450 volts and instead 65% of the sample did! Also, it can be very difficult to quantify the cost and the benefits. Moreover, susceptibility of the analysis to researcher bias is high and this is not necessarily removed by the ethical committees as the value of the research tends to be favoured over the participants or the group represented by the participants. The ethical committees have a little more power in real life as the individual would have to find another institution to support their research if it was rejected by the committee. However, the committees could be biased, particularly if the research was likely to bring financial and/or status rewards. Saying that, ethical committees do reject more socially sensitive research than other types of research.

Paragraph 7

Assess the extent to which ethnocentrism and androcentrism have been overcome by using your knowledge of gender and culture bias.

Paragraph 8 Conclusion

Weigh up/assess the extent to which they have been successful/unsuccessful. The overcommercialism of psychology is a current issue that supports the criticism that there are not enough safeguards and so the ethical committes are not a completely successful solution. In fact the BPS is currently campaigning for an external statutory regulatory body that would be backed by government. This suggests that they recognise the limitations of the present initiatives to resolve ethical issues. External assessment is common practice in teaching and medicine and would increase the objectivity of the cost–benefit analysis and could have greater powers of censure to stop psychologists practising altogether if they violate the guidelines.

4 Critically consider the arguments for and against the use of non-human animals in psychological research. (30 marks)

A key criticism of students' answers is that they are too emotional and lack psychological content. So avoid giving a personal answer and stick to the informed arguments for and against as this will receive more credit than personal opinion.

Paragraph 1 Introduction

Consider that this is a contentious issue and that agreement is unlikely to be reached by the opposing movements, e.g. the pro-animal research campaigners and the animal rights activists. Arguments for and against are varied and often very selective.

Paragraph 2

Discuss the utilitarian argument (Singer, 1991, 2005) and how it rejects animal research that cannot be undertaken on humans but does support animal research in some circumstances. Compare this with Regan's Animal Rights argument, which rejects animal research.

Paragraph 3

Consider the different moral obligations and discuss speciesism. Use research, such as Selye (1936), Brady (1958), Jouvet (1967), and Rechtschaffen et al. (1983) as examples of speciesism as animals were used as expendable commodities.

Paragraph 4

Consider the continuity/discontinuity argument both in terms of the validity of the comparisons and whether they are ethically justifiable, i.e. compare evolutionary and humanistic perspectives as they have differing views on the nature of the difference—is it quantitative or qualitative?

Paragraph 5

Consider the scientific and practical arguments for and against, including the strengths and weaknesses of laboratory research. Discuss the fact that shorter breeding cycles enable genetic inheritance to be studied, e.g. H. J. Eysenck and Broadhurst's (1964) research on the genetic basis of anxiety. Animals can be used when humans would not legally be permitted, e.g. Harlow's (1959) research. Use the criticisms of extrapolation and anthropomorphism as arguments against justification on scientific grounds.

Paragraph 6

Assess the research contributions and practical applications of animal research. Use the criticisms to evaluate these. For example, consider whether the ends justify the means by assessing the value of research versus the criticism that the research findings of much animal research are self-evident. For example, it can be argued that Brady's findings were transparent *but* it is easy to conclude this in retrospect and not always possible to accurately predict outcomes at the outset. Furthermore, even if we accept the research findings as self-evident, the research itself is still of value as it is *scientific evidence* of the expected findings.

Paragraph 7

Critically consider the effectiveness of the safeguards, including the cost–benefit analysis.

Paragraph 8 Conclusion

The pro-animal research lobby criticises the selectivity of the animal rights movement as they only draw attention to the most vivid cases of animal suffering and ignore the majority of studies where animals are treated humanely. However, those who favour the utilitarian argument and animal rights criticise the pro-animal research movement on the grounds of speciesism and because they downplay or conceal the suffering inherent in the research. We would not have the knowledge we have today without animal research but it has come at a high cost. Fortunately the situation for animals in research today has greatly improved but this is not enough for some, and too much for others who strongly believe that human advancement justifies animal suffering. The most unethical examples would not be considered justifiable today but this is not strict enough for the utilitarian and animal rights arguments. Thus, the use of animals is extremely contentious and the opposing views may never be reconcilable.

Perspectives

What's it about?

As you will already be aware by this stage in your course, there are many contentious issues in psychology. In this section we consider four of these debates. First, we ponder the extent to which our behaviour is under our personal control. Our intuitive private impression is that we decide what we want to do; we make free choices. But is this the case—what do the different schools of psychology have to say about this issue? Second, we contemplate the issue of reductionism: whether it is useful or misleading to explain complex behaviour by reducing it to a combination of simpler components. Third, we look at psychology in the context of science. Psychology has been defined as the science of mind and behaviour, but what exactly is meant by science and can psychology reasonably be said to fit this description? Finally, we revisit an issue that pervades many areas of psychology—the debate over the relative importance of nature and nurture in determining behaviour and how these factors interact.

What's in this unit?

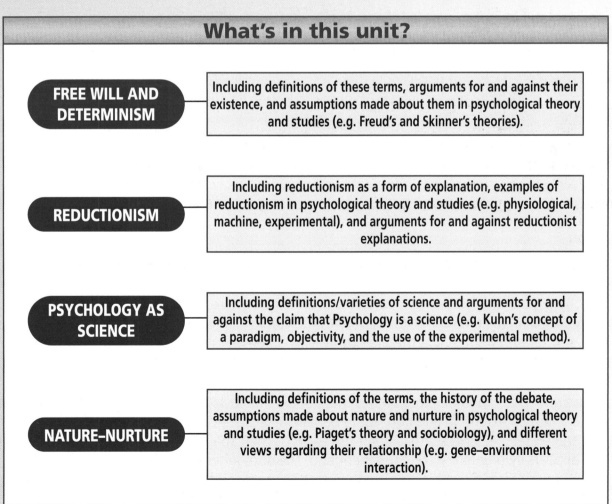

FREE WILL AND DETERMINISM

Including definitions of these terms, arguments for and against their existence, and assumptions made about them in psychological theory and studies (e.g. Freud's and Skinner's theories).

REDUCTIONISM

Including reductionism as a form of explanation, examples of reductionism in psychological theory and studies (e.g. physiological, machine, experimental), and arguments for and against reductionist explanations.

PSYCHOLOGY AS SCIENCE

Including definitions/varieties of science and arguments for and against the claim that Psychology is a science (e.g. Kuhn's concept of a paradigm, objectivity, and the use of the experimental method).

NATURE–NURTURE

Including definitions of the terms, the history of the debate, assumptions made about nature and nurture in psychological theory and studies (e.g. Piaget's theory and sociobiology), and different views regarding their relationship (e.g. gene–environment interaction).

FREE WILL AND DETERMINISM

To read up on free will and determinism, refer to pages 485–493 of A2PKT.

WHAT IS MEANT BY FREE WILL AND DETERMINISM?

The extent to which we are free to choose how we behave has occupied philosophers and psychologists for many years. Those who argue for *free will* view people as responsible for their own actions, free to choose how they want to behave. Those who advocate *determinism* believe that actions come from forces over which people have no control. These forces may be internal, such as hormones, or external, such as being rewarded for a certain action.

Determinism

Determinists argue that human behaviour is orderly, obeys laws, and is explainable and predictable. This approach is therefore entirely in accord with the scientific method, which presupposes that behaviour is determined. Indeed, the whole purpose of psychology is to ascertain the causes of behaviour—researchers try to measure how a variable influences, and therefore determines, behaviour. One of the implications of the assumption that behaviour has a cause is that it is then theoretically possible to control behaviour. Skinner believed that we should design an environment in which behaviour could be controlled in a way that was socially desirable.

PROBLEMS WITH DETERMINISM

- It is untrue to say that accurate predictions about human behaviour can be made. Even in physics, there is always a degree of uncertainty (hence chaos theory). With respect to human behaviour, the problems of predictions are far greater. This may, however, be due to the measuring instruments used, but it is still difficult to see how human behaviour could ever be entirely predictable.

- The idea of determinism is unfalsifiable. Determinists argue that if a cause is not found, it is not because it does not exist but because it has yet to be discovered. There is no way of proving or refuting this argument.

Free will

Intuitively, most of us believe that we have some control over our lives; that we are free, within certain limits, to choose how we want to act. However, logically speaking, if we have complete free will then our behaviour has no cause and is entirely random. This is not, however, the interpretation of free will advanced by psychologists. Rather, free will is seen as an act resulting from someone's character or personality, including their morals, and is therefore predictable to a certain extent. This represents a position known as *soft determinism*, first advocated by William James.

SOFT DETERMINISM AND HARD DETERMINISM

Soft determinism is an approach that argues that people's behaviour is constrained by the environment, but only to a certain extent. In addition, some behaviour is more constrained than others. For example, if a child apologises because she has been threatened, then this behaviour is highly constrained and therefore appears involuntary. If, on the other hand, she apologises because she is genuinely sorry, then her behaviour appears less constrained and therefore appears voluntary. Behaviour is determined in both cases but in one the constraints are more obvious than in the other.

It is useful to contrast soft determinism and hard determinism. Soft determinism holds that there is an element of free will in people's behaviour and that, except on the few occasions when they are greatly constrained by external forces, they are free to choose between a number of courses of action. A hard determinist would argue that all behaviour is constrained and there is no element of choice, only an illusion of personal control. According to this view, *all* behaviour is entirely determined; it simply differs in the source of the cause.

PROBLEMS WITH FREE WILL

- It is difficult to provide a precise account of what is meant by free will. No one seriously argues that behaviour is random and has no cause, but that leaves the problem of what part free will plays in causing behaviour.

- Most sciences are based on some form of determinism. If human behaviour is not subject to determinism in the way the rest of the natural world is, then this has enormous implications for psychology and calls into question any attempts by researchers to discover the reasons why people behave as they do.

Where the Main Approaches Stand on Free Will and Determinism

- ***The biological approach*** represents ***physiological determinism***—the belief that our behaviour is determined by our biological systems. Obviously humans are to some extent controlled by their biology but less so than nonhuman animals. This ties in with the arguments for and against the biological approach (see Chapter 12, Approaches in Psychology).

- ***The behaviourist approach*** represents ***environmental determinism*** and proposes that all behaviour is determined by learning, and its causes can therefore be explained in terms of environmental stimuli. Skinner took an uncompromising view on this issue and argued that behavioural freedom is an illusion because in reality we have no freedom but are controlled by our environment.

- ***The social learning approach*** is more of a compromise position. Bandura advocates *reciprocal determinism*: the belief that whilst the environment is an important determinant of behaviour, in turn, behaviour is also a determinant of the environment. We influence our environment by, for example, seeking out certain experiences rather than passively responding to environmental stimuli. The social learning theory view also takes account of the influence of cognitive factors such as hopes, ambitions, and values on our behaviour. According to this view, we are neither entirely free to choose our own fate, nor are we completely controlled by factors beyond our control.

- ***The psychodynamic approach*** represents ***psychic determinism*** because it stresses that we are at the mercy of unconscious forces over which we have no control. Like Skinner, Freud believed that free will was an illusion but he did believe that people have the potential for free will—psychoanalysis is based on the belief that people can change.

- ***The evolutionary approach*** is very deterministic, the fundamental belief being that genes, which are naturally selected from one generation to another, have control over behaviour as well as over physiological processes. This approach, while being deterministic, is less so in humans than in animals lower down the evolutionary scale since it acknowledges the influence of cultural evolution in humans.

- ***The humanistic approach*** differs from the others in that it puts considerable emphasis on free will. It holds that people are free to choose their own destinies and they have the capacity to change. Carl Rogers, a prominent humanist, has, however, incorporated the notion of determinism into this approach by saying that we choose our actions but within a "framework" that dictates certain behaviours. The emphasis on free will can be seen in the belief of humanists that we must take moral responsibility for our actions.

Conclusions

There are several conclusions that can be made about this argument.

- The issue of the extent to which we have free will is more of a philosophical question than a scientific one because we have no way of designing studies that test it. This is due to the fact that we can never know whether an individual's behaviour in any given situation could have been different had they chosen it to be.

- All psychologists are agreed on the fact that behaviour is, to a certain extent, determined by our biology, our past experiences, and the present environment. Factors such as personality or character may be internal but they have still been the result of causal sequences stretching back into the past so they are no more or less the product of free will than are other internal factors. The argument therefore is not so much between free will and determinism but between soft and hard determinism.

- It is possible to go a step further and argue that there is no real incompatibility between determinism and free will (see A2PKT p.491). According to the determinist position, behaviour is the result of physical activity in the brain. If free will, in the form of conscious decision making, forms part of these brain activities, it is possible to believe in determinism at the same time as believing that we have some freedom to choose how we want to act.

SO WHAT DOES THIS MEAN?

This issue, like many other debates in psychology, has its roots in philosophy and has important implications for human society. If behaviour is entirely determined, then this removes responsibility from the individual. The free will or moral view is that people are responsible for many of their actions and it is this responsibility that leads to concepts of praise or blame. If actions are determined then such concepts become meaningless. Reward and punishment still have a role but only as a means of changing future behaviour rather than as a source of congratulation or retribution. Few people believe in the extremes of free will and determinism. Rather, if these are seen as positions on a continuum, the issue of responsibility is not an all or nothing issue but a case of deciding just how much responsibility an individual should take for his or her actions.

OVER TO YOU

1. Describe and evaluate assumptions about free will and determinism made by psychological theories and research. **(30 marks)**

2. Describe and critically assess the arguments for and against the existence of determinism in psychology. **(30 marks)**

REDUCTIONISM

To read up on reductionism, refer to pages 493–500 of A2PKT.

REDUCTIONISM AS A FORM OF EXPLANATION

Reductionism is the belief that the subject matter of psychology can be best explained by breaking it down into separate, simpler parts. It refers to two different theoretical approaches:

- The reduction of psychological phenomena in terms of the more basic sciences or disciplines, for example, in terms of physiology. This is based on the belief that there is no need to use complex psychological and sociological explanations since behaviour can be adequately explained in terms of biochemistry or physiology.

- The explanation of complex behaviour in terms of simple principles. For example, reducing behaviour to S–R (stimulus–response) units, or processes such as memory to an information-processing system.

The Reduction of Psychological Phenomena in Terms of More Basic Sciences

Psychologists study a huge variety of different behaviours, and their field of interest overlaps with several other sciences and social sciences. Because psychology is multidisciplinary, it is necessary to consider the ways in which it is related to other disciplines. These other areas of study can be viewed as a hierarchy, the top ones taking a more global perspective and the lower ones taking a more focused and narrow view:

- **Sociology**—the study of groups and societies.
- **Psychology**—the study of human and animal behaviour.
- **Physiology**—the study of the functional working of the healthy body.
- **Biochemistry**—the study of the chemistry of the living organism.

Reductionists believe that it is possible to explain psychological and social phenomena in terms of physiology or biochemistry. But does this work? Although neurology and biochemistry underlie all behaviour, many would argue that we need more than one level of explanation to fully understand behaviour, e.g. to explain what happens when someone watches a sunset (see A2PKT p.494). The physiological explanation would involve how the reflected light from the landscape forms an image on the retina, which is transmitted to the brain. This is a true and essential explanation but arguably not a full or sufficient one because it neglects various important influences, e.g. it takes no account of the emotion felt by the watcher or the personal and social significance of such an event.

Evaluating Reductionism

ADVANTAGES

- There may be an increased understanding of psychology by taking full account of the relevant contribution of the other sciences. This may eventually lead to *theoretical unification* in which the theories advanced by psychology, physiology, and biochemistry become increasingly similar, or at least are based on the same empirical findings.

- Psychology could benefit from the more well-established facts and theories that exist in such sciences as physiology and biochemistry. Even if a reductionist approach is not adopted, by taking account of physiological research findings, psychological theories will be more accurate and complete.

DISADVANTAGES

- Most human behaviour simply cannot be reduced to physiology because it is complex, varied, and based on the beliefs and values of the society in which people are raised. You may be able to describe in detail the muscle movements involved when one person shakes hands with another but this conveys little about why they did it or the meaning it holds for them.

- Valentine (1992, see A2PKT p.494) points out that physiology and psychology are often concerned with different aspects of a behaviour. For example, with respect to visual perception, physiologists are concerned with the *structures* involved (the nerve pathways, parts of the brain, and so on) whereas psychology is more concerned with the *processes* involved in it (what aspects of the environment are being perceived, what part the brain plays, whether the processing is "bottom-up" or "top-down", and so on). In other words, physiologists are interested in *where*; psychologists are concerned with *how*.

- The reductionist approach simply does not work very well. There are very few examples of psychological phenomena which have been adequately explained in terms of physiology and it is extremely difficult to see how such an explanation could usefully be applied to, for example, Freud's theories or to Milgram's agency theory, to name but two.

Examples of Reductionism in Psychological Theory and Research

As mentioned earlier, reductionism also refers to the explanation of complex behaviour in terms of simple principles. In addition, it refers to the ways in which research in psychology has been conducted. We will now consider some examples of reductionism in both theory and research. Bearing in mind that this is a synoptic part of the Specification, we will use examples you will have studied in other parts of the course.

- *Physiological reductionism* offers explanations of behaviour based on physiological mechanisms. An example would be explaining the causes of schizophrenia simply in terms of excess activity of dopamine receptors in the brain and other brain abnormalities, with no reference to social factors that may have contributed to the condition.

- *Biological reductionism* advocates that behaviour can best be understood through the study of less complex animals. Lorenz (1966, see A2PKT pp.89–90) explained the causes of human aggression by studying the reasons why other animals are aggressive.

- *Evolutionary reductionism* explains behaviour in terms of how a particular behavioural pattern helps the individual adapt to its environment and pass on its genes. The controversial theory of sociobiology (which is not advocated by all evolutionary biologists) reduces the cause of human (as well as nonhuman) behaviour to the most advantageous way of passing on genes. In the section on Mate Selection (see Chapter 7, Evolutionary Explanations in Human Behaviour), we saw how sociobiologists believe that men prefer younger, attractive females, as they are good breeders, while women seek men who are older than them with good prospects, so they can be good providers for them and their children.

- *Environmental reductionism* represents the behavioural (learning) approach because behaviourists reduce the causes of human behaviour to simple environmental factors such as reinforcement and punishment. They also reduce the components of the mind to simple behavioural components such as stimulus–response links. The major problem with such an approach can be expressed by the saying "the whole is greater than the sum of its parts". Water can be reduced to its constituent elements of hydrogen and oxygen but these chemicals have completely different characteristics from those of water. This is an example of reductionism confusing rather then clarifying.

- *Machine reductionism* is used by the cognitive approach when it likens the human mind to a computer. This type of information-processing approach explains behaviour in terms of encoding–storage–retrieval, exemplified in some models of memory. Whilst this approach can be useful in trying to explain human cognitive functioning, there are obvious limitations since, unlike humans, computers do not forget, they do not get tired or bored, they do not reconstruct memories, and they are not affected by emotions. On the other hand, even the most sophisticated computers cannot perform any of a host of everyday tasks that humans take for granted, like recognising the meaning of certain phrases by their context. In essence, computers can never reproduce the unique qualities that make human behaviour so complex, brilliant, and unpredictable.

- *Experimental reductionism* is concerned with methodology rather than theory. When laboratory studies are conducted, psychologists work on the assumption that it is legitimate to study behaviour under controlled conditions in order to gain understanding of similar behaviours in the natural environment. This reduces behaviour to a simple set of variables that offer the possibility of identifying a cause and an effect. The major problem with such an approach is that of ecological validity. Such studies can provide valuable information but they do not necessarily tell us much about how people behave in real-life situations, especially when studying social behaviour. The study of such behaviours as obedience and helping need to be conducted both in the field as well as under controlled conditions if we are ever to be able to draw conclusions about ordinary behaviour from them.

Alternatives to Reductionism

- *The humanistic approach* is vociferously anti-reductionist. This approach (see A2PKT, p.490) is a holistic one, opposed to any attempt to reduce humans to a set of simple elements. Psychologists of a humanist persuasion argue that in order to understand people you must study the whole person, taking full account of individual experience, emotion, choice, and the world as the individual sees it. Critics of this approach argue that the humanist rejection of the influence of physiological and biological factors is unrealistic, since these factors do have a significant effect and therefore need to be taken into account.

- *The eclectic approach* is an alternative that takes account of various approaches in psychology and operates by gathering data from as many relevant sources as possible. For example, when considering schizophrenia or, indeed, any mental disorders, it would take account of all the possible physiological, psychological, and social factors that may be implicated in the disorder and how these factors might interact. With respect to therapies, such an approach would look to a multi-treatment approach, considering the appropriateness of various types of biological and psychological therapies as well as family support. The main problem with the eclectic approach is that it is difficult to combine information from all the relevant sources into one coherent theory. However, this may be because human behaviour is so complex that such theories are inevitably going to be difficult to formulate. It certainly does not mean that we should ignore valuable information in a futile attempt to make things simpler.

- *Methodological alternatives.* The "slice of life" school, as it is sometimes referred to, holds that human behaviour can never be fully understood by using the scientific method and that people should be studied in the real world by "taking a slice of their life". These descriptive methods, such as observational methods, provide rich but complex data and it is often difficult to ascertain which factors, amongst a great array of contenders, are responsible for determining behaviour.

SO WHAT DOES THIS MEAN?

Many psychologists believe that any attempt to offer a single causal explanation for human behaviour is futile and misleading. For example, by describing mental disorders in terms of biological processes, the contribution of social and cultural factors is ignored. Similarly, if we explain aggression in terms of levels of hormones, we neglect social constructionist ways of explaining it and this, in turn, means we may be tempted not to consider social means of coping with aggressive behaviour. Nevertheless, it may be reasonable to assume that some issues within psychology lend themselves to the reductionist perspective. According to Eysenck (see A2PKT p.497), "All forms of reductionism serve the useful function of encouraging us to consider factors that are relevant to an understanding of human behaviour".

OVER TO YOU

1.(a) Describe examples of reductionism in psychological theory and research. **(15 marks)**

(b) Critically assess the appropriateness of the reductionist approach for these areas of theory and research. **(15 marks)**

2. Discuss the extent to which reductionism has helped to explain human behaviour. **(30 marks)**

PSYCHOLOGY AS SCIENCE

To read up on psychology as science, refer to pages 500–511 of A2PKT.

THE DEVELOPMENT OF PSYCHOLOGY IN RELATION TO SCIENCE

The philosopher Descartes (1596–1650) had an important influence on the discipline of psychology, helping to distinguish it from philosophy. Before Descartes, the human mind was viewed as being unique and beyond rational explanation. Two very different scientific discoveries of the time had a profound effect on the speculation of the workings of the human mind. First, the discovery by Copernicus (1473–1543) that the Earth was not the centre of the universe removed the idea of humans being exclusive in all creation. Second, the discovery by Harvey (1578–1657) of the blood circulatory system led to the recognition that the human body was basically the same as that of other animals (albeit more complex) and, more importantly, could be reduced to something as ordinary as a machine.

Descartes was the first philosopher to distinguish between mind (thinking, reasoning, remembering) and body (biological processes), in a theory known as *dualism*. He believed that the interaction of mind and body took place in the brain (although the part he pinpointed was inaccurate). This distinction was important in that it allowed scientists to treat matter as distinct from themselves as observers of it and meant that the world could be described *objectively*. Objectivity became a major goal of science. Out of this grew a philosophy called *positivism*, the belief that we should not go beyond the boundaries of what can be observed, that science should be concerned only with questions that can be investigated using the scientific method. With respect to psychology, the approach that resulted from positivism was behaviourism, which concerned itself only with behaviour that could be observed. A variation of positivism, *logical positivism,* held that all approaches that provided knowledge that could not be scientifically verified, such as Freud's ideas on the id, ego, and superego, were meaningless.

The British Empiricist movement, led by the philosophers Hobbes (1588–1679) and Locke (1632–1704), was another milestone in the history of psychology because it advocated the use of systematic and objective methods of study rather than reasoning and intuition.

In the 1870s the first psychology laboratories were set up by Wundt (1832–1920) in Germany and James (1842–1910) in the USA. 1879 can be viewed as the date when psychology became a discipline in its own right since it was in that year that Wundt established an institute of experimental psychology. Wundt used a technique known as introspection, a carefully controlled technique for looking inward at conscious experiences and attempting to analyse them into the basic elements of sensations and feelings. In the USA, William James, having written a book (*The Principles of Psychology*, 1890) in which he described psychology as "the Science of Mental Life", became disillusioned with what psychology could offer as a science.

John Watson (1878–1958), the founder of behaviourism, who did not believe that the study of "consciousness" had any part in psychology, instigated the next major movement. He rejected the method of introspection on the grounds that it was unreliable and the knowledge obtained from it was difficult, if not impossible, to verify. Watson substituted the study of observable behaviour for the study of the mind as the only suitable subject matter for scientific psychology. Behaviourism, with its emphasis on rigorous scientific methodology and objectivity, represents the positivist approach in psychology.

For many years, behaviourism had an important impact on psychology, but since the 1950s its influence has waned as other approaches have become more prominent. For example, cognitive psychology has stressed the importance of thinking and brought the study of the mind, albeit in a different way, back into mainstream psychology. In addition, the use of many nonscientific methods, such as field studies, case studies, and discourse analysis, have been recognised as legitimate ways of studying human behaviour.

Definition/Varieties of Science

In the traditional sense, a science is concerned with what we *know* to be true as opposed to what we simply *believe* to be true. Science is a way of amassing knowledge and its broad aims are description, understanding, prediction, and control. The traditional view of science, as put forward by the behaviourists, is summarised by Eysenck and Keane (1990, see A2PKT p.500) as having the following features:

- It is objective.
- This objectivity is ensured by careful observation and experimentation.
- The knowledge obtained by scientists is turned into law-like generalisations.

It is now accepted that there are problems with this behaviourist view of science. First, as discussed below, it is virtually impossible to measure behaviour objectively. Second, there are valid nonscientific methods by which data can be collected. Third, as Popper (1945) argued, "The ultimate aim of science is not to establish general or other kinds of law, but to establish (or at least approach) the truth—what is, was and always will be the case".

Arguments For and Against the Claim that Psychology is a Science

Given the inadequacy of the behaviourist definition of science, a new definition became necessary. This was a difficult enterprise and there is no absolute agreement on what constitutes a science, but the following features are usually included:

- Objectivity
- Falsifiability
- Paradigm
- Replicability

OBJECTIVITY

Data (information) should be collected as objectively as possible with the minimum of bias, prejudice, and expectation from researchers. However, Popper (1969, 1972, see A2PKT p.502) argues that observation is always selective and pre-structured because, before an observation can be made, the researcher has to decide *what* is to be observed. No-one ever observes without some idea of what they are looking for, so observations are *selective*. Psychologists also have preconceived ideas depending on their theoretical orientation, so what they see depends to an extent on what they expect to see, so observations are *interpretative*.

Wallach and Wallach (1994, see A2PKT p.503), while they acknowledge that perfect objectivity is not possible, argue that nevertheless we can be confident in the interpretation of behaviour if there is plenty of other supporting evidence.

FALSIFIABILITY

Popper (1969, see A2PKT p.503) argued that the hallmark of science is the formulation of ideas that are potentially capable of being falsified. The idea of falsifiability is related to the extent to which *predictions* can be made from the theory.

If predictions are specific then it is possible to test them to see if they are false. For example, the theory that STM holds 7 items + or − 2 leads to clear predictions that can be tested. If people can generally only remember 3 items, or they can regularly remember at least 11, the theory is false.

On the other hand, if a theory is very general and unspecified, then predictions are vague and multiple and the theory is impossible to falsify. A classic example is Freud's theory. Take the example of a boy raised by a harsh, rejecting mother and a weak father. He may, according to the theory, seek dominating women who will denigrate him because they remind him of his mother, or a warm, comforting wife who can provide the mothering he lacked in infancy. Another nonscientific aspect of Freud's theory is that there are many aspects of it, such as the id, ego, and superego, which are unfalsifiable since it is not possible to imagine any findings that would refute them.

PARADIGM

A paradigm is a *shared set of assumptions, methods, and terminology about what should be studied and how*. Kuhn (1962, see A2PKT pp.505–506) states that "a field of study can only be properly considered a science if a majority of its workers subscribe to a common global theory or perspective". He suggests that the progression of science takes place in three historical stages:

- **Pre-science**—no universally accepted paradigm.
- **Normal science**—researchers work by sharing the same paradigm.
- **Revolutionary science**—the evidence becomes so overwhelming that a "paradigm shift" occurs and a new perspective is adopted (e.g. moving from believing in a flat earth to it being a sphere). The transition from an old to a new paradigm is not smooth. Some scientists cling to the old paradigm and ignore conflicting evidence.

As regards psychology, Kuhn argues that it is still at the pre-science stage with no overall paradigm for two main reasons. First, there are many conflicting approaches (psychodynamic, behaviourist, humanistic, and so on). Second, the subject matter of psychology is so diverse, ranging from topic areas bordering on sociology, biology, biochemistry, neurology, and more, that researchers in different fields have little in common.

Valentine (1982, see A2PKT p.507) takes a different view, arguing that behaviourism constitutes a science because it has a clear paradigm. Behaviourism uses the scientific method, only studying what can be objectively measured, and making precise predictions. However, only a minority of psychologists are advocates of behaviourism. In addition to this, although it has had a considerable influence on psychology, this is mainly in the realm of methodology rather than theory. At present, it is fair to say that psychology is at the pre-science stage and has far to go before it reaches the revolutionary science stage.

REPLICABILITY

Replicability refers to repeatability of studies in order to see if results are consistent and therefore reliable. The only method in psychology that is replicable is the experimental method. Laboratory experiments permit high control and reasonably good replicability. But do they tell us much about ordinary human behaviour? Heather (1976, see A2PKT p.505) argues that all they tell us is how strangers act in unusual situations.

Laboratory studies have *high internal validity* because if repeated, the same results are found time and again. However, they have *low external or ecological validity* because they tell us little about how people act in ordinary, everyday situations. In a laboratory, the researcher rather than the participant controls the situation, whereas in everyday life we spend a great deal of time responding to and coping with our environment.

Even the replicability of the experimental method cannot be guaranteed when studying human behaviour since no two samples of people are the same. Factors such as culture, gender, and the particular era are all going to affect the results.

Methods such as the case study, field study, or naturalistic observation are not replicable at all, yet they provide invaluable information about human behaviour. Psychology would be a far less valid means of finding out how and why people behave as they do if the laboratory experiment was the only means of investigation. Many researchers therefore argue that it is inappropriate to use a scientific method in psychology, or indeed to attempt to make psychology a pure science.

SO WHAT DOES THIS MEAN?

Since psychology has many different theories, approaches, and methodologies, it can be argued that it does not as yet constitute a science. Some areas do fulfil some of the criteria of science, with theories that are falsifiable and research findings that are replicable. However, this certainly does not apply to all aspects of psychology. What needs to be considered is whether it *could* and whether it *should* be a science. Some people argue that humans are so complex and variable that psychology can never be a science with a single overriding paradigm. They also point to problems such as lack of ecological validity of studies, the bias of researchers in their interpretation of findings, and the bias of the samples of participants used for research. Still others argue that psychology should make no attempt to be a science. The humanists, for example, argue that the nonscientific method in which individuals report their conscious experiences gives deep insight into what the experience has meant to them. Therefore, at present there is not only an argument concerning whether psychology is a science but a more deep-seated philosophical one concerning whether or not it should ever attempt to be.

OVER TO YOU

1. Discuss the extent to which psychology fits into the definition of science.   **(30 marks)**

2. Describe the development of psychology as a separate discipline, and critically assess whether modern psychology can now be considered a science. **(30 marks)**

Question 1 adapted from AQA A2 [Summer 2002] Psychology Examination Papers.

NATURE–NURTURE

To read up on nature–nurture, refer to pages 511–520 of A2PKT.

THE NATURE–NURTURE DEBATE

The nature–nurture debate in psychology concerns the extent to which human behaviour is determined by heredity (nature) and to what extent it is the product of learned experiences (nurture). The nature–nurture issue is pervasive in psychology and you will have already come across it in many areas of study, such as aggression (antisocial behaviour), gender differences, causes of mental disorders, and intelligence. The section on Development of Measured Intelligence in Chapter 5, Cognitive Development, is worth particular consideration because of the significance of the implications, and should be re-read before going further.

The nature–nurture controversy has a long history in philosophy and psychology. Around 1800, a debate began amongst learned people about the true nature of the human species. One extreme was represented by the British philosopher John Locke (1632–1704) who espoused a doctrine known as *empiricism*. This held that babies are born with a mind that is like a blank slate (a *tabula rasa*) and it is experience that etches itself on the slate and gives everyone their unique characteristics. On the other side of the debate was the French philosopher Jean Rousseau (1712–1778), who presented the *nativist* argument. This stated that inherited characteristics are by far the most important influence on personality and behaviour. According to this view, babies are born with an inherited blueprint and it is this that shapes development.

Nowadays, few, if any, philosophers and psychologists would take such an extreme view. They recognise that every type of complex behaviour is shaped by both an individual's biological inheritance and by their experiences, including learning. Heredity and environment have a continuing influence on one another. No longer do we ask the simplistic question, does nature or nurture shape behaviour? Indeed, as pointed out by Anastasi (1958), the either/or argument makes no sense at all. As we said in Chapter 5 (Cognitive Development), both are essential—it's like arguing whether the seed or soil is more important when a plant grows. Without both, nothing grows. In a similar vein, Hebb says that it is like arguing about whether the breadth or length is more important in deciding area. Given that we acknowledge that both sets of influences are important and that they influence each other, what we need to examine is the way in which this interaction operates. Before we consider this, we will look at ways of investigating the nature–nurture issue.

Researching Nature and Nurture

Psychologists use a variety of methods to explore the extent to which a characteristic is inherited. These methods were mentioned in Chapter 5, Cognitive Development, in the section Development of Measured Intelligence.

- **Concordance rate** is the extent to which two measures are in agreement. For example, if 20 pairs of twins are studied and in 12 of the pairs both twins have developed a certain condition such as schizophrenia, this would produce a concordance rate of 12/20 or 60%. If concordance rates are higher for pairs of people that are more closely related genetically than for pairs of people who are less closely related, it is reasonable to assume that there is a genetic element operating for that characteristic, all other things being equal.

- **Twin studies** are commonly used to investigate the nature–nurture issue. Identical (MZ) twins have the same genetic make-up, whereas non-identical (DZ) twins share only half their genes (like any pair of siblings). If the concordance rate for MZ twins is higher than for DZ twins then we can assume some genetic influence on the characteristic being assessed. We have, for example, seen this is the case in schizophrenia (Chapter 8, Psychopathology) and intelligence (Chapter 5,

Cognitive Development). However, we need to be cautious about drawing conclusions because, although higher concordance rates for MZ than for DZ twins strongly implicate heredity, the concordance rate for MZ twins is never 100% and often considerably less. Therefore, other factors, namely environment and experience, must also play a part. It is also possible that MZ twins, being identical, may be treated more similarly than are DZ twins.

- *Studies of twins reared apart* have also been conducted, so as to rule out the role of a shared environment. However, in the past these studies were often seriously flawed. Faber (1981) reported that twins supposedly reared apart were often raised by relatives in the same town, saw quite a lot of each other, and sometimes even went to the same school. So their environments were nowhere near as different as two people chosen at random. A more recent large-scale study in Minnesota (Bouchard et al., 1990, see A2PKT p.205) is far less flawed but not without its methodological problems.

- *Family studies* are also useful in investigating nature and nurture. The concordance rate within a family line can show whether or not a characteristic is liable to be inherited. Such studies have, for example, implicated genetic factors in schizophrenia (Gottesman, 1991).

- *Adoption studies.* One of the problems of any comparison of concordance rates between people in the same family is that they share a similar environment, so it is never clear to what extent shared experience rather than heredity has contributed to a condition. One way to try to separate out the effects of heredity and environment is to look at individuals who were not raised in their biological families. Adoption studies provide this opportunity.

The Interaction of Nature and Nurture

We said earlier that the environment and heredity do not act independently of one another, but interact. We will consider ways in which this interaction may occur.

THE DIATHESIS–STRESS MODEL

You will already have come across the diathesis–stress model in Chapter 8, Psychopathology. This model states that *both* a genetic predisposition to a mental disorder *and* environmental stressors are necessary for the condition to affect an individual. What is inherited in some cases of mental disorder is a *predisposition to be vulnerable* to it, not the disorder itself. In order for the disorder to emerge, an individual has to have the genetic vulnerability to the disorder and a particular stressor that brings it about. In some cases this stressor needs only to be very mild, such as a teenager leaving home for the first time. In other cases, the stressor needs to be quite extreme, such as a very troubled family life, in order for the condition to occur. So even within the genetic vulnerability there is wide individual variation (which may account for the fact that even people from loving, well-balanced families can develop schizophrenia).

PHENOTYPE AND GENOTYPE

When considering the nature–nurture issue it is important to distinguish between an individual's genotype and their phenotype. The total genetic makeup of an individual is known as the *genotype*. Genes contain the instruction for producing a physical body, which in turn have an effect on psychological characteristics. The *phenotype* is the observable physical and behavioural characteristics of an individual; in other words, the phenotype is what an individual actually becomes. This phenotype is the result of both genetic and environmental influences. For example, two children may be born with a similarly high predisposition to suffer anxiety. If one then experiences a very stressful environment, he or she may become a very anxious adult and perhaps be prone to anxiety disorders such as phobias. The other may, in contrast, have a supportive and benign upbringing that results in a well-adjusted adult capable of coping well with anxiety-provoking situations. Their genotypes are similar, but their phenotypes are very different.

THE FORM OF INTERACTION

If genetics and environment interact, then it is useful to consider ways in which this interaction could occur. In recent years, behavioural geneticists have argued that our genes may actually influence the type of environment we experience. Plomin, DeFries, and Loehlin (1977, see A2PKT pp.514–515) identified three different kinds of interaction between nature and nurture, described in terms of how a child may be affected by his or her environment:

1. ***Passive heredity–environment interaction.*** The kind of environment that parents provide for their child may be influenced, at least in part, by the parents' genotype. For example, parents who are predisposed genetically to be musical may provide a very musical environment for their children, encouraging them to listen to music and play musical instruments. Similarly, intelligent parents may provide an environment that encourages learning. The environment is related to the parents' genetic make-up and the effect of these genes is transmitted passively to the children via the environment the parents create.

2. ***Reactive heredity–environment interaction.*** Parents react in different ways to different children, depending on the child's temperament and looks. People tend to react more positively to an attractive child than an unattractive one and, in a similar way, smiling, active babies are likely to receive more attention and positive stimulation than moody and passive ones. Thomas and Chess (1977, see A2PKT p.514) suggested that parents find it easier to form a good relationship with a child who has an easy temperament than one who has a difficult one. The child's inherited characteristics create a reaction in others that leads to differences in the child's environment. In this way the child's genetic make-up affects the type of social environment in which the personality develops.

3. ***Active heredity–environment interaction.*** A child's genetic make-up is likely to influence the type of environment they prefer and seek out. For example, a friendly child is likely to seek out other children and prefer sociable activities while a shyer child may prefer solitary activities like reading. So people with different genetic temperaments seek out different environments, which may then have a powerful effect on their later development. This is related to a concept mentioned earlier in this chapter: Bandura's notion of *reciprocal determinism*—the belief that whilst the environment is an important determinant of behaviour, in turn, behaviour is also a determinant of the environment.

Nature and Nurture in Psychological Theory

- ***The biological approach*** obviously emphasises the importance of nature. Biological psychologists are primarily interested in investigating physiological activity. The approach, however, does recognise that the environment is influential and that no individual is entirely a prisoner of his or her genes.

- ***Sociobiology*** takes the view that any organism has evolved to maximise the passing on of its genes and that humans are no exception to this rule. They are therefore also on the nature side of the argument. Many sociobiologists nevertheless concede that human behaviour is also influenced by cultural transmission—the passing on of behaviours, attitudes, values, and information from one generation to the next via socialisation, but they believe it would be wrong to neglect what they consider to be the strong influence of evolution in shaping our behaviour.

- *The behaviourist approach* represents the extreme of the nurture side of the debate. John Watson, one of the founders of this movement, said "Give me a dozen healthy infants…and my own specified world to bring them up in and I'll guarantee to take any one at random and train him to become any type of specialist I might select—doctor, lawyer…and yes, even beggarman and thief". Nevertheless, recent research indicates that both humans and other animals are predisposed to learn biologically useful behaviours (such as learning to associate food with sickness) rather than unhelpful ones. The approach also recognises that the potential for learning is innate.

- *The cognitive approach* acknowledges that we are products of both nature and nurture. The more recent analogy of comparing the workings of the brain with that of a computer draws a parallel between the way the brain is "hard-wired" (our biology) and the ways in which it has been "programmed" (our learning). It therefore acknowledges that we are both the product of our nature and our nurture.

- *The psychodynamic approach* combines both nature and nurture in that it believes our experiences in early childhood modify the natural innate urges of the id to produce the adult personality.

- *The humanistic approach* emphasises nurture but also makes basic assumptions about human nature—i.e. that it is positive, inclined towards psychological good health, and has the potential for self-actualisation.

Resolving the Nature–Nurture Controversy

The nature–nurture debate has important practical and political implications as discussed in Chapter 5 (Cognitive Development) in the section Development of Measured Intelligence. Gottesman's (1963, see A2PKT p.517) concept of a *reaction range* could be the best solution to the nature–nurture question. According to Gottesman, genes do not determine behaviour but they establish a range of possible responses that a person will show to different kinds of life experiences. What this means is that the genotype sets the boundaries on the type of phenotype that will develop. With respect to intellectual performance, Shaffer (1996) provides an example of the effects of varying degrees of environmental enrichment on three children, one who has high genetic potential for intellectual development, one whose genetic endowment for intelligence is average, and one whose potential for intellectual growth is far below average. The first child has the widest reaction range, varying from well below average in a deprived environment to far above average in an enriched one. In contrast the child with the least potential has a much more limited reaction range and shows a smaller variation across different environments. The most important implication of this is that, even though an individual's genotype sets a range of possible outcomes, a good environment can make the most of this potential. Contrary to the argument of the nativists, regardless of their genetic endowment, all children benefit from a stimulating and loving environment.

SO WHAT DOES THIS MEAN?

There are important implications arising from the nature–nurture debate. If behaviour is mainly determined by heredity then intervention in the form of an enriched environment has little effect. In contrast, if nurture has a profound effect then a person's experience, especially in early life, is crucial. The implications for social policy are profound. As far as intelligence is concerned, programmes like Operation Headstart (see A2PKT p.209) were based on the idea that children could be enriched by positive experiences and stifled by negative ones and that such enrichment programmes were a worthwhile investment in children's futures. On the other hand, Herrnstein and Murray (1994, see A2PKT p.518), in the book *The Bell Curve,* argue that since intelligence is mainly inherited, then intervention programmes are largely a waste of resources. As Wade and Tavris (1990) comment, the issue is one of great complexity and "unsophisticated assumptions about nature and nurture can influence the formation of social and educational policies that affect millions of lives."

OVER TO YOU

1.(a) Outline what is meant by the "nature–nurture" debate.   **(5 marks)**

  (b) Discuss psychological research in terms of its contribution to the
      "nature–nurture" debate.   **(25 marks)**

2. Critically consider different views regarding the relationship between
nature and nurture in psychology.   **(30 marks)**

Question 1 adapted from AQA A2 [Summer 2002] Psychology Examination Papers.

QUESTIONS AND ESSAY PLANS

Since this is the synoptic part of the Specification, the essays carry more marks than on other areas of the paper (30 as opposed to 24), equally weighted between AO1 and AO2. You should spend about 40 minutes on each of the questions below. Since they are synoptic, remember that you need to draw on other areas of the Specification. You will notice that in the preceding chapter, reference is frequently made to other areas of the Specification and this is what is required in your answers.

1 Describe and analyse how theoretical approaches in psychology have addressed the free will/determinism issue. (30 marks)

This question provides a very good opportunity to address the synoptic requirements of the Specification since it requires you to look at the different approaches in psychology with respect to their stance of free will and determinism. Bear in mind that for each approach, you are required to describe and analyse, so you must consider the implications of each approach to this issue.

Paragraph 1 Introduction

Outline the debate with respect to free will and determinism.

Paragraph 2

Mention that the extreme free will position is not advocated by any approach and explain what is meant by soft determinism.

Paragraph 3

The learning approach as represented by classic behaviourism is extremely deterministic—describe this approach. The analysis could include Skinner's views and the content of *Walden Two*, the novel he wrote in 1948 (see A2PKT p.461) describing the use of operant conditioning to create an ideal society. The social learning approach is far less deterministic, advocating the idea of reciprocal determinism. In the analysis, say how this is a more sophisticated approach since it takes account of how we each, within the limits of opportunity, help to determine our own environment and therefore do have an element of control.

Paragraph 4

The biological approach is deterministic in a different way as, according to this, we are constrained by our biology. However, the diathesis–stress model shows how the environment also has an effect and this is not entirely out of our control. No complex behaviour is entirely determined by biological factors, so you need to analyse the other ways in which behaviour is affected and whether or not these are under our control.

Paragraph 5

The evolutionary approach is very deterministic. You can analyse this with reference to sociobiology, using examples from different topic areas such as interpersonal relationships and/or prosocial behaviour. You then have plenty of opportunity to critically evaluate this approach for the AO2 part.

Paragraph 6

The psychodynamic approach is another deterministic one because it stresses that our behaviour is determined by unconscious forces over which we have little or no control. The analysis of this can be two-pronged. First, the theory itself can be criticised for the vagueness of the concepts involved and the possible lack of empirical evidence, so there is no compelling reason to believe that we are controlled by unconscious forces, although there is some evidence to suggest that we don't always fully understand why we behave the way we do. But a rather different type of analysis is that the use of psychoanalytic therapy helps free people from the control of their unconscious mind and enables them to take control of their own lives. So the knowledge of how our lives are determined provides the opportunity to become freer.

Paragraph 7

The humanistic approach differs from the other approaches in its emphasis on free will. It does, however, acknowledge that this freedom only exists in a framework of constraint. This has important implications because it makes people morally responsible for their own behaviour in a way that many of the other approaches do not. By the therapies it uses, this approach also offers people the freedom to change their lives and gain fulfilment. On the other hand, such an approach can be criticised since for many people free will is not a reality. There are a great many things in our lives that dictate how we must behave and the humanistic approach is perhaps rather unrealistic in this respect.

Paragraph 8 Conclusion

It is now necessary to analyse the whole debate. This issue is more philosophical than psychological because there is no way of designing research studies into the extent to which we can choose our actions. Therefore the different approaches are, to a degree, expressing a philosophical viewpoint rather than an evidence-based one.

2(a) Examine reductionist approaches in different areas of psychology. **(15 marks)**

(b) Critically assess the appropriateness of the reductionist approach to these areas of psychology. **(15 marks)**

In the first part of this essay you need to describe different examples of reductionism in psychology, taking care to use a variety of types of reductionism and covering each in reasonable detail so you have depth as well as width. In the second part you are required to consider the strengths and limitations (appropriateness) in the areas you have covered in (a), so don't rush headlong into writing part (a) until you have considered part (b).

Part (a)

Start by very briefly outlining what is meant by reductionism in a psychological context. Then consider which approaches to use. Since they cover different types of reductionism, it is useful to mention the physiological, evolutionary, and learning approaches. Then select an anti-reductionist approach, such as the humanistic. For each of these, outline the ways in which they are reductionist and provide an example, if possible from different areas of the Specification as this includes synopticity. For example, you could use the dopamine hypothesis for the physiological approach, the criteria men and women use for selecting sexual partners for the evolutionary approach, and so on. (You will notice that there is a good deal of overlap between this, free will/reductionism, and nature–nurture since they are all addressing similar issues.)

Part (b)

The limitation of the appropriateness of physiological reductionism is that rarely in psychology are behaviour and/or a mental disorder determined entirely by biology. The diathesis–stress model demonstrates that a lot of factors other than biology need to be taken into account. This is not to say that consideration of physiology is not essential to the understanding of human behaviour but we must also consider how it interacts with environmental factors, and how environmental factors may affect physiology. To make this point, you may find it useful to consider some of the work on stress you covered in the AS course.

Evolutionary reductionism has been heavily criticised in psychology but can also be evaluated from the perspective of its usefulness. Do not get bogged down in criticism of the sociobiological explanation of specific theories, rather concentrate on the overall criticism of its emphasis on evolution being a major determinant of human behaviour that takes little account of free will, cultural transmission, or specific learning.

When discussing the appropriateness of reductionism in the learning approach, it would be useful to consider not only the limitations of the theory and the use of animals (which is reductionist because it reduces human behaviour to that of less complex animals), but also experimental reductionism and its limitations and advantages.

The humanistic approach, or third force in psychology, was a reaction to the reductionisms of other areas of psychology, advocating a holistic approach. This may seem laudable in principle and has certainly offered a new and refreshing perspective on how to view humans but there are times, especially with respect to certain mental disorders, when the solutions offered are very vague and we need to look at the specific causes of that disorder rather than only considering the whole person in his or her social context.

Conclude by briefly considering the general advantages and limitations of any reductionist approach.

3 Discuss the extent to which psychology fits into the definition of science. (30 marks)

Paragraph 1 Introduction

Begin by asking the question "What is a science?" including its broad aims of description, understanding, prediction, and control. *The main body of the essay involves a consideration of the nature of science in more detail and the extent to which psychology fits into those criteria.*

Paragraphs 2–3 Objectivity

Discuss the problems for psychologists in attempting to be completely objective. You may want to contrast psychology with the "pure" sciences in which there are objective measuring instruments. Consider whether the study of human behaviour can or should be entirely objective.

Paragraph 4 Falsifiability

Present Popper's argument that science should comprise ideas that are falsifiable and offer examples from psychology of cases when this is and is not true, for example, behaviourism and Freudian theory.

Paragraphs 5–6 Replicability

Discuss the methodological problems inherent in psychology and the limitations of using methods that permit replication, such as the laboratory experiment. Discuss whether this type of method is appropriate given its severe limitations. It would then be a good idea to discuss the nonscientific methods such as discourse analysis and give some consideration to the advantages and limitations of using these methods in preference to the more scientific ones.

Paragraph 7 A paradigm

Present Kuhn's argument that a field of study can only be considered a science if a majority of its workers subscribe to a common global theory or perspective. There are various branches of psychology that do have their own perspective, such as behaviourism, evolutionary psychology, and perhaps even the psychodynamic perspective. However, these are not shared by other approaches, indeed some of them are vociferously rejected, so at present psychology has no overall paradigm.

Paragraph 8 Conclusion

It would be appropriate to conclude with reference not only to whether psychology *is* a science but whether it should strive to be. There are several branches of psychology, such as humanistic and social constructionist, which believe that science is not an appropriate goal in the study of human behaviour.

4 Discuss the nature–nurture debate in psychology.   (30 marks)

There is a great deal of potential AO1 material that could be included in this essay (such as examples from different areas of psychology or how the different approaches view the debate), and you must be careful not to give too much breadth (don't try to cover too many areas) so you have enough time to present AO2 material—the evaluation. Since there is so much material, you may approach this answer in a different way to the suggested answer that follows. This is not a problem as long as you include sufficient AO2.

Paragraph 1 Introduction

Describe what is meant by the nature–nurture debate and provide some background to it in terms of the nativist–empiricist dichotomy.

Paragraph 2

You could now consider the methods used to research this debate. Include the problems of using concordance rates, twin studies, and so on in order to assess heritability.

Paragraph 3

Introduce the idea of the interaction between nature and nurture being more relevant than an either/or concept to lead into a discussion of the ways in which this interaction might occur. Then start with the diathesis–stress model. In order to include synopticity, you could discuss this in terms of mental disorders, using an example of a disorder you have studied (such as schizophrenia or eating disorders).

Paragraph 4

Now move onto genotype and phenotype, with emphasis on the fact that the genotype cannot be measured, only the phenotype. Provide an example from another area of psychology in order to illustrate this point (perhaps intelligence or aggression), mentioning how the environment acts on the genotype to produce the phenotype.

Paragraphs 5–7

Discuss Plomin et al.'s (1977) model of the different kinds of interaction between nature and nurture. Mention how all these three processes take place simultaneously, so any attempt to tease out the separate effects of nature and nurture is nonsensical. Nevertheless, we need to acknowledge these effects.

Paragraph 8 Conclusion

A useful conclusion would be Gottesman's (1963) idea of a reaction range. The AO2 content would include the implications from this. The area of intelligence is useful to illustrate the point. No essay on the nature–nurture debate is complete without a consideration of the practical and political consequences. You may want to mention the issue of socially sensitive research and the dangers of simplistic, unsophisticated arguments regarding nature–nurture. The race and IQ debate (see Chapter 5, Cognitive Development) is an ideal vehicle by which to discuss this.

Questions 3 and 4 adapted from AQA A2 [Summer 2002] Psychology Examination Papers.
The authors are responsible for the solutions and (a) they have neither been provided nor approved by AQA and (b) they may not necessarily constitute the only possible solutions.

Perspectives

APPROACHES IN PSYCHOLOGY
Specification 14.2

What's it about?

By the time you've reached this stage in your revision, you will be aware that there are various approaches to addressing the problem of explaining behaviour. In this section we will consider five major approaches: biological, behavioural, psychodynamic, cognitive, and evolutionary. In some cases there are psychologists who consistently prefer to explain behaviour in terms of a single approach, such as in terms of biology or learning. However, it is likely that even those who consistently take one particular stance nevertheless acknowledge the influence of other approaches—it is simply that their focus of interest is on a specific type of influence. In other cases, a psychologist may prefer one explanation for some behaviours while explaining others in a different way. For example, they may be drawn to a biological explanation of schizophrenia, a psychodynamic interpretation of aggressive behaviour, and an evolutionary approach to account for sexual attraction. Again, although drawn to one approach to explain each of these behaviours, it is still unlikely that they would accept that one approach could ever provide a complete account. Most psychologists accept that human behaviour is immensely complex and is affected by a wide variety of interrelated influences.

Candidates will be required to apply their knowledge and understanding of any **two** theoretical approaches/methodological approaches to a novel situation or psychological phenomenon presented in the stimulus material given in the examination questions. These approaches might be selected from:

(a) Biological/medical, behavioural, psychodynamic, and cognitive (as specified in AS/A2 Individual Differences).

(b) Other psychological approaches, not named in the Specification, such as social constructionism, Humanistic Psychology, Evolutionary Psychology, etc.

(c) Those deriving from other, related disciplines, such as Sociology, Biology, and Philosophy (for example, symbolic interactionism and functionalism). These may overlap with samples from (b).

This part of Perspectives will be assessed through a stimulus material question. The way in which this is done is covered at the end of the chapter, which contains sample questions and answers.

How does this chapter differ?

Since the question regarding Approaches in Psychology has a rather different format from the other questions in the examination, the style of this chapter will differ slightly from that of the others. The exact format of the questions asked about Approaches is discussed at the beginning of the last section of the chapter, although you may find it helpful to read this before going further. This will enable you to appreciate how you need to use the information on each Approach to answer a specific examination question.

At the end of each Approach you are given guidance as to what to look for when attempting to answer the question from the viewpoint of that particular Approach. It may be useful to practise this on any piece of everyday stimulus material you come across and then check your ideas with your teacher. For example, how different approaches might account for why a particular individual wants to trek to the South Pole; why crime novels are top of the bestseller list; why carrying guns has become increasingly popular. The more you can apply different approaches to a variety of behaviours, the more likely you are to be able to do this with the stimulus material in the exam.

THE BIOLOGICAL APPROACH

To read up on the biological approach, refer to pages 526–532 of A2PKT.

DESCRIPTION AND ASSUMPTIONS

As the name implies, the biological approach considers how genetics and the workings of the body can explain behaviour.

The main assumptions are:

- All behaviour can be explained and understood at the level of functioning of biological systems.
- Both behaviour and experience can be reduced to the functioning of biological systems.

There are several branches of the biological approach, including the following:

- *The physiological approach,* which concentrates on the ways in which bodily activity can explain behaviour. For example, a physiological explanation of dreaming looks at what happens in the brain during REM sleep and explains dreams in terms of activation of certain parts of the brain (see Chapter 4, Biological Rhythms, Sleep, and Dreaming). A physiological explanation of stress, which you looked at during the AS course, would focus on the bodily responses to stress, such as increased adrenaline levels, increased heart rate, and increased rate of breathing.
- *The medical approach,* which explains and treats mental disorders in terms of physical illnesses. It assumes that mental illness can be described in terms of clusters of symptoms and treated by means of medication. A medical explanation for depression is that it is caused by abnormal levels of certain neurotransmitters in the brain and could be treated by means of antidepressant drugs.
- *The nativist view* (see Chapter 11, Debates) is that behaviour can be explained in terms of inherited behaviour. Since genes have evolved over millions of years to best adapt us to our environments, our individual characteristics, including personality, abilities, and behaviour, are strongly influenced by these genes. A nativist view of gender differences is that such differences are genetic and have evolved so as to best adapt each sex to reproductive success (as described in Chapter 7, Evolutionary Explanations of Human Behaviour).

TYPICAL METHODOLOGY

- *The experimental method* lends itself well to the biological approach because this approach reduces behaviour to simple components. The effect of an independent variable on a dependent variable can be measured, so cause and effect can be established. For example, such a method could be used to measure the effect of alcohol (the IV) on reaction time (the DV). The laboratory experiment would often be the most suitable form of experiment because conditions can be carefully controlled and the behaviour can be measured objectively.
- *Family studies, twin studies, and adoption studies* are used to investigate concordance rates in people who share genes or environment or both. These measurements are used to see if genes are implicated in causing certain characteristics and behaviour (see, for example, the section on development of measured intelligence in Chapter 5, Cognitive Development).
- *Brain scans, such as CAT scans, PET scans, and MRIs,* are used to look at the structure and functioning of the brain.

EVALUATION OF THE BIOLOGICAL APPROACH

Strengths

 A great deal of objective, quantitative data can be obtained. Since the methods used in the biological approach (especially the physiological approach) are scientific, the data obtained is objective and quantitative.

 It can be used to establish cause and effect. Because the experimental method is used, it is possible to establish cause and effect.

 It has many practical applications. Because this approach provides an understanding of the influence of biology on our behaviour, it has many practical applications such as the use of drugs to treat mental illness or conditions such as stress. Knowledge of genetic transmission can also be used to provide genetic counselling, although this is sometimes controversial.

Weaknesses/Limitations

It is a reductionist, deterministic, machine-like approach. It tends to neglect or underestimate the role of nurture (of experience) and of the influence of free will on our behaviour. It gives the impression of humans as powerless in the face of their biological endowment.

It is rather simplistic. It does not give full credit to the complex interplay of body and mind or the role of emotion and consciousness on our thoughts and behaviour. It is more appropriate in explaining some behaviours, such as the working of the visual system, than higher-order thinking, but even vision depends on factors other than just biology.

SO WHAT DOES THIS MEAN?

It is very important for psychologists to take account of the biological influences on behaviour and to consider the contribution that genetic factors can make. However, as with other approaches, it is not possible to reduce the explanation for behaviour to one set of factors and it is essential that we consider the complex interplay of biology, the environment, and cognition in determining behaviour. The biological approach, though useful, is inadequate as a sole means of explaining behaviour.

Examples of the Biological Approach in the Specification

AS

Specification 11.1:   Physiological psychology, with emphasis on stress.
Specification 11.2:   Individual differences: the medical model of abnormality, including the biological explanation of eating disorders.

A2

Specification 13.2:   Physiological psychology, including biological explanations of sleep and dreaming.
Specification 13.4:   Developmental psychology, cognitive development: Piaget's account of cognitive development emphasises the role of biologically determined stages of development. Social and personality development: the biological explanation of gender development.
Specification 14.1:   Individual differences: biological explanations of multiple personality disorder, schizophrenia, depression, and anxiety disorders as well as biological (somatic) treatments for mental disorders.

Using the Biological Approach to Explain a Behaviour in the "Approaches" Question

If you want to consider a biological explanation, think about the answers to the following questions:

1. Is there any evidence of genetic transmission, such as an indication that the behaviour runs in a family?
2. Is there any behaviour that can be accounted for in terms of the ANS (autonomic nervous system) and physiological activity, such as that it gives the individual a natural "high" (e.g. addictive behaviour or risk-taking behaviour)?
3. Is there any behaviour that indicates a malfunctioning of the CNS so that the person cannot function properly, or requires some support from drugs (whether prescribed or "recreational")?

THE BEHAVIOURAL APPROACH

To read up on the behavioural approach, refer to pages 532–538 of A2PKT.

DESCRIPTION AND ASSUMPTIONS

The behavioural approach in psychology is based on the belief that behaviour is determined by conditions in the environment. It was founded by Watson (1878–1958) and was a very radical approach at the time since it rejected any ideas of unconscious mind or introspective methods and concentrated only on the use of strictly experimental methods to investigate observable behaviour. Its aim was to make psychology a pure science in the same way that physics and chemistry are sciences. In the nature–nurture debate it represents the extreme of the nurture side.

The main assumptions are:

- All behaviour is learned. When we are born we are like a blank slate (*tabula rasa*) and it is experience and interaction with the environment that make us what we are.

- All behaviour can be explained in terms of conditioning theory: stimulus–response links that build up to produce more complex behaviours.

- Psychologists should only study observable behaviour since this is all that is required in order to understand and explain how all animals, including humans, operate. There is no need to look at what goes on in the mind.

- Different species of animals only differ from each other *quantitatively*. This means that they only differ in terms of having more or less of something rather than differing in quality. It is therefore appropriate to study other species, such as rats and pigeons, in order to understand human learning since it is possible to generalise from nonhuman behaviour to human behaviour.

- Psychology should be a pure science, so the research method should be scientific.

Since the start of behaviourism, there have been several developments from the original ideas. There are therefore now several perspectives within behaviourism:

- *Radical (or classical) behaviourism* is the original approach, advocated by Skinner throughout his life. It rejects all considerations of the mind as a subject of study, and strictly adheres to the view that psychology should be the study of observable behaviour and that all behaviour can be explained in terms of learning.

- *Neobehaviourism* is a more recent, modified form of behaviourism, one of the most prominent forms being social learning theory as advanced by Bandura. One of the most important assumptions of social learning theory is that learning can occur through observation and does not need to be a consequence of direct experience. Social learning theory takes account of *cognitive* factors in learning (the roles of ambition, emotion, perceptions, and expectations in influencing behaviour), so it spans both the behavioural and the cognitive approaches. It does adhere to the strict scientific methodology advocated by radical behaviourists, but is involved in investigating human behaviour rather than the behaviour of nonhuman animals.

- *Methodological behaviourism* is a very mild version of behaviourism. It does not view the behavioural approach as capable of explaining *all* behaviour but does hold that learning provides a partial explanation for all behaviour. So when trying to explain aggressive behaviour, for example, it would explain it partly in terms of operant conditioning but would take account of other explanations, such as it being a response to frustration.

TYPICAL METHODOLOGY

Laboratory experiments are the main method used in the behavioural approach. Radical behaviourists used animals in their research; social learning theorists investigated human behaviour. In either case, an independent variable was manipulated to assess its effect on a dependent variable, with careful control being exercised over any extraneous or confounding variables. The methodology is nomothetic—it is based on the attempt to establish general laws of behaviour.

EVALUATION OF THE BEHAVIOURAL APPROACH

Strengths

- **It emphasises the importance of learning on behaviour.** There is no doubt that learning plays a fundamental part in the behaviour of all animals, especially humans. This approach has contributed greatly to our understanding of psychological functioning.

- **It has many important practical applications.** There is a wide variety of uses of the behavioural approach. The principles of learning have been used to deal with serious childhood behavioural problems, in anger management programmes, in improving motivation of managers, and in prisons. In addition, one of the most important applications you will have studied is its use in clinical psychology to change unwanted behaviour, such as in the treatment of phobias and obsessive-compulsive disorders.

- **It lends itself well to scientific methodology.** Since the approach concentrates on observable and measurable behaviour, quantitative data can be gathered in a controlled setting.

Weaknesses/Limitations

- **It is a mechanistic approach that ignores important aspects of human functioning.** The behavioural approach, by concentrating on observable behaviour, takes no heed of consciousness, subjective experience, or the role of emotions.

- **Radical behaviourism is overly deterministic.** It portrays humans (and other animals) as passive responders to environmental influences with no free will. (This is not true of social learning theory.)

- **It is reductionist.** It explains all behaviour in terms of stimulus–response connections. Although this may be appropriate for some simple learning, especially in lower-order animals, it is insufficient to explain the complexity of much human behaviour, for example, language acquisition.

- **It underestimates the role of biology.** By placing great emphasis on the role of learning, it underestimates the importance of biological factors in influencing behaviour.

- **Radical behaviourism is overly dependent on the study of a few species of animals.** Many psychologists argue that it is inappropriate to generalise the findings of research on one species in order to explain behaviour in another species. Behaviourists such as Skinner studied rats and pigeons and then generalised the findings to human behaviour.

SO WHAT DOES THIS MEAN?

The behavioural approach has been one of the important influences in the history of psychology. The extreme position taken by radical (classical) behaviourists has been largely superseded by the more moderate views of neobehaviourist approaches such as social learning theory. The main characteristics of radical behaviourism—mechanistic, deterministic, and reductionist—can be seen as weaknesses or strengths. They are weaknesses in that they are too simplistic but strengths in that they have made a considerable contribution to making psychology a scientific discipline. Moreover, such explanations are probably very appropriate to certain simple forms of behaviour.

It is important to take account of the ethical considerations involved in the practical applications of learning theory, especially when used in situations such as prisons or psychiatric institutions in which people have very limited choice. Again, this is a two-sided argument, in which we need to consider the degree of control it is fair to exercise over individuals placed in behavioural programmes but also the serious consequences for themselves and others if no such programmes are implemented.

Examples of the Behavioural Approach in the Specification

AS

Specification 11.2:   Individual differences: the behavioural model of abnormality, including the learning theory explanation of eating disorders.

A2

Specification 13.1:   Social psychology: learning theory explanations of the formation and maintenance of relationships. Learning theory explanations of pro- and anti-social behaviour.
Specification 13.3:   Cognitive psychology: learning theory explanations of language development.
Specification 13.4:   Developmental psychology: learning theory explanations of gender development.
Specification 13.5:   Comparative psychology: classical and operant conditioning.
Specification 14.1:   Individual differences: learning theory explanations of schizophrenia, depression, and anxiety disorders as well as behavioural therapies for mental disorders.

Using the Behavioural Approach to Explain a Behaviour in the "Approaches" Question

The behavioural approach is probably one of the most straightforward approaches to use in the Approaches question, since it is not difficult to account for most behaviour in terms of learning, and to then point out the limitations of such an explanation. If you want to consider a behavioural explanation to the stimulus material, think about the answers to the following questions:

1. Is it possible to account for the behaviour in terms of classical and operant conditioning? Could the behaviour be the result of association of two factors (CC)? Could it be the result of the individual being directly rewarded for the behaviour by, for example, members of the family, and/or is it a type of behaviour encouraged and admired in the culture or subculture in which the person lives? Is the absence of a behaviour (like not drinking when all your group do) a source of disapproval that acts as a punisher?

2. Could social learning theory play a part, in that the individual has observed the behaviour being performed by significant people in their life? Is it likely that the observed behaviour has been vicariously rewarded?

THE PSYCHODYNAMIC APPROACH

To read up on the psychodynamic approach, refer to pages 539–545 of A2PKT.

DESCRIPTION AND ASSUMPTIONS

Dynamics are the forces that drive us (or machines) to do things. The term "psychodynamic" refers to the way in which mental forces (especially unconscious ones) determine our personality and emotion. The originator of this approach was Freud whose work you have already considered. The term "psychoanalytic" refers to Freud's approach and is concerned with the interplay of innate drives and early experience.

The main assumptions are:

- Early experience has a strong influence on behaviour in later life. Our behaviour as adults is greatly influenced by our experiences in early childhood.

- The forces of the unconscious mind motivate much of our behaviour. We are born with certain innate urges (two of the most important being sexual and aggressive urges), which eventually become unconscious but still have a profound influence on our behaviour. If the ego is prevented from directly expressing unconscious urges then it uses defence mechanisms such as repression, regression, and reaction formation to cope with the urges.

- Unconscious urges are revealed in a symbolic form. The unconscious mind "leaks" into consciousness by means of dreams, slips of the tongue, forgetting, and irrational behaviour. It is possible to access the unconscious mind by analysing these symbolic expressions.

Neo-Freudians are psychologists whose theories are based on Freud's essential ideas but with certain significant differences. For example, Erik Erikson considered the whole of the life span to be influential rather than just the early years, and placed greater emphasis on social factors and less on sexual urges than did Freud.

TYPICAL METHODOLOGY

Case studies are particularly useful in the psychodynamic approach. A case study is a detailed description of a particular individual. The methods used to obtain the information vary from approach to approach; in the psychodynamic approach a *clinical interview* would be used. This is likely to be done by psychoanalysis (see Chapter 9, Treating Mental Disorders) as a means of obtaining information about early childhood experiences and their influence on the unconscious, which, in turn, involves the *analysis of symbols* in order to gain access to the contents of the unconscious mind.

The case study method is *idiographic*—it emphasises the uniqueness of each individual. Nevertheless, Freud's general methodology could also be seen as using a nomothetic approach in that he tried to establish general laws about human development (such as the stages of psychosexual development that we pass through).

EVALUATION OF THE PSYCHODYNAMIC APPROACH

Strengths

☺ **Freud's theory changed the Western view of human nature.** In particular, it led to recognition of the importance of early childhood experience on later behaviour and of the importance of the unconscious mind.

Freud's theory recognises that personality has more than one aspect. Jarvis (2000, see A2PKT p.541) points out that this explains why we all sometimes experience "mixed feelings" about a possible action—"one part of me wants to, but another doesn't". It allows for the fact that we can be rational and irrational, and that we sometimes predict that we will act in one way but actually do something quite different.

 The approach recognises the need to acknowledge basic urges. The psychodynamic approach has helped us recognise that we have urges that are dangerous to ignore, but that there is a difference between acknowledging these urges and acting on them.

 Psychoanalysis has been helpful in therapy for some abnormal conditions. However, this type of therapy has its limitations in that it is only suitable for the well-educated and articulate who are capable of insight (see Chapter 9, Treating Mental Disorders).

 The methodology provides great insight into behaviour. Although the case study method has limitations, the idiographic nature of it provides a unique insight into human behaviour because of the depth of the information collected.

Weaknesses/Limitations

 The theory lacks empirical support. Freud mainly studied a small number of Viennese women suffering from neurotic disorders. It is not possible to build a theory of normal development based on a few case studies of abnormality.

The theory is unfalsifiable. In psychoanalysis, any interpretation by the therapist is impossible to deny, since denial is taken as an indication of resistance by the unconscious mind, thus confirming the therapist's interpretation. There is therefore no way of knowing whether the psychoanalyst's analysis of symbols is correct.

There is evidence that contradicts the theory. In cases where it is possible to gather evidence to test the theory, some of this evidence has not supported it. For example, there is little evidence for the Oedipus complex or for penis envy.

It is a very deterministic theory. The psychodynamic approach sees childhood behaviour as dependent on innate forces, and adult behaviour as dependent on early childhood experience and its effect on the unconscious mind. This allows little, if any, room for free will.

SO WHAT DOES THIS MEAN?

The psychodynamic approach has had a profound influence on Western thought with this influence extending far beyond psychology to art, literature, and everyday life. It encouraged a far more compassionate attitude to the mentally ill and to irrational behaviour in general, and emphasised the fact that we ignore and repress our basic urges at our peril. It is difficult to reach an unbiased opinion over the work of Freud and his followers as demonstrated by the sharply divided attitudes towards the approach. These vary from those who dismiss the basic assumptions as nonscientific, sexist nonsense, through those who regard the work as culturally biased and outdated but with some important nuggets of truth, to yet others who regard the theory as universally correct and the work of a genius. Whatever the view, there is no denying that the approach has had an enormous influence on the history of psychology and on social attitudes.

Examples of the Psychodynamic Approach in the Specification

AS

Specification 10.1:   Cognitive psychology: repression as an explanation of forgetting.

Specification 11.2:   Individual differences: psychodynamic model of abnormality; psychodynamic explanation of eating disorders.

A2

Specification 13.2:   Physiological psychology: Freud's theory of the function of dreaming.

Specification 13.4:   Developmental psychology: psychodynamic explanation of personality development.

Specification 14.1:   Individual differences: psychodynamic explanations of schizophrenia, depression, and anxiety disorders as well as psychodynamic therapies for mental disorders.

Using the Psychodynamic Approach to Explain a Behaviour in the "Approaches" Question

If you want to consider a psychodynamic explanation of the behaviour described in the stimulus material of the Approaches question, think about the answers to the following questions:

1. Can it be explained in terms of early childhood experiences, such as being frustrated (fixated) in any of the first three stages of psychosexual development?
2. Could it be accounted for in terms of the use of defence mechanisms to cope with any unacceptable unconscious urges?
3. Could the behaviour be symbolic of a deep-seated psychological problem, in the way that Little Hans' fear of horses biting him was considered to be symbolic of the fear of castration by his father?
4. Could the behaviour be explained in terms of the balance (or imbalance) between the id, ego, and superego?

THE COGNITIVE APPROACH

To read up on the cognitive approach, refer to pages 546–552 of A2PKT.

DESCRIPTION AND ASSUMPTIONS

The cognitive approach in psychology is concerned with internal mental explanations of behaviour. In contrast to the traditional behavioural approach with its emphasis on passive responses to external events, the cognitive approach views humans as actively thinking about events and considering their meaning. Unlike the previous approaches we have discussed, there is no single body of theory in the cognitive approach. The common element is the focus on mental processes—how people take in information, how they mentally represent it, and how they store it.

The main assumptions are:

- Behaviour can largely be explained in terms of how the mind operates.
- It is useful to use the computer processing model to explain human cognition. The computer is used as an *analogy* (comparison or likeness) for human thought processes. Both the computer and the brain receive information, store it in a particular way, and retrieve it. Human thinking is assumed to involve the *processing of information* in the way a computer processes the data put into it.
- Psychology is a pure science and should use scientific methodology, mainly laboratory experiments.

Although the information processing metaphor is an important one in cognitive psychology, as a perspective it does not only rely on this. Any explanation of behaviour in terms of mental concepts is using a cognitive perspective. For example, Piaget's theory is one of cognitive development since it is concerned with how mental operations and schemas develop and change as children mature; Beck's approach to the causes of depression is cognitive because it accounts for depression in terms of certain patterns of thinking.

TYPICAL METHODOLOGY

The *laboratory experiment* is the main methodology of the cognitive approach. This has the advantage of demonstrating cause and effect and being able to see the specific effect of an independent variable on a dependent variable. However, it does lack ecological validity (see below).

EVALUATION OF THE COGNITIVE APPROACH

Strengths

- **It takes account of the influence of mental processes on behaviour.** In particular, the approach focuses on processes involved in perception and thinking, in what happens between a stimulus and response. It has also provided very useful models of memory and attention.
- **It has many useful practical applications.** It has, for example, offered advice on improving memory, particularly improving and checking the accuracy of eyewitness testimony, on how to concentrate in safety-critical situations such as air traffic control, in improving problem-solving skills, and in the application of therapies for mental disorders.

Weaknesses/Limitations

 It is a very mechanistic approach, which compares humans to machines. The computer analogy is limited since computers do not, like humans, get bored, tired, and make mistakes. Computers are also far more limited than humans in the actions they can perform—the human brain has far, far greater abilities than even a very sophisticated computer.

 The use of laboratory experiments has certain limitations. Much of the behaviour studied is carefully controlled and stripped of the context of ordinary behaviour. This means that the research lacks ecological validity in that the behaviour shown in these situations is not necessarily the behaviour that would occur in everyday situations. This method also tends to fragment the type of behaviour studied. For example, memory is often studied by attempts to recall facts, whereas in real life there are many types of memory, all of which interact.

SO WHAT DOES THIS MEAN?

Although theories of cognitive psychology are pervasive, there is no coherent theory that links the different strands, just a very general and rather vague concept concerning mental processes. Although this could be viewed as a weakness, the pervasiveness of such an approach can also be viewed as a strength. Cognitive psychology has influenced almost all areas of psychology, including theories of emotion, motivation, social cognition, attitude formation, and abnormality.

Examples of the Cognitive Approach in the Specification

AS

Specification 10.1:   Cognitive psychology: human memory.
Specification 11.1:   Physiological psychology: cognitive methods of coping with stress.
Specification 11.2:   Individual differences: cognitive models and therapies for abnormality.

A2

Specification 13.1:   Social psychology: attribution theory.
Specification 13.3:   Cognitive psychology.
Specification 13.4:   Developmental psychology: cognitive development.
Specification 14.1:   Individual differences: cognitive explanations for depression; cognitive-behavioural therapies for mental disorders.

Using the Cognitive Approach to Explain a Behaviour in the "Approaches" Question

This is a less straightforward approach than the previous three approaches since there is no overall cognitive theory. If you want to consider a cognitive explanation of the behaviour described in the stimulus material of the Approaches question, think about the answers to the following questions:

1. Can the behaviour be understood in terms of any theory of cognitive activity? For example, could a person's *schemas* account for the behaviour? Alternatively, could *attribution theory*—an individual's interpretation of what causes a particular behaviour—offer an explanation? If using any of these cognitive theories, make sure you put them in the context of the stimulus material; don't simply describe them.
2. Could the behaviour be accounted for in terms of changes in cognitive processes as a child matures?
3. If the stimulus material describes abnormal behaviour, could it be accounted for in terms of irrational thinking?
4. Could any problems of memory, or particular schemas, account for the behaviour?

319

THE EVOLUTIONARY APPROACH

To read up on the evolutionary approach, refer to pages 552–558 of A2PKT.

DESCRIPTION AND ASSUMPTIONS

The evolutionary approach seeks to explain behaviour in terms of how it has helped animals, including humans, to best adapt to their environments and thereby survive and reproduce. You have seen many examples of such explanations: the whole of Chapter 7 (Evolutionary Explanations of Human Behaviour) is concerned with the evolutionary approach. It may be helpful to recap on this and/or the section on sociobiological explanations of sexual attraction in Chapter 2 (Relationships).

The theory of evolution is based on the fact that organisms undergo continual change from one generation to the next as a result of sexual reproduction and mutation. Those organisms that inherit characteristics liable to improve their "fitness" (their survival) are likely to live a little longer and be slightly more reproductively successful than other competing organisms of the same species. Because there is often competition for resources, through survival of the fittest, these characteristics are more likely to be passed on to the next generation. In this way, slowly and over the course of a great many generations, organisms evolve. Behaviour patterns as well as physical characteristics become adapted by evolution in such a way that those that aid survival and reproduction are most likely to survive. The end result is that *genes* of the individuals with traits that best "fit" their environment are naturally selected.

Evolutionary Psychologists are interested in why particular behaviours have evolved. They seek to account for behaviour in a way that can be explained in terms of how it helps the animal reproduce (see A2PKT p.553 for an example of how this may operate).

Darwin's theory of evolution was based on the principle of individual fitness, that is, that behaviour that helped an individual survive would be naturally selected. Whilst this is obviously true, it did not provide a complete answer because some behaviours, such as animals risking their lives for others, could not be explained in these terms (as Darwin recognised). *Sociobiology* is a branch of evolutionary theory that explains these paradoxical behaviours. It states that behaviour that helps the *genes* of the individual, rather than the individual itself, survive are selected. After all, if an animal acts to protect its offspring (or other genetic relatives), then its own genes will survive even if the individual dies. So while Darwin focused on individual fitness, sociobiology focuses on *kin selection*. In a nutshell, sociobiological theory states that any behaviour that promotes the survival of the kin (genetic relatives) will be selected. (It is important to remember that evolution does not involve forward planning by a higher being. No one is doing the selecting—it occurs "naturally" by means of survival of the fittest.)

As noted in Chapter 7 (Evolutionary Explanations of Human Behaviour), we need to differentiate between evolution as fact (which it is) and the theories based on evolution. These theories are usually based on conjecture rather than fact and are often extremely controversial. For this reason, in the evaluation, we refer to the evolutionary approach rather than evolutionary theory.

The main assumptions are:

- All behaviour can be explained in terms of genetic determinism. Ethologists, who study behaviour in its natural environment, assume that all types of behaviour have an adaptive function or they would not have survived in the gene pool.

- Genetically determined traits evolve through natural and kin selection. Any behaviour that helps the individual survive and reproduce will be "selected" and the genes for that trait will survive. Changes in the environment and competition for resources exert selective pressure and the individual who best adapts to their particular environmental niche will survive.

TYPICAL METHODOLOGY

Ethologists use *naturalistic observation* to study animals in their natural environment. They also conduct *field experiments*, in which they manipulate aspects of the environment to investigate the effects of these changes on the behaviour of the animals. Ethologists do not usually study humans, so their methods are not relevant for studying human behaviour.

Sociobiologists look at traits that are universal across cultures and then attempt to explain these in terms of the theory of kin selection. Because human behaviour is so greatly influenced by culture, and because cross-cultural studies are difficult to conduct in an unbiased fashion, the hypotheses generated are often found to be controversial (as you saw in Chapter 7, Evolutionary Explanations of Human Behaviour).

Evolutionary theorists also use *natural experiments* in their investigations. They look at how naturally occurring independent variables (changes in the environment) affect the behaviour of organisms, including humans.

EVALUATION OF THE EVOLUTIONARY APPROACH

Strengths

 This approach has drawn attention to how the pressures of natural selection can affect behaviour. It is especially relevant for explaining nonhuman animal behaviour but may, as seen below, be less useful in explaining human behaviour.

 It has certain practical applications. The acknowledgement of the importance of genetic factors in influencing behaviour has led to some important but controversial applications in the form of genetic engineering.

Weaknesses/Limitations

 The approach is reductionist. Evolutionary theory holds that all behaviour is a result of natural selection and is embedded in our genes. With respect to human behaviour this is highly unlikely to be true. There is an enormous variety in the behaviour of humans both within and between cultures because they are influenced by culture and society. Cultural transmission (the passing of information from one generation to another) is hugely influential in all human societies, yet the evolutionary approach takes little account of it.

 It ignores conscious thought. Humans are capable of conscious thought and active decision making, yet this approach, which is very deterministic, takes little account of this. It views humans as helpless victims of their evolutionary history. A controversial example is the recent attempt by evolutionary theorists to justify rape, which has met with strenuous criticism.

 There are problems of methodology. The method of natural experiments does not establish cause and effect because there are always a host of factors other than the independent variable that might be influencing behaviour.

 There is a serious lack of evidence to support theories of evolutionary psychology. The blurb of the book *Alas Poor Darwin* (Rose & Rose, 2000) summarises the criticisms of evolutionary psychology thus: "the claims of evolutionary psychology rest on shaky empirical evidence, flawed premises and unexamined political suppositions". This book challenges the reductionist stance of evolutionary psychology and offers, via academics from many disciplines, a fuller biosocial view of human behaviour. Many critics argue that these theories are simply the equivalent of the *Just So* stories, with no empirical evidence as their basis.

Examples of the Evolutionary Approach in the Specification

A2

Specification 13.1:   Social psychology: sociobiological theory of the formation of relationships. Sociobiological explanations of pro- and anti-social behaviour.

Specification 13.5:   Comparative psychology: determinants of animal behaviour. Evolutionary explanations of animal behaviour. Evolutionary explanations of human behaviour.

Using the Evolutionary Approach to Explain a Behaviour in the "Approaches" Question

If you want to offer an evolutionary explanation of the behaviour described in the stimulus material you need to consider whether the behaviour can be accounted for in terms of evolutionary advantage. Can you account for the behaviour described in the stimulus material in terms of how it helps to increase the individual's fitness and/or helps the survival of genetically related individuals? If you think about the topic areas for which an evolutionary explanation has been offered—sexual attraction, pro-social and anti-social behaviour, mental disorders, intelligence—then this may help you in explaining other examples of behaviour in such a way.

SAMPLE QUESTIONS AND ANSWERS

The Approaches question is different from all others in the examination. You will have about 40 minutes to answer this question and it is worth a total of 30 marks. Each question consists of a piece of stimulus material followed by the same basic four-part question. The question will be in the following format:

(a) Describe how the subject presented in the stimulus material might be explained by two different approaches. **(6 + 6 marks)**

(b) Assess one of these explanations of the subject presented in the stimulus material in terms of its strengths and limitations. **(6 marks)**

(c) How might the subject presented in the stimulus material be investigated by one of these approaches? **(6 marks)**

(d) Evaluate the use of this method of investigating the subject material presented in the stimulus material. **(6 marks)**

It is essential that when you answer the question you refer consistently to the stimulus material—you will gain few marks if you simply describe an approach, or list its limitations and strengths. You need to think carefully about how the different approaches would explain what is described in the stimulus material. Although you only need to use two approaches, it is advisable to learn at least the four basic approaches, that is, biological, behavioural, psychodynamic, and cognitive. You need to know these approaches well to answer questions in all areas of the Specification, therefore it would be short-sighted and restrictive to confine yourself to being able to answer this question with reference to only two approaches. In addition, depending on the stimulus material, it is often easier to answer with reference to some approaches rather than others.

Below are two sample questions, both taken from the AQA-A examination paper of June 2002 (with slight modifications to allow for small changes in the Specification), in which two approaches are used to explain the behaviour in the stimulus material. In the examination you will be given a choice of two pieces of stimulus material but you only use one. Before you decide on which of the two questions to tackle, think about *all* parts of the question so you ensure that you are offering the best overall answer you can give.

Over the two examples, we have offered explanations based on the four main perspectives. They are not necessarily the most straightforward ones to use but have been written to illustrate each of these main approaches. Before you read the answers, think about how you might tackle the questions and when you have read them, consider how the two approaches not used might offer an explanation. You could, if you wish, also think about how you could use other explanations, such as evolutionary, or a nonpsychological approach such as sociology.

QUESTION 1 (AQA-A JUNE 2002)

All the people who know Errol agree that he is a very attractive young man. He has a fine dress sense and muscular physique and handsome features. Errol is also short-sighted. He tried wearing contact lenses but found them uncomfortable. He was prescribed a pair of glasses but only rarely wears them because he thinks they spoil his good looks. Some people think he is extremely vain.

(a) Describe how Errol's behaviour might be explained by two different approaches. **(6 + 6 marks)**

An answer based on the behavioural approach could offer explanations for Errol's behaviour in terms of classical conditioning (CC), operant conditioning (OC), and social learning theory. In terms of CC, Errol has learnt to associate admiration with a muscular physique and an attractive face. He views an attractive face as one that does not require glasses. In terms of OC, admiration from others is a powerful positive reinforcer. His good looks may bring him other positive reinforcers like sex. According to social learning theory, Errol could be vain because he has seen others, including powerful and sexually attractive male media figures, being admired. By vicarious conditioning, he associates his own good looks with the potential to gain rewards and does not want them ruined by wearing glasses. It is also possible that Errol has observed other people's reaction to physically unattractive people, such as men who are "weedy" and thin rather than muscular, and/or wear glasses, and by vicarious punishment, is conditioned to not wanting to look like this.

In terms of the cognitive approach, it is possible to see Errol's vanity in terms of the schemas he has concerning what makes people sexually attractive to others. In Western society, the schema for an attractive male is one with a muscular physique and the other kinds of features that Errol possesses. He has also acquired a schema that the wearing of spectacles makes a person less attractive. This could have arisen from such expressions as "men do not make passes at girls who wear glasses"—although this refers to female attractiveness, the principle is the same. The cognitive approach is concerned with what goes on in the mind—the way data is processed. Errol probably processes the fact that he receives a lot of compliments and admiring glances as being caused by his physical attractiveness rather than any of his other attributes. If we consider Western society in general, people are socialised to attach a great deal of importance to physical attractiveness and to believe that this is crucial to having a successful marriage and a happy life. This is not necessarily a schema (an attitude) that exists in other cultures and demonstrates how important cognitive processes can be in influencing behaviour.

(b) **Assess one of these explanations of Errol's vanity in terms of its strength *and* limitations.**

(6 marks)

With respect to the learning approach, a strength of this explanation is that there is considerable empirical evidence obtained from controlled experiments to support the various elements of the theory. Pavlov showed, albeit in animals, that we learn by association, so this supports the idea that Errol could have learnt to associate admiration with his looks. Skinner, also using animals, showed from experimental research that positive reinforcement increases the probability of a response. Since admiration is a positive reinforcer, this would also account for the fact that Errol has become more and more vain. There is also empirical evidence, based on studies of humans, that people are influenced by significant role models including media figures, especially if these role models are reinforced for their behaviour (Bandura, 1977). In terms of weaknesses, the traditional learning approach takes no account of the cognitive influences on Errol's behaviour. It regards him rather as a puppet of external environmental influences, helplessly controlled by the admiring glances of others. However, Errol may seek out these responses and consciously decide to do things, such as dressing very well, in order to boost his self-esteem, a concept that the behavioural approach does not acknowledge since it does not concern observable behaviour. Other cognitive aspects that may influence Errol's behaviour but are neglected by the behavioural approach are his ambitions and plans for the future. His vanity may reflect an active decision to seek certain goals, which can be obtained by looking good, rather than a reaction to previous admiration.

(c) **How might Errol's behaviour be investigated by one of these approaches?** **(6 marks)**

The learning approach would use the experimental method for investigating Errol's vanity. It could select a certain behaviour, such as the wearing of spectacles, and see if this does reduce someone's attractiveness, thereby providing a test of whether wearing glasses actually acts as a punishment in that it decreases the probability of admiration. You could use an experimental design in which participants, in a repeated measures design, are asked to assess the attractiveness, on a scale of 1–10, of a set of photographs in which people are wearing glasses or not wearing glasses. The preferable design would use a large number of photographs in which the same people were seen wearing glasses or not wearing glasses, well ordered so it is not obvious to participants that they are viewing the same person twice. Alternatively, still using a repeated measures design, you could use a series of photographs in which two groups of people are matched for attractiveness and then one group is photographed wearing glasses and the other group is assessed while not wearing then. You can then compare the two sets of scores and see if there is a statistically significant difference in the ratings of attractiveness. Yet another experimental design would be an independent groups design in which the same people were assessed by two different groups, one who assessed the individuals while wearing glasses and the other without them.

(d) Evaluate the method of investigating Errol's vanity that you referred to in part (c). **(6 marks)**

The experimental method has the advantage that it can measure whether the independent variable (whether or not the person is wearing glasses) is the cause of changes in the dependent variable (the assessment of attractiveness). In this way cause and effect can be established. However, this method has certain disadvantages. As with many studies in the behavioural approach, you are only studying one small aspect of Errol's vanity. His vanity may depend on the interaction of several types of behaviour and this method does not easily lend itself to investigating this interaction. Several types of behaviour may affect his vanity, such as his choice of clothes and his muscular physique. The method also lacks ecological validity: in ordinary life, there are many ways in which people judge attractiveness, and simply asking people to rate "still" pictures of others does not do this justice. We judge attractiveness by a lot of characteristics, including the degree to which people have self-confidence, smile, and make eye contact, to name but a few. This type of method does not take account of this, so even if people judge those in photographs as being less attractive when they wear glasses than when they do not, this may not be reflected in their assessments of people they meet in an everyday context.

QUESTION 2 (AQA-A JUNE 2002)

Anne enjoys fast driving. She enjoys it when she is in someone else's car going fast but she enjoys it even more when she is driving fast herself. She finds high speeds exhilarating. Within a year of passing her test Anne has been charged with breaking motorway speed limits three times and is now in danger of losing her licence.

(a) Describe how Anne's exhilaration from speeding might be explained by two different approaches. **(6 + 6 marks)**

The biological approach would look at the physiological effects on Anne of her speeding behaviour. Driving fast is physiologically arousing, creating a sense of excitement and pleasure in certain individuals, of whom Anne appears to be one. The dangerous situation would trigger the "fight or flight" response and it is possible that the surge of adrenaline that Anne receives in response to fast driving gives her a real "high" and she wishes to repeat the experience, despite being caught for speeding on several occasions. In fact, the very danger of being caught may increase her arousal level and add to the exhilaration she experiences. You may also consider the reasons why Anne finds this behaviour exciting while others would not enjoy being in a car that was travelling very fast. Anne may have inherited a genetic predisposition to be easily bored and need excitement and danger in her life in order to enjoy herself. This may be the same reason why some people enjoy the type of ride we have in theme parks whereas others are scared witless by them. It may be that the CNS (central nervous system) of some individuals is so "damped down" that they need constant change and challenge, especially if this involves high risk-taking, whereas others are so "wound up" that they prefer a quiet life and a calm environment. The explanation is rooted in genetic differences in the working of the CNS, particularly the ANS (autonomic nervous system).

The psychodynamic approach may see Anne's behaviour as rooted in the Oedipus complex. According to Freud, all females suffer penis envy, and fast driving, which is far more commonly seen and admired in men than in women, may be a way in which her unconscious mind is trying to deal with this inevitable jealousy. The media, especially the advertising industry, equates fast driving with masculinity and fast cars are often considered to be phallic symbols. Anne's car may act as a penis substitute and her fast and dangerous driving may be symbolic of the fact that she wants to act like a rebellious and dynamic man, and thereby have the same attributes as he does.

The psychodynamic approach may also view Anne as having problems of impulse control, caused by strong urges of the id. The fast driving may be a way that the ego can try to balance the urges of the id with those of the superego. Although this way of satisfying the id may not be entirely acceptable to the superego, at least it does not lead to the anxiety that more direct uncontrolled expression of the id, such as inappropriate sexual or aggressive behaviour, might entail.

(b) **Assess one of these explanations of Anne's exhilaration from speeding in terms of its strengths *and* limitations.**　　　　　　　　　　　　　　**(6 marks)**

The biological view takes full account of how physiological processes can affect our behaviour, for example, in this case it explains how surges in hormone levels can lead to particular emotional responses. This explanation is particularly useful when describing adaptive responses to situations that threaten survival, but in this case it is rather a puzzle to explain Anne's enjoyment of danger because this obviously does not aid survival—rather the reverse. In the case of humans, we also need to look at social influences, for example, the admiration that Anne may obtain for engaging in such risky behaviour. In modern Western society, driving fast cars is a behaviour that is respected and admired by certain subcultures, especially the young, but a biological explanation takes little account of this. In this case, the behavioural approach offers a good explanation in terms of reinforcement.

The biological approach offers a good *description* of what is happening at the physiological level of nerves and hormones but it does not fully *explain* why Anne enjoys doing something dangerous, especially as evolutionary forces would be expected to channel behaviour towards survival, not pointless risk taking.

(c) **How might Anne's exhilaration from speeding be investigated by one of these approaches?**　　　　　　　　　　　　　　**(6 marks)**

The biological approach lends itself well to the experimental method. One way of investigating Anne's behaviour would be to look at the physiological responses of a number of participants to different situations involving physiological arousal, including fast driving. Since it would be neither practical nor ethical to do this in reality, a virtual reality machine would provide a suitable apparatus. Measures of physiological functioning such as heart rate, galvanic skin response, and breathing rate would be taken beforehand to provide a baseline against which measures during the study could be compared. The physiological measures taken give an indication of the degree of autonomic arousal and would give a good indication of the types of situations that increase arousal and the extent to which particular individuals differ in the degree of such arousal.

(d) Evaluate the method of investigating Anne's exhilaration from speeding that you referred to in part (c). **(6 marks)**

As the study would be conducted in a laboratory using apparatus that is not true to life, it would lack ecological validity. It may not reflect how someone would respond if driving or being driven in a real car in dangerous conditions. In this particular study it would be difficult to carry out a very realistic field experiment for both practical and ethical reasons. Nevertheless, it may be possible to carry out a field study in a more realistic situation than a laboratory, such as using a disused airfield. Field studies increase ecological validity but decrease internal validity. However, there are still ethical and practical problems because you need volunteers who are willing to be in this situation, so you may not get a representative sample.

Another limitation of this method is that you are also only measuring observable behaviour. Therefore it only takes account of physiological measures and does not provide a means of measuring cognitive responses to the situation, such as the degree of excitement or fear experienced. Therefore, whatever experimental design is used, it is likely to have limitations.

Questions 1 amd 2 adapted from AQA A2 [Summer 2002] Psychology Examination Papers.
The authors are responsible for the solutions and (a) they have neither been provided nor approved by AQA and (b) they may not necessarily constitute the only possible solutions.